MACBETH

Leaving Certificate English

Text, analysis, commentary notes and sample essays

MARTIN KIERAN AND FRANCES ROCKS

g GILL EDUCATION

Gill Education
Hume Avenue
Park West
Dublin 12
www.gilleducation.ie

Gill Education is an imprint of M.H. Gill & Co.

ISBN: 978-0-7171-7326-6

Cover design: O'Brien Creative

At the time of going to press, all web addresses were active and contained information relevant to the topics in this book. Gill Education does not, however, accept responsibility for the content or views contained on these websites. Content, views and addresses may change beyond the publisher or author's control. Students should always be supervised when reviewing websites.

For permission to reproduce photographs, the authors and publisher gratefully acknowledge the following:

© Alamy: i, 2, 26, 33, 44, 101, 133, 180, 200, 219, 249, 251, 254, 256, 257, 259, 261, 266, 267, 268, 273, 276, 278, 282, 284, 289, 291, 293, 294, 296, 299, 300, 302, 305, 307; © Arcangel: 10, 17, 35, 47, 55, 64, 74, 85, 90, 100, 107, 111, 123, 131, 151, 165, 172, 176, 182, 192, 195, 199, 203, 210, 216, 223, 229, 231, 235, 237, 239, 240; © Colm Hogan: 6, 29, 48, 75, 86, 121, 183, 224, 246, 247, 252, 280; © Folger Digital Image Collection: 4; © Getty Images: 243; © iStock: 9, 28, 43, 63, 126, 144, 186, 226, 228, 234, 241, 242, 244, 245; © Photostage: 7, 62, 65, 99, 129, 185, 270, 274, 277, 285, 295, 297; © REX/Shutterstock: Alastair Muir: 288, Geraint Lewis: 39, See Saw Films/ Studio Canal: 213; © Royal Shakespeare Company: ii, 11, 36, 56, 69, 108, 112, 143, 145, 167, 187, 193, 194, 196, 204, 221, 227, 230, 248, 264; © T Charles Erickson: 57, 83, 92, 124, 127, 173, 177; © 2013 Temple University. Design by Bridget Currie: 262; © Utah Shakespeare Festival: 18, 233.

The authors and publisher have made every effort to trace all copyright holders, but if any has been inadvertently overlooked we would be pleased to make the necessary arrangement at the first opportunity.

The paper used in this book is made from the wood pulp of managed forests. For every tree felled, at least one tree is planted, thereby renewing natural resources.

Contents

* N.B. Key scenes requiring close, detailed study

* N.B. Key scenes requiring close, detailed study

Introduction

- *Macbeth* is one of Shakespeare's most powerful tragedies. The play raises fascinating questions about human nature, ambition, corruption and power. Other key themes include deception, violence, masculinity and the supernatural.

- Drama is a story – usually involving human conflict – relayed through dialogue and actions and performed by actors. Most Leaving Cert exam questions on the Shakespearean text relate to characters, relationships, themes and dramatic techniques, all of which are closely interlinked. A good knowledge of the play's key or revealing scenes will provide a solid basis for answering exam questions.

- When studying the play, it is worth remembering that the text was written specifically for theatrical performance. Despite any peculiarities or inconsistencies regarding the plot, audiences must accept the 'new reality' that Shakespeare has created in order to fully appreciate this intriguing stage drama.

The Real Macbeth

Shakespeare's portrayal of Macbeth bears little resemblance to the original Macbeth, an eleventh-century Scottish king who was known as Mac Bethad and nicknamed the Red King. He was born in 1005, the son of an earl. In 1040, he killed the ruling king, Duncan I, in battle near Elgin, Morayshire, and replaced him as the new monarch. Duncan's wife fled Scotland with her two sons, Malcolm (who would become Malcolm III of Scotland) and Donald.

Macbeth's long reign as king of the Scots was relatively peaceful. There are no records from the period that refer to him as a tyrant.

For about seventeen years, he appears to have ruled fairly, imposing law and order and encouraging Christianity. In 1050, he is known to have travelled to Rome for a papal jubilee. He was also a courageous leader who fought successful battles against England along Scotland's border.

In 1054, Macbeth was challenged by Siward, Earl of Northumbria, who was attempting to return Duncan's son Malcolm to the throne. In August 1057, Macbeth was killed at the Battle of Lumphanan in Aberdeenshire by Malcolm, who succeeded him as king.

Shakespeare's Story of Macbeth

Three witches confront the great army general Macbeth on his victorious return from battle, telling him that he will become king. Filled with ambition and encouraged by his wife, Macbeth kills King Duncan and claims the Scottish throne for himself. He is immediately consumed with guilt and paranoia. He becomes a tyrannical ruler, committing more and more murders to secure his grip on power. The resulting bloodshed drives Macbeth and Lady Macbeth towards madness and death.

'The Scottish Play'

One of the best-known theatre superstitions surrounds Shakespeare's *Macbeth*. It is seen as bad luck to say the name of the drama, which is usually referred to as 'the Scottish Play' instead. The origins of this superstition are unknown, although there are several theories, ranging from the practical (the story contains a lot of swordplay, so injuries are more likely) to the fanciful (the play was cursed by witches because it revealed their secrets). Although rumours of a curse are now generally dismissed as nonsense, the play is famously associated with reports of misfortune.

During a 1672 production in Amsterdam, the actor playing Macbeth substituted a real dagger for the blunted stage dagger and killed the actor playing Duncan in full view of the audience.

In 1849, a long-standing rivalry between fans of British actor William Charles Macready and American actor Edwin Forrest became violent during a production at New York's Astor Place Opera House, reportedly leaving more than twenty dead and many more seriously injured.

Even the great English actor Laurence Olivier couldn't escape the curse. When he played the Scottish king, a heavy weight mysteriously dropped from above the stage, missing him by inches. His performance was further jinxed by the use of real swords on stage – one flew into the audience, striking a theatre-goer and causing him to have a heart attack.

The 1942 run of the play with John Gielgud notched up one of the highest body counts: three of the actors died in unexplained circumstances and the costume designer committed suicide on set on the opening night.

Another Shakespearean performer, Harold Norman, who reportedly did not believe in the superstition, also died while playing Macbeth in 1947 after his stage battle became a little too realistic. When Charlton Heston took the lead in 1953, he suffered a motorcycle crash during rehearsals and his legs were left horrifically burned during a performance. It later emerged that his costume had been mysteriously soaked in kerosene. In a 2001 production by the Cambridge Shakespeare Company, Macduff injured his back, Lady Macbeth bumped her head, Ross broke a toe, and two cedar trees from Birnam Wood toppled over, destroying the set.

Of course, Shakespeare seems to have warned any actor brave enough to take on 'the Scottish play' when he wrote the famous line: 'Something wicked this way comes.'

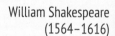

William Shakespeare
(1564–1616)

Shakespeare's Life *(Dates of plays are approximate)*

1564	Born in Stratford-upon-Avon
1582	Marries Anne Hathaway
1583	His daughter Susannah is born
1584	Birth of twins, Judith and Hamnet
1585	Moves to London
1590s	Writes first plays, *Richard III* and *Henry VII*
1593–96	Continues to write, including *Richard II* and *Romeo and Juliet*
1596	Death of his son Hamnet
1599	Invests in the Globe Theatre
1605	Writes *Macbeth*
1609	Becomes part-owner of the new Blackfriars Theatre
1612	Retires and returns to Stratford
1616	Dies aged 52

Shakespeare's Theatre

Throughout Shakespeare's lifetime, professional theatre was a highly successful business that provided popular entertainment for people of all backgrounds. Shakespeare wrote for a specific acting company, known first as the Lord Chamberlain's Men and later as the King's Men.

Plays were performed in the royal courts, as well as in town squares, churches and guildhalls around the country. In London, the largest theatres were open-air arenas with room for several thousand people. These playhouses were made mainly of wood.

Indoor playhouses accommodated up to 500 people, all of whom were given seats. Lighting was provided by candles, making indoor theatres suitable for winter and evening productions.

The Swan

Built in 1595–6, the Swan Theatre was located in the Southwark district of London, close to the River Thames. It had a capacity for 3,000 spectators and was described by Johannes De Witt, a Dutchman visiting the English capital, as the 'finest and biggest of the London theatres'. De Witt also drew a sketch of the building and a copy of this famous drawing is probably the single most reliable source of information about the interior layout of Elizabethan London theatres.

The Globe

From 1599, London's most important outdoor theatre was the Globe, also in Southwark, where Shakespeare's best-known dramas were first produced. The building was about 36 feet high and had a diameter of about 84 feet. The inside of the structure contained three tiers of galleries that surrounded an uncovered yard roughly 56 feet in diameter.

The grounds surrounding the theatre would have been bustling with play-goers and local people. Stallholders sold merchandise and refreshments, creating a lively market-day atmosphere. The Globe would have particularly attracted young people and there were many complaints of apprentices avoiding work in order to go to the theatre.

Staging

The bare stages of Shakespeare's day had very little scenery and few props except for objects required by the plot, such as a table or a throne. Setting and mood were suggested by the power of the play's language. In *Macbeth*, this is particularly evident in the scenes involving the witches.

There was a roof over the stage, but no curtain. Rhyming couplets signalled the end of a scene. Colourful costumes were common, often denoting a character's social status or nationality. Exits and entrances were in plain view of the audience, but actors could also descend from the 'heavens' above the stage or enter and exit from the 'hell' below through a trapdoor.

The Actors

Women never performed in stage dramas (acting was seen as a disreputable profession), and young boys usually played female characters. During

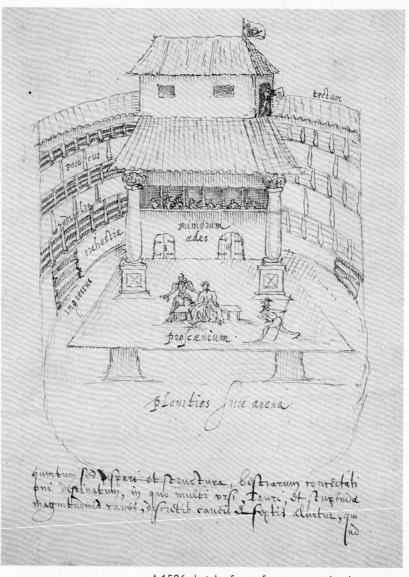

A 1596 sketch of a performance on the thrust stage (a stage that extends into the auditorium) of the Swan.

Elizabethan times, there was a fast turnover of plays – and little or no time for rehearsal – so actors needed to have excellent recall. Indeed, they sometimes received scripts just before the play started and relied on prompters who sat behind the curtains and whispered the lines.

Actors performed on a stage space that thrust into the yard area and had three sides where audience members could watch the action. Acoustics were poor and the actors were often forced to shout their lines and use exaggerated theatrical gestures. Speech patterns were heightened for dramatic effect.

Audiences

Shakespeare's theatre was full of life. Poorer people ('groundlings') would pay a few pennies to stand in front of the stage while the better-off paid more for places in the sheltered side galleries. Plays were staged in the afternoon and the audience would talk, wander around and eat and drink during the play, so authors had to come up with ways of holding their attention.

Since there were no backdrops or artificial lighting, audiences used their imagination to accept the 'new reality' being presented on the stage. Although Shakespeare gave his plays different settings, the way his characters spoke and acted is now believed to have been very similar to how English people in the sixteenth and seventeenth centuries would have spoken and behaved.

Shakespeare's Text and Line Numbers

Over the years, Shakespeare's plays have been printed in various formats. Most popular versions of *Macbeth* have some modernised spelling and punctuation. Line numbers may also differ slightly, depending on particular editions.

Before Reading *Macbeth*

When preparing for the Single Text *Macbeth* question, it is important to become familiar with the entire play through a close reading of the text. Your written work should show evidence of effective analysis. You will be expected to support relevant points with suitable reference to key scenes. Some moments in the drama are particularly significant and worth studying thoroughly.

Remember that all commentaries and study guides are there to be challenged. There is no single 'correct way' to interpret *Macbeth*.

In responding to exam questions, have confidence in developing your own ideas and always express yourself clearly. Identify the main elements of the question, so that your answer is coherent and well structured. Make sure to avoid unfocused narrative. Wherever possible, find your own examples from the text to support your views and use accurate quotations when appropriate.

Characters

The Royal House of Scotland
DUNCAN – King of Scotland
MALCOLM – his elder son and heir
DONALBAIN – his younger son

Thanes (Scottish noblemen), their households and supporters
MACBETH – Thane of Glamis, an army general
LADY MACBETH – The wife of Macbeth
BANQUO – Thane of Lochaber, another general
FLEANCE – his son
MACDUFF – Thane of Fife, a nobleman of Scotland
LADY MACDUFF
BOY – son of Macduff
LENNOX – Scottish nobleman
ROSS – Scottish nobleman
MENTEITH – Scottish nobleman
ANGUS – Scottish nobleman
CAITHNESS – Scottish nobleman
CAPTAIN in Duncan's army
PORTER at Macbeth's castle
AN OLD MAN
A DOCTOR
SEYTON – attendant to Macbeth
THREE MURDERERS

The English
SIWARD – Earl of Northumberland,
general of the English forces
YOUNG SIWARD – his son

The Supernatural World
THREE WITCHES – the weird sisters
THREE APPARITIONS
HECATE – Queen of Witchcraft

(Lords, Gentlemen, Officers, Soldiers, Servants,
Attendants and Messengers)

OVERVIEW

In the midst of a gathering thunderstorm, three witches appear on a desolate Scottish heath. They plan to meet again after the battle, when they will confront Macbeth. As quickly as they arrive, these creatures of the night are called away by evil spirits, their demonic companions, and quickly depart into the foggy air.

An open place

Thunder and lightning. Enter three Witches

First Witch

When shall we three meet again?

In thunder, lightning, or in rain?

Second Witch

When the hurlyburly's done,

When the battle's lost and won.

Third Witch

That will be ere the set of sun.   5

First Witch

Where the place?

Second Witch

Upon the heath.

Third Witch

There to meet with Macbeth.

First Witch

I come, Graymalkin!

Second Witch

Paddock calls.   10

Third Witch

Anon!

All

Fair is foul, and foul is fair: ~~that~~ turning Mrgs

Hover through the fog and filthy air.

Exeunt

diabolical trinity △
Witches - agents of evil

2 In thunder, lightning or in rain?:
   In what kind of bad weather?

3 hurlyburly: *confusion and chaos*

4 lost and won: *one side will have
   succeeded, the other will have failed*

5 ere the set of sun: *before evening*

9 Graymalkin: *grey cat*

10 Paddock: *toad*

11 Anon: *soon*

Study Notes

Contradictions (lines 1–13)

Shakespeare's short, dramatic opening instantly captures the audience's attention. The ambivalent tone of the play is established from the start. Appearances are deceptive: 'Fair is foul, and foul is fair'. The witches appear to have the ability to control the weather ('In thunder, lightning, or in rain') and to have the gift of prophecy ('When the battle's lost and won'). The stormy conditions and the witches' demonic companions (Graymalkin and Paddock) add to the evil atmosphere. To Shakespeare's superstitious audience, this would be a frightening spectacle.

The playwright increases the tension by exciting our curiosity. What battle is taking place? Who will win? Who is Macbeth? And why are the witches meeting him? This sinister scene sets the play's supernatural tone and introduces the theme of duplicity. The witches represent confusion and moral uncertainty. Is there about to be a reversal of the natural order?

Shakespeare's language

In a staccato exchange of just twelve short lines, Shakespeare succeeds in creating an **unsettling atmosphere**: 'Where the place?' The witches speak in a highly stylised manner – at first individually and then delivering a conclusion in unison. Their language throughout is ambiguous. The use of rhyme intensifies a disturbing sense of chanting and magical charms.

Much of what they say seems contradictory or **paradoxical:** 'When the battle's lost and won', 'Fair is foul, and foul is fair'. The alliterative phrase is like a spell-binding incantation and the force of opposites creates further tension. The witches inhabit neither sky nor earth, but 'Hover through the fog and filthy air'. Their evasive language **foreshadows** an uncertain future when everything will be called into question.

Upon the heath

Second Witch, Act 1 Scene 1, l.7

❝❝ Key Quotes

In thunder, lightning, or in rain? (First Witch) l.2	The supernatural power of the three witches allows them to see the future and control the weather. The use of the number three is also traditionally associated with magic. These creatures are only interested in disorder and meeting in foul weather.
When the hurlyburly's done (Second Witch) l.3	A serious confrontation between warring factions is dismissed as a noisy uproar. As instruments of evil, the witches delight in disorder.
When the battle's lost and won (Second Witch) l.4	This paradoxical phrase typifies the double-dealing of the witches. They are associated with Macbeth from the start. Do they now intend to defeat him and bring about his downfall?
Fair is foul, and foul is fair (All three witches) l.12	The alliterative phrase chanted by the witches calls attention to the morally ambiguous world they inhabit. Does this menacing paradox foreshadow future events in the play?

OVERVIEW

In an army camp near Forres, Duncan, King of Scotland, and his two sons are given the latest news from the battlefield by a wounded officer. Several battles are taking place. Macdonwald, a Scottish rebel, is fighting Duncan's forces. Meanwhile, Sweno, King of Norway, has invaded Scotland, aided by the disloyal Thane of Cawdor. Macbeth and Banquo are highly praised for their bravery in battle and are credited with leading the king's army to victory. Duncan orders the Thane of Cawdor's immediate execution and awards Macbeth with his title.

* A key scene requiring close, detailed study

A camp near Forres

*Alarum within. Enter King Duncan, Malcolm, Donalbain,
Lennox and attendants, meeting a bleeding Captain*

Duncan

What bloody man is that? He can report,

As seemeth by his plight, of the revolt

The newest state.

Malcolm

        This is the sergeant

Who like a good and hardy soldier fought

'Gainst my captivity. – Hail, brave friend!   5

Say to the king the knowledge of the broil

As thou didst leave it.

Captain

        Doubtful it stood;

As two spent swimmers that do cling together

And choke their art. The merciless Macdonwald –

Worthy to be a rebel, for to that   10

The multiplying villanies of nature

Do swarm upon him – from the Western Isles

Of kerns and gallowglasses is supplied,

And Fortune, on his damned quarrel smiling,

Showed like a rebel's whore. But all's too weak,   15

For brave Macbeth – well he deserves that name –

Disdaining Fortune, with his brandished steel,

Which smoked with bloody execution –

Like Valour's minion – carved out his passage,

Till he faced the slave;   20

Which ne'er shook hands, nor bade farewell to him,

Till he unseamed him from the nave to th' chops,

And fixed his head upon our battlements.

Duncan

O valiant cousin, worthy gentleman!

Captain

As whence the sun 'gins his reflection,   25

Shipwrecking storms and direful thunders break,

So from that spring whence comfort seemed to come

Discomfort swells. Mark, King of Scotland, mark:

No sooner Justice had, with Valour armed,

Compelled these skipping kerns to trust their heels,   30

---

1 report: *give an account of the latest news from the battlefield*

4–5 fought/ 'Gainst my captivity: *prevented my arrest*

6 broil: *fight*

7 Doubtful it stood: *the outcome was uncertain*

8 spent: *worn out*

9–11 merciless Macdonwald … nature: *the ruthless rebel leader*

13 kerns and gallowglasses: *mercenary foot soldiers and horsemen*

14–15 Fortune … like a rebel's whore: *Fate behaved like a faithless woman, favouring one side, then the other*

15 all's too weak: *nothing could stand in Macbeth's way*

17 Disdaining Fortune: *contemptuous of what might happen*

17 brandished steel: *raised sword*

19 Valour's minion: *Courage's favourite*

19 carved out his passage: *cut down all who stood in his way*

20 the slave: *the rebel Macdonwald*

21 unseamed him from the nave to th' chops: *cut him open from the navel to the jaw*

30 trust their heels: *run away*

But the Norweyan Lord, surveying vantage,
With furbished arms and new supplies of men,
Began a fresh assault.

Duncan

Dismayed not this
Our captains, Macbeth and Banquo?

Captain

Yes;
35 As sparrows eagles, or the hare the lion.
If I say sooth, I must report they were
As cannons overcharged with double cracks,
So they doubly redoubled strokes upon the foe;
Except they meant to bathe in reeking wounds,
40 Or memorise another Golgotha,
I cannot tell –
But I am faint, my gashes cry for help.

Duncan

So well thy words become thee, as thy wounds;
They smack of honour both. Go get him surgeons.
Exit Captain, attended
Enter Ross and Angus
Who comes here?

Malcolm

45 The worthy Thane of Ross.

Lennox

What a haste looks through his eyes! So should he look
That seems to speak things strange.

Ross

God save the king!

Duncan

Whence camest thou, worthy thane?

Ross

From Fife, great King;
Where the Norweyan banners flout the sky,
50 And fan our people cold.
Norway himself, with terrible numbers,
Assisted by that most disloyal traitor
The Thane of Cawdor, began a dismal conflict,

31 surveying vantage: *seizing an opening*

32 furbished arms: *improved weapons*

36 say sooth: *tell the truth*

37 overcharged with double cracks: *prepared with double quantities of gunpowder*
39 Except they meant to bathe in reeking wounds: *as if they intended to wash in the foul blood of their enemies*
40 memorise another Golgotha: *make this place as memorable as the site of Christ's crucifixion (Golgotha meaning 'the place of the skull')*
42 gashes: *wounds*

44 They smack of honour both: *both his words and his injuries suggest heroism*

45 Thane: *Scottish nobleman*

49 flout: *defy*

50 fan our people cold: *terrify our own population*

53 dismal conflict: *depressing fight*

54 Bellona's bridegroom: *Macbeth is fit to be the husband of the Roman goddess of war*

56 Point: *sword*

Till that Bellona's bridegroom, lapped in proof,

Confronted him with self-comparisons, 55

Point against point, rebellious arm 'gainst arm,

Curbing his lavish spirit; and, to conclude, — Macbeth

The victory fell on us. *beaten them*

Duncan

Great happiness!

Ross

That now

Sweno, the Norways' king, craves composition.

59 craves composition: *pleads for a peace treaty*

60 deign: *agree to*

61 disbursed: *paid*

61 Saint Colme's Inch: *an island in the Firth of Forth*

Nor would we deign him burial of his men 60

Till he disbursed, at Saint Colme's Inch,

Ten thousand dollars to our general use.

Duncan — *King*

No more that Thane of Cawdor shall deceive — *kill him*

64 bosom interest: *deepest good*

64 present: *instant*

Our bosom interest. Go pronounce his present death,

And with his former title greet Macbeth. — *give Macbeth* 65 *title*

Ross

I'll see it done.

Duncan

What he hath lost, noble Macbeth hath won.

Exeunt

Study Notes

The report of the battle (lines 1–44)

The ferocious confrontation between King Duncan's forces and the traitors takes place offstage. A wounded captain who had rescued the king's son, Malcolm, from 'captivity', graphically describes the action. At first, the rebel Macdonwald, his forces swollen by mercenaries ('kerns and gallowglasses'), seemed to have the upper hand. But a determined Macbeth 'carved out his passage' through the enemy ranks until he confronted Macdonwald. Discarding all formality, he then 'unseamed him from the nave to th' chops' and placed his head upon the battlements for all to see.

This graphic report highlights Macbeth's fierce heroism and increases the audience's interest in a man at the height of his powers, lavishly praised as loyal and fearless: 'Bellona's bridegroom', 'worthy gentleman'. But he also displayed excessive zeal in killing. Macbeth's sword 'smoked with bloody execution'. He and Banquo were intent on creating another Golgotha, a comparison with the scene of Christ's crucifixion. The extensive blood imagery establishes the play's violent atmosphere and ensures that we now link Macbeth with slaughter and an enthusiasm for killing.

The outcome (lines 45–67)

Another of the loyal Scottish thanes, the Earl of Ross, brings news of victory against the treacherous Thane of Cawdor and the Norwegians. Both Ross and the captain perform the dramatic function of a chorus, reporting and commenting on the play's action. Once again, Macbeth is highly praised for confronting Scotland's enemies. Duncan expresses his 'Great happiness' that his country is at peace and he feels that he is now secure: 'No more that Thane of Cawdor shall deceive/ Our bosom interest.'

Shakespeare presents King Duncan as an honourable monarch – but suggests that he is weak and a poor judge of character. Although Scotland is in a state of open rebellion, Duncan is not providing leadership on the battlefield, but relies on others to do that for him. However, he orders the rebellious Thane of Cawdor's 'present death' and grants the title to Macbeth. In every battle, there is a winner and a loser. Audiences will be acutely aware of the allusion to the weird sisters' refrain, 'Fair is foul, and foul is fair.'

A key purpose of this scene is to continue the dramatic build-up of Macbeth before he actually makes his first appearance. It also shows the unsettled state of Scotland and portrays the ineffectual Duncan. To date, the audience has been given a complex impression of Macbeth as a man who is both a loyal subject and a ferocious soldier.

Shakespeare's language

From the graphic description, 'the bloody man', to Macbeth's sword, which 'smoked with bloody execution', audiences are invited into a turbulent and merciless world. Brutal verbs convey the viciousness of the fighting: 'carved out', 'unseamed'. Shakespeare uses **images of heroism** to emphasise the unequal battle, 'As sparrows eagles, or the hare the lion'.

Emphatic repetition describes the force of the attack by Macbeth and Banquo against the Norwegian invaders: 'As cannons overcharged with double cracks,/ So they doubly redoubled strokes upon the foe'. The vigorous 'd' sound mimics the raining down of blows on the enemy. Effective **similes** describe the twisting fortunes of the struggle: 'Doubtful it stood;/ As two spent swimmers that do cling together/ And choke their art'. We can sense the two exhausted armies struggling to gain advantage, the level of their fatigue stressed by the alliterative phrase 'spent swimmers'.

Scotland's uncertain times are shown by the **juxtaposition of opposites**: 'comfort'/ 'Discomfort', 'lost' and 'won'. Nothing is quite as it seems. On the one hand, Macbeth is a courageous soldier, yet he is firmly linked to the weird sisters through the scene's concluding line, 'What he hath lost, noble Macbeth hath won.' Ironically, Duncan is unaware of any disloyal ambitions Macbeth might have and believes that he is now safe from further betrayal. Is he entirely oblivious of the risk he has taken? Will awarding Macbeth the title Thane of Cawdor incite his hidden ambitions?

Critical Analysis

1. Based on your study of Act 1 Scene 2, describe the world in which the play *Macbeth* is set. Refer closely to the text in your response.

2. What picture of Macbeth himself is conveyed in Act 1 Scene 2? Support your answer with reference to the text.

Sample Paragraph 1 (Q1)

I think this is a very bloody world. Everyone is drenched in blood, the captain, Macbeth and Banquo. The army general Macbeth seems to enjoy killing people from the 'navel to the chops' like a butcher. The wounded soldier explains about how brave Macbeth was in battle. 'Bellona's bridegroom'. He fights Duncan's rival enemies and puts their heads on sticks. The captain is wounded and has to be helped. It is a very bloody battlefield. When Macbeth does win he asks for money before he lets the king of Norway bury his soldiers. Duncan is not clued in or aware of what is going on. He praises Macbeth as a great fighter. He gives the traitor's title to Macbeth as a reward for his brave fighting during the battle scenes. *(130 words)*

Examiner's Comment

* This basic low-grade response is more of a random summary than a considered response to the question.
* While there are references to the violence, there is little or no focus on the key issue of 'world' and atmosphere.
* Expression is note-like, repetitive and poorly controlled.

Sample Paragraph 2 (Q1)

In Act 1 Scene 2, Shakespeare creates a blood-soaked violent world where nothing is as it first appears. The first visual image of the wounded captain, a 'bloody man' whose 'gashes cry for help', sets an uneasy tone. This frenzied world is also seen in the blood-thirsty Macbeth who cuts his way through enemies with a sword that 'smoked with bloody execution'. The carnage continues while Macbeth slashes the traitor Macdonwald from the 'nave to the chops'. Like 'cannons over-charged with double cracks', Macbeth and Banquo bravely confront the Norwegian army.

The uncertain atmosphere is found in the captain's description of the outcome of the battle as 'Doubtful'. The armies are 'spent swimmers', unable to move. Comfort seems to come and then discomfort. The mercenary soldiers don't fight but flee. But 'Bellona's bridegroom' wins in the end. An echo of the weird sisters concludes the scene, 'What he hath lost, noble Macbeth hath won.' Because of his loyalty to the king, Macbeth becomes the new Thane of Cawdor, replacing the former traitor. The tragic irony is that he will prove much more treacherous. Nothing is exactly as it seems in this violent blood-stained world. *(195 words)*

Examiner's Comment

* This is a much more focused top-grade answer that addresses the question directly.
* Clear discussion points (about violence and treachery) are well developed and supported with apt quotation throughout.
* The expression is closely controlled and fluent – and varied vocabulary (such as 'frenzied', 'carnage', 'tragic irony') is particularly impressive.

Key Quotes

What bloody man is that? (Duncan) l.1	The bloodstained captain provides a striking visual image of the gory battle being waged between Duncan's army and the rebels.
Doubtful it stood;/ As two spent swimmers that do cling together/ And choke their art (Captain) l.7–9	This vivid simile of the two exhausted swimmers holding each other so that neither can swim graphically portrays the ferocity of the conflict being fought offstage. We get a real sense of the tension surrounding the outcome of the battle.
from the Western Isles/ Of kerns and gallowglasses is supplied (Captain) l.12–13	Duncan's enemies are relying on mercenary soldiers – unlike the king's army, who are fighting for their country out of loyalty. The suggestion is that the mercenaries will not put up as strong a battle.
Till he unseamed him from the nave to th' chops,/ And fixed his head upon our battlements (Captain) l.22–3	Macbeth's fighting spirit and violent nature is portrayed in this gruesome account of his prowess in battle. Does the excessive fervour raise questions about Macbeth's character? Has he a love of sadistic violence?
So they doubly redoubled strokes upon the foe (Captain) l.38	Repetition highlights the desperate struggle. In Shakespeare's plays, battle scenes were usually offstage, so audiences had to imagine such ferocious scenes, helped by the language used.
Bellona's bridegroom (Ross) l.54	Previously Macbeth was spoken of in extravagantly heroic terms ('Valour's minion'). Now he is described as a fitting husband for the Roman goddess of war.
What he hath lost, noble Macbeth hath won (Duncan) l.67	The scene's concluding ironic line predicts Macbeth's future position in the kingdom. Duncan is still somewhat naive and appears to be totally unaware that Macbeth might eventually prove to be a more effective conspirator than the former Thane of Cawdor.

OVERVIEW

The three witches await the arrival of Macbeth. They chant a spell, boasting of their malicious acts. The witches then predict Macbeth's accession to the title of Thane of Cawdor and subsequently King of Scotland. They also foretell that Banquo's descendants shall be kings. Ross and Angus arrive to confirm that King Duncan has given Macbeth the title of Thane of Cawdor. Although Banquo is concerned that the witches' prophecies may lead to trouble, he agrees to meet later with Macbeth to discuss their predictions.

* **A key scene requiring close, detailed study**

A heath

Thunder. Enter three Witches

First Witch

Where hast thou been, sister?

Second Witch

Killing swine.

Third Witch

Sister, where thou?

First Witch

A sailor's wife had chestnuts in her lap,

5   And munched, and munched, and munched: 'Give me,' quoth I.

'Aroint thee, witch!' the rump-fed ronyon cries.

Her husband's to Aleppo gone, master o' the *Tiger*.

But in a sieve I'll thither sail,

And like a rat without a tail

10   I'll do, I'll do, and I'll do.

Second Witch

I'll give thee a wind.

First Witch

Th'art kind.

Third Witch

And I another.

First Witch

I myself have all the other,

15   And the very ports they blow,

All the quarters that they know

I'th' shipman's card.

I will drain him dry as hay.

Sleep shall neither night nor day

20   Hang upon his penthouse lid,

He shall live a man forbid.

Weary sev'nights nine times nine

Shall he dwindle, peak and pine.

Though his bark cannot be lost,

25   Yet it shall be tempest-tost.

Look what I have.

1 Killing swine: *slaughtering pigs*

6 Aroint thee: *clear off*
6 rump-fed ronyon: *fat kitchen maid fed on scraps*
7 Aleppo: *ancient city in the Middle East*
7 the *Tiger*: *name of a ship*
8 sieve: *strainer, cooking utensil with holes*

15 ports they blow: *storm winds*
16 quarters: *billets, shelters*
17 shipman's card: *naval compass*
18 drain him dry as hay: *make him weak*

20 penthouse lid: *eyelid*
21 forbid: *cursed*
22 sev'nights: *seven nights*
23 dwindle, peak and pine: *become thinner and thinner*
24 bark cannot be lost: *ship cannot be sunk*

28 pilot's thumb: *severed thumb of a ship's helmsman*

32 weird sisters: *agents of destiny who can predict the future*
33 Posters: *swift travellers*

37 charm: *spell*

39 called: *said to be*

40 withered: *shrivelled*
40 wild in their attire: *disorderly in their dress*
42 aught: *anything*

46 beards: *hairy chins*

51 hereafter: *at some time in the future*

Second Witch

Show me, show me.

First Witch

Here I have a pilot's thumb,

Wracked as homeward he did come.

Drum within

Third Witch

A drum, a drum –   30

Macbeth doth come.

All

The weird sisters, hand in hand,   *writes spell like rhyming*

Posters of the sea and land,

Thus do go about, about;

Thrice to thine, and thrice to mine,   35

And thrice again, to make up nine.

Peace, the charm's wound up.

Enter Macbeth and Banquo

Macbeth   — *Witches said same Act 1 Scene 1*

So foul and fair a day I have not seen.

Banquo

How far is't called to Forres? – What are these,

So withered, and so wild in their attire,   40

That look not like the inhabitants o' th'earth,

And yet are on't? – Live you? Or are you aught

That man may question? You seem to understand me,

By each at once her choppy finger laying

Upon her skinny lips. You should be women,   45

And yet your beards forbid me to interpret

That you are so.

Macbeth

Speak, if you can: what are you?

First Witch

All hail, Macbeth! Hail to thee, Thane of Glamis!   *he is*

Second Witch

All hail, Macbeth! Hail to thee, Thane of Cawdor!   *he is not but will be*   *predicted*   50

Third Witch

All hail, Macbeth, that shalt be king hereafter!

far fetched

prophecy

Banquo

Good sir, why do you start, and seem to fear

Things that do sound so fair? I'th' name of truth,

Are ye fantastical, or that indeed

55   Which outwardly ye show? My noble partner

You greet with present grace, and great prediction

Of noble having and of royal hope,

That he seems rapt withal: to me you speak not.

If you can look into the seeds of time,

60   And say which grain will grow and which will not,

Speak then to me, who neither beg nor fear

Your favours nor your hate.

[handwritten: What about me]

First Witch

Hail!

Second Witch

Hail!

Third Witch

65   Hail!

First Witch

Lesser than Macbeth, and greater. *[handwritten: ? what suggesting]*

Second Witch

Not so happy, yet much happier.

Third Witch

Thou shalt get kings, though thou be none.

So all hail, Macbeth and Banquo!

First Witch

70   Banquo and Macbeth, all hail!

Macbeth

Stay, you imperfect speakers, tell me more.

By Sinel's death I know I am Thane of Glamis;

But how of Cawdor? The Thane of Cawdor lives,

A prosperous gentleman; and to be king

75   Stands not within the prospect of belief,

No more than to be Cawdor. Say from whence

You owe this strange intelligence? Or why

Upon this blasted heath you stop our way

With such prophetic greeting? Speak, I charge you.

Witches vanish

54 fantastical: *unreal, imaginary*

56 present grace: *current title (Thane of Glamis)*

56 great prediction: *the promise of becoming Thane of Cawdor*

57 royal hope: *possibility of becoming king*

57 rapt: *absorbed*

68 get: *be the father of*

71 imperfect: *incomplete, ambivalent*

72 Sinel: *Macbeth's father*

75 prospect: *possibility*

77 strange intelligence: *surprising knowledge*

78 blasted: *windblown*

79 charge: *command*

Banquo

The earth hath bubbles, as the water has, 80

And these are of them. Whither are they vanished?

Macbeth

Into the air, and what seemed corporal

Melted as breath into the wind. Would they had stayed!

Banquo

Were such things here as we do speak about?

Or have we eaten on the insane root 85

That takes the reason prisoner?

Macbeth

Your children shall be kings.

Banquo

                               You shall be king.

Macbeth

And Thane of Cawdor too; went it not so?

Banquo

To th' self-same tune and words. Who's here?

Enter Ross and Angus

Ross

The king hath happily received, Macbeth, 90

The news of thy success; and when he reads

Thy personal venture in the rebels' fight,

His wonders and his praises do contend

Which should be thine or his. Silenced with that,

In viewing o'er the rest o' th' self-same day, 95

He finds thee in the stout Norweyan ranks,

Nothing afeard of what thyself didst make,

Strange images of death. As thick as hail

Came post with post, and every one did bear

Thy praises in his kingdom's great defence, 100

And poured them down before him.

Angus

                             We are sent

To give thee from our royal master thanks;

Only to herald thee into his sight,

Not pay thee.

83 corporal: *physical, solid*

85 insane root: *a herb causing madness, possibly hemlock*

91 reads: *takes note of*

92 Thy personal venture: *your own action*

93 contend: *clash, compete*

97 Nothing afeard: *not at all afraid*

99 post with post: *many messages*

103 herald: *escort*

Ross

105   And, for an earnest of a greater honour,

He bade me, from him, call thee Thane of Cawdor,

In which addition, hail, most worthy thane,

For it is thine.

Banquo

              What, can the devil speak true?

Macbeth

The Thane of Cawdor lives; why do you dress me

In borrowed robes?

Angus

110   Who was the thane, lives yet;

But under heavy judgement bears that life

Which he deserves to lose. Whether he was combined

With those of Norway, or did line the rebel

With hidden help and vantage, or that with both

115   He laboured in his country's wrack, I know not;

But treasons capital, confessed and proved,

Have overthrown him.

Macbeth

Aside

             Glamis, and Thane of Cawdor!

The greatest is behind! *[to Ross and Angus]* Thanks for

      your pains.

[to Banquo] Do you not hope your children shall be kings,

120   When those that gave the Thane of Cawdor to me,

Promised no less to them?

Banquo

                That, trusted home,

Might yet enkindle you unto the crown,

Besides the Thane of Cawdor. But 'tis strange,

And oftentimes, to win us to our harm,

125   The instruments of darkness tell us truths,

Win us with honest trifles, to betray us

In deepest consequence.

[to Ross and Angus] Cousins, a word, I pray you.

---

105 earnest: *promise*

107 addition: *new title*

110 borrowed robes: *clothes which do not rightfully belong*

111 heavy judgement: *death sentence*

112 combined: *allied, in league with*

113 line: *reinforce*

116 treasons capital: *momentous betrayals*

121 trusted home: *believed absolutely*

122 enkindle: *fire*

125 instruments of darkness: *evil powers*

126 Win us with honest trifles: *entice us with small truths*

126 betray: *deceive*

127 deepest consequence: *great issues*

128 Cousins: *kinsmen*

Macbeth

Aside

Two truths are told

As happy prologues to the swelling act   130

Of the imperial theme. – *[aloud]* I thank you, gentlemen. –

[aside] This supernatural soliciting

Cannot be ill, cannot be good. If ill,

Why hath it given me earnest of success,

Commencing in a truth? I am Thane of Cawdor.   135

If good, why do I yield to that suggestion

Whose horrid image doth unfix my hair

And make my seated heart knock at my ribs

Against the use of nature? Present fears

Are less than horrible imaginings.   140

My thought, whose murder yet is but fantastical,

Shakes so my single state of man that function

Is smothered in surmise, and nothing is

But what is not.

Banquo

Look, how our partner's rapt.

Macbeth

Aside

If chance will have me king, why, chance may crown me,   145

Without my stir.

Banquo

New honours come upon him,

Like our strange garments, cleave not to their mould

But with the aid of use.

Macbeth

Aside

Come what come may,

Time and the hour runs through the roughest day.

Banquo

Worthy Macbeth, we stay upon your leisure.   150

Macbeth

Give me your favour. My dull brain was wrought

With things forgotten. Kind gentlemen, your pains

Are registered where every day I turn

The leaf to read them. Let us toward the king.

155 *[aside to Banquo]* Think upon what hath chanced; and, at more time,

The interim having weighed it, let us speak

Our free hearts each to other.

Banquo

Very gladly.

Macbeth

Till then, enough. *[to Ross and Angus]* Come, friends.

Exeunt

156 The interim having weighed it:
after time for further thought

Study Notes

The weird sisters (lines 1–37)

The three witches spitefully boast of their malevolent exploits. The second witch has been killing pigs while the first has decided to torture a sailor by creating storms. She takes her revenge on the 'master o' the *Tiger*' because of his wife's refusal to give her a chestnut. Together, they perform a spell before Macbeth's entrance; 'the charm's wound up'. This atmospheric scene now brings the worlds of the supernatural and the human together.

The first meeting (lines 38–89)

Macbeth unknowingly aligns himself with the witches by echoing their comment from the opening scene: 'So foul and fair a day I have not seen.' Indeed, his words are so close to the witches' speech, 'Fair is foul, and foul is fair', as to suggest that he is already under their spell.

Everything, including the weather, is in a state of flux and nothing is exactly what it seems. The witches should be 'women', yet their 'beards' contradict this. They immediately turn their attention directly to Macbeth, addressing him as 'Thane of Cawdor' and forecasting that he will be 'king hereafter'. Banquo is troubled by Macbeth's startled reaction to such good news, 'why do you start, and seem to fear?' He notes that Macbeth becomes totally withdrawn, 'rapt withal'. The audience is left to wonder at his extraordinary behaviour.

To a large extent, the witches ignore Banquo, who in turn remains sceptical of them. In contrast, Macbeth is much more energised and anxious to know more; 'Say from whence/ You owe this strange intelligence?' But the 'imperfect speakers' disappear, 'as breath into the wind', leaving Macbeth to remark wistfully, 'Would they had stayed!'

The second meeting (lines 90–158)

Ross and Angus arrive with news from King Duncan confirming that Macbeth has been made Thane of Cawdor as a reward for his loyalty and courage on the field of battle. Macbeth argues that he is not entitled to this position, 'why do you dress me/ In borrowed robes?' He is then informed that the former Thane of Cawdor has confessed to his treason and been sentenced to death for aiding the rebels.

Banquo's and Macbeth's reactions differ greatly. The cautious Banquo tries to warn Macbeth to be wary of the witches' prophecies, reminding him that evil powers seduce men into dangerous situations by tempting them 'with honest trifles'. But thoughts of becoming king, 'happy prologues to the swelling act', appeal to Macbeth's imagination. His first soliloquy clearly shows that he has become obsessed with the witches' predictions. He attempts to rationalise their prophecies, weighing the different options; 'If ill', then 'If good'. Yet it seems almost certain that the possibility of murdering Duncan had already occurred to him, 'Present fears/ Are less than horrible imaginings.'

For a second time, Banquo comments on Macbeth's distracted state, 'Look, how our partner's rapt.' But after considering the prospect of becoming Scotland's next ruler, Macbeth reaches the decision that he will leave everything to destiny: 'If chance will have me king, why, chance may crown me,/ Without my stir.' He then privately suggests that he and Banquo should meet later to discuss all that has happened. For the audience, this important scene raises the crucial question: will Macbeth have to act to ensure that he becomes king?

Shakespeare's language

The play's murky, **ambivalent atmosphere** is heightened by the supernatural witches and the uncertainty which surrounds everything. The witches even defy the laws of nature: 'what seemed corporal/ Melted as breath into the wind.'

Peace, the charm's wound up

The Witches,
Act 1 Scene 3, l.37

The 'foul and fair' weather serves as a **pathetic fallacy** (attributing human feelings to inanimate objects), hinting at the inner storm brewing in Macbeth's mind. A staccato exchange of malicious acts performed by the witches and the emphasis on the magic numbers of three, seven and nine add to the surreal atmosphere. Impossible physical feats (setting sail in a sieve, predicting the future, looking into 'the seeds of time') all serve to unsettle the audience.

Other **echoes foreshadow** Macbeth's possible fate. He, like the sailor, will be drained 'dry as hay', emotionally and morally, by the witches and their predictions. He will find it difficult to rest, 'Sleep shall neither night nor day/ Hang upon his penthouse lid'. He will 'dwindle', becoming less than the man he was. Not only is Macbeth linked to the witches through his opening remark, he also indulges in their equivocation.

During his **soliloquy**, he mulls over 'Things that do sound so fair'. He tries to make sense of everything he has heard by teasing out the possible consequences of what the witches have promised: 'If good, why do I yield to that suggestion/ Whose horrid image doth unfix my hair ... ?'

Macbeth also identifies his character flaw of procrastination, his inability to act through over-thinking a problem: 'function/ Is smothered in surmise'. The use of **asides** shows that he is beginning to act secretively, 'nothing is/ But what is not'. He even suggests that Banquo and he should meet to 'speak/ Our free hearts each to other'. Is he possibly suggesting that they form an alliance against Duncan so that both can profit? Shakespeare leaves us wondering what will happen next. Will Macbeth become king? And by what means?

Critical Analysis

1. 'Appearances are deceptive.' Discuss this statement in relation to Act 1 Scene 3 of *Macbeth*. Refer closely to the text in your response.

2. Act 1 Scene 3 develops our understanding of the relationship between the two comrades-in-arms, Macbeth and Banquo. In your opinion, what picture of their relationship emerges from this scene? Give reasons for your response, supporting your answer with reference to the play.

Sample Paragraph 1 (Q1)

In this scene on the windswept heath nobody's sure of what is happening. For a start, can the witches really tell the future? The weather is good and bad at the same time, 'foul and fair'. Impossible. Banquo doesn't know what Macbeth is thinking. Macbeth himself doesn't know what to think. The witches are not what they seem or appear. They look like women but have men's beards. So Banquo can't take them too seriously, but Macbeth half believes in them. They speak in complete riddles, mixing up the truth with the future without ever explaining themselves properly. I think everyone's confused but especially Macbeth himself who is dying to be king some day but not sure about killing the old King Duncan. Appearances are totally deceptive in this scene. *(130 words)*

Examiner's Comment

- This very limited attempt outlines some of the deceptive aspects of the scene, such as the uncertainty about the witches and Macbeth's reaction to them.
- Points lack development and reflection.
- There is no effective use of supportive quotation.
- Expression is note-like and repetitive throughout this basic-grade response.

Sample Paragraph 2 (Q1)

In this dramatic scene, what 'seems' is not necessarily so. Macbeth wryly comments near the scene's conclusion, 'nothing is/ But what is not'. The witches, their prophecies, people's attitudes and reactions, the very earth itself, all appear illusive. The witches' appearance belies their nature, they should 'be women' – yet their 'withered' physical appearance, 'choppy fingers' and 'beards' all suggest the opposite. They 'look not like the inhabitants o' th' earth/ And yet are on't'. These weird creatures seem 'corporal', but are capable of disappearing like insubstantial 'bubbles', so much so that Banquo wonders, 'Were such things here as we do speak about?' He seems to distrust the evidence of his own eyes. He is also amazed at Macbeth's startled reaction to their news. Macbeth seems to fear 'Things that do sound so fair'. In Macbeth's soliloquy, he reveals that he is unable to make up his mind about what to do. His 'seated' heart, which was so strong on the battlefield, now shakes, his hair stands on end. He is paralysed into inaction; what a contrast to the fearless warrior! Which is the real Macbeth? Yet outwardly he does not express his true emotions and just seems 'rapt withal'. After the predictions, there is an atmosphere of secrecy, conveyed by many asides. This misleading scene leaves the audience in a state of suspense, wondering what the next twist will be in this disturbing drama. *(235 words)*

Examiner's Comment

- This is a much more focused answer which addresses the question directly, using apt references and quotations throughout.
- Good range of developed discussion points about the ambivalence of the witches and Macbeth.
- Close interaction with the text, e.g. 'Which is the real Macbeth?'
- Impressive expression ('all appear illusive', 'paralysed into inaction') adds to the quality of this incisive, top-grade response.

❝❝ Key Quotes

So foul and fair a day I have not seen *(Macbeth to Banquo) l.38*	Macbeth unwittingly echoes the witches' chant, 'Fair is foul, and foul is fair'. While this paradoxical comment refers to the harsh weather and victory in battle, the audience will now link him with the forces of evil.
All hail, Macbeth, that shalt be king hereafter! *(Witches to Macbeth) l.51*	The witches greet Macbeth with his present title, his new title and the promise of kingship in the future. They have the ability to foretell the future and their predictions will have a crucial effect on Macbeth's life.
he seems rapt withal *(Banquo to Witches) l.58*	Banquo's comment about Macbeth's preoccupied state of mind is revealing. Clearly shocked by what he has heard, Macbeth withdraws into himself and seems oblivious to his surroundings.
why do you dress me/ In borrowed robes? *(Macbeth to Ross) l.109-10*	A disbelieving Macbeth challenges Ross, saying that he cannot be Thane of Cawdor because that gentleman is still alive. This vivid clothing imagery highlights the idea of assuming an illegal position.
The instruments of darkness tell us truths,/ Win us with honest trifles, to betray us/ In deepest consequence *(Banquo to Macbeth) l.125-7*	Banquo is suspicious of the witches and their predictions. Ironically, he warns Macbeth that evil powers often tempt people along a certain path with superficial truths, only to let them down when they are most needed.
This supernatural soliciting/ Cannot be ill, cannot be good *(Macbeth soliloquy) l.132-3*	This paradox again underlines the unstable times. If the prophecy is evil, why did it start with a truth? Macbeth *has* been made Thane of Cawdor. If it is good, why does he imagine himself as Duncan's murderer? Macbeth is already experiencing the torture of indecision.
New honours come upon him,/ Like our strange garments, cleave not to their mould/ But with the aid of use *(Banquo to Ross and Angus) l.146-8*	Using another clothing image, Banquo remarks that just as clothes fit better when they have been worn for a while, so Macbeth has not yet had the chance to adjust to his new title. Might he also be suggesting that Macbeth does not deserve to become king?
Come what come may,/ Time and the hour runs through the roughest day *(Macbeth aside) l.148-9*	Macbeth's philosophical comment reiterates his decision to wait and see what the future brings. Shakespeare's use of the rhyming couplet indicates that Macbeth is in denial and uncomfortable with thinking about the kingship.

OVERVIEW

Duncan enquires whether the disloyal Thane of Cawdor's execution has been carried out, and Malcolm reports that the rebellious thane was repentant and dignified in the end. The king expresses his gratitude to Macbeth and Banquo for defeating his enemies and securing his kingship. He officially honours Macbeth with the title Thane of Cawdor. Immediately, he proclaims that his son, Malcolm, will be the heir to the Scottish throne. Macbeth is horrified because he realises that this is a serious obstacle to his ambition. Duncan also announces his intention to spend time at Macbeth's castle in Inverness.

* **A key scene requiring close, detailed study**

Flourish: *fanfare of trumpets*

1 execution: *death sentence for treason*

2 Those in commission: *those commanded to carry out the execution*

2 liege: *lord*

5 frankly: *candidly, honestly*
5 treasons: *betrayal of one's country*
6 Implored: *begged for*

8 Became him: *did him proud*
9 studied in his death: *rehearsed his moment of death*
10 owed: *owned*
11 careless trifle: *item of little importance*

12 mind's construction: *inner thoughts*

15 ingratitude: *thanklessness, lack of appreciation*
16 so far before: *so beyond my power to pay you*
17 swiftest wing of recompense: *the most immediate repayment*
17–18 slow/ To overtake thee: *insufficient to reward you*
19 proportion: *balance*

21 thy due: *owed to you*

23 pays itself: *is its own reward*

Forres. The palace

Flourish. Enter King Duncan, Malcolm, Donalbain, Lennox and Attendants

Duncan

Is execution done on Cawdor? Are not

Those in commission yet returned?

Malcolm

My liege,

They are not yet come back. But I have spoke

With one that saw him die, who did report

That very frankly he confessed his treasons,   5

Implored your highness' pardon and set forth

A deep repentance. Nothing in his life

Became him like the leaving it. He died

As one that had been studied in his death

To throw away the dearest thing he owed,   10

As 'twere a careless trifle.

Duncan

There's no art

To find the mind's construction in the face.

He was a gentleman on whom I built

An absolute trust.

Enter Macbeth, Banquo, Ross, and Angus

O worthiest cousin!

The sin of my ingratitude even now   15

Was heavy on me. Thou art so far before

That swiftest wing of recompense is slow

To overtake thee. Would thou hadst less deserved,

That the proportion both of thanks and payment

Might have been mine! Only I have left to say,   20

More is thy due than more than all can pay.

Macbeth

The service and the loyalty I owe,

In doing it, pays itself. Your highness' part

Is to receive our duties; and our duties

Are to your throne and state, children and servants,   25

Which do but what they should, by doing everything

Safe toward your love and honour.

Duncan

                                        Welcome hither:

I have begun to plant thee, and will labour

To make thee full of growing. Noble Banquo,

30   That hast no less deserved, nor must be known

No less to have done so, let me enfold thee

And hold thee to my heart.

Banquo

                                  There if I grow,

The harvest is your own.

Duncan

                                My plenteous joys,

Wanton in fullness, seek to hide themselves

35   In drops of sorrow. Sons, kinsmen, thanes,

And you whose places are the nearest, know

We will establish our estate upon

Our eldest, Malcolm, whom we name hereafter

The Prince of Cumberland; which honour must

40   Not unaccompanied invest him only,

But signs of nobleness, like stars, shall shine

On all deservers. From hence to Inverness,

And bind us further to you.

Macbeth

The rest is labour, which is not used for you.

45   I'll be myself the harbinger, and make joyful

The hearing of my wife with your approach;

So humbly take my leave.

Duncan

                              My worthy Cawdor!

Macbeth

Aside

The Prince of Cumberland! that is a step

On which I must fall down, or else o'erleap,

50   For in my way it lies. Stars, hide your fires!

Let not light see my black and deep desires;

The eye wink at the hand, yet let that be

Which the eye fears, when it is done, to see.

Exit

---

27 hither: *here*

28 plant thee: *promote you*
28 labour: *work, endeavour*
29 full of growing: *enhance your status*

31 enfold: *embrace*

32 if I grow: *if my position is advanced*
33 harvest: *return, yield*

33 plenteous: *many*
34 Wanton: *unruly, unrestrained*

37 establish our estate: *pass on my title and power*

40 Not unaccompanied ... only: *he alone is to be honoured*

42 Inverness: *location of Macbeth's castle*

43 bind us further: *become even closer*

44 The rest ... for you: *everything else is tiresome*
45 harbinger: *messenger*

48 step: *obstacle*

49 o'erleap: *overcome*

51 my black and deep desires: *Macbeth's secret wish to kill Duncan*
52 The eye wink at the hand: *let conscience ignore actions*
52 let that be: *allow*
53 when it is done, to see: *observe the outcome after the deed is done*

54 valiant: *heroic*

55 commendations: *praises, recommendations*

55 fed: *comforted, sustained*

57 peerless: *unrivalled, without equal*

Duncan

True, worthy Banquo; he is full so valiant,

And in his commendations I am fed;   55

It is a banquet to me. Let's after him,

Whose care is gone before to bid us welcome:

It is a peerless kinsman.

Flourish. Exeunt

Study Notes

Deception and treachery (lines 1–15)

The Thane of Cawdor has received swift punishment for his treachery, 'Is execution done on Cawdor?' We learn that he has died nobly and expressed 'deep repentance' for his treason. Malcolm acknowledges Cawdor's final graciousness, 'Nothing in his life/ Became him like the leaving it.' However, Duncan shows himself to be much more credulous: 'There's no art/ To find the mind's construction in the face.' He is not a good judge of character and admits to being bitterly disappointed in the former Thane of Cawdor, 'He was a gentleman on whom I built/ An absolute trust.' Ironically, Macbeth enters at this precise moment. Is Duncan about to show his naivety again?

Public compliments and private thoughts (lines 15–58)

The generous king expresses his appreciation to his loyal supporters, Macbeth and Banquo, 'The sin of my ingratitude even now/ Was heavy on me.' Macbeth appears to be the most reliable of followers, 'Your highness' part/ Is to receive our duties'.

The public compliments continue. Although there is a genuine warmth between Duncan and Banquo ('let me enfold thee/ And hold thee to my heart'), the king has not rewarded him directly. Duncan continually exhibits a lack of judgement. He chooses this moment to make the dramatic announcement that his eldest son, Malcolm, will succeed him as king.

In trying to establish political stability, Duncan risks alienating other contenders for the throne of Scotland – particularly Macbeth, the hero of the hour. Although a generous man, the king appears to lack strong leadership skills. He has not played an active part in the battle and is not fully aware of the atmosphere around him.

Macbeth, in his private thoughts, expressed in his soliloquy, shows a very different side to his character; his devious nature emerges. He has quickly realised that Malcolm's promotion is a serious obstacle to his own ambitions, 'a step/ On which I must fall down, or else o'erleap.' He requires darkness to carry out his terrible deed, 'Let not light see my black and deep desires'. Macbeth is now divided within himself, wanting desperately to be king, yet concerned with what has to be done to get the throne, succinctly expressed in the phrase, 'The eye wink at the hand'. Even one part of the body has to be unaware of what another part is doing.

Shakespeare's language

The witches' words 'Fair is foul, and foul is fair' dominate this scene of echoes and **dramatic irony**. Cawdor's fate foreshadows Macbeth's own tragic downfall: 'Nothing in his life/ Became him like the leaving it.' Duncan once regarded Cawdor as someone in whom he could place 'absolute trust'. Now he regards Macbeth as a 'peerless kinsman'. Shakespeare confounds his audience with such bewildering links.

This scene is **rich in imagery**. Duncan employs images from building when describing how hard it is to get beyond superficial appearances, 'There's no art/ To find the mind's *construction* in the face,/ He was a gentleman on whom I *built*/ An absolute trust.' The king also uses imagery from nature to show how he is going to reward Macbeth, 'I have begun to *plant* thee, and will labour/ To make thee full of *growing*.'

Duncan's references to **light** express how he is going to reward others, 'signs of nobleness, like stars, shall shine'. However, when Macbeth picks up this imagery in his soliloquy, it is to express the exact opposite, 'Stars, hide your fires!' This contrast between light and darkness highlights the difference between good and evil, openness and hypocrisy.

A clear distinction in **speech patterns** contrast the different characters. Duncan's extravagant speech is answered by the public Macbeth's formal conventional tones as he appears to be the loyal subject, 'I'll be myself the harbinger', 'So humbly take my leave'. The honest Banquo is much more succinct, 'There if I grow,/ The harvest is your own.'

Shakespeare also uses **dramatic irony** (a device used to let the audience know more than the characters onstage) to increase tension. The sly Macbeth enters just as Duncan has expressed his disappointment at Cawdor's treason and is greeted by 'O worthiest cousin'. Yet the audience is already well aware that Macbeth has been harbouring malicious thoughts against the king. Immediately after Macbeth's soliloquy, in which he has been agonising over Malcolm's succession as heir to the throne ('in my way it lies'), Duncan describes him as a 'peerless kinsman'.

My worthy Cawdor!
Duncan, Act 1 Scene 4, l.47

Critical Analysis

1. In your opinion, is Duncan a wise and astute leader or a naive and gullible character? Give reasons for your view and support your response with accurate quotation from the text.

2. Act 1 Scene 4 develops our understanding of the theme of appearance and reality. In your opinion, how effectively is this theme explored throughout the scene? Explain your response and support your answer with reference to the play.

Sample Paragraph 1 (Q2)

Duncan is a decent but simple king who believes everyone should be as they appear. He is unable to see into people's minds. He has already been betrayed and is going to be betrayed again by Macbeth who is angry and furious that he has chosen his son Malcolm to be next king. This is what sets off Macbeth's 'dark and black desires'. In Scotland the eldest son of a ruling king did not automatically have the right to be the next heir. Duncan just thinks if he hands out 'signs of nobility', then there will be no more rebellion. It's a gamble that backfires. Macbeth becomes more secretive and decides he has to do something now to gain royal power for himself, 'Stars put out your lights'. There's a lot of deception going on in this scene for the audience to notice. *(140 words)*

Examiner's Comment

- This basic response includes some potentially good discussion of appearance and reality.
- Points are not developed, however, and misquotes further reduce the quality of response.
- The essential element concerning how the playwright explores the theme of deception is almost entirely ignored.
- Expression is repetitive at times and poorly controlled, e.g. the third sentence.

Sample Paragraph 2 (Q2)

The credulous Duncan, already completely duped by the traitors Macdonwald and the Thane of Cawdor, regretfully remarks, 'There's no art/ To find the mind's construction in the face'. At that moment, Shakespeare has the duplicitous Macbeth enter to be greeted by Duncan as 'O worthiest cousin'. The audience is left astounded. This king has learned nothing. But it is when Duncan then announces that he intends to 'establish our estate upon/ Our eldest, Malcolm' that we really see the distinction between appearance and reality. Macbeth, the 'peerless kinsman', unnerves us with a soliloquy in which his soaring ambition is expressed in dramatic language, 'that is a step/ On which I must fall down, or else o'erleap'. The playwright involves us in the murky atmosphere of plotting and hypocrisy through the effective use of light and darkness imagery. Shakespeare also cleverly uses personification to show how Macbeth is aware of the necessity for self-deceit, 'The eye wink at the hand'. Deception fills the air and nobody is aware of what Macbeth is thinking. His final tortuous comments add to the suspense in this crucial scene. *(185 words)*

Examiner's Comment

- This focused top-grade response shows genuine engagement with both the question and the play.
- Clear discussion points highlight the recurring effects of deceit within the scene – and these are well developed and supported with accurate quotations.
- There is also a commendable focus on how the playwright involves the audience.
- The expression is assured, well controlled; vocabulary is impressive ('the duplicitous Macbeth', 'cleverly uses personification', 'tortuous comments').

❝❝ Key Quotes

Nothing in his life/ Became him like the leaving it (Malcolm to Duncan) l.7–8	The Thane of Cawdor's final dignified moments are the best of his life. Malcolm's comment is gracious, but is also realistic about Cawdor's earlier disloyalty.
There's no art/ To find the mind's construction in the face (Duncan to Malcolm) l.11–12	The credulous Duncan regrets being unable to discern what lies beneath the surface of an individual's outward appearance. Such lack of insight is particularly dangerous in a king. The audience is aware that he might well be repeating the same mistake with Macbeth.
More is thy due than more than all can pay (Duncan to Macbeth) l.21	Duncan shows himself to be gracious and trusting, thankful that the rebels have been defeated. He openly admits that he is completely in Macbeth's debt for his magnificent acts of bravery on the battlefield.
We will establish our estate upon/ Our eldest, Malcolm (Duncan) l.37–8	The king happily nominates his son, Malcolm, as his heir. He assumes that the Scottish crown is hereditary. Duncan may be thinking that he is securing power, but his timing is appalling. Both Macbeth and Banquo have fought bravely so that Duncan can retain his crown. The king's judgement is questionable.
The Prince of Cumberland! that is a step/ On which I must fall down, or else o'erleap (Macbeth) l.48–9	A furious Macbeth considers the unexpected obstacle that appears to thwart his ambition to be king. The audience will now be aware that (in Macbeth's view) Duncan has signed his own death warrant by appointing his son as successor.
Stars hide your fires!/ Let not light see my black and deep desires (Macbeth) l.50–1	The theme of light and dark is threaded throughout the entire play. Macbeth calls on the heavens to darken the skies lest light illuminates his hidden longing to be king. Once again, his language echoes that of the witches.
It is a peerless kinsman (Duncan to Banquo) l.58	A naive Duncan comments that Macbeth is without equal among the Scottish thanes. This deeply ironic statement shows how little the king has learned from his experience with the devious Cawdor and other rebels.

OVERVIEW

At Macbeth's castle in Inverness, Lady Macbeth reads a letter from her husband telling her of the witches' prophecies and his new title. Her intense ambition is apparent immediately and her only concern is that her husband lacks the necessary ruthlessness to fulfil his destiny and seize the Scottish crown. When informed of Duncan's impending visit, she prays to evil spirits to transform her into a pitiless, inhuman being. As soon as Macbeth arrives, she greets him warmly and takes control straightaway, advising him on how to act when the king arrives. In contrast to his decisive wife, Macbeth seems less certain.

* A key scene requiring close, detailed study

Inverness. Macbeth's castle

Enter Lady Macbeth with a letter

Lady Macbeth

Reads

'They met me in the day of success, and I have
learned by the perfectest report, they have more in
them than mortal knowledge. When I burned in desire
to question them further, they made themselves air, into

5   which they vanished. Whiles I stood rapt in the wonder
of it, came missives from the king, who all-hailed me,
"Thane of Cawdor"; by which title, before, these weird
sisters saluted me, and referred me to the coming on of time,
with, "Hail, king that shalt be!" This have I thought

10   good to deliver thee, my dearest partner of greatness,
that thou mightst not lose the dues of rejoicing by being
ignorant of what greatness is promised thee. Lay it to thy
heart, and farewell.'
Glamis thou art, and Cawdor; and shalt be

15   What thou art promised. Yet do I fear thy nature,
It is too full o' the milk of human kindness
To catch the nearest way. Thou wouldst be great,
Art not without ambition, but without
The illness should attend it. What thou wouldst highly,

20   That wouldst thou holily; wouldst not play false,
And yet wouldst wrongly win. Thou'dst have, great Glamis,
That which cries 'Thus thou must do', if thou have it,
And that which rather thou dost fear to do
Than wishest should be undone. Hie thee hither,

25   That I may pour my spirits in thine ear,
And chastise with the valour of my tongue
All that impedes thee from the golden round,
Which fate and metaphysical aid doth seem
To have thee crowned withal.

Enter Messenger

                       What is your tidings?

Messenger

The king comes here tonight.

---

1 day of success: *victory against the rebels*
2 perfectest report: *most reliable information*
3 mortal knowledge: *limits of human understanding*
5 rapt: *spellbound, engrossed*
6 missives: *messengers*
8 coming on of time: *future*
10 deliver: *tell*
11 dues of rejoicing: *your right to feel great delight*
12 ignorant: *unaware*
12–13 Lay it ... heart: *place it carefully in your heart (to ponder it and keep it secret)*
15 I fear thy nature: *I worry about your gentle character*
16 milk of human kindness: *human feelings of compassion and mercy*
17 catch the nearest way: *take the direct route (kill Duncan and seize power)*
17 Thou wouldst be great: *you want to be king*
18–19 without ... should attend it: *lacking the ruthlessness required*
20 holily: *by fair means*
20 wouldst not play false: *do not wish to do wrong*
21 wouldst wrongly win: *want to win what is not yours*
21–2 Thou'dst have ... have it: *your desires require you to commit regicide*
23–4 that which ... be undone: *your fear of committing murder is more powerful than any regret you might have after carrying out the act*
24 Hie thee hither: *hurry here to me*
25 spirits: *feelings of courage*
26 chastise ... my tongue: *reprimand with the strength of my words*
27 impedes ... golden round: *prevents you from gaining the crown*
28 Which fate ... withal: *with which destiny and the supernatural appear to have already crowned you*
29 tidings: *news*

32 informed for preparation: *told me so that I could prepare for Duncan's visit*

34 had the speed of him: *rode faster than him*

36 Give him tending: *look after him*

37 raven: *a bird of ill omen, thought to foretell death*
37 hoarse: *rough-voiced*
38 fatal entrance: *final visit (Duncan will not leave Macbeth's castle)*
39-40 you spirits ... mortal thoughts: *you evil spirits who encourage murderous plans*
40 unsex me here: *remove my womanly feelings of tenderness*
42 Make thick my blood: *give me strength*
43 Stop up ... remorse: *do not allow me to feel pity or regret*
44 compunctious visitings of nature: *natural guilty feelings*
45 Shake my fell purpose: *weaken my fierce determination*
45-6 keep peace ... Th'effect and it: *prevent its accomplishment*
47 take my milk for gall: *replace my mother's milk with bile*
47 murdering ministers: *agents of slaughter*
48 sightless substances: *invisible forms*
49 wait ... mischief: *assist nature's malice*
50 pall thee: *cover yourself*
50 dunnest: *darkest, murkiest*
51 keen: *sharp*
52-3 Nor heaven ... 'Hold, hold': *May heaven be unable to see through the darkness so that it cannot prevent the murder*
54 by the all-hail hereafter: *by the prophecy of your future greatness*
55-6 transported me ... present: *brought me beyond this current moment*

Lady Macbeth

> Thou'rt mad to say it. 30

Is not thy master with him? Who, were't so,
Would have informed for preparation.

Messenger

So please you, it is true: our thane is coming;
One of my fellows had the speed of him,
Who, almost dead for breath, had scarcely more 35
Than would make up his message.

Lady Macbeth

> Give him tending:

He brings great news.

Exit Messenger

> The raven himself is hoarse

That croaks the fatal entrance of Duncan
Under my battlements. Come, you spirits
That tend on mortal thoughts, unsex me here, 40
And fill me from the crown to the toe top-full
Of direst cruelty. Make thick my blood,
Stop up th'access and passage to remorse,
That no compunctious visitings of nature
Shake my fell purpose, nor keep peace between 45
Th'effect and it. Come to my woman's breasts,
And take my milk for gall, you murdering ministers,
Wherever in your sightless substances
You wait on nature's mischief. Come, thick night,
And pall thee in the dunnest smoke of hell, 50
That my keen knife see not the wound it makes,
Nor heaven peep through the blanket of the dark
To cry 'Hold, hold!'

Enter Macbeth

> Great Glamis! Worthy Cawdor!

Greater than both, by the all-hail hereafter.
Thy letters have transported me beyond 55
This ignorant present, and I feel now
The future in the instant.

Macbeth

> My dearest love,

Duncan comes here tonight.

Lady Macbeth

> And when goes hence?

Macbeth

Tomorrow, as he purposes.

Lady Macbeth

                    O, never

60   Shall sun that morrow see.

Your face, my thane, is as a book, where men

May read strange matters. To beguile the time,

Look like the time. Bear welcome in your eye,

Your hand, your tongue; look like the innocent flower,

65   But be the serpent under it. He that's coming

Must be provided for; and you shall put

This night's great business into my dispatch,

Which shall to all our nights and days to come

Give solely sovereign sway and masterdom.

Macbeth

We will speak further.

Lady Macbeth

                    Only look up clear;

70   To alter favour ever is to fear.

Leave all the rest to me.

Exeunt

59 purposes: *intends*

62 read strange matters: *observe sinister complications*

62-3 To beguile the time/ Look like the time: *to deceive other people, appear to be as innocent as everyone else*

66 provided for: *dealt with (Duncan is both guest and victim)*

67 into my dispatch: *into my management*

69 solely sovereign sway: *total power*

70 Only look up clear: *you only have to appear unconcerned*

71 To alter ... to fear: *if you seem troubled, you will create suspicion*

look like the innocent flower,/
But be the serpent under it
Lady Macbeth, Act 1 Scene 5, l.64-65

Study Notes

Hopes of greatness (lines 1–29)

Lady Macbeth reads a letter from her husband informing her of his recent encounter with the witches and his spellbound reaction to their predictions, 'I stood rapt in the wonder of it'. His wife's response is instant and resolute, 'and shalt be/ What thou art promised', her words echoing those of the witches, 'that shalt be king hereafter'. Her only concern is her husband's character, which is 'too full o' the milk of human kindness' to do what must be done – the murder of Duncan. She is well aware of how much he wishes to be king, 'Thou wouldst be great', but also realises that he does not want to 'play false'. So she decides to strengthen his resolve. This terrifying woman has no doubts about her ability to manipulate her husband.

Fears of doom (lines 37–53)

Lady Macbeth's second soliloquy is a chilling invocation to the spirits of evil. She invites them to remove any vestiges of her feminine nature, 'unsex me here', and asks to be filled with 'direst cruelty', desiring nothing to come between her 'fell purpose' and its execution. Like Macbeth, she needs to operate under the cover of darkness, 'thick night'. Although her demonic language is similar to that of the witches, the audience might wonder if she is forcing herself to act against her real nature.

Partners in deceit (lines 53–72)

Macbeth arrives to a rapturous welcome from his wife. Once again, Lady Macbeth's speech echoes the witches, 'Greater than both, by the *all-hail hereafter*'. This links her with dark supernatural powers. Macbeth's genuine affection for his wife, 'My dearest love', is clearly evident. At this point, their relationship is very close. She takes the lead in 'This night's great business', advising her husband to behave like the perfect host, 'Bear welcome in your eye'. Meanwhile, while he acts like a hypocrite ('the innocent flower'), she will take care of Duncan. Macbeth hesitates, 'We will speak further', thus giving credence to his wife's uneasiness about his character in her first soliloquy. Characteristically, she does not listen to his concerns but emphatically commands, 'Leave all the rest to me'.

Shakespeare's language

The playwright creates a powerfully **ominous atmosphere** throughout this scene. Macbeth's letter links the past ('these weird sisters saluted me') and the future ('Hail, king that shalt be'). There is an underlying tension between good and evil throughout. This sense of ambiguity was first referenced in the witches' chant of 'Fair is foul, and foul is fair' and is continued in Lady Macbeth's critical appraisal of her husband's paradoxical nature, 'Thou wouldst', 'wouldst not'. Macbeth craves the great prize of kingship, but does not want to have to do what is required to achieve it.

Lady Macbeth's soliloquy reverberates with the **appalling imagery and sound effects** which signify what must be done to secure the crown. Onomatopoeia emphasises the arrival of the doomed Duncan, 'The raven himself is *hoarse*/ That *croaks* the fatal entrance'. Such unsettling description shows the lengths to which she is prepared to go. Long vowel sounds ('direst cruelty') and alliteration ('murdering ministers') underline the unearthly nature of the evil spirits she addresses.

Effective use of **personification** accentuates the evil required to perform the dreadful deed of regicide, 'Come, thick night,/ And pall thee in the dunnest smoke of hell'. Her chilling language has close similarities with Macbeth's references to light and darkness. This parallel use of imagery stresses the close union of the couple's secret desires.

Half-line breaks intensify the drama as each character picks up the rhythm of the other's speech, 'Duncan comes here tonight', 'And when goes hence?' Lady Macbeth issues orders to her indecisive husband in a series of curt imperatives, 'Look', 'bear', 'put'.

The **contrast between reality and illusion** is graphically portrayed in the image of the 'innocent flower' and 'the serpent'. This embodiment of wickedness waits quietly before striking its victim with its deadly blow. The scene ends on a resolute note expressing Lady Macbeth's assumption that she and her husband will soon seize absolute power, and her final terse command, 'Leave all the rest to me', prepares the audience for the nerve-wracking events to come.

Critical Analysis

1. 'Shakespeare uses a range of contrasts to create a darkly fascinating world in the course of the play *Macbeth*.' Discuss this statement in relation to Act 1 Scene 5, supporting your answer with close reference to the text.

2. 'Act 1 Scene 5 makes effective use of the soliloquy as a dramatic technique to reveal Lady Macbeth's true character.' Discuss this view, supporting your answer with close reference to the text.

Sample Paragraph 1 (Q1)

Shakespeare contrasts Lady Macbeth with the witches. She says almost the same words as they use, 'hail here-after'. Lady Macbeth is like a fourth witch who wants to be like the other three 'murdering minsters'. She wants to live in the same darkly fascinating world as they do, 'thickest night'.
I think this scene is also fascinating because it contrasts Lady Macbeth with her husband, Macbeth. She uses the same ideas as he does with the hope of becoming the new rulers of Scotland, but he is weak and half-hearted. She is strong and completely evil. He wants to kill Duncan in the dark, 'Stars hide all your fires'. So does she, 'no light will see my keen knife'. This is a scene of fascinating contrasts. *(125 words)*

Examiner's Comment

• This low-grade answer is made up primarily of unfocused narrative and fails to address the full question.

• While there are references to contrasts, the point on the 'darkly fascinating world' is stated but lacks development.

• There are some misquotes and the expression is poorly controlled.

ACT 1 | **Scene 5 – Critical Analysis**

Sample Paragraph 2 (Q1)

Lady Macbeth is a real contrast to her husband Macbeth, who is 'full o' the milk of human kindness'. This evil woman is not. She wants her 'milk' to be replaced with 'gall'. She is ferocious in her determination to see Macbeth king, 'shalt be/ What thou art promised'. He is not so sure, 'We will speak further'. But she is not going to let anything stand in her way. She commands him, 'Leave all the rest to me'. She echoes her husband's wish 'Stars hide your fires' by summoning 'thick night' to come and cover everything in darkness so that the wicked deed of murder cannot be seen. Through this effective contrast of a strong-minded wife with an unsure husband, Shakespeare has created an interesting play. *(130 words)*

Examiner's Comment

- This mid-grade answer has concentrated on the effective difference in character between Lady Macbeth and Macbeth. But it has also failed to address the entire question. There is only a brief reference to 'an interesting play' in the concluding sentence.
- The contrast between husband and wife is developed and is supported with relevant quotation.
- However, the reference to the echo of her husband's wish shows a lack of precise focus on the question asked.

Sample Paragraph 3 (Q1)

In Act 1 Scene 5, Lady Macbeth and Macbeth, who both crave power, are starkly contrasted. In a shocking soliloquy, Lady Macbeth prays to the powers of darkness to change her compassionate female nature, to 'unsex me here'. Her demands reflect her ruthless evil, 'make thick my blood'. She is even willing to exchange her mother's milk for 'gall'. In contrast to his manipulative wife's overwhelmingly dramatic language ('look like the innocent flower, / But be the serpent under it'), a hesitant Macbeth seems subdued, and replies in short, flat sentences. He announces 'Duncan comes here tonight', which contrasts with his wife's chilling image of the 'hoarse' raven. Duncan will leave 'tomorrow as he purposes' which is very different to Lady Macbeth's 'fatal entrance'. His timid 'We will speak further' is juxtaposed against his wife's self-assured 'Leave all the rest to me'. Faced with these two distinctly different characters, the audience is left wondering who will triumph. Will it be the cautious Macbeth who 'wouldst wrongly win'? Or will it be the seemingly obsessive Lady Macbeth, filled 'from the crown to the toe top-full/ Of direst cruelty'? *(190 words)*

Examiner's Comment

- This is a much more focused response that includes very good emphasis on the contrasting language used by the two central characters.
- Clear discussion points are well developed and supported effectively with apt quotation throughout.
- Expression is well controlled and fluent – and wide-ranging vocabulary (such as 'overwhelmingly dramatic language', 'juxtaposed', 'seemingly obsessive') adds to the top-grade quality of the response.

42

❝❝ Key Quotes

my dearest partner of greatness (Macbeth's letter to Lady Macbeth) l.10	Macbeth is anxious to share his good fortune (his promotion to Thane of Cawdor and the witches' prophecies) with his wife. The endearment shows a strong relationship between equals.
Yet do I fear thy nature,/ It is too full o' the milk of human kindness/ To catch the nearest way (Lady Macbeth's soliloquy) l.15–17	This insightful assessment of Macbeth's contradictory character reveals a sensitive moral dimension; he is someone who lacks the ruthlessness to fulfil his ambition. Lady Macbeth's language shows her complete contempt for human decency.
The raven himself is hoarse/ That croaks the fatal entrance of Duncan/ Under my battlements (Lady Macbeth's soliloquy) l.37–9	Lady Macbeth's unnerving imagery shows that she considers that Duncan's tragic fate is sealed. The raven was traditionally associated with death, and Lady Macbeth imagines this bird of ill omen warning of the king's arrival at her castle. He will not leave alive.
take my milk for gall (Lady Macbeth's soliloquy) l.47	Lady Macbeth's desire to deny her feminine nature is particularly shocking. She would prefer that her own breast milk were replaced with bitter bile, which was believed to increase callousness in a person.
Come, thick night,/ And pall thee in the dunnest smoke of hell (Lady Macbeth's soliloquy) l.49–50	Echoing Macbeth's earlier soliloquy (Act 1 Scene 4 l.50–1), Lady Macbeth paints a picture of night enveloped in the murky smoke of hell. The reference to a shroud ('pall') is a further indication of Duncan's fate.
look like the innocent flower,/ But be the serpent under it (Lady Macbeth to Macbeth) l.64–5	The theme of appearance and reality recurs throughout the play. Lady Macbeth is advising her husband to act inoffensively while being ready to strike when the opportunity is right.
Leave all the rest to me (Lady Macbeth to Macbeth) l.72	Lady Macbeth has the last word. Her curt monosyllabic statement indicates that she chooses to ignore her husband's hesitation and is determined to take control.

OVERVIEW

King Duncan and his entourage arrive at Macbeth's castle in Inverness. The king praises its scenic location and is charmed that his loyal supporters are prepared to show their respect for him. The king has come to visit the Macbeths because he regards them highly. He is welcomed warmly by Lady Macbeth, who appears to be the perfect hostess.

Inverness. Before Macbeth's castle

*Hautboys and torches. Enter King Duncan, Malcolm,
Donalbain, Banquo, Lennox, Macduff, Ross, Angus, and
Attendants*

Duncan

This castle hath a pleasant seat; the air
Nimbly and sweetly recommends itself
Unto our gentle senses.

Banquo

      This guest of summer,
The temple-haunting martlet, does approve,
5 By his loved mansionry, that the heaven's breath
Smells wooingly here: no jutty, frieze,
Buttress, nor coign of vantage, but this bird
Hath made his pendent bed and procreant cradle.
Where they most breed and haunt, I have observed,
The air is delicate.

Enter Lady Macbeth

Duncan

10   See, see, our honoured hostess.
The love that follows us sometime is our trouble,
Which still we thank as love. Herein I teach you
How you shall bid God 'ield us for your pains,
And thank us for your trouble.

Lady Macbeth

      All our service
15 In every point twice done, and then done double,
Were poor and single business to contend
Against those honours deep and broad wherewith
Your majesty loads our house. For those of old,
And the late dignities heaped up to them,
We rest your hermits.

Duncan

20 I → *referring to himself* Where's the Thane of Cawdor?
We coursed him at the heels, and had a purpose
To be his purveyor; but he rides well,
And his great love, sharp as his spur, hath holp him
To his home before us. Fair and noble hostess,
We are your guest tonight.

Hautboys: *oboes*

1 seat: *location*

2 Nimbly: *quickly*

4 temple-haunting martlet: *house martin; a bird often found in old church buildings*
5 mansionry: *nesting*
6 wooingly: *enticing*
6 jutty: *projection*
6 frieze: *sculpted decoration*
7 Buttress: *stone support*
7 coign of vantage: *suitable corner*
8 pendent: *hanging*
8 procreant cradle: *nest*
10 delicate: *mild*

11 trouble: *care*

13 'ield: *profit*

16 single: *minor, trifling*

19 late dignities: *recent honours*

20 rest your hermits: *welcome you*

21 coursed: *hunted, chased*

23 hath holp: *has helped*

26 compt: *readiness*

27 audit: *review, stocktaking*

30 graces: *kindness*

Lady Macbeth

Your servants ever   25

Have theirs, themselves and what is theirs, in compt,

To make their audit at your highness' pleasure,

Still to return your own.

Duncan

Give me your hand;

Conduct me to mine host: we love him highly,

And shall continue our graces towards him.   30

By your leave, hostess.

Exeunt

Study Notes

Harmony and treachery (lines 1–31)

This brief scene opens with a series of ironic observations from the unsuspecting Duncan. The king is completely unaware of the dire fate in store for him at the hands of the Macbeths. Duncan comments on the favourable setting of their impressive home, 'This castle hath a pleasant seat'. Banquo speaks of the 'temple-haunting martlet', the house martin. This small bird often nests in old churches and other peaceful locations. It is highly ironic, considering that Macbeth and his wife are planning to murder Duncan.

The deceptiveness of appearances permeates the entire scene. As Lady Macbeth and the king exchange formal pleasantries, Duncan is his usual courteous self, 'honoured hostess', 'Fair and noble hostess'. The respectful tone and repeated references to Lady Macbeth's hostess role emphasise the enormity of the crime that is about to take place.

Meanwhile, Lady Macbeth follows her own advice to Macbeth and acts as the 'innocent flower', adopting a submissive tone, 'We rest your hermits'. The unsuspecting king promises to further advance Macbeth's fortunes and to 'continue our graces towards him'. On the surface, the atmosphere appears to be tranquil and serene. The audience awaits the outcome of Duncan's misguided trust.

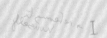

Key Quotes

This castle hath a pleasant seat (Duncan to Banquo) l.1	The naive king utters a bitterly ironic comment which tellingly resounds with the tense audience. Lady Macbeth has just made a chilling reference to Duncan's 'fatal entrance' under her battlements.
Where they most breed and haunt, I have observed,/ The air is delicate (Banquo to Duncan) l.9–10	Banquo, like Duncan, is associated with positive natural language. This is in sharp contrast to the dark, supernatural imagery associated with the Macbeths.
We rest your hermits (Lady Macbeth to Duncan) l.20	A humble hostess acknowledges the Macbeths' indebtedness to their king. Hermits were beggars who depended on the charity of others for their survival. Her natural hypocrisy is astounding.
shall continue our graces towards him (Duncan to Lady Macbeth) l.30	The generous Duncan promises to further advance Macbeth's position. The audience is left to wonder whether or not Macbeth will be satisfied with additional titles – or if he will want even more power.

OVERVIEW

Macbeth reflects on the crime of murdering Duncan. After considering the consequences that will inevitably follow, he decides against it. However, Lady Macbeth dismisses his fears, accusing him of cowardice. She quickly persuades her husband to change his mind and Macbeth agrees to carry out her ruthless plan to kill the king.

* **A key scene requiring close, detailed study**

Inverness. Macbeth's castle

Hautboys and torches. Enter a Sewer, and divers Servants with dishes and service, and pass over the stage. Then enter Macbeth

Macbeth

If it were done, when 'tis done, then 'twere well

It were done quickly. If th'assassination

Could trammel up the consequence, and catch

With his surcease, success; that but this blow

5   Might be the be-all and the end-all here – ~ *saying nowadays*

But here, upon this bank and shoal of time –

We'd jump the life to come. But in these cases

We still have judgement here, that we but teach

Bloody instructions, which, being taught, return

10 To plague the inventor. This even-handed justice

Commends th'ingredients of our poisoned chalice

To our own lips. He's here in double trust:

First, as I am his kinsman and his subject –

Strong both against the deed; then, as his host,

15 Who should against his murderer shut the door,

Not bear the knife myself. Besides, this Duncan

Hath borne his faculties so meek, hath been

So clear in his great office, that his virtues

Will plead like angels, trumpet-tongued against

20 The deep damnation of his taking-off;

And pity, like a naked new-born babe,

Striding the blast, or heaven's cherubim, horsed

Upon the sightless couriers of the air,

Shall blow the horrid deed in every eye,

25 That tears shall drown the wind. I have no spur

To prick the sides of my intent, but only

Vaulting ambition, which o'erleaps itself

And falls on the other.

Enter Lady Macbeth

        How now! what news?

Lady Macbeth

He has almost supped: why have you left the chamber?

Macbeth

Hath he asked for me?

1-2 If...quickly: *the sooner the murder is committed, the better*
3 trammel: *catch, enmesh*
4 With his surcease, success: *triumph resulting from Duncan's death*
6 bank and shoal of time: *earthly life*
7 jump the life to come: *risk eternal happiness after death*
7 cases: *situations, crimes*
8 judgement here: *the ability to make good decisions*
9 Bloody instructions: *violent lessons*
10 plague the inventor: *punish the wrong-doer*
10 even-handed justice: *fair law*
11-12 Commends ... lips: *ensures we get our due punishment*
12 double trust: *Duncan has two reasons to trust Macbeth*
13 his kinsman and his subject: *his relation and his supporter*
17 borne his faculties so meek: *used his powers so humbly*
18 clear in his great office: *honest in carrying out his kingly duties*
19 plead: *advocate*
19 trumpet-tongued: *loudly*
22 blast: *wind*
22 cherubim: *angels*
22 horsed: *mounted*
23 sightless couriers: *invisible winds*
24 horrid deed: *terrible act*
25 tears ... wind: *rain will calm the storm*
25 spur: *interest, incentive*
26 intent: *purpose, ambition*
27 Vaulting ambition: *soaring desire for success*
27 o'erleaps: *over-reaches*
29 supped: *finished eating*

Sewer: *a servant who tasted the king's food before it was given to him*
divers: *several*

49

31 business: *plot (to murder the king)*

32 bought: *gained*

33 Golden opinions: *great praise*

34 newest gloss: *brand-new shine*

35 cast aside: *discarded*

35-6 Was the hope ... dressed yourself: *Was it only drink talking?*

37 green and pale: *hungover, sick and cowardly*

42 ornament of life: *greatest achievement (kingship)*

44 Letting ... 'I would': *allowing fear to replace desire*

45 adage: *well-known proverb (the cat never caught fish because it was afraid to get its paws wet)*

45 Prithee, peace: *be quiet*

46 that may become: *is appropriate for*

47 Who dares ... is none: *no man is braver*

48 this enterprise: *the plan to kill Duncan*

49 durst: *dared*

50-1 to be more ... the man: *to stretch yourself to do more would only increase your manliness*

52 adhere: *suit*

52 you would make both: *you would organise the two*

53-4 their fitness ... unmake you: *their suitability weakens you*

54 given suck: *breastfed*

58 so sworn: *made as solemn a promise*

Lady Macbeth

Know you not he has? 30

Macbeth

We will proceed no further in this business:
He hath honoured me of late, and I have bought
Golden opinions from all sorts of people,
Which would be worn now in their newest gloss,
Not cast aside so soon.

Lady Macbeth

Was the hope drunk 35
Wherein you dressed yourself? Hath it slept since?
And wakes it now to look so green and pale
At what it did so freely? From this time
Such I account thy love. Art thou afeard _afraid?_
To be the same in thine own act and valour 40
As thou art in desire? Wouldst thou have that
Which thou esteem'st the ornament of life,
And live a coward in thine own esteem,
Letting 'I dare not' wait upon 'I would,'
Like the poor cat i'th'adage?

Macbeth

enough
Prithee, peace. 45
I dare do all that may become a man;
Who dares do more, is none.

Lady Macbeth

What beast was't, then,
That made you break this enterprise to me?
When you durst _dared_ do it, then you were a man;
And to be more than what you were, you would _unless u do it / your not a man_ 50
Be so much more the man. Nor time nor place
Did then adhere, and yet you would make both:
They have made themselves, and that their fitness now
Does unmake you. I have given suck, and know _um a mother_
How tender 'tis to love the babe that milks me – _had child / ↳ what happened to child?_ 55
I would, while it was smiling in my face,
Have plucked my nipple from his boneless gums,
And dashed the brains out, had I so sworn as you _(if) had / ↳ sworn / would have done it_
Have done to this.

Macbeth

If we should fail?

Lady Macbeth

We fail!

60 But screw your courage to the sticking-place,
    And we'll not fail. When Duncan is asleep –
    Whereto the rather shall his day's hard journey
    Soundly invite him – his two chamberlains
    Will I with wine and wassail so convince

65 That memory, the warder of the brain,
    Shall be a fume, and the receipt of reason
    A limbeck only. When in swinish sleep
    Their drenchèd natures lie as in a death,
    What cannot you and I perform upon

70 Th'unguarded Duncan? What not put upon
    His spongy officers, who shall bear the guilt
    Of our great quell?

Macbeth

Bring forth men-children only:
    For thy undaunted mettle should compose
    Nothing but males. Will it not be received,

75 When we have marked with blood those sleepy two
    Of his own chamber and used their very daggers,
    That they have done't?

Lady Macbeth

Who dares receive it other,
    As we shall make our griefs and clamour roar
    Upon his death?   ~ shock, horror → reaction

Macbeth

I am settled, and bend up   I'll do it
80 Each corporal agent to this terrible feat.
    Away, and mock the time with fairest show: – pretend normal
    False face must hide what the false heart doth know.

Exeunt

---

60 screw: *fasten tightly*
60 sticking-place: *mark*

63 chamberlains: *servants*

64 wassail: *drinking*

65 warder: *guardian*

66 receipt of reason: *logical thought*

67 limbeck: *container for alcohol*
67 swinish sleep: *asleep like pigs*

68 drenchèd: *soaked in drink*

71 spongy: *intoxicated*

72 great quell: *huge suppression*

73 undaunted mettle: *fearless strength*

74 received: *accepted*

77 receive it other: *take it any other way*

79 am settled: *have decided*

80 corporal agent: *physical part of myself*

81 mock the time: *deceive*

82 false heart: *hypocrite*

Study Notes

Internal torment – Macbeth's soliloquy (lines 1–28)

In this crucial soliloquy, Shakespeare presents Macbeth as a complex character who is deeply troubled by inner conflict. He believes that if the murder of Duncan was all it would take to replace him as king, then it would be better if he did the deed swiftly, 'If it were done, when 'tis done, then 'twere well/ It were done quickly'. But Macbeth has doubts. He is fearful of the spiritual significance of such a great sin and the risk of eternal damnation. He also acknowledges that his assassination of Duncan might teach a lesson ('Bloody instructions') to others, who would attempt to kill him if he were to become king. This opening section deals with Macbeth's selfish concerns about the impact of murdering Duncan.

Macbeth then specifies all the reasons why he should not kill the king. He is Duncan's cousin as well as his subject – and he should show due allegiance. As the king's host, he should also guard his guest from danger, 'Not bear the knife myself'. Macbeth reflects that Duncan has been an honourable ruler who 'Hath borne his faculties so meek' and that his death would cause uproar throughout Scotland. Finally, Macbeth accepts that his sole motivation for considering the crime of regicide is his 'Vaulting ambition'. Ironically, he is aware that by over-reaching himself in the pursuit of power, he could cause his own downfall. He has talked himself out of committing murder.

The fatal decision (lines 28–82)

Macbeth tells his wife, 'We will proceed no further in this business'. He is grateful for Duncan's support and wishes to enjoy 'Golden opinions from all sorts of people'. He is immediately met by a savage attack from a bitterly disappointed Lady Macbeth, who accuses him of cowardice, 'Art thou afeard/ To be the same in thine own act and valour/ As thou art in desire?'

Macbeth insists that he is as courageous as any man, 'Who dares do more, is none'. But Lady Macbeth is completely unscrupulous in manipulating her husband by repeatedly questioning his masculinity, saying that the murder would make him 'so much more the man'. Her final strategy is to remind him of his failure to keep his word. Using all her powers of emotional blackmail, she tells Macbeth that she would be prepared to kill her own child rather than break a promise.

Her persuasive words succeed in weakening Macbeth's resolve and he is reduced to self-doubt once more, 'If we should fail?' Unlike her husband, Lady Macbeth thinks only of the present and will not entertain the idea of failure, 'But screw your courage to the sticking-place,/ And we'll not fail'.

She has been transformed into the epitome of cold-hearted cruelty. Her simple plan is to fill Duncan's personal bodyguards 'with wine and wassail' so that they are unable to remember anything, 'memory, the warder of the brain,/ Shall be a fume'. Then when they are unconscious, she and Macbeth can kill the 'unguarded Duncan' and blame his murder on the 'spongy officers'.

Macbeth is overwhelmed with admiration for his wife. He suggests that they smear the bodyguards with Duncan's blood and use their daggers to incriminate them. Lady Macbeth agrees and adds that the couple's show of grief will convince everyone that they had nothing to do with the murder, 'Who dares receive it other?' Macbeth has now submitted to his wife's resolute will, against his better judgement. He even echoes her words on the necessity for deception, 'Away, and mock the time with fairest show'. The couple's fatal decision has been made.

Shakespeare's language

This pivotal scene sets in motion the act which will unleash a series of tragic consequences. The indecisive Macbeth is tortured by hesitation. A series of short **staccato phrases** illustrate his fervent wish that one quick act of murder would complete the business, 'If it were done, when 'tis done, then 'twere well/ It were done quickly'. The repetition of the monosyllabic verb 'done' emphasises his paradoxical situation; the enormous crime of regicide will not necessarily be completed when the actual murder has taken place.

The soliloquy reveals Macbeth's poetic sensibilities. His innovative language use reflects a vivid imagination. **Personification** highlights Duncan's many qualities as king, 'his virtues/ Will plead like angels'. The use of a compound adjective ('trumpet-tongued') and the hard consonants 't' and 'd' mimic the noise of the angels' outcry. Another dramatic example of personification envisions what will happen on earth, as well as in heaven, when Duncan is murdered. Pity will assume the shape of 'a naked new-born babe' and all of Scotland will be engulfed in grief. Borrowing imagery from horse-riding ('spur', 'Vaulting', 'o'erleaps', 'falls'), Macbeth admits that the only reason for his murderous act is personal ambition.

Lady Macbeth's entrance initiates a series of **tense questions and answers** in half-lines as the couple quickly pick up each other's thoughts, 'Hath he asked for me?', 'Know you not he has?' Clothing imagery expresses how Macbeth wishes to enjoy what he has obtained from Duncan for his exploits in battle, 'Which would be worn now in their newest gloss, / Not cast aside so soon'. But Lady Macbeth seizes the image and turns it against her husband, accusing him of drunken bragging when he 'dressed' himself in the king's clothes.

Her final attempt to persuade Macbeth is utterly depraved. The **graphic description** of one of life's most natural and loving moments (a mother breastfeeding her child) being torn apart is expressed in some of the most disturbing lines that Shakespeare has ever written. The horrific image of a young mother denying all her maternal instincts and viciously killing her own infant is a shocking illustration of Lady Macbeth's evil nature.

The audience sees Macbeth begin to buckle in his **faltering question**, 'If we should fail?' Lady Macbeth, through the force of her dire arguments, has succeeded in overturning her husband's moral anxieties to the more practical details of murder. This dark scene concludes with a submissive Macbeth echoing his wife's former advice: 'False face must hide what the false heart doth know'. Nothing is as it appears in the reckless world of the Macbeths.

Critical Analysis

1. 'Macbeth and Lady Macbeth share a variety of character traits that contribute to the dramatic and tragic aspects of the play *Macbeth*.' To what extent do you agree with this view? Support your answer with close reference to Act 1 Scene 7.

2. 'Act 1 Scene 7 is a key scene that reveals many aspects of Macbeth's conflicted character.' Discuss this statement and support your answer with reference to the scene.

Sample Paragraph 1 (Q1)

I think this is a very dramatic, tragic scene. Macbeth has a very good idea of the reasons why he should not murder his king, but he gives in to his wife because she questions his manhood comparing him to a frightened kitten. They are both extremely ambitious, but she is far stronger. He has guilty feelings about King Duncan's murder but she is much more evil. She is very critical of his inability to decide on a decision and stick to it. I thought it was very dramatic when she said she would kill her new-born baby rather than break her promise. This is what did it for Macbeth. He certainly admired his wife, believing she should only have 'men-children' because she is so tough. I also liked how he echoed the witches 'fair is foul' when he says 'mock the time with fairest show'. This was very dramatic. *(150 words)*

Examiner's Comment

- This basic-grade paragraph touches on some potentially worthwhile discussion points (e.g. shared ambition), but fails to develop the discussion effectively.
- Little or no attempt to address the tragic outcome of this critical scene.
- Scant use of relevant quotations.
- Awkward expression ('decide on a decision') and over-use of 'very'.

Sample Paragraph 2 (Q1)

Both Macbeth and Lady Macbeth share the personality characteristics of ruthless ambition and personal bravery which add to the drama and tragedy of the play. 'Vaulting ambition' will eventually destroy the couple. This leads Macbeth to abandon his moral scruples about killing the king. He is no longer concerned that Duncan is his 'kinsman', nor that he is Duncan's 'subject'. He puts aside his recognition of Duncan's good qualities, 'faculties so meek'. Similarly, Lady Macbeth denies her femininity when she callously states that she would kill her innocent baby rather than break a solemn vow. Her dramatic language will shock audiences. Like her husband, she suppresses her natural instincts to advance a hunger for power. Macbeth is a physically brave man who can truthfully claim that he dares 'do all that may become a man'. However, he is emotionally weak and submits to his wife's savage onslaught on his character. With Lady Macbeth's 'undaunted mettle' strengthening his wavering ambition, he decides to commit murder, 'I am settled ... to this terrible feat'. While the deceptive couple 'mock the time with fairest show', they are unaware that they are taking the first steps on their tragic downfall. *(195 words)*

Examiner's Comment

- A successful response that includes some good commentary on the shared character traits of both protagonists.
- Clear engagement with the text; higher-order discussion points developed and supported effectively with apt quotation.
- Incisive observations of the scene's various dramatic features (such as Lady Macbeth's startling language).
- Expression is controlled – and wide-ranging vocabulary (e.g. 'abandon his moral scruples', 'suppresses her natural instincts') adds to the top-grade quality of this impressive response.

🗨🗨 Key Quotes

If it were done, when 'tis done, then 'twere well/ It were done quickly *(Macbeth soliloquy) l.1–2*	Macbeth reflects on the momentous deed of killing the king. His initial hesitancy suggests a troubled conscience. He would prefer that the murder was over and done with as swiftly as possible.
but only/ Vaulting ambition, which o'erleaps itself/ And falls on the other *(Macbeth soliloquy) l.27–8*	Macbeth realises the possible consequences of killing Duncan and the fact that murdering a good man would cause outrage both here on earth and in heaven. Using the language of the hunt, he describes his desire to be king, comparing himself to an over-enthusiastic rider who tries to leap too high to get into the saddle only to fail and fall on the other side.
We will proceed no further in this business *(Macbeth to Lady Macbeth) l.31*	Having reflected on why he should not commit the murder, a seemingly determined Macbeth communicates his decision to his astonished wife. The language is plain and matter-of-fact, in contrast to his earlier poetic speech.
I dare do all that may become a man;/ Who dares do more, is none *(Macbeth to Lady Macbeth) l.46–7*	Macbeth is hurt by his wife's insults and ironically retorts that he is as brave as any other man. Lady Macbeth's attack on his masculinity has obviously unnerved him.
I would, while it was smiling in my face,/ Have plucked my nipple from his boneless gums,/ And dashed the brains out, had I so sworn as you/ Have done to this *(Lady Macbeth to Macbeth) l.56–9*	In some of the most shocking lines in literature, Lady Macbeth conjures up a tender scene of innocence and maternal love – and then shatters it cruelly. It is a last desperate attempt to get Macbeth to carry out the murder of the king. She is filled with viciousness and all her feminine instincts have been repressed.
If we should fail? *(Macbeth to Lady Macbeth) l.59*	The influence of his wife's ferocious persuasion overwhelms Macbeth, who wavers in his earlier decision not to kill Duncan.
False face must hide what the false heart doth know *(Macbeth to Lady Macbeth) l.82*	Macbeth is now prepared to commit the murder. In a chilling echo of his wife's former advice ('Look like the innocent flower,/ But be the serpent under it'), he declares that a deceptive appearance must hide the guilty heart.

Key Points | Act 1

- Act 1 introduces the audience to the strange world of evil and ambiguity which the Macbeths inhabit. It is a world of equivocation where nothing is certain. The play begins in mid-action; the battle between good and evil is already being waged.

- Three witches appear on a stormy heath. Nature is in turmoil. We immediately associate them with wickedness and double-dealing – and with Macbeth.

- On the battlefield, treachery is defeated by loyalty. Macbeth is extraordinarily heroic.

- Vivid images of blood, light and darkness create an ominous atmosphere.

- Another side of Macbeth's character (ambitious, devious, secretive) is evident in his exchange with the witches.

- Macbeth's powerful soliloquies reveal an anguished, divided inner-self, in contrast to the lawful king, Duncan, who is gracious and trusting.

- Banquo, who is also contrasted with Macbeth, warns him to be wary of the witches.

- The Macbeths are a loving couple, united in their ruthless ambition. But Lady Macbeth's practicality and lack of scruples are in sharp contrast with her husband's conflicted nature.

- At the end of Act 1, the balance between good and evil has been reversed.

Class/Homework Exercise

Based on your study of Act 1, what is your initial impression of Macbeth? Write a short paragraph (150–200 words), supporting your answer with reference to the text.

Prithee, peace./ I dare do all that may become a man

Macbeth, Act 1 Scene 7, l.45-46

OVERVIEW

Banquo and his son Fleance meet with Macbeth in the dark castle courtyard. An uneasy discussion takes place between the two troubled men. Macbeth pretends that he has given little thought to the witches' prophecies. Banquo asserts his allegiance to the king and bids goodnight to Macbeth. As soon as Macbeth is alone, he has an extraordinary vision of a ghostly dagger leading him to Duncan. He resolves to act. A bell rings – a signal from Lady Macbeth – and he sets off towards the king's quarters.

Inverness. Courtyard of Macbeth's castle

Enter Banquo, and Fleance holding a torch before him

Banquo

How goes the night, boy?

Fleance

The moon is down; I have not heard the clock.

Banquo

And she goes down at twelve.

Fleance

                    I take't 'tis later, sir.

Banquo

Hold, take my sword. There's husbandry in heaven;

Their candles are all out. Take thee that, too.   5

A heavy summons lies like lead upon me,   *exhausted*
                                        but can't sleep
And yet I would not sleep. Merciful powers,

Restrain in me the cursèd thoughts that nature

Gives way to in repose!

Enter Macbeth, and a Servant with a torch

                    Give me my sword –

Who's there?   10

Macbeth

A friend.

Banquo

What, sir, not yet at rest? The king's a-bed.

He hath been in unusual pleasure, and

Sent forth great largess to your offices.

This diamond he greets your wife withal   15

By the name of most kind hostess, and shut up

In measureless content.   *wants to kill*

Macbeth

                    Being unprepared,

Our will became the servant to defect,

Which else should free have wrought.

Banquo

                    All's well.

I dreamt last night of the three weird sisters. → *still thinking* 20
                                            about witches
To you they have showed some truth.

        part of it true

Macbeth

                    I think not of them.

            pretending

Glossary (left margin):

3 she goes down at twelve: *the moon sets at midnight*

4 husbandry: *thriftiness, economy*

5 candles: *stars*
5 that: *his shield and dagger*

7 Merciful powers: *Good spirits, guardian angels*
8 cursèd: *damnable, evil*
9 Gives way to in repose: *experiences while resting*

14 great largess to your offices: *many gifts to honour you*

16–17 shut up ... content: *ended very happily*

17–19 Being unprepared ... wrought: *Duncan's visit was unexpected, so it was not possible to entertain him as we would have wished*

Yet, when we can entreat an hour to serve,

We would spend it in some words upon that business,

If you would grant the time.

Banquo

At your kind'st leisure.

Macbeth

25 If you shall cleave to my consent, when 'tis,

It shall make honour for you. — will be rewarded   bribe?

Banquo

So I lose none

In seeking to augment it, but still keep   — we can talk

My bosom franchised and allegiance clear,   — My allegiance to king

I shall be counselled.

Macbeth

Good repose the while.

Banquo

30 Thanks, sir. The like to you.

Exeunt Banquo and Fleance

Macbeth

Go bid thy mistress, when my drink is ready,

She strike upon the bell. Get thee to bed.

Exit Servant   Vision?

Is this a dagger which I see before me,

The handle toward my hand? Come, let me clutch thee.

35 I have thee not, and yet I see thee still.

Art thou not, fatal vision, sensible

To feeling as to sight? Or art thou but

A dagger of the mind, a false creation,   am I imagening

Proceeding from the heat-oppressèd brain?

40 I see thee yet, in form as palpable

As this which now I draw.

Thou marshall'st me the way that I was going,

And such an instrument I was to use.   — It was a sight this should happen

Mine eyes are made the fools o'th'other senses,

45 Or else worth all the rest: I see thee still;   dagger has blood

And on thy blade and dudgeon gouts of blood,   — cops on

Which was not so before. There's no such thing:

It is the bloody business which informs   — mind playing tricks

Thus to mine eyes. Now o'er the one half-world

50 Nature seems dead, and wicked dreams abuse   — only nightmares

---

22 entreat: *spare*

25-6 If you … for you: *if you fit in with my plans when the time is right, it will benefit you*

26 So: *as long as*

27 seeking to augment it: *trying to improve my position*

28 bosom franchised: *heart free of guilt*

28 allegiance: *loyalty to the king*

29 I shall be counselled: *I will listen to what you have to say*

29 Good repose the while: *sleep well*

32 bell: *the signal to proceed with the murder*

36 fatal vision: *deadly sight*

36 sensible: *perceivable*

38 false creation: *deception*

39 heat-oppressèd: *feverish*

40 palpable: *real, tangible*

41 this: *his own dagger*

42 marshall'st: *guide*

44-5 Mine eyes … the rest: *Either my eyes deceive me or they show what is real*

46 dudgeon: *handle*

46 gouts: *large drops*

48-9 bloody business … mine eyes: *the thought of killing is causing me to hallucinate*

49 one half-world: *this hemisphere*

50 Nature seems dead: *nothing can be seen in the dark*

51 curtained: *drawn, veiled*

51-2 Witchcraft ... offerings: *the witches solemnly perform sacrifices to the goddess of evil*

52-6 withered Murder ... ghost: *the wrinkled spirit of murder is summoned to creep about in the darkness like the evil Roman prince, Tarquin*

56-8 Thou sure ... whereabout: *Macbeth hopes that his footsteps will not be heard*

59 present horror: *the imminent act of murder*

60 suits with it: *is appropriate for it*

60 Whiles I threat, he lives: *while I'm making plans, Duncan is still alive*

61 Words ... gives: *mere talk is not enough for the passionate deed of murder*

63 knell: *funeral bell*

The curtained sleep. Witchcraft celebrates

Pale Hecate's offerings; and, withered Murder, *goddess of witchcraft.*

Alarumed by his sentinel, the wolf,

Whose howl's his watch, thus with his stealthy pace,

With Tarquin's ravishing strides, towards his design   55

Moves like a ghost. Thou sure and firm-set earth,

Hear not my steps, which way they walk, for fear

Thy very stones prate of my whereabout,

And take the present horror from the time,

Which now suits with it. Whiles I threat, he lives: 60

Words to the heat of deeds too cold breath gives.

A bell rings — *signal*

I go, and it is done. The bell invites me.

Hear it not, Duncan, for it is a knell *— funeral bell*

That summons thee to heaven, or to hell.

Exit

Study Notes

Uneasy conversation (lines 1–32)

Banquo's nervousness and the midnight setting create a restless atmosphere of impending evil. His conversation with Fleance is in stark contrast to the murderous dialogue between the Macbeths in the previous act. Obviously troubled by his conscience, Banquo prays that he can withstand the tempting ambitious thoughts that are disrupting his sleep.

The tense mood is heightened when he adopts the position of guard inside Macbeth's own castle, challenging its owner, 'Who's there?' The earlier camaraderie of the two defenders of Duncan's kingdom is now absent. Banquo comments on the king's generosity to Lady Macbeth, 'This diamond he greets your wife withal' and he reminds Macbeth how Duncan regards her as a 'most kind hostess'. The compliment is particularly chilling as the audience already knows that Duncan's entrance under Lady Macbeth's battlements will be 'fatal'. Banquo cryptically remarks that the witches 'have showed some truth' to Macbeth. He is now Thane of Cawdor.

In response, Macbeth tells a blatant lie, 'I think not of them'. He is aware that Banquo is the only other person who has heard the witches' prophecies. As a result, he can be either an ally or a threat to Macbeth's ambition. In another frosty exchange, Banquo states that he is choosing to keep his 'allegiance clear' to his king, although he would be prepared to hear what Macbeth has to say. As soon as Banquo and Fleance retire to bed, however, Macbeth orders his servant to instruct Lady Macbeth to ring the bell when his drink is ready. This is yet another example of deception. The sound of the bell will notify him that the king's servants are in a drunken sleep and he can proceed with the plan to murder Duncan.

Inner turmoil (lines 33–64)

The tragedy of Macbeth's ambition is evident in the intensity of his imagination as he wrestles with the act of murder. His moral confusion and murderous thoughts form the key parts of the soliloquy. Lines 33–49 concentrate on the vision of the dagger while lines 49–56 disclose Macbeth's contemplation of a world filled with deception and evil. In lines 56–60, he asks the ground beneath him to keep his footsteps quiet as he carries out the killing. Finally, lines 60–4 show Macbeth acknowledging that words are no substitute for actions.

His ambition has ultimately won. Macbeth has made a crucial choice and knows that he is damning himself. The vision of the dagger is the first of many bloody visions which both he and his wife will see, all unleashed by the unnatural act of regicide. The last traces of the honourable Macbeth vanish at the end of this compelling speech, which reveals both his desire for and revulsion at the act he is about to perform. The funeral bell tolls for Macbeth as well as Duncan.

Shakespeare's language

This intensely dramatic scene is suffused in blood and darkness. Nothing is as it seems and **dramatic irony** is present throughout. Once again Duncan is oblivious to the danger surrounding him, generously rewarding the murderous couple and sleeping in 'measureless content'. Macbeth will decide to act, desperately trying to convince himself that he will end all his problems with a single act of violence, 'I go, and it is done'; but both he and the audience know that they are only beginning.

The **symbol of the dagger** can be viewed ambiguously. Is it an omen that Macbeth should proceed, 'the handle toward my hand?' Or is it a final warning from his conscience, a 'fatal vision' not only for Duncan, but for the couple? The onomatopoeic verb 'clutch' highlights not only Macbeth's desperation to do the deed, but also his anxiety over whether or not the dagger is real. A stark paradox, 'I have thee not, and yet I see thee still', underlines Macbeth's puzzled frustration.

The playwright is forcing the audience to visualise the dagger as though it were a character present on the stage. This 'false creation' is doubly deceptive. Is it real or unreal? Is it, like the witches' words, to be trusted or not? Macbeth's 'heat-oppressèd' language vividly conveys his feverish imagination, gripped by the disease of ambition. The **repetition** of the refrain, 'I see', 'I see thee still' and 'I see thee yet', builds up the tension for both the protagonist and the audience.

Questions, exclamations and qualifications are unsettling, culminating in Macbeth physically drawing his own dagger to create supporting **visual imagery**, 'As this which now I draw'. The playwright also makes has the audience visualise the dagger as it might appear after the murder has been committed, covered with 'gouts of blood'.

Personification allows objects and abstract ideas, rather than people, to assume control. Banquo's 'cursèd thoughts' resound in 'wicked dreams'. The reference to 'Pale Hecate' foreshadows Macbeth's future encounter with the witches and their goddess. The gruesome vision of murder as a gaunt spectre stalking the land accompanied by his howling guard, the wolf, conjures up the horrifying world into which Macbeth is about to descend. He fears that even the stones will 'prate' about his secret manoeuvres.

The tension is eventually relieved by the stark realisation, 'Whiles I threat, he lives'. The resolution seems casual and mechanical, almost too good to be true, 'I go, and it is done'. Is Macbeth now consciously fooling himself? For whom does the 'knell' toll? As on so many other occasions, Shakespeare leaves the audience – like Macbeth himself – in a fever of anxiety.

Critical Analysis

1. 'Shakespeare's *Macbeth* invites us to look into the disturbed mind of a man consumed by ambition and guilt.' Give your response to this statement, supporting your answer with particular reference to Act 2 Scene 1.

2. Shakespeare uses foreshadowing to powerful effect throughout Act 2 Scene 1 to increase the dramatic tension. In your opinion, how successful is this technique in enhancing the audience's dramatic experience? Explain your response, supporting your answer with reference to the scene.

Sample Paragraph 1 (Q1)

Macbeth is a man eaten up by all-out ambition. He tells Banquo that he has not thought about the witches. A complete lie. The minute Banquo leaves, Macbeth's confused brain begins playing tricks on him. He wants to kill King Duncan so much that he can almost see the dagger already leading him to Duncan's royal room, 'Thou marshallest'. He can even see the blood stains, 'dudgeon clots'. This is proof of a totally unstable character and his brain is running away with him. One minute he sees the dagger, the next he is saying it's all a fantasy of his brain. Macbeth is extremely unstable, changing his mind all the time. He thinks of himself as a killing machine, like a great warrior going 'towards his great design'. Macbeth really can't wait to commit the murder of Duncan. When he hears Lady Macbeth's bell ringing, he says, 'I go and it's done'. To him, it sounds like a funeral bell for King Duncan. Macbeth is eaten up by ambition. *(165 words)*

Examiner's Comment

- This basic-grade answer relies mainly on unfocused narrative and fails to address the full question.
- While there are several worthwhile references to Macbeth's confusion and ambition, there is no focus on his guilt.
- Some quotations are slightly inaccurate.
- Expression is repetitive and poorly controlled at times.

*Is this a dagger which I
see before me*

Macbeth, Act 2 Scene 1, l.33

Sample Paragraph 2 (Q1)

Shakespeare effectively uses the dramatic device of the soliloquy in Act 2 Scene 1 to allow the audience to see Macbeth's unsettled mind before the killing. After the witches' prophecy and Lady Macbeth's scathing criticisms of her husband ('When you durst do it, then you were a man'), Macbeth is torn between desperately desiring to be king and being equally repelled by the idea of murder. Even his senses are in revolt. He imagines a dagger which he can visualise, but cannot feel: 'I have thee not, yet I see thee still'. The powerful paradox reveals his confused mental state. He is acutely self-aware, and knows that he is over-wrought and that the vision could be 'a false creation'. He imagines – or wants to imagine – that the dagger is inviting him, the alliterative phrase, 'the handle toward my hand', suggesting the ease with which he could do the deed. But his mind immediately conjures up the hellish world awaiting him if he commits the murder. Yet, despite his vivid misgivings, he forces himself to act. A curt but alarming final comment seals the fate of both Duncan and Macbeth: 'I go, and it is done'. The imaginative Macbeth has vanished, replaced by a determination to be king regardless of the cost. But even now, he seems to be regretting the act, hoping Duncan cannot hear the bell. This foreshadows his bitter guilt after the murder, 'Wake Duncan with thy knocking'.
(240 words)

Examiner's Comment

- Highly successful, focused response that addresses the question directly and uses apt supporting reference.
- Ranges purposefully over the soliloquy, making well-developed points (e.g. 'Even his senses are in revolt', 'powerful paradox reveals his confused mental state').
- Insightful discussion throughout – e.g. that Macbeth 'imagines – or wants to imagine – that the dagger is inviting him'.
- Excellent expression throughout further enhances the top-grade standard.

Key Quotes

Merciful powers,/ Restrain in me the cursèd thoughts that nature/ Gives way to in repose! *(Banquo to Fleance) l.7–9*	In contrast to Macbeth, Banquo is resisting the allure of the witches' promises. He prays that the powers of good will get rid of the evil thoughts that trouble his dreams. Is Shakespeare reminding us that Macbeth has a choice about how he responds to the witches?
He hath been in unusual pleasure, and/ Sent forth great largess to your offices *(Banquo to Macbeth) l.13–14*	Banquo remarks on Duncan's extraordinary delight with the Macbeths' hospitality and his generous gifts to the couple. This is bitterly ironic because the audience is aware of the fate that awaits the king at the hands of the murderous couple.
I think not of them *(Macbeth to Banquo) l.21*	Macbeth tells his friend a deliberate lie in response to Banquo's confession that he had dreamt of the witches. Already he is practising Lady Macbeth's advice, to 'look like the innocent flower'.
Is this a dagger which I see before me,/ The handle toward my hand? *(Macbeth soliloquy) l.33–4*	Macbeth imagines that he sees the murder weapon, its handle inviting him to clasp it. His intense turmoil is graphically conveyed in this powerful hallucination.
There's no such thing:/ It is the bloody business which informs/ Thus to mine eyes *(Macbeth soliloquy) l.47–9*	For a moment, Macbeth fights against his over-active imagination and turbulent conscience. He decides that it is the thought of killing the king that is deceiving his eyes. Is he a reluctant murderer?
Whiles I threat, he lives *(Macbeth soliloquy) l.60*	This plain comment cuts through the imaginative reverie of Macbeth's previous uncertainty. As an experienced soldier, he is used to taking decisive action. The longer Macbeth talks, the longer Duncan lives.
I go, and it is done *(Macbeth soliloquy) l.62*	At the pre-arranged signal of the bell rung by Lady Macbeth, a resolute Macbeth goes to commit the momentous crime. The phrase echoes a previous comment, 'If it were done when 'tis done', at a time when Macbeth feared that the one act would not be an end to the business.

OVERVIEW

Alone on stage, Lady Macbeth anxiously awaits Macbeth's return from committing the murder. She had earlier drugged Duncan's guards. Macbeth arrives with bloodstained hands, fearing that he will never get rid of his guilt. Lady Macbeth takes charge, ordering him to remain calm. The success of their plot is also in danger because Macbeth has brought back the daggers with him. Lady Macbeth rushes back to the scene of the murder to return the weapons and to smear the king's sleeping guards with blood. As the scene closes, there is a loud and persistent knocking at the outer door of the castle.

* A key scene requiring close, detailed study

1 them: *Duncan's bodyguards*
1 bold: *brave, unflinching*
2 What hath quenched ... fire: *what has silenced them has made me courageous*
2 Hark: *listen*
3–4 fatal bellman ... good night: *deadly watchman who rang the bell before executions*
4 He is about it: *Macbeth is now murdering Duncan*
5–6 surfeited ... snores: *the drunken servants demean their guard duties by being drunk and asleep*
6 possets: *warm drinks laced with alcohol*
7–8 That death ... die: *The guards are so intoxicated that they are in danger of dying*

9 Alack: *Alas*
10–11 The attempt ... Confounds us: *An unsuccessful murder bid would ruin us*

15 owl ... crickets: *creatures associated with death*
16 Did not you speak?: *a reference to Macbeth's earlier cries offstage*

17 second chamber: *room beside Duncan's*

Inverness. Macbeth's castle

Enter Lady Macbeth

Lady Macbeth

That which hath made them drunk hath made me bold.

What hath quenched them hath given me fire. Hark!

Peace! It was the owl that shrieked, the fatal bellman,

Which gives the stern'st good night. He is about it:

The doors are open, and the surfeited grooms   5

Do mock their charge with snores. I have drugged their
  possets,

That death and nature do contend about them,

Whether they live or die.

Macbeth

[within]

                Who's there? What, ho!

Lady Macbeth

Alack, I am afraid they have awaked,

And 'tis not done. The attempt and not the deed   10

Confounds us. Hark! I laid their daggers ready;

He could not miss 'em. Had he not resembled

My father as he slept, I had done't.

Enter Macbeth

                My husband!

Macbeth

I have done the deed. Didst thou not hear a noise?

Lady Macbeth

I heard the owl scream and the crickets cry.   15

Did not you speak?

Macbeth

          When?

Lady Macbeth

          Now.

Macbeth

           As I descended?

Lady Macbeth

                Ay.

Macbeth

Hark! Who lies i' the second chamber?

Lady Macbeth

Donalbain. — son _younger_ — Duncan

Macbeth

   This is a sorry sight.

Lady Macbeth

A foolish thought, to say a sorry sight.

Macbeth

20 There's one did laugh in 's sleep, and one cried 'Murder!'
That they did wake each other. I stood and heard them;
But they did say their prayers, and addressed them
Again to sleep.

Lady Macbeth

    There are two lodged together.

Macbeth

One cried 'God bless us', and 'amen' the other,
25 As they had seen me with these hangman's hands.
Listening their fear, I could not say 'amen',
When they did say 'God bless us'.

Lady Macbeth

Consider it not so deeply.

Macbeth

But wherefore could not I pronounce 'amen'?
30 I had most need of blessing, and 'amen'
Stuck in my throat.

Lady Macbeth

    These deeds must not be thought
After these ways. So, it will make us mad.

Macbeth

Methought I heard a voice cry 'Sleep no more! 7 _guilty conscience_
Macbeth does murder sleep' – the innocent sleep,
35 Sleep that knits up the ravelled sleave of care,
The death of each day's life, sore labour's bath,
Balm of hurt minds, great nature's second course,
Chief nourisher in life's feast –

Lady Macbeth

    What do you mean?

---

18 sorry sight: *Macbeth looks regretfully at his bloodstained hands*

19 foolish thought: *Lady Macbeth dismisses Macbeth's regrets*

20–1 There's one ... other: *the servants were sleeping restlessly*

22–3 addressed ... sleep: *settled back to sleep*

23 lodged together: *staying in the same room*

24 amen: *'So be it' – said at the end of a prayer*

25 hangman's hands: *bloodstained hands*

28 Consider ... deeply: *don't think about it so intensely*

29 wherefore: *why*

31–2 These deeds ... ways: *these acts must not become an obsession*

33–4 Methought ... sleep: *Macbeth imagines an inner voice saying that he will have no more peace of mind*
35 knits ... care: *heals the disturbed mind*

36 death of each day's life: *rest follows every active day*
36 sore labour's bath: *sleep soothes weary workers*
37 Balm of hurt minds: *ointment to heal mental anguish*
38 Chief nourisher: *sleep sustains people*

Macbeth

Still it cried 'Sleep no more' to all the house:
'Glamis hath murdered sleep, and therefore Cawdor
Shall sleep no more; Macbeth shall sleep no more.'

[handwritten: Macbeth haunted & tormented forever & doomed & never have piece of Mind] 40

Lady Macbeth

Who was it that thus cried? Why, worthy thane,
You do unbend your noble strength, to think
So brainsickly of things. Go get some water,
And wash this filthy witness from your hand.
Why did you bring these daggers from the place?
They must lie there: go carry them, and smear
The sleepy grooms with blood.

[handwritten: wash blood away / water will not wash murder deed away]

Macbeth

                    I'll go no more:
I am afraid to think what I have done;
Look on't again I dare not.

Lady Macbeth

                    Infirm of purpose!   50
Give me the daggers. The sleeping and the dead
Are but as pictures: 'tis the eye of childhood
That fears a painted devil. If he do bleed,
I'll gild the faces of the grooms withal,
For it must seem their guilt.

[handwritten: frame servants]

Exit. Knocking within

Macbeth

                    Whence is that knocking?   55
How is't with me, when every noise appals me?
What hands are here? Ha, they pluck out mine eyes.
Will all great Neptune's ocean wash this blood
Clean from my hand? No, this my hand will rather
The multitudinous seas incarnadine,   60
Making the green one red.

Re-enter Lady Macbeth

Lady Macbeth

My hands are of your colour; but I shame
To wear a heart so white.

Knocking within

                    I hear a knocking
At the south entry. Retire we to our chamber.
A little water clears us of this deed.   *[handwritten: wash away evidence]*   65

---

43 unbend … strength: *reduce your vigour*
44 brainsickly: *frantically, foolishly*
45 witness: *evidence (Macbeth's bloody hands)*
46 place: *Duncan's room*
47 smear … blood: *cast suspicion on the guards*

50 Infirm of purpose!: *lacking courage*
51–2 The sleeping … pictures: *people who are asleep or dead are like unreal images*
52–3 'tis the eye … devil: *only children are afraid of scary pictures*
54 gild: *paint with blood*

55 Whence: *where from*

58–9 Will all … hand?: *can all the world's oceans wash away my guilt? (Neptune was the Roman god of the sea)*
59–61 this my hand … red: *my blood will dye the oceans red and the green sea will become crimson*

62 of your colour: *as bloody and guilty as yours*
63 To wear … so white: *to be so cowardly*

How easy is it, then! Your constancy
Hath left you unattended.

Knocking within

                   Hark! More knocking.
Get on your nightgown, lest occasion call us,
And show us to be watchers. Be not lost
70 So poorly in your thoughts.

Macbeth

To know my deed, 'twere best not know myself.

Knocking within

Wake Duncan with thy knocking! I would thou couldst!

Exeunt

66-7 constancy ... unattended: *strength has abandoned you*

68-9 lest occasion call us: *in case we are looked for*

71 To know ... myself: *I cannot bear to acknowledge what I have done*

72 I would thou couldst!: *I wish you could*

Go get some water,/ And wash this filthy witness from your hand

Lady Macbeth, Act 2 Scene 2, l.44-45

Study Notes

A practical wife and a hysterical husband (lines 1–67)

Lady Macbeth anxiously awaits her husband's return from Duncan's chamber. She has been drinking and claims that this has given her courage. When she hears Macbeth's cry, she fears that the murder will not be successful. Her admission that the sleeping king's resemblance to her father prevented her from carrying out the killing herself would indicate that she has some human feelings.

When Macbeth returns, it's clear that he is both psychologically and emotionally shattered by the 'deed' he has committed. His mind jumps erratically from his bloodied hands to the memory of the restless servants to his own inability to pray. Lady Macbeth attempts to calm him, but already his mind is obsessed with haunting visions of sleep. Their conversation shows how edgy they both are.

Lady Macbeth is perplexed at her husband's wild imagination. Her focus is firmly fixed on practical concerns and dealing with the aftermath of the murder. She is anxious to remove any incriminating evidence, advising Macbeth to wash his bloodstained hands and to return the servants' daggers to Duncan's bedroom. But Macbeth is incapable of doing anything more, 'Look on't again I dare not.' Lady Macbeth curtly dismisses his anxieties, 'Infirm of purpose!', and goes to 'gild' the guards with Duncan's blood so as to incriminate them. When she returns, she criticises Macbeth again for being so cowardly.

Knocking at the gate (lines 67–72)

The knocking at the castle gates increases the dramatic tension, conveying a sense of inevitable doom. Macbeth can only stand paralysed at the sight of his bloody hands, shocked at the knowledge that he can never be cleansed from the guilt of his wicked crime. Further knocking results in Lady Macbeth displaying her remarkable composure, insisting that the couple return to their own bedroom and pretend that they were completely unaware of the murder. She casually blocks out the awful truth, saying that 'A little water clears us of this deed.' Macbeth's only comment is that he cannot bear to think that he is now a murderer. He already understands the enormity of what he has done and wishes desperately that the killing had never happened, 'Wake Duncan with thy knocking! I would thou couldst!'

Shakespeare's language

The playwright makes interesting choices in the staging of this intense scene. Duncan's murder is committed offstage. This ensures that the shocking action will appear much worse because it is filtered through the imagination of the audience by **the power of suggestion**. It also allows the focus of the scene to be on the internal drama taking place in Macbeth's mind and the changing dynamic of the Macbeths' personal relationship. The scene concludes with the repeated knocking at their gate. Shakespeare is reminding his audience that real life will assert itself even after the most horrendous deeds. The Macbeths will have to deal with the consequences of the murder and so, once again, they resort to deception, 'Get on your nightgown, lest occasion call us,/ And show us to be watchers.' The audience waits to see how long their pretence will succeed.

A staccato exchange between the couple on Macbeth's return ('Did not you speak?'/'When?'/'Now') reflects their desperate need for communication. The shared lines are a reminder of an earlier – and stronger – relationship between them. Yet their **contrasting responses** to Duncan's murder reveal the conflicting aspects of their personalities, which foreshadows further divisions ahead. A strong, domineering Lady Macbeth attends to the practicalities of the enterprise, 'I laid their daggers ready'. She provides extraordinary support when her husband returns in an agitated state after committing the murder.

At first she scolds her husband, treating him like a child, 'A foolish thought'. She then comforts him, 'Consider it not so deeply'. When this has no effect on the panic-stricken Macbeth, she changes tactics, directly ridiculing him, ''tis the eye of childhood/ That fears a painted devil'. She takes command when he refuses to return the servants' daggers and decisively goes off to 'gild the faces of the grooms'. Lady Macbeth's **language and actions are rational and detached.**

When she returns, she again chastises Macbeth's manhood, 'I shame/ To wear a heart so white'. Shakespeare further involves the audience in the horrifying reality by revealing Macbeth's boiling imagination. In a powerful trance-like state, the guilt-ridden murderer lists the benefits of sleep, 'Chief nourisher in life's feast'. Macbeth's **emotional, figurative language** and inability to act, 'I'll go no more', is in stark contrast to his pragmatic wife.

Dramatic irony adds another layer to this tense scene. Lady Macbeth's advice that obsessing over an action 'will make us mad', and her belief that 'A little water clears us of this deed', will both prove deeply ironic in the course of the play. Similarly, Macbeth's nightmare that an unnamed voice cried out 'Sleep no more!/ Macbeth does murder sleep' will prove only too true. His tragic fate is that he will never again experience peace of mind. In Shakespeare's world, sleep is the privilege of the good and the reward of the innocent. Tragically, it has been put to death and there is no goodness left in Macbeth's disordered mind.

Shakespeare has created a memorable scene of intense turmoil, not only for the actors on stage but also for the audience, aghast at the unfolding consequences of regicide.

Critical Analysis

1. 'Macbeth and Lady Macbeth are both evil characters who never succeed in winning our sympathy.' To what extent do you agree or disagree with this statement? Support your answer with reference to Act 2 Scene 2 of the play *Macbeth*.

2. 'The relationship between Macbeth and Lady Macbeth is fascinating because it is both intimate and complex.' Discuss this view of the relationship between Macbeth and his wife. Support your answer with reference to the play *Macbeth*, Act 2 Scene 2.

Sample Paragraph 1 (Q1)

I think Macbeth and Lady Macbeth are both extremely evil. Macbeth himself committed the murder of King Duncan of Scotland. But Lady Macbeth had planned it. 'I have drugged their possets'. She goes back to Duncan's room to leave the daggers back in which Macbeth had taken by mistake. These belonged to the two servants. They were supposed to be left there that the blame for the murder would be put on the two servants, not the Macbeths. She doesn't care about the dead of whom she thinks of. 'But as pictures'. Lady Macbeth comes back with her hands red like Macbeth and immediately starts giving grief to him. She says she isn't a coward like him. I would have no sympathy at all for her. Maybe Macbeth could deserve sympathy because he has a weak conscience. Macbeth is looking at his guilty hands. But he still knew what he was doing. It's no use feeling sorry when Duncan's dead. Macbeth had thought about all the rights and wrongs of killing King Duncan in other speeches. So I don't have much time for him either. *(185 words)*

Examiner's Comment

- This low-grade response attempts to address the question, but relies mainly on summary.
- There is evidence of a basic knowledge of the scene, but little illustration of the evil nature of both central characters.
- Lack of suitable quotation to support points.
- Poor language control weakens the answer considerably – particularly awkward expression ('in which Macbeth', 'of whom she thinks') and slang ('giving grief', 'much time').

Sample Paragraph 2 (Q1)

I felt sympathy for Lady Macbeth even though I agree she is evil in this scene, 'If he do bleed,/ I'll gild the faces of the grooms withal'. She has been placed in the situation of having to arrange everything, 'I have drugged their possets' because Macbeth keeps changing his mind about committing the murder. Despite asking the powers of darkness to 'Unsex' her, she still has some softer feelings, 'had he not resembled/ My father as he slept, I had done it'. Her husband returns in bits, 'This is a sorry sight'. Immediately she has to swing into action to help him, 'A foolish thought'. She has to hold it together for both of them, 'These deeds must not be thought/ After these ways'. She even has to go to return the incriminating daggers to Duncan's bedroom while Macbeth refuses. When knocking is heard at the castle gate, it is Lady Macbeth who must resume control, 'Get on your nightgown', while at the same time comforting her nervous husband, 'A little water clears us of this deed'. I think Shakespeare was very subtle in the portraying of this strong woman who deserves sympathy for staying calm after the fall-out from the murder by her husband, but also dealing with his nervous guilt. *(230 words)*

Examiner's Comment

- A mid-grade response. While the candidate has taken an unusual point about Lady Macbeth which is well supported with relevant quotations, only one part of the question has been addressed.
- Little or no focus on whether Macbeth is a sympathetic character.
- Inappropriate language use ('returns in bits', 'She has to hold it together for both of them') and an awkward concluding sentence also lower the standard.

Sample Paragraph 3 (Q1)

It would be almost impossible for a playwright to evoke sympathy for such an evil couple as the Macbeths. This scene focuses mainly on the mental turmoil experienced by the murderer. Yet, ironically, Macbeth's distraught state manages to slowly diminish the audience's initial revulsion. He is shown fixated by the 'sorry sight' of his 'hangman's hands'. He realises that he is blocked from redemption, he had 'most need of blessing, and Amen/ Stuck in my throat'. His powerful language ('pluck', 'Stuck') enables the audience to share the horror he is feeling. Through his poetic images describing sleep which he personifies as the 'balm of hurt minds', the audience is drawn into his nightmare. The final lines seal the audience's sympathy for this frantic man. Macbeth despises what he has become, a vile murderer. He is merely a common killer unable to cope with what he has done. Both he and the audience realise that the real tragedy is that he understands this himself, 'to know my deed 'twere best not know myself'. Unlike Lady Macbeth, who only briefly shows any human emotion, 'Had he not resembled/ My father as he slept', Macbeth's distress awakens a certain amount of audience empathy. *(215 words)*

Examiner's Comment

- An informed, focused paragraph that explores interesting high-order analysis about the audience reaction to Macbeth.
- The central point tracing the playwright's depiction of Macbeth as a traumatised victim of his own weakness is very well developed.
- Excellent expression – impressive vocabulary ('initial revulsion', 'blocked from redemption') and controlled syntax.
- Effective use of apt, accurate quotations also contributes to this top-grade response.

🙶 Key Quotes

That which hath made them drunk hath made me bold (Lady Macbeth soliloquy) l.1	Lady Macbeth has plied the servants guarding Duncan with drink so that Macbeth will have unrestricted access to commit the murder while they lie in a drunken stupor. Drink has had the opposite effect on her making her fearless.
Had he not resembled/ My father as he slept, I had done't (Lady Macbeth soliloquy) l.12–13	This is the first apparent weakness in Lady Macbeth's steely determination to proceed with the planned murder. It shows how even she, who has prayed to the 'spirits' to 'unsex' her, cannot fully extinguish all feeling.
This is a sorry sight (Macbeth to Lady Macbeth) l.18	Macbeth appears on stage with bloodstained hands just after the killing of Duncan. Soft sibilant alliteration increases the anguish of the assassin's regret at what he has done.
These deeds must not be thought/ After these ways. So, it will make us mad. (Lady Macbeth to Macbeth) l.31–2	Lady Macbeth attempts to calm her agitated husband and stop him obsessing over the regicide. Her composed, sensible advice that this over-thinking leads to insanity has a bitterly ironic edge.

'tis the eye of childhood/ That fears a painted devil *(Lady Macbeth to Macbeth) l.52–3*	A caustic Lady Macbeth dismisses with ridicule Macbeth's fear of returning the daggers to Duncan's room. Only a child, she reasons, could fear a scary image.
Will all great Neptune's ocean wash this blood/ Clean from my hand? *(Macbeth to Lady Macbeth) l.58*	Macbeth is becoming all too aware of the enormity of his crime. Nothing can cleanse him from guilt. The broad vowels imitate the great surge of the sea, but even the ocean cannot undo the consequences of what has happened.
A little water clears us of this deed *(Lady Macbeth to Macbeth) l.65*	Another ironic comment by Lady Macbeth. She attempts to soothe her increasingly frantic husband, who is convinced that his guilt will pollute all the oceans of the world.
Wake Duncan with thy knocking! I would thou couldst! *(Macbeth soliloquy) l.72*	Responding to insistent knocking at the castle gate, a bitterly regretful Macbeth wishes that Duncan were still asleep and could be awakened by the noise. His desperate tone is so filled with shame that he seems to care little whether or not his crime is discovered.

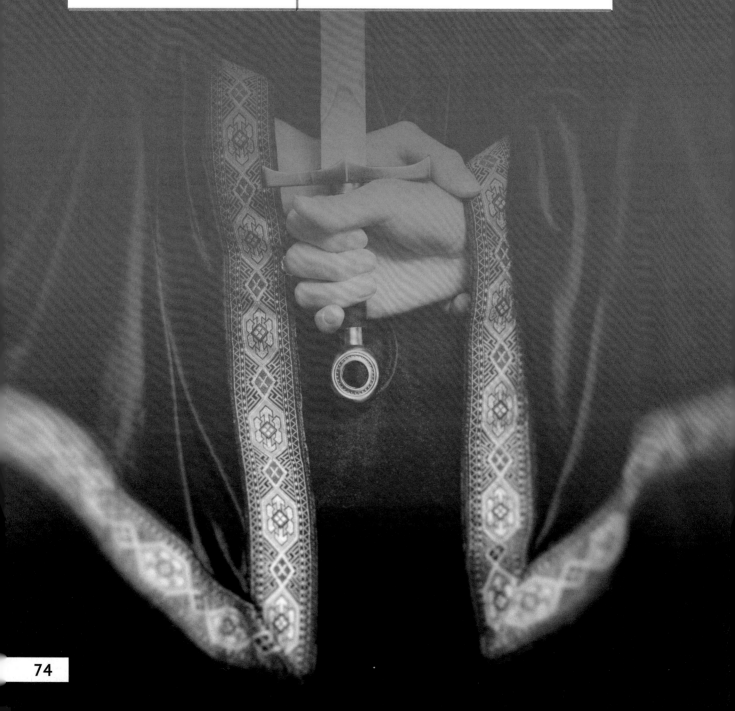

Scene 3*

OVERVIEW

The drunken porter of Macbeth's castle imagines that he is the gatekeeper to hell. He slowly responds to the repeated knocking, finally admitting Macduff and Lennox, with whom he jokes about the effects of drunkenness. As dawn breaks, Macduff goes to the king's chamber and discovers that Duncan has been murdered. The alarm bell rings out and Macbeth pretends to be horrified by the tragic news. He tells Duncan's sons of their father's murder, lying to them that he killed the king's bodyguards in a fit of fury. As Malcolm and Donalbain prepare to flee the country for their own safety, the Scottish thanes resolve to avenge the act of treason.

Inverness. Macbeth's castle

Knocking within. Enter Porter

Porter ⌐drunk ⌐   *Macduff + Lennox arrive*

Here's a knocking indeed! If a man were porter of hell-
gate, he should have old turning the key.

Knocking within

Knock, knock, knock! Who's there, i' the name of
Beelzebub? Here's a farmer that hanged himself on
the expectation of plenty: come in time; have napkins   5
enough about you, here you'll sweat for't.

Knocking within

Knock, knock! Who's there, i'the other devil's name? Faith,
here's an equivocator that could swear in both the scales
against either scale, who committed treason enough for
God's sake, yet could not equivocate to heaven: O, come   10
in, equivocator.

Knocking within

Knock, knock, knock! Who's there? Faith, here's an English
tailor come hither for stealing out of a French hose: come
in, tailor, here you may roast your goose.

Knocking within

Knock, knock; never at quiet! What are you? But this place 15
is too cold for hell. I'll devil-porter it no further; I had
thought to have let in some of all professions that go the
primrose way to the everlasting bonfire.

Knocking within

Anon, anon! I pray you, remember the porter.

Opens the gate. Enter Macduff and Lennox

Macduff

Was it so late, friend, ere you went to bed,   20
That you do lie so late?

Porter

Faith, sir, we were carousing till the second cock; and
drink, sir, is a great provoker of three things.

Macduff

What three things does drink especially provoke?

Porter

Marry, sir, nose-painting, sleep, and urine. Lechery, sir, it 25
provokes, and unprovokes: it provokes the desire, but it

Porter: *gatekeeper, janitor*

4 Beelzebub: *devil; second in command to Satan*
4–5 farmer ... plenty: *a farmer who killed himself when his crops were less profitable than he had hoped*
5 napkins: *handkerchiefs*

8 equivocator: *untrustworthy person who speaks with deliberate ambiguity*
8–9 swear ... scale: *hypocritically support both sides of an argument*
9 treason: *treachery against king and country*

13 stealing ... hose: *skimped on cloth when making fashionable trousers*

18 primrose ... bonfire: *attractive road to destruction*

20 ere: *before*

21 lie: *sleep in*

22 carousing ... cock: *drinking until three a.m.*

23 provoker: *instigator*

25 Marry: *indeed*
25 nose-painting: *makes a nose red – caused by drinking too much*
25 Lechery: *lust*

takes away the performance. Therefore, much drink may be said to be an equivocator with lechery: it makes him, and it mars him; it sets him on, and it takes him off; it
30 persuades him, and disheartens him; makes him stand to, and not stand to. In conclusion, equivocates him in a sleep, and, giving him the lie, leaves him.

Macduff

I believe drink gave thee the lie last night.

Porter

That it did, sir, i' the very throat on me; but I requited him
35 for his lie, and, I think, being too strong for him, though he took up my legs sometime, yet I made a shift to cast him.

Macduff

Is thy master stirring?

Enter Macbeth

Our knocking has awaked him; here he comes.

Lennox

Good morrow, noble sir.

Macbeth

Good morrow, both. → normal, confident pretending

Macduff

Is the king stirring, worthy thane?

Macbeth

40   Not yet.

Macduff

He did command me to call timely on him;
I have almost slipped the hour.

Macbeth

I'll bring you to him.

Macduff

I know this is a joyful trouble to you,
But yet 'tis one.

Macbeth

45 The labour we delight in physics pain.
This is the door.

Macduff

I'll make so bold to call,
For 'tis my limited service.

28 equivocator with lechery: *alcohol makes a fool of desire*
29 mars: *stops*
30-1 stand to: *desire, want*
31-2 equivocates ... sleep: *tricks him into falling asleep*
32 giving him ... leaves him: *initiates desire, then abandons it*

34-6 i' the very throat ... cast him: *drink stayed in his throat until he vomited it out*

41 timely: *early*

42 almost slipped the hour: *nearly let the time pass*

43 joyful trouble: *rewarding work*

45 labour ... pain: *work we enjoy heals us*

47 limited service: *official duty*

48 appoint so: *arrange*

49 unruly: *stormy, violent*

51 Lamentings: *sorrowful cries*

53 dire combustions: *terrible disorder*
54 obscure bird: *owl – a sign of death*
55 Clamoured: *protested loudly*

57–8 My young ... to it: *my young memory cannot recollect anything like it*

60 conceive: *comprehend*

62 sacrilegious murder: *an offence against a sacred person (the king was seen as God's representative)*
63 Lord's anointed temple: *Duncan – God's appointed representative*

68 Gorgon: *mythical monster who turned humans to stone*

Exit

Lennox

Goes the king hence today?

Macbeth

He does: he did appoint so.

Lennox

The night has been unruly: where we lay,

Our chimneys were blown down; and, as they say,   50

Lamentings heard i' the air, strange screams of death,

And – prophesying with accents terrible

Of dire combustion, and confused events,

New hatched to th' woeful time – the obscure bird

Clamoured the livelong night. Some say, the earth   55

Was feverous and did shake. → *super natural signs*

Macbeth

'Twas a rough night.

Lennox

My young remembrance cannot parallel

A fellow to it.

Enter Macduff

Macduff   *found dead Duncan*

O horror, horror, horror! Tongue nor heart

Cannot conceive nor name thee!

Macbeth, Lennox

What's the matter?   60

Macduff

Confusion now hath made his masterpiece!

Most sacrilegious murder hath broke ope

The Lord's anointed temple, and stole thence

The life o' the building!

Macbeth

What is't you say? The life?   65

Lennox

Mean you his majesty?

Macduff

Approach the chamber, and destroy your sight

With a new Gorgon. Do not bid me speak.

See, and then speak yourselves.

devinely ordained → crime against king is crime against god

Exeunt Macbeth and Lennox

Awake, awake!

70 Ring the alarum-bell. Murder and treason!

Banquo and Donalbain! Malcolm! Awake!

Shake off this downy sleep, death's counterfeit,

And look on death itself! Up, up, and see

The great doom's image! Malcolm! Banquo!

75 As from your graves rise up, and walk like sprites,

To countenance this horror!

Bell rings. Enter Lady Macbeth

Lady Macbeth

What's the business,

That such a hideous trumpet calls to parley

The sleepers of the house? Speak, speak!

Macduff

O gentle lady, → more able to hear than the rest

→ referring to feminity stereotype

'Tis not for you to hear what I can speak:

80 The repetition, in a woman's ear,

Would murder as it fell.

Enter Banquo

O Banquo, Banquo,

Our royal master 's murdered!

Lady Macbeth

Woe, alas!

What, in our house?

Banquo

Too cruel anywhere.

Dear Duff, I prithee, contradict thyself,

85 And say it is not so.

Enter Macbeth, Lennox and Ross

Macbeth

Had I but died an hour before this chance, *I wish I never lived to see the day*

↳ hipocracy

I had lived a blessèd time; for, from this instant,

There's nothing serious in mortality:

All is but toys; renown and grace is dead;

90 The wine of life is drawn, and the mere lees

Is left this vault to brag of.

Enter Malcolm and Donalbain

Donalbain

What is amiss?

---

74 great doom's image: *exact likeness of the Last Judgement*

75 sprites: *ghosts*

76 countenance: *face, see*

77 hideous ... parley: *alarm signalling a warlike discussion*

81 murder as it fell: *prove fatal for the listener*

88 serious in mortality: *worthwhile in human existence*

89 toys: *trivialities, tricks*

89-91 renown ... brag of: *now the noble king is dead, this world is worthless*

92 amiss: *wrong*

93 fountain: *source*

Macbeth

        You are, and do not know it.

The spring, the head, the fountain of your blood

Is stopped; the very source of it is stopped.

[handwritten: > father dead.]

Macduff

Your royal father's murdered.

Malcolm

        O! By whom?   95

Lennox

Those of his chamber, as it seemed, had done't.

[handwritten: > servents have done it.]

97 badged: *marked, crested*

Their hands and faces were all badged with blood;

So were their daggers, which unwiped we found

Upon their pillows. They stared, and were distracted;

No man's life was to be trusted with them.   100

Macbeth

[handwritten: doesnt make sense]

O, yet I do repent me of my fury,

[handwritten: > admitting to killing servents, but he said king is not awake yet.]

That I did kill them.

Macduff

        Wherefore did you so?

Macbeth

Who can be wise, amazed, temperate and furious,

103 amazed, temperate and furious: *surprised, calm and frenzied*

Loyal and neutral, in a moment? No man:

Th'expedition of my violent love   105

105–6 expedition … reason: *the course of my vengeful love for the king overtook logic*

Outrun the pauser, reason. Here lay Duncan,

His silver skin laced with his golden blood;

And his gashed stabs looked like a breach in nature

108–9 breach … entrance: *a gap allowing devastation to enter*

For ruin's wasteful entrance. There, the murderers,

Steeped in the colours of their trade, their daggers   110

111 Unmannerly … gore: *coarsely covered in blood*

Unmannerly breeched with gore. Who could refrain

That had a heart to love, and in that heart

Courage to make 's love known?

Lady Macbeth

        Help me hence, ho!

Macduff

Look to the lady.

Malcolm

Aside to Donalbain

Why do we hold our tongues, that most may claim   115

116 argument: *situation, development*

This argument for ours?

Lady Macbeth unusually quiet

Donalbain

afraid → might be next → is next to be king

Aside to Malcolm

What should be spoken
Here, where our fate, hid in an auger-hole,
May rush, and seize us? Let's away;
Our tears are not yet brewed.

117 our fate ... auger-hole: *we are in great danger*

119 brewed: *ready*

Malcolm

Aside to Donalbain

Nor our strong sorrow
Upon the foot of motion.

119-20 sorrow ... motion: *grief has not yet been expressed*

Banquo

120 Look to the lady –

Lady Macbeth is carried out → *Faking fainting to distract*

And when we have our naked frailties hid,
That suffer in exposure, let us meet,
And question this most bloody piece of work,
To know it further. Fears and scruples shake us:

125 In the great hand of God I stand and thence
Against the undivulged pretence I fight
Of treasonous malice.

121 naked frailties: *human weaknesses*

124 scruples: *doubts*

126 undivulged pretence: *hidden plots*

Macduff

And so do I.

All

So all.

Macbeth

Let's briefly put on manly readiness,
And meet in the hall together.

128 manly readiness: *preparedness*

All

Well contented.

Exeunt all but Malcolm and Donalbain

Malcolm

130 What will you do? Let's not consort with them.
To show an unfelt sorrow is an office
Which the false man does easy. I'll to England.

130 consort with: *associate with*

131 office: *task, duty*

Donalbain

separating for survival

To Ireland, I. Our separated fortune
Shall keep us both the safer. Where we are,

135 There's daggers in men's smiles: the near in blood,
The nearer bloody.

135 daggers ... smiles: *people can be hypocritical*

135-6 near in ... bloody: *those closely related to us are most dangerous*

136 murderous shaft: *deadly arrow*

139 dainty: *courteous, particular*

140 shift away: *secretly leave*

140-1 warrant ... mercy left: *there's good reason to escape danger*

Malcolm

This murderous shaft that's shot

Hath not yet lighted, and our safest way

Is to avoid the aim. Therefore, to horse,

And let us not be dainty of leave-taking,

But shift away. There's warrant in that theft   140

Which steals itself when there's no mercy left.

Exeunt

Study Notes

Knocking (lines 1-58)

The knocking heard at the end of the last scene continues. Macbeth's drunken porter slowly makes his way to the castle gate, imagining himself the gatekeeper to hell who invites in various sinners in the name of 'Beelzebub'. He ridicules a greedy farmer who hanged himself after his crops failed to make as much profit as he had wished. During his rambling talk, he complains of other types of sinner – including those who engage in prevarication and theft. When he finally opens the gate to Macduff and Lennox, the porter jokes about the side effects of drink. Despite the light-hearted atmosphere, tension returns when Macduff asks about the king. Meanwhile, Lennox comments on the 'unruly' night. The audience will, of course, link the catalogue of unnatural events with what has happened within the castle and will be all too aware of the dramatic irony of these lines.

Report of regicide (lines 59-141)

A clearly distraught Macduff returns to report the 'sacrilegious murder' of Duncan. The alarm bell is rung and Lady Macbeth appears, demanding to know 'What's the business' that has so disturbed her house. Does she make a rare mistake by responding to the news with the words, 'What, in our house?' A curt Banquo replies, 'Too cruel anywhere.' Macbeth then delivers two lengthy and carefully composed speeches designed to impress on his listeners the extent of his grief, 'renown and grace is dead'. He also confesses to murdering Duncan's bodyguards in a wild fit of grief at the sight of the dead monarch, 'I do repent me of my fury, / That I did kill them'. Interestingly, Macduff is suspicious about why Macbeth should have done this. Lady Macbeth faints, perhaps in astonishment that her husband has killed the guards – this was not part of their plan in murdering Duncan. It is also possible that she is putting on an act to divert attention from him, 'Help me hence'.

Banquo accepts that Lady Macbeth is genuinely unwell and tries to help her, 'Look to the lady'. He also takes control of the situation in the immediate aftermath of such 'treasonous malice'. In contrast, Macbeth does not show leadership at this point, merely echoing Banquo's instruction, 'Let's ... meet in the hall together.' Throughout the scene, we have witnessed his increasing moral decline as he resorts to gross hypocrisy.

Malcom and Donalbain are acutely aware that they are in danger, possibly suspecting Macbeth, 'the near in blood, / The nearer bloody.' They know that their lives are at risk and decide to leave without delay, Donalbain to Ireland and Malcolm to England.

Shakespeare's language

The **dramatic significance** of Act 2 Scene 3 has often been the subject of debate. Most critics agree that while it provides comic relief, it has other important functions. In theatrical terms, the Porter interlude allows time for Macbeth and his wife to change into their nightclothes and for Macduff to make his entrance. The purpose of this scene could also be to reinforce the diabolical nature of the Macbeths' castle. The intoxicated porter sees himself as hell's gatekeeper, admitting sinners to damnation. Macbeth and his wife have committed the terrible sin of murder. Macbeth also craved power and indulges in equivocation, asking who can be 'loyal and neutral in a moment' as he seeks to excuse himself for killing Duncan's bodyguards. Macbeth and Lady Macbeth, like the tailor, steal what is not theirs. There are numerous echoes from the previous scene – the references to the dagger ('there's daggers in men's smiles'), the owl ('obscure bird') and sleep ('downy sleep, death's counterfeit') – all of which add to the tension.

> *Murder and treason!*
>
> *Macduff, Act 2 Scene 3, l.70*

The **violent descriptions** of the night's storm would have made Shakespeare's audience shiver. People believed that 'dire combustion' in the state was echoed in nature. Lennox's detailed account of the 'unruly night' is curtly answered by a tense Macbeth: ''Twas a rough night.' The audience is reminded of the anguish this man suffered while he agonised over the murder of his king. Other biblical references reflect the Elizabethan belief that the king was appointed by God, 'The Lord's anointed temple'.

Elaborate images are used in Macbeth's report of Duncan's murder, 'The wine of life is drawn', 'the fountain of your blood/ Is stopped'. His language becomes increasingly extravagant as he describes the king's lifeless body, 'His silver skin laced with his golden blood'. The daggers of the grooms are 'Unmannerly breeched with gore'. Macbeth is desperate to convince. In response, the audience is conscious of the **dramatic irony** in his speech, 'Had I but died an hour before this chance,/ I had lived a blessèd time.' From now on, 'There's nothing serious in mortality' for the murderer Macbeth, who will be embroiled in trying to cover up the king's death.

Macbeth's carefully rehearsed speeches are in stark **contrast** to the genuine response of Macduff, 'Your royal father's murdered'. Images drawn from war abound, adding to the violent atmosphere, 'daggers in men's smiles', 'gashed stabs looked like a breach in nature/ For ruin's wasteful entrance', 'murderous shaft'. Shakespeare uses comparisons, contrasts, echoes, foreshadowing and rich imagery to craft a scene which not only advances the plot but increases the bloody violence of the play for an already tense audience.

83

Critical Analysis

1. 'Shakespeare makes effective use of disturbing imagery in the play *Macbeth*.' Discuss this view, supporting your answer with reference to Act 2 Scene 3.

2. 'Dramatic irony is effectively used to add to the audience's experience of *Macbeth*.' Discuss this statement, supporting your answer with reference to Act 2 Scene 3.

Sample Paragraph 1 (Q1)

Macbeth is a disturbed man who has committed the terrible criminal act of regicide, assassinating his appointed king. He uses long speeches full of hypocrisy to plead innocence. But he fools no-one, so that Lady Macbeth has to distract the others by fainting, 'Help me hence'. There is tension through the whole of Act 2 Scene 3. Lennox speaks of the terrible unnatural overnight storm, with 'chimneys blown down'. There was also some 'strange lamentations of death'. The others, Malcolm and Donalbain, who do not know Macbeth has murdered Duncan, speak in short sentences, asking 'What is amiss?' But Macbeth keeps his nerve, explaining about how all that is left is the dregs, 'the lees'. He then adds a little about Duncan's 'golden skin and silver blood', but he is desperate. Even Duncan's twin sons suspect him and decide to go away without saying goodbye, one to England and the other to Ireland. This is a very unnatural scene that is filled with disturbing images. *(165 words)*

Examiner's Comment

- This basic response only occasionally succeeds in addressing the question of disturbing imagery in the drama.
- Points are haphazard and there is a reliance on unfocused narrative.
- More developed discussion on the tension within the scene would have raised the standard.
- Expression is poorly controlled and some of the references are inaccurate.

Sample Paragraph 2 (Q1)

In Act 2 Scene 3, the playwright uses ominous imagery to evoke the evil world of the Macbeths. The drunken Porter is playing at being the 'porter of hell-gate'. Reference is made to Beelzebub, the devil who revolted against Satan. This is an unnerving parallel to Macbeth. Lennox remarks that an alarming overnight storm blasted its way through the country, 'prophesying…dire combustion'. A disquieting image, 'strange screams of death' contributes to the restless atmosphere. Equally, the reference to the 'obscure bird' also adds to the menacing atmosphere. Biblical references, 'The great doom's image' and Greek myth, 'destroy your sight/ With a new Gorgon' are employed to disquiet the audience. Violent language adds further distress. The sons of Duncan fear the 'daggers in men's smiles' and a possible 'murderous shaft'. Shakespeare uses dark diabolical language, foreboding images from nature and mythological references to unsettle the audience in this highly dramatic scene. *(150 words)*

Examiner's Comment

- A much more focused top-grade answer that shows excellent understanding of the scene.
- The emphasis throughout is on the playwright's choice of images and the effect on the audience ('ominous', 'unnerving', 'disquiet', 'unsettle').
- Accurate quotations and reference used well to support key points.
- Impressive language use, varied expression and controlled syntax add to the high standard.

❝❝ Key Quotes

here's an equivocator that could swear in both the scales against either scale *(Porter soliloquy) l.8–9*	The drunken porter imagines the types of sinner who would be likely to enter hell. One such is the equivocator, someone who indulges in vagueness, double-speak. No matter which way an argument goes, he will be able to say he is on that side. This references the theme of deceit which permeates the entire play.
The night has been unruly *(Lennox to Macbeth) l.49*	Lennox reports on the violent storms that have just rocked Scotland. This was particularly significant to an Elizabethan audience who believed that disorder in the state was mirrored by disorder in nature.
There's nothing serious in mortality:/ All is but toys *(Macbeth to Macduff) l.88–9*	Macbeth hypocritically declares that since the king has been killed, there is nothing worthwhile left in this life. Ironically, he will soon learn how true this statement will be for him and Lady Macbeth.
Here lay Duncan,/ His silver skin laced with his golden blood *(Macbeth) l.106–7*	The king's lifeless body is described by Macbeth as a richly decorated garment. This image of clothing is woven throughout the drama. But his carefully chosen words do not impress the listeners. Lady Macbeth faints – possibly to divert attention from her husband's hollow-sounding words.
And when we have our naked frailties hid,/ That suffer in exposure, let us meet *(Banquo) l.121–2*	Extraordinarily, Banquo assumes control of events in Macbeth's castle. It should be Macbeth who takes command. Everyone – apart from the newly arrived Macduff and Lennox – is dressed in flimsy nightclothes. There is also a suggestion of deceit in the comment.
Where we are,/ There's daggers in men's smiles *(Malcolm to Donalbain) l.134–5*	Unlike their trusting father, Duncan's sons are suspicious. They understand that people are not what they seem. Duncan died because he believed that 'There's no art/ To find the mind's construction in the face.' His sons are more cautious and therefore more likely to survive.

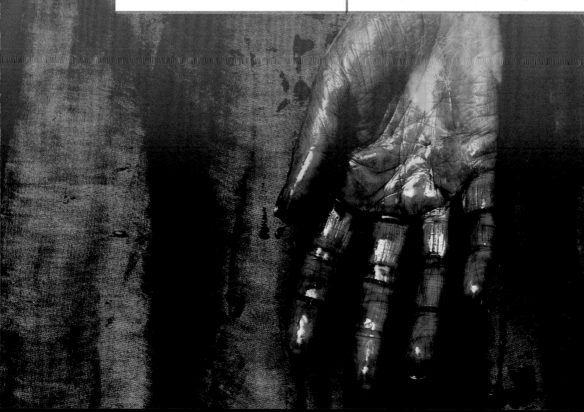

OVERVIEW

On the day after the murder of Duncan, Ross and an Old Man discuss the unnaturally dark morning and the strange events that are occurring in Scotland. Duncan's two absent sons, Malcolm and Donalbain, seem to be under suspicion for the murder of their father. Macduff decides that he will not go to Scone to see Macbeth crowned as the new king of Scotland.

Inverness. Outside Macbeth's castle

Enter Ross and an Old Man

Old Man — Wise, seer, oracle
70

Threescore and ten I can remember well, — biblical language.

Within the volume of which time I have seen — never seen anything so terrible

Hours dreadful and things strange; but this sore night

Hath trifled former knowings.

Ross

                Ah, good father,

5   Thou seest the heavens, as troubled with man's act,

Threatens his bloody stage: by the clock 'tis day,

And yet dark night strangles the travelling lamp.

Is it night's predominance, or the day's shame,

That darkness does the face of earth entomb,

When living light should kiss it?

Old Man

                        'Tis unnatural, — natural order over turned those less powerful > become more dominant

10

Even like the deed that's done. On Tuesday last,

A falcon, towering in her pride of place,

Was by a mousing owl hawked at and killed.

Ross

And Duncan's horses – a thing most strange and certain – — something terrible is happening

15   Beauteous and swift, the minions of their race, — chaos — supernatural occurrences

Turned wild in nature, broke their stalls, flung out,

Contending 'gainst obedience, as they would

Make war with mankind.

Old Man

               'Tis said they ate each other.

Ross

They did so, to the amazement of mine eyes

That looked upon't.

Enter Macduff

20   Here comes the good Macduff.

How goes the world, sir, now?

Macduff

              Why, see you not?

Ross

Is't known who did this more than bloody deed?

---

1 Threescore and ten: *seventy years*

2 volume: *length*

4 Hath trifled former knowings: *is the worst I have ever experienced*

5 act: *human behaviour*

7 travelling lamp: *the sun*

8–10 Is it night's … kiss it?: *is night in control or is day ashamed to appear?*

12 towering … place: *soaring before attacking*

13 mousing: *hunting for mice*

15 minions … race: *finest specimens of their breed*

17 Contending … mankind: *revolting against their natural master, man*

24 pretend: *gain (from killing Duncan)*

24 suborned: *bribed*

28 Thriftless: *wasteful*

31 named: *appointed*
31 Scone: *the palace where Scottish kings were crowned*

33 Colmekill: *the island of Iona in the Inner Hebrides*

36 Fife: *Macduff is thane of Fife*

36 thither: *to there (Scone)*

38 Lest … new: *in case Duncan's reign was better than Macbeth's will be*

40-1 God's … foes: *God's blessing to you and to all who make peace*

Macduff

Those that Macbeth hath slain.

Ross

                                    Alas, the day!

What good could they pretend?

Macduff

                              They were suborned:

Malcolm and Donalbain, the king's two sons,   25

Are stolen away and fled; which puts upon them

Suspicion of the deed. →fled scene ⇒ ~~body~~ suspicion

Ross   *Macbeth*   'Gainst nature still!
                    ↑

Thriftless ambition, that will ravin up

Thine own life's means! Then 'tis most like

The sovereignty will fall upon Macbeth.   30

Macduff

He is already named, and gone to Scone

To be invested.

Ross

                        Where is Duncan's body?

Macduff

Carried to Colmekill,

The sacred storehouse of his predecessors,

And guardian of their bones.

Ross

                                    Will you to Scone?   35

Macduff

No, cousin, I'll to Fife.

Ross

                              Well, I will thither.

Macduff

Well, may you see things well done there: adieu,

Lest our old robes sit easier than our new.

Ross

Farewell, father.

Old Man

God's benison go with you; and with those   40

That would make good of bad, and friends of foes!

Exeunt

Study Notes

Unnatural events (lines 1–20)

An old man of seventy remarks that he has never witnessed such a severe storm, 'this sore night/ Hath trifled former knowings'. Ross comments on the unnatural darkness of the morning, 'night's predominance'. Shakespeare's audience would have believed that human wickedness is reflected by turbulence in nature. Since Duncan's death, there have been reports of unnatural occurrences among animals. Predator becomes prey; a falcon has been killed by an owl. Duncan's horses have gone wild and eaten one another. The mayhem throughout Scotland is a reminder of the witches' evil powers and that Macbeth is now under their spell.

Unnatural deeds (lines 20–41)

Macduff, Thane of Fife, confirms the official line that Duncan's grooms are believed to have killed the king. It is also thought that they were paid by Duncan's sons to commit the murder. The fact that Malcolm and Donalbain have fled 'puts upon them/ Suspicion of the deed'. But Ross expresses his uneasiness; what could Duncan's sons have hoped to gain? Why would they kill their own father and cut off their source of income, their 'own life's means'?

Macbeth has been named Duncan's successor. Since the old king's sons have fled, he is next in line because he is Duncan's cousin. He will be crowned at Scone, while Duncan's body is to be buried with his ancestors on the island of Iona. Macduff does not plan to attend the coronation and intends to return home. He suspects that Duncan's reign will turn out to have been much better than Macbeth's will be. His cryptic remark 'Lest our old robes sit easier than our new' indicates his growing distrust of Macbeth. For the audience, this strikes an ominous note, suggesting trouble ahead.

Shakespeare's language

This short scene provides information about upcoming events and also **reinforces the horror of the king's death**. The metaphor of the earth as a 'bloody stage' references Macbeth's earlier remark that his murderer's guilty hands will 'incarnadine' the earth's oceans. Hideous **personification** vividly conveys the overturning of the natural order, 'dark night strangles the travelling lamp' of day. This darkness will 'entomb' daylight. Even the morning is personified as a guilt-ridden face and ambition is seen as a monster eating what gave it life ('ravin up').

The animal world has also been thrown into chaos. The owl flies up to kill the bigger bird, rather than down to kill its natural prey, the mouse. It is a creature of the night, wild and untameable. But even disciplined animals, the king's horses, react against their nature, turning wild and making 'war with mankind'. The **symbolism** of such disorder highlights the moral collapse of the Macbeths, who were once 'minions' of the king, favourites showered with gifts and honours, yet they too broke out in revolt.

Clothing imagery strikes an uneasy note at the end of the scene, 'Lest our old robes sit easier than our new.' Macduff is hinting that Macbeth is implicated in the murder and will initiate a reign of terror. Other thanes have been wary of openly expressing their opinions in this new dangerous atmosphere. Ross is a minor character who represents the concerns of the ordinary people of Scotland. What could the grooms or Duncan's sons gain by killing the king? The Old Man's final blessing is particularly **ironic**, 'God's benison go with you; and with those/ That would make good of bad, and friends of foes!' Scotland is about to descend into a nightmare of evil and moral ambiguity, the antithesis of peace.

💬 Key Quotes

Thou seest the heavens, as troubled with man's act,/ Threatens his bloody stage *(Ross to Old Man) l.5–6*	Shakespeare's audience believed that unnatural acts by man (in this case regicide) cause disturbance in the universe. This in turn harms the earth, the scene of man's bloody deeds. Ross's remark increases the sense of tension and foreboding in the play.
'Tis said they ate each other *(Old Man to Ross) l.18*	Even the animal kingdom is in revolt. Duncan's horses have gone wild. Everything is in chaos after the horrendous murder of Duncan. Violence and anarchy are now predominant.
Thriftless ambition, that will ravin up/ Thine own life's means! *(Ross to Old Man) l.28–9*	The imagery of cannibalism continues. Reckless ambition is a monster which will devour even its own source of life. Ross doubts that Duncan's sons have murdered their father. It would not only be unnatural, but also foolish, since they would lose all that he could have given them.

Key Points | Act 2

- Act 2 focuses on the murder of Duncan, the pivotal act in the play. Shakespeare presents a sequence of intensely dramatic scenes before, during and after the killing.
- In his soliloquies, Macbeth struggles with his conflicted feelings about murdering the king.
- Unlike Macbeth, Banquo refuses to compromise his loyalty to Duncan.
- Self-controlled and practical, Lady Macbeth continues to exert her influence on her husband.
- The murder of Duncan takes place offstage, leaving the audience to imagine its full significance.
- In the aftermath of the killing, Macbeth is paralysed by regret. His resolute wife remains composed, concentrating on providing the Macbeths with a plausible alibi and ironically dismissing his guilt.
- Shakespeare relieves the oppressive tension with a short interlude involving a drunken porter. While the scene is darkly comic, it also increases the audience's sense of horror.
- Malcolm and Donalbain flee Scotland for their own safety. Macduff begins to grow suspicious of Macbeth and does not attend the new king's coronation at Scone.
- Evil has now overpowered good. This upheaval of the natural order is mirrored in the weather and the animal world.

Class/Homework Exercise

How does Shakespeare create dramatic tension in the aftermath of Duncan's murder? Write a short paragraph (150–200 words), supporting your answer with reference to the text.

Act 3
Scene 1

OVERVIEW

Banquo is suspicious that Macbeth has become Scotland's new king through evil means, but he takes some comfort from the witches' predictions for his own descendants. He is also persuaded by the Macbeths to return later that evening to their palace at Forres for a special feast. However, Macbeth has already decided that Banquo and his son must die, so that he can continue to reign securely. He hires two professional murderers to carry out the foul deed.

Forres. The palace

Enter Banquo

Banquo

Thou hast it now: king, Cawdor, Glamis, all,

As the weird women promised; and I fear

Thou played'st most foully for it. Yet it was said

It should not stand in thy posterity, –

5   But that myself should be the root and father

Of many kings. If there come truth from them –

As upon thee, Macbeth, their speeches shine –

Why, by the verities on thee made good, –

May they not be my oracles as well, →

10 And set me up in hope? But hush, no more.

Sennet sounds. Enter Macbeth as king, Lady Macbeth as queen, Lennox, Ross, Lords, Ladies, and Attendants

Macbeth

Here's our chief guest.

Lady Macbeth

                    If he had been forgotten,

It had been as a gap in our great feast,

And all-thing unbecoming.

Macbeth

Tonight we hold a solemn supper, sir,

And I'll request your presence.

Banquo

15   Let your highness

Command upon me; to the which my duties

Are with a most indissoluble tie

For ever knit.

Macbeth

Ride you this afternoon? →

Banquo

                 Ay, my good lord.

Macbeth

20 We should have else desired your good advice –

Which still hath been both grave and prosperous –

In this day's council; but we'll take tomorrow.

Is it far you ride?

1 it: *the crown*

2 weird women: *witches*

3 played'st most foully: *acted falsely*

4 stand in thy posterity: *continue in your family*

5 root: *source, origin*

8 verities: *truths*

9 oracles: *prophets*

Sennet: *trumpet call*

11 chief guest: *Banquo*

13 all-thing unbecoming: *completely improper*

14 solemn supper: *formal banquet*

15–18 Let … knit: *I will do whatever you ask out of duty and loyalty*

22 council: *meeting of the royal council*
22 take: *consult*

Banquo

As far, my lord, as will fill up the time

'Twixt this and supper. Go not my horse the better,   25

I must become a borrower of the night

For a dark hour or twain.

Macbeth

                    Fail not our feast.

Banquo

My lord, I will not.

Macbeth

We hear, our bloody cousins are bestowed

In England and in Ireland, not confessing   30

Their cruel parricide, filling their hearers

With strange invention; but of that tomorrow,

When therewithal we shall have cause of state

Craving us jointly. Hie you to horse: adieu,

Till you return at night. Goes Fleance with you?   35

Banquo

Ay, my good lord: our time does call upon us.

Macbeth

I wish your horses swift and sure of foot;

And so I do commend you to their backs.

Farewell.

Exit Banquo

Let every man be master of his time   40

Till seven at night: to make society

The sweeter welcome, we will keep ourself

Till supper-time alone; while then, God be with you!

Exeunt all but Macbeth and Servant

Sirrah, a word with you: attend those men

Our pleasure?   45

Servant

They are, my lord, without the palace gate.

Macbeth

Bring them before us.

Exit Servant

                To be thus is nothing,

But to be safely thus. Our fears in Banquo

Stick deep; and in his royalty of nature

Reigns that which would be feared. 'Tis much he dares,   50

And, to that dauntless temper of his mind,

He hath a wisdom that doth guide his valour

To act in safety. There is none but he

Whose being I do fear; and under him,

35 My genius is rebuked as, it is said,

Mark Antony's was by Caesar. He chid the sisters

When first they put the name of king upon me,

And bade them speak to him; then prophet-like

They hailed him father to a line of kings.

60 Upon my head they placed a fruitless crown,

And put a barren sceptre in my gripe,

Thence to be wrenched with an unlineal hand,

No son of mine succeeding. If it be so,

For Banquo's issue have I filed my mind;

65 For them the gracious Duncan have I murdered;

Put rancours in the vessel of my peace

Only for them; and mine eternal jewel

Given to the common enemy of man

To make them kings – the seed of Banquo kings!

70 Rather than so, come, Fate, into the list,

And champion me to the utterance! Who's there?

Re-enter Servant and two Murderers

Now go to the door, and stay there till we call.

Exit Servant

Was it not yesterday we spoke together?

First Murderer

It was, so please your highness.

Macbeth

                              Well then, now

75 Have you considered of my speeches? Know

That it was he in the times past which held you

So under fortune, which you thought had been

Our innocent self? This I made good to you

In our last conference; passed in probation with you,

80 How you were borne in hand, how crossed, the
        instruments,

Who wrought with them, and all things else that might

To half a soul and to a notion crazed

Say 'Thus did Banquo.'

First Murderer

                              You made it known to us.

54–6 under him ... Caesar: *Macbeth compares himself to the Roman general Mark Antony and Banquo to Octavius Caesar. He fears that his genius (guardian angel) is frightened, just as Mark Antony's angel supposedly feared Octavius Caesar.*

56 chid: *scolded*

60 fruitless: *unsatisfactory, disappointing*

62 unlineal hand: *someone not in the family*

64 issue: *descendants*

66 rancours: *resentments*

67 eternal jewel: *immortal soul*

68 enemy: *Satan*

70–1 come, Fate ... utterance: *let Destiny fight me to the last*

76 he: *Banquo*

79 passed in probation with you: *gave you detailed proofs*

80 borne in hand: *manipulated*

80 crossed: *hindered*

80–1 instruments ... them: *agents who used these devices*

81–2 all things ... Banquo': *everything that would persuade another person to say 'Banquo did it'*

95

Macbeth

I did so; and went further, which is now
Our point of second meeting. Do you find   85
Your patience so predominant in your nature
That you can let this go? Are you so gospelled
To pray for this good man and for his issue,
Whose heavy hand hath bowed you to the grave
And beggared yours for ever?

First Murderer

                      We are men, my liege.   90

Macbeth

Ay, in the catalogue ye go for men;
As hounds and greyhounds, mongrels, spaniels, curs,
Shoughs, water-rugs and demi-wolves are clept
All by the name of dogs. The valued file
Distinguishes the swift, the slow, the subtle,   95
The housekeeper, the hunter, every one
According to the gift which bounteous nature
Hath in him closed; whereby he does receive
Particular addition from the bill
That writes them all alike: and so of men.   100
Now, if you have a station in the file,
Not in the worst rank of manhood, say it;
And I will put that business in your bosoms
Whose execution takes your enemy off,
Grapples you to the heart and love of us,   105
Who wear our health but sickly in his life,
Which in his death were perfect.

Second Murderer

                     I am one, my liege,
Whom the vile blows and buffets of the world
Have so incensed that I am reckless what
I do to spite the world.

First Murderer

                And I another   110
So weary with disasters, tugged with fortune,
That I would set my lie on any chance,
To mend it, or be rid on it.

Macbeth

              Both of you
Know Banquo was your enemy.

Second Murderer

        True, my lord.

Macbeth

115 So is he mine; and in such bloody distance,

That every minute of his being thrusts

Against my nearest of life. And though I could

With barefaced power sweep him from my sight

And bid my will avouch it, yet I must not,

120 For certain friends that are both his and mine,

Whose loves I may not drop, but wail his fall

Who I myself struck down. And thence it is

That I to your assistance do make love,

Masking the business from the common eye

For sundry weighty reasons.

Second Murderer

125   We shall, my lord,

Perform what you command us.

First Murderer

        Though our lives –

Macbeth

Your spirits shine through you. Within this hour at most

I will advise you where to plant yourselves,

Acquaint you with the perfect spy of the time,

130 The moment on it; for it must be done tonight,

And something from the palace; always thought

That I require a clearness. And with him –

To leave no rubs nor botches in the work –

Fleance his son, that keeps him company,

135 Whose absence is no less material to me

Than is his father's, must embrace the fate

Of that dark hour. Resolve yourselves apart;

I'll come to you anon.

Second Murderer

        We are resolved, my lord.

Macbeth

I'll call upon you straight: abide within.

Exeunt Murderers

140 It is concluded. Banquo, thy soul's flight,

If it find heaven, must find it out tonight.

Exit

---

115 distance: *disagreement, estrangement*

119 bid … avouch it: *justify it simply because I wanted to do it*

121 loves … drop: *friendships I need*

124 business: *the murder*
124 common eye: *public view*

128 plant: *hide*

129 Acquaint: *inform*

131 something: *some distance*

132 clearness: *freedom from suspicion*

133 rubs nor botches: *flaws or bungling*

135 absence: *death*

138 resolved: *decided*

140 concluded: *settled, finished*

[Handwritten annotations: "tell them what to do, where to go."; "must kill tonight"; "If he is with"; "must die as well."; "Death notice"]

Study Notes

Private concerns (lines 1–10)

Banquo's short soliloquy has several functions. It reminds the audience of the witches' prophecies and also reveals Banquo's deep suspicions that Macbeth murdered Duncan to obtain the throne, 'Thou played'st most foully for it'. Yet Banquo is in an ambiguous situation. He is tempted by the witches' prediction that he will 'be the root and father/ Of many kings'. His tone is clearly ambitious, 'May they not be my oracles as well'. Unlike Macbeth, however, he does not give in to these thoughts, but swiftly banishes them, 'hush, no more'.

Masks (lines 11–43)

The newly crowned king and queen make a grand entrance. Macbeth has already begun to use the plural pronoun 'we' to denote his royal status and authority. He informs the assembly, 'we hold a solemn supper'. Banquo immediately acknowledges Macbeth's superiority, addressing him as 'my good lord'. The confident monarch in kind refers to his friend as 'our chief guest'. Lady Macbeth adds her own gracious words of welcome. Yet Banquo, just like the Macbeths, masks his true feelings. His speech is formal, but artificial in tone, 'my duties/ Are with a most indissoluble tie/ For ever knit'. This is in stark contrast to his warm declaration of loyalty to Duncan, 'There if I grow,/ The harvest is your own.'

Despite his fine sentiments, Macbeth's duplicity is still evident. Three short questions cunningly elicit Banquo's immediate plans: 'Ride you this afternoon?', 'Is it far you ride?', 'Goes Fleance with you?'. The new king is following Lady Macbeth's advice to 'look like the innocent flower,/ But be the serpent under it.' Banquo's responses are reserved, 'Let your highness/ Command upon me.' The formality adds to the underlying tension. Neither man trusts the other in this uneasy exchange. Interestingly, Macbeth announces his intention to spend some time alone.

Hidden insecurities (lines 44–72)

Despite his assured public performance as monarch, Macbeth is riddled with doubts. It is no longer enough that he is king; he now wishes to extend his power and secure the Scottish throne in his family's name, 'to be safely thus'. As his ambition grows and becomes increasingly uncontrolled, his 'fears in Banquo/ Stick deep'. The violent verb reminds the audience of both the vicious attack on Duncan and Macbeth's latest murderous plans. Banquo's 'royalty of nature' makes him a more noble and deserving ruler, further diminishing Macbeth's right to be king. He also recognises Banquo's 'dauntless temper', which is enhanced by his shrewdness of character. Macbeth knows that he cannot achieve his full potential while Banquo lives.

Murderous intent (lines 73–138)

It seems certain that Macbeth has met with the murderers before this. He has also convinced them that Banquo is their enemy and is largely responsible for their downfall, 'This I made good to you/ In our last conference.' He provokes them with sarcastic comments about their manliness – 'Ay, in the catalogue ye go for men;/ As hounds and greyhounds'. His insults show that he considers them little more than animals – but, of course, he himself has become as debased as these 'reckless' assassins.

Using a mixture of threats and encouragement, Macbeth persuades the two murderers to kill Banquo and Fleance. The deceitful and unscrupulous king we now see is a very different man from the courageous 'Bellona's bridegroom' at the beginning of the play. The scene ends with a harsh rhyming couplet that sums up the treacherous thoughts of Scotland's tyrannical ruler: 'It is concluded. Banquo, thy soul's flight,/ If it find heaven, must find it out tonight.'

Shakespeare's language

Shakespeare's use of **soliloquies** increases the tension in the play and illustrates how power can corrupt individuals. Banquo's tone is both critical and resentful. We are left to wonder about the extent of his morality. Meanwhile, Macbeth's soliloquy shows the dire consequences of murder. He cannot rest ('Put rancours in the vessel of my peace') and realises that 'this blow' of killing Duncan is not the 'be-all and end-all'. Increasingly paranoid and preoccupied with the future, he is convinced that he must now kill Banquo to secure his position, 'under him,/ My genius is rebuked'.

The great tragedy of Macbeth is that he fully realises how evil his actions are, as well as their terrible cost, and yet he still commits them. He is haunted by the **irony** of his position. He has risked everything for nothing, a 'fruitless crown'. His searing language ('barren sceptre', 'filed my mind') indicates the level of his growing frustration.

The audience is struck with **conflicting emotions** about his character. We are horrified by Macbeth's casual barbarity when he insists that Banquo's son must also be killed ('embrace the fate/ Of that dark hour') to prevent the witches' prophecy coming true. Yet we cannot help but empathise with this tormented, driven man who defies Fate in pursuit of his dream, 'come, Fate, into the list,/ And champion me to the utterance!'

During Macbeth's exchange with the murderers, his speech is filled with **animal imagery**. He has already reduced humanity through his own moral choices. He now classifies men and dogs as similar, 'and so of men'. Having learned his lesson from the clumsy murder of Duncan, he seems obsessed with ensuring that Banquo's death will be the perfect crime, 'no rubs nor botches in the work'. The scene concludes with an unnerving echo for the audience. Before the murder of his king and cousin, Macbeth spoke of a 'knell/ That summons thee to heaven or to hell'. He now anticipates the vicious murder of his friend and thinks of Banquo's 'soul's flight,/ If it find heaven, must find it out tonight.'

We are men, my liege

First Murderer, Act 3 Scene 1, l.90

❝❝ Key Quotes

Thou hast it now: King, Cawdor, Glamis, all,/ As the weird women promised; and I fear/ Thou played'st most foully for it *(Banquo soliloquy) l.1–3*	Banquo lists Macbeth's new titles – just as the witches predicted. Is he enraged or envious? He had been wary of the witches, in contrast to Macbeth, who welcomed their predictions. Banquo suspects that Macbeth is involved in murder, yet he has publicly approved the new king's election.
we will keep ourself/ Till supper-time alone *(Macbeth to the court) l.42–3*	A dramatic change has occurred in the relationship between Macbeth and Lady Macbeth. Instead of sharing everything with his 'dearest partner of greatness', he now isolates himself to plan his next move.
He hath a wisdom that doth guide his valour/ To act in safety *(Macbeth soliloquy) l.52–3*	Macbeth is wary of Banquo. As army generals on the battlefield and old friends, they know each other well. Banquo is both brave and noble (having 'royalty of nature'), so Macbeth fears him all the more. Does he also think that Banquo might act to ensure that his son Fleance will eventually accede to the throne in accordance with the witches' prophecy?
For Banquo's issue have I filed my mind *(Macbeth soliloquy) l.64*	Increasingly, Macbeth is tormented by the knowledge, gained from the witches, that no descendant of his will be king. Instead, Banquo's family will inherit the crown. Bitterly, he realises that he has destroyed his peace of mind and defiled his soul to benefit another man's children.
For certain friends that are both his and mine,/ Whose loves I may not drop, but wail his fall/ Who I myself struck down *(Macbeth to Murderers) l.120–2*	Macbeth is becoming ever more devious and treacherous. He gives a reason to explain why he is not committing the murders himself: it is because he and Banquo have friends in common and Macbeth needs to retain their support to secure his position as king. He will therefore have to pretend to grieve over Banquo's death even though he was the one who ordered it – a reminder of his false protestations of sorrow after Duncan's murder.

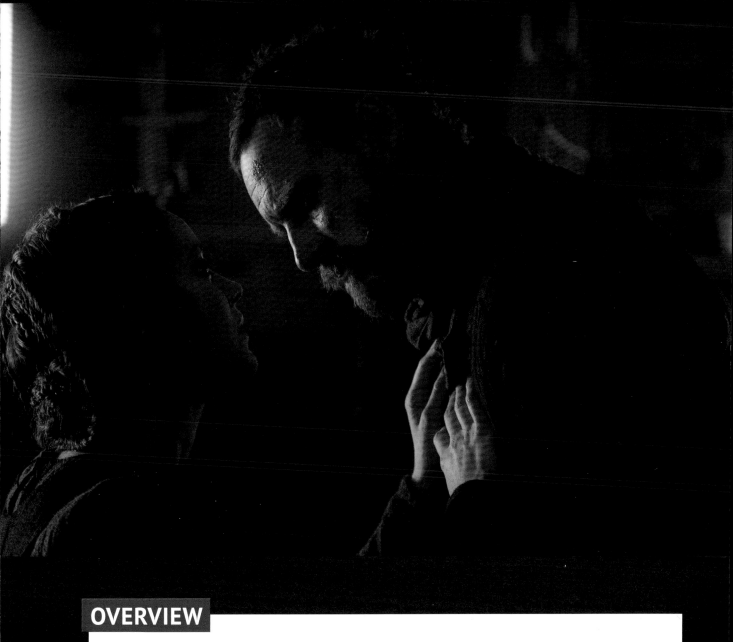

OVERVIEW

A dejected Lady Macbeth now realises that kingship and power have not brought peace of mind. Macbeth is also deeply troubled and is increasingly concerned about his future as king. He envies Duncan, who rests peacefully in death, while he remains tortured by anxiety day and night. His wife tries in vain to comfort him, but Macbeth is becoming estranged from her. He no longer takes her into his full confidence, but hints that something terrible is about to happen.

---

* **A key scene requiring close, detailed study**

The palace

Enter Lady Macbeth and Servant

Lady Macbeth

Is Banquo gone from court?

Servant

Ay, madam, but returns again tonight.

Lady Macbeth

Say to the king, I would attend his leisure

For a few words.

Servant

Madam, I will.   5

Exit

Lady Macbeth

Nought's had, all's spent,   *Duncan is lucky he is at peace*

Where our desire is got without content.

'Tis safer to be that which we destroy

Than by destruction dwell in doubtful joy.

Enter Macbeth

How now, my lord! Why do you keep alone,   10

Of sorriest fancies your companions making,

Using those thoughts which should indeed have died

With them they think on? Things without all remedy

Should be without regard: what's done is done.

Macbeth

We have scorched the snake, not killed it.   15

She'll close and be herself, whilst our poor malice

Remains in danger of her former tooth.

But let the frame of things disjoint, both the worlds suffer,

Ere we will eat our meal in fear, and sleep   *we will be troubled*

In the affliction of these terrible dreams   20

That shake us nightly. Better be with the dead,

Whom we, to gain our peace, have sent to peace,

Than on the torture of the mind to lie   *restless torment*

In restless ecstasy. Duncan is in his grave;   *Duncan at peace Macbeth not.* 25

After life's fitful fever he sleeps well.

Treason has done his worst: nor steel, nor poison,

Malice domestic, foreign levy, nothing

Can touch him further.

---

3 attend: *look forward to*

6 spent: *used up*

8–9 safer ... doubtful joy: *better be the victim than a killer living in fear*

11 sorriest fancies: *depressing thoughts*

14 without regard: *without any consideration*

15 scorched: *wounded*

16 close: *heal*
16 poor malice: *ineffective attempts to cause harm*
18 let the frame ... disjoint: *let the world be destroyed*
18 both the worlds: *heaven and earth*

24 restless ecstasy: *anxious delirium*

27 Malice domestic: *treason from within Scotland*
27 foreign levy: *armies from abroad*

Lady Macbeth

Come on;

Gentle my lord, sleek o'er your rugged looks;

30 Be bright and jovial among your guests tonight.

Macbeth

So shall I, love; and so, I pray, be you.

Let your remembrance apply to Banquo;

Present him eminence, both with eye and tongue –

Unsafe the while, that we

35 Must lave our honours in these flattering streams,

And make our faces vizards to our hearts,

Disguising what they are.

False sense security

disguise emotion on face

Lady Macbeth

You must leave this.

Macbeth

O, full of scorpions is my mind, dear wife!

Thou knowest that Banquo, and his Fleance, lives.

Lady Macbeth

40 But in them nature's copy's not eterne.

Macbeth

There's comfort yet; they are assailable.

we can get rid of them.

Then be thou jocund: ere the bat hath flown

His cloistered flight, ere to black Hecate's summons

The shard-borne beetle with his drowsy hums

45 Hath rung night's yawning peal, there shall be done

A deed of dreadful note.

Lady Macbeth

What's to be done?

Macbeth

Be innocent of the knowledge, dearest chuck,

Till thou applaud the deed. – Come, seeling night,

Scarf up the tender eye of pitiful day,

50 And with thy bloody and invisible hand

Cancel and tear to pieces that great bond

Which keeps me pale! – Light thickens, and the crow

Makes wing to the rooky wood.

Good things of day begin to droop and drowse;

55 While night's black agents to their preys do rouse.

Thou marvellest at my words: but hold thee still;

Things bad begun make strong themselves by ill.

So, prithee, go with me.

Exeunt

---

29 sleek … looks: *smooth over your frowns*

30 jovial: *cheerful*

32 remembrance: *attention, consideration*

33 eminence: *special honour and respect*

35 lave: *wash*

36 vizards: *masks*

38 scorpions: *stinging creatures*

40 nature's … eterne: *they will not live for ever*

41 assailable: *vulnerable to attack*

42 jocund: *jolly*

43 cloistered flight: *flying through buildings*
43 Hecate's summons: *command of the goddess of witchcraft*
44 shard-borne: *scaly-winged*
45 peal: *bell*
46 deed of dreadful note: *action of hideous importance*

47 innocent: *unaware*
47 dearest chuck: *my dear*
48 seeling: *concealing*

51-2 Cancel … pale!: *end Banquo and Fleance's frightening grip on life*
52 Light thickens: *it's getting dark*

55 night's … rouse: *nocturnal animals start to hunt*
56 marvellest: *are astonished*
57 bad: *immoral*
57 ill: *further evil-doing*

Study Notes

A growing split (lines 1–9)

Lady Macbeth's prominent position in Macbeth's life is fading since her husband has become king. She is no longer aware of Macbeth's latest arrangements and has to question a servant for information: 'Is Banquo gone from court?' She also has to wait until it is convenient for Macbeth to spare her a 'few words'. Earlier Macbeth could not wait to tell his wife about the witches and he hurried home to involve her in his plans. As she reflects on the secrets that are coming between them, a bitter Lady Macbeth is slowly realising that 'Nought's had, all's spent'. The thought is a chilling echo of her husband's unhappiness, 'To be thus is nothing'. Both are beginning to recognise that the price of kingship is to lose 'content' and the prospect of living not 'safely', but in 'doubtful joy'.

Role reversal (lines 10–58)

The arrival of Macbeth causes Lady Macbeth to revert to her former self. She slips into her familiar role, scolding him about his aloofness and advising him to put his gloomy thoughts behind him, 'which should indeed have died/ With them they think on'. Her earlier practicality resurfaces with her curt assertion, 'what's done is done'.

However, Macbeth is more alert to the danger facing them. He uses the image of the wounded snake that will recoil and then strike again to describe their alarming situation. Once again, his bravery surges and he refuses to live a life of fear. Yet he still envies the dead Duncan, who 'sleeps well' in contrast to Macbeth himself, tortured with 'terrible dreams'. Ironically, he works himself up into a frenzy imagining all the woes of life which Duncan no longer has to face. Lady Macbeth comes to the rescue once more, counselling him to 'sleek o'er your rugged looks'.

In a sharp reversal of roles, Macbeth hints at what is to be done, 'A deed of dreadful note', but he refuses to include Lady Macbeth in what he is planning. He has become more and more brutalised, decisively dismissing his wife, 'Be innocent of the knowledge'. Macbeth's unnerving declaration that they must continue to commit evil acts to strengthen their position concludes this crucial scene. The treacherous tone of his closing speech, seeking out darkness and associating himself with 'night's black agents', underlines his rapid moral decline. For the Macbeths, the price of ambition has been very high.

Shakespeare's language

In the **tortuous phrases** used throughout their soliloquies, the play's two central characters vividly demonstrate the disastrous consequences of their murderous actions. The hesitant exchange between Lady Macbeth and her husband reflects their growing estrangement. The new queen struggles with her troubled consciousness: ''Tis safer to be that which we destroy/ Than by destruction dwell in doubtful joy'; while, caught in a trap of his own making, Macbeth is now convinced that death would be preferable to 'restless ecstasy'.

Shakespeare makes effective use of **animal imagery** to increase the hellish atmosphere that Macbeth has created. His language is filled with references to the predatory world of nature: 'snake', 'scorpions', 'bat', 'crow', 'night's black agents'. Through Macbeth's poetic imagination, the audience is brought into this furtive environment where nocturnal creatures stalk their prey under cover of darkness. Their rustling sounds are delivered through emphatic onomatopoeia, 'The shard-borne beetle with his drowsy hums/ Hath rung night's yawning peal'.

Personification captures the violent nature of Macbeth's dark world; its 'invisible hand' will obliterate all that holds him back. A sinister description of oncoming dusk is vividly evoked through assonance, 'rooky wood'. The heavy alliterative 'd' in the phrase 'droop and drowse' features the eclipsing of the 'Good things of day'. The overall effect is to leave audiences aghast at the nerve-wracking prospect of even more evil to come, 'Things bad begun make strong themselves by ill'.

Critical Analysis

1. 'Shakespeare dramatically explores the changing relationship between Macbeth and Lady Macbeth.' Discuss this statement, supporting your answer with suitable reference from Act 3 Scene 2 of the play Macbeth.

2. 'Macbeth is portrayed as a man who is fully aware not just of the evil of his moral choices, but of their disastrous consequences.' Discuss this view, supporting your answer with suitable reference from Act 3 Scene 2.

Sample Paragraph 1 (Q1)

I think Macbeth and Lady Macbeth were strong together at the beginning of the play. He wrote to his 'dearest partner in greatness'. The witches had appeared to Macbeth and told him he would be king. Macbeth believed them and shared the news with Lady Macbeth, his dominant wife in greatness. But since the murder of Duncan everything was changed. In act 3 scene 2, he is the one in control now. She just doesn't know what is going on with the plans to kill Banquo. I don't think either of them are happy either. They don't sleep and are afraid night and day. I think she is lonely too. She doesn't seem to have any friends. But for him. He still calls her his 'dear chuck', but they are no longer a close couple. *(135 words)*

Examiner's Comment

- This basic response includes some relevant discussion about the Macbeths' deteriorating relationship.
- However, points lack development and are poorly controlled.
- More coherent and focused reference to Act 3 Scene 2 would be expected.
- Misquotes and mechanical errors further reduce the standard.

Be innocent of the knowledge, dearest chuck

Macbeth, Act 3 Scene 2, l.47

Sample Paragraph 2 (Q1)

Lady Macbeth and Macbeth were partners when they dreamed of the crown, planned Duncan's murder and helped each other to commit it. But now 'Nought's had, all's spent'. The lesson seems to be: Be careful of what you wish for! They are now Scotland's king and queen, yet they are in 'doubtful joy'. Not exactly a success story. Lady Macbeth keeps trying to regain her old role as Macbeth's soul-mate and his full-on co-conspirator. Unfortunately, they have reached a critical turning-point, a bit of a crossroads on their rocky marriage. Their roles are almost reversed. She advises him not to be alone and not to keep living in the past, to look cheerful, to stop angsting. He uses his imagination to describe the dark world they inhabit, so I think they are both pretty much drifting far apart, divided by secrets and just basically unhappy. *(145 words)*

Examiner's Comment

- Solid middle-grade standard. Some close engagement, but drifted at times from the question.
- Focused points on the couple's changing relationship ('roles are almost reversed').
- Effective use of accurate quotations to support points.
- Expression is reasonably good – apart from some use of slang (e.g. the concluding sentence).

Sample Paragraph 3 (Q1)

At first, the playwright presented his audience with a very modern relationship, a partnership of equals. But, having achieved their goal, the energy has evaporated from their relationship. Macbeth's once powerful partner is reduced to begging for time with her husband. Her request trails weakly away, 'For a few words'. How different from her confident assertion 'And we'll not fail'. Macbeth now assumes control, issuing instructions to her about her required behaviour towards Banquo, 'Present him eminence'. He sets out the plan for the future, 'Things bad begun make strong themselves by ill'. She no longer has the 'night's great business' in her 'dispatch'. Instead she is relegated by him to a supportive onlooker, 'till thou applaud the deed'. Act 3 Scene 2 illustrates the new dynamic between an increasingly insecure wife and the king she now addresses as 'my Lord'. Their once close relationship, like their peace of mind, has become an unwitting casualty of their evil actions as Macbeth assumes her earlier role as the dominant marriage partner. *(170 words)*

Examiner's Comment

- Excellent top-grade answer engaging closely with the Macbeths' volatile relationship.
- Focused comparative approach, contrasting the couple's initial interdependence with their present estrangement.
- Effective use of relevant quotations provides strong support for key discussion points.
- Impressive control of language throughout – wide-ranging vocabulary and fluent expression (e.g. 'evaporated from their relationship', 'new dynamic', 'unwitting casualty').

🙸 Key Quotes

Say to the king, I would attend his leisure/ For a few words (Lady Macbeth to Servant) l.3–4	An isolated Lady Macbeth is forced to wait on her husband's convenience to speak with him. She is now almost in the position of subject, rather than partner, and must request a few moments of his time. This contrasts strongly with her former influential position.
We have scorched the snake, not killed it (Macbeth to Lady Macbeth) l.15	Using a powerfully sibilant image, Macbeth describes how perilous is his position as king. Yet he is determined to finish the job so that he can reign securely. The reference to the snake has overtones of the devil in the Garden of Eden – a story that ended in doom for Adam and Eve.
But let the frame of things disjoint, both the worlds suffer (Macbeth to Lady Macbeth) l.18	A disdainful Macbeth refuses to be confined by fear. He would rather destroy the universe than continue to be filled with dread. The length of the line breaks the shape and rhythm of the iambic pentameter of the verse, mirroring the destruction Macbeth will cause in his desire to rule Scotland unchallenged.
make our faces vizards to our hearts (Macbeth to Lady Macbeth) l.36	The atmosphere of deception continues. Macbeth has learned Lady Macbeth's earlier lesson about acting falsely ('look like the innocent flower'). In a reversal of roles, he now advises her to eagerly welcome Banquo, just as she had counselled him to do when Duncan visited their castle.
Be innocent of the knowledge, dearest chuck (Macbeth to Lady Macbeth) l.47	A much more independent Macbeth is determined to exclude Lady Macbeth from the terrible double murder he is planning for Banquo and Fleance. Although he no longer relies on the steely character of his wife for support, he still has feelings for her and desires her approval, 'Till thou applaud the deed'.

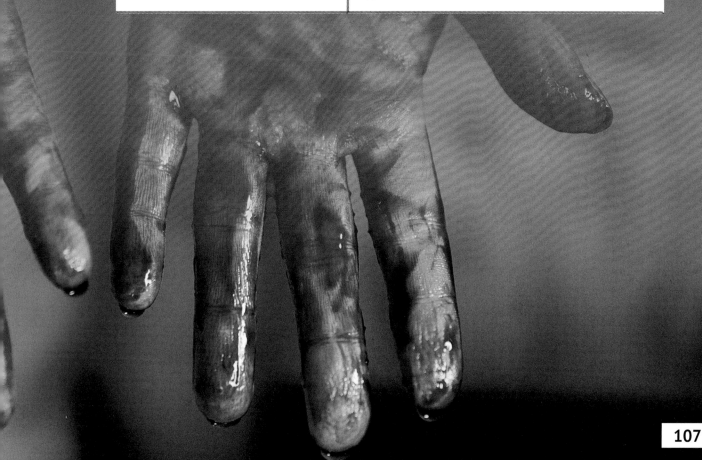

Act 3
Scene 3

OVERVIEW

As the murderers wait for Banquo, they are joined by a third man, who has been sent by Macbeth. They decide to trust him because he knows the local countryside well. In the darkness and confusion, Banquo is killed, but Fleance escapes. The murderers leave to report what has happened to Macbeth.

Forres. Near the palace

to murder Banquo +
Fleance.

Enter three Murderers

→ half succeed, only ~~King~~ Banquo dead.
→ While Fleance lives, prophecy can come true.

First Murderer

But who did bid thee join with us?

Third Murderer

Macbeth.

Second Murderer

He needs not our mistrust, since he delivers

Our offices and what we have to do,

To the direction just.

3 offices: *duties*

4 To the direction just: *precisely*

First Murderer

Then stand with us.

5 The west yet glimmers with some streaks of day;

Now spurs the lated traveller apace

To gain the timely inn; and near approaches

The subject of our watch.

8 subject of our watch: *Banquo and Fleance*

Third Murderer

Hark! I hear horses.

Banquo

[Within]

Give us a light there, ho!

Second Murderer

Then 'tis he: the rest

10 That are within the note of expectation

Already are in the court.

11 court: *king's palace*

First Murderer

His horses go about.

Third Murderer

Almost a mile: but he does usually –

So all men do – from hence to the palace gate

Make it their walk.

Second Murderer

[Aside]

A light, a light!

Enter Banquo, and Fleance with a torch

Third Murderer

'Tis he.

15 Stand to it: *get into position*

16 Let it come down: *the murderers strike Banquo*

17 fly: *flee, escape*
18 mayst revenge: *can exact retaliation*
18 slave: *villain (term of abuse referring to Macbeth)*

son getting revenge ⇒ similar to Hamlet.

19 way: *right thing to*

20 one down: *only one person killed*

21 best ... affair: *the most important task (to kill Fleance)*

First Murderer

Stand to it.   15

Banquo

It will be rain tonight.

First Murderer

                                    Let it come down.

First murderer strikes out the torch. The others attack Banquo

Banquo

O, treachery! Fly, good Fleance, fly, fly, fly!

Thou mayst revenge. – O slave!   *— revenge my murder*

Dies. Exit Fleance

Third Murderer

Who did strike out the light? → *Banquo was the light ⇒ only moral light in dark world*

First Murderer

                                    Was it not the way? → *not supposed to?*

Third Murderer

There's but one down; the son is fled.   20

Second Murderer

We have lost best half of our affair. ⇒ *Witches prophecy he, Fleance will be king*

First Murderer

Well, let's away, and say how much is done.

Exeunt

Study Notes

Murder most foul (lines 1–22)

In the growing dark, the two hired assassins are joined by a third. Does Macbeth not trust those he initially hired to carry out his orders? The 'night's black agents' wait to perform their dreadful deed in the gathering gloom. But, because Fleance escapes, Macbeth's position becomes more dangerous than ever. Banquo, according to the witches' prophecy, was never going to be king, but his descendants were. So the murderers have lost the 'best half of our affair'.

The audience is left not only horrified at the callous murder of Macbeth's close friend, but mystified. Who is the Third Murderer? Will Fleance eventually exact revenge for the murder of his father? The dramatic tension increases.

This brutal scene shows that Macbeth trusts no one around him. Doubt and deception have taken hold in Scotland. Ironically, Fleance's escape means that Macbeth will continue to fear the witches' prophecy that Banquo's heirs will be future kings. The scene ends with a call for retaliation. Macbeth's rule remains under threat.

❝❝ Key Quotes

There's but one down; the son is fled (Third Murderer) l.20	The murderers are symbols of Macbeth's brutal reign, which is dominated by the forces of darkness. These hired killers have only managed to murder Banquo. Ironically, Fleance is the real cause of worry to Macbeth – and he manages to escape.
We have lost best half of our affair (Second Murderer) l.21	The new king desperately needed Fleance killed because it is the thought of Banquo's descendants inheriting (as foretold by the witches) which is tormenting Macbeth's peace of mind.

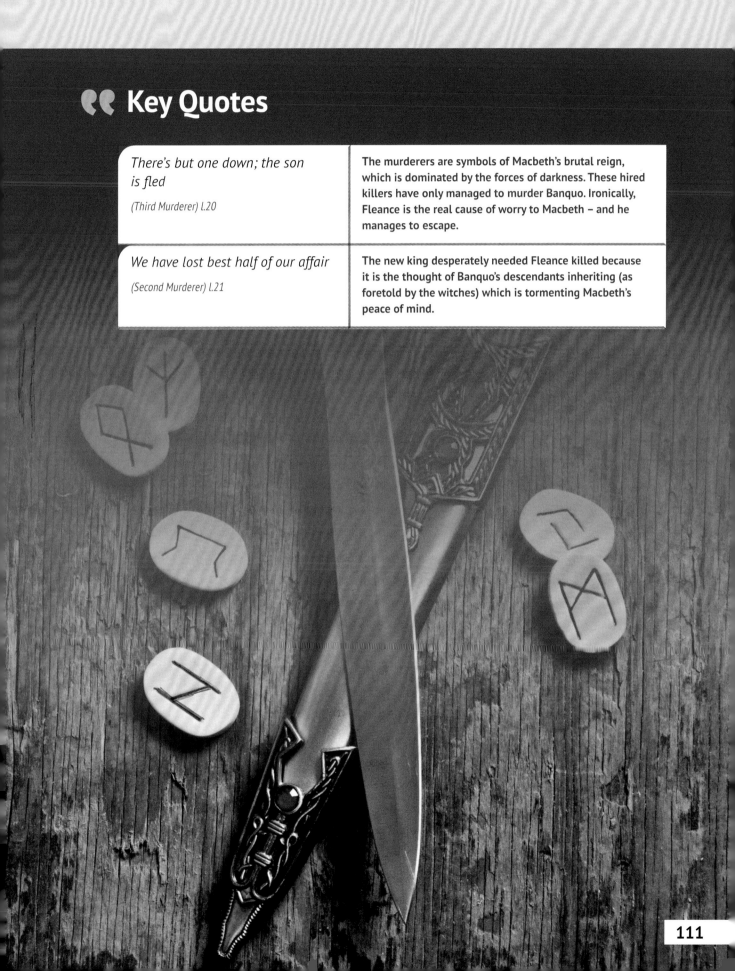

OVERVIEW

The 'banquet scene' opens with the newly established king and queen welcoming their guests. One of the murderers informs Macbeth about Banquo's murder and Fleance's escape. The news devastates him, but he consoles himself with the thought that Banquo's son is still too young to be an immediate threat. Lady Macbeth reminds her husband of his official duties as host. However, when Banquo's Ghost suddenly appears to Macbeth, he becomes highly distraught. Lady Macbeth attempts to restore order, but fails. The feast ends in disarray and she is forced to dismiss the thanes. She advises her paranoid husband to rest, but he is already planning to meet the witches in the hope that they will help him to secure his power in Scotland.

* **A key scene requiring close, detailed study**

Forres. The palace

A banquet prepared. Enter Macbeth, Lady Macbeth, Ross, Lennox, Lords and Attendants

Macbeth

You know your own degrees; sit down: at first

And last, the hearty welcome.

Lords

                              Thanks to your majesty.

Macbeth

Ourself will mingle with society,

And play the humble host.

5   Our hostess keeps her state, but in best time

We will require her welcome.

Lady Macbeth

Pronounce it for me, sir, to all our friends;

For my heart speaks they are welcome.

First Murderer appears at the door

Macbeth

See, they encounter thee with their hearts' thanks.

10   Both sides are even. Here I'll sit, in the midst.

Be large in mirth; anon, we'll drink a measure

The table round.

Approaches the door. Aside, to First Murderer

                    There's blood upon thy face.

First Murderer

'Tis Banquo's then.

Macbeth

'Tis better thee without than he within.

15   Is he dispatched?

First Murderer

My lord, his throat is cut; that I did for him.

Macbeth

Thou art the best o' the cut-throats. Yet he's good

That did the like for Fleance. If thou didst it,

Thou art the nonpareil.

First Murderer

                    Most royal sir,

20   Fleance is escaped.

---

1 degrees: *social rank*
2 at first and last: *from start to finish*

3 society: *the guests*

5 keeps her state: *stays seated*

7 Pronounce it: *make the speech (of welcome)*

9 encounter: *address*

11 large in mirth: *very merry*

14 'Tis better … he within: *Banquo's blood is better on you than in him*
15 dispatched: *murdered*

19 nonpareil: *best, without equal*

113

Macbeth

Then comes my fit again; I had else been perfect,

Whole as the marble, founded as the rock,

As broad and general as the casing air.

But now I am cabined, cribbed, confined, bound in

To saucy doubts and fears. – But Banquo's safe?   25

First Murderer

Ay, my good lord: safe in a ditch he bides,

With twenty trenchèd gashes on his head;

The least a death to nature.

Macbeth

                  Thanks for that.

There the grown serpent lies; the worm that's fled

Hath nature that in time will venom breed,   30

No teeth for the present. Get thee gone: tomorrow

We'll hear ourselves again.

Exit Murderer

Lady Macbeth

                My royal lord,

You do not give the cheer. The feast is sold

That is not often vouched, while 'tis a-making,

'Tis given with welcome. To feed were best at home;   35

From thence, the sauce to meat is ceremony;

Meeting were bare without it.

Macbeth

                  Sweet remembrancer!

Now, good digestion wait on appetite,

And health on both!

Lennox

            May it please your highness sit?

Macbeth

Here had we now our country's honour roofed,   40

Were the graced person of our Banquo present;

 The Ghost of Banquo enters, and sits in Macbeth's place

Who may I rather challenge for unkindness

Than pity for mischance.

Ross

                His absence, sir,

Lays blame upon his promise. Please it your highness

45 To grace us with your royal company?

Macbeth

The table's full.

Lennox

Here is a place reserved, sir.

Macbeth

Where?

Lennox

Here, my good lord. What is it that moves your highness?

Macbeth

Which of you have done this?

Lords

What, my good lord?

Macbeth

50 Thou canst not say I did it. Never shake

Thy gory locks at me.

Ross

Gentlemen, rise: his highness is not well.

Lady Macbeth

Sit, worthy friends: my lord is often thus,

And hath been from his youth. Pray you, keep seat;

55 The fit is momentary; upon a thought

He will again be well. If much you note him,

You shall offend him and extend his passion.

Feed, and regard him not. –

Aside to Macbeth

Are you a man?

Macbeth

Ay, and a bold one, that dare look on that

Which might appal the devil.

Lady Macbeth

60 O proper stuff!

This is the very painting of your fear:

This is the air-drawn dagger which, you said,

Led you to Duncan. O, these flaws and starts –

Impostors to true fear – would well become

65 A woman's story at a winter's fire,

44 promise: *promise to attend*

48 moves: *disturbs, stirs*

51 gory locks: *bloodied hair*

54 keep seat: *stay seated*

55 a thought: *an instant*

56 note: *watch*

59 bold: *brave*

60 proper stuff: *nonsense*

61 painting: *image, representation*

62 air-drawn: *unreal*

63 flaws and starts: *outbursts*

64 Impostors: *false signs*

65-6 story ... grandam: *like an old tale told by a grandmother*

115

Authorised by her grandam. Shame itself!

Why do you make such faces? When all's done,

You look but on a stool.

Macbeth

Prithee, see there!

Behold! Look! Lo! How say you?

Why, what care I? If thou canst nod, speak too.   70

If charnel-houses and our graves must send

Those that we bury back, our monuments

Shall be the maws of kites.

Ghost of Banquo vanishes

Lady Macbeth

What, quite unmanned in folly?

Macbeth

If I stand here, I saw him.

Lady Macbeth

Fie, for shame!

Macbeth

Blood hath been shed ere now, in the olden time,   75

Ere human statute purged the gentle weal;

Ay, and since too, murders have been performed

Too terrible for the ear. The times have been

That when the brains were out, the man would die,

And there an end; but now they rise again,   80

With twenty mortal murders on their crowns,

And push us from our stools. This is more strange

Than such a murder is.

dead rise again
steal my
seat.

Lady Macbeth

My worthy lord,

Your noble friends do lack you.

Macbeth

I do forget.

Do not muse at me, my most worthy friends,   85

I have a strange infirmity, which is nothing

To those that know me. Come, love and health to all;

Then I'll sit down. Give me some wine; fill full.

I drink to the general joy of the whole table,

And to our dear friend Banquo, whom we miss;   90

Would he were here! — *hipocracy → if he was here*
↓ he dead in
forest

Re-enter Ghost of Banquo

To all, and him, we thirst,

And all to all.

Lords

Our duties, and the pledge.

Macbeth

Avaunt, and quit my sight! Let the earth hide thee!

Thy bones are marrowless, thy blood is cold; — go away

95   Thou hast no speculation in those eyes you arent real

Which thou dost glare with!

Lady Macbeth

Think of this, good peers,

But as a thing of custom: 'tis no other; happens all the time

Only it spoils the pleasure of the time.

Macbeth

What man dare, I dare.

100   Approach thou like the rugged Russian bear,

The armed rhinoceros, or the Hyrcan tiger;

Take any shape but that, and my firm nerves

Shall never tremble. Or be alive again,

And dare me to the desert with thy sword.

105   If trembling I inhabit then, protest me

The baby of a girl. Hence, horrible shadow!

Unreal mockery, hence!

Ghost of Banquo vanishes

Why, so: being gone,

I am a man again. Pray you, sit still.

Lady Macbeth

You have displaced the mirth, broke the good meeting,

With most admired disorder.

Macbeth

110   Can such things be,

And overcome us like a summer's cloud,

Without our special wonder? You make me strange

Even to the disposition that I owe,

When now I think you can behold such sights, shes not scared

115   And keep the natural ruby of your cheeks, but she doesnt

When mine is blanched with fear. see ghost.

---

91 thirst: *want to drink*

92 Our duties ... pledge: *to loyalty and service*

93 Avaunt: *get away*

95 speculation: *power of sight*

96 peers: *noblemen, equals*

97 thing of custom: *routine occurrence*

101 Hyrcan: *Persian*

102 that: *Banquo's ghost*

109 displaced the mirth: *spoiled the party*

110 admired disorder: *astonishing fuss*

111 overcome: *pass*

112–13 make ... owe: *confuse me*

116 blanched: *turned pale*

Ross

What sights, my lord?

Lady Macbeth

I pray you, speak not. He grows worse and worse;
Question enrages him. At once, good night:
Stand not upon the order of your going,
But go at once.

Lennox

Good night; and better health   120
Attend his majesty!

Lady Macbeth

A kind good night to all!

Exeunt all but Macbeth and Lady Macbeth

Macbeth

It will have blood; they say, blood will have blood.
Stones have been known to move, and trees to speak;
Augurs and understood relations have
By maggot-pies and choughs and rooks brought forth   125
The secret'st man of blood. What is the night?

Lady Macbeth

Almost at odds with morning, which is which.

Macbeth

How say'st thou, that Macduff denies his person
At our great bidding?

Lady Macbeth

Did you send to him, sir?   130

Macbeth

I hear it by the way; but I will send:
There's not a one of them but in his house
I keep a servant fee'd. I will to-morrow –
And betimes I will – to the weird sisters: *will go back to witches.*
More shall they speak; for now I am bent to know,   135
By the worst means, the worst. For mine own good
All causes shall give way: I am in blood   *no way back from here.*
Stepped in so far that, should I wade no more,   *Turning back*
Returning were as tedious as go o'er: *worthless.*
Strange things I have in head, that will to hand;   140
Which must be acted ere they may be scann'd.

119 Stand not: *don't delay*

122 It will have blood: *the ghost will take revenge*
123 Stones: *gravestones*
124 Augurs: *secrets revealed in the movements of birds*

127 at odds: *in conflict*

128-9 denies ... bidding: *refused to come to the banquet*

131 by the way: *in passing*

133 servant fee'd: *paid spy*
134 betimes: *speedily*
135 bent: *determined*
136 worst means: *the witches' power*
137 causes: *considerations*
138 Stepped in: *involved, immersed*

140 to hand: *soon be done*

Lady Macbeth

You lack the season of all natures, sleep.   *You're fine, just sleep.*

> 142 season ... sleep: *rest, the basic natural requirement*

Macbeth

Come, we'll to sleep. My strange and self-abuse   → *we are still new to crime we just have to get used it.*

Is the initiate fear that wants hard use:

145   We are yet but young in deed.

> 143-5 My strange ... deed: *these delusions are the immature fears of a novice who needs to become much more evil*

Exeunt

Study Notes

A proud king and queen (lines 1–12)

The impressive banquet scene shows the newly crowned Macbeth and Lady Macbeth glorying in their success. It is an opportunity to establish their authority publicly. Macbeth wishes to be seen as the triumphant monarch while still having the approval of his invited guests, 'Ourself will mingle with society,/ And play the humble host'. Throughout the play, Macbeth desires the 'golden opinions' of others. Portraying himself as relaxed and approachable, he opts to sit informally 'in the midst' of his thanes rather than occupying the head of the table. The Macbeths' delight in their elevated status is accentuated by the king's continual use of the royal plural pronoun 'we' and Lady Macbeth's delay in vacating her throne. Initially, the atmosphere is relaxed as the couple present their hospitable public faces. Yet what kind of hosts were they to their king and cousin, Duncan?

Dark secrets (lines 12–32)

The opulence of the banquet scene contrasts sharply with the sinister shadows of the circumstances surrounding Banquo's murder. We are reminded of the dark reality of Macbeth's reign when the First Murderer appears with the incriminating evidence of his victim's blood on his face. It is a symbolic representation that murder will be exposed. The new king's cruel joke and euphemism ('dispatched') for Banquo's killing link him irrevocably to the assassins. The once-noble Macbeth is now on the same level as the hired cut-throats. At first he is delighted to hear about Banquo's murder, but this soon turns to anguish at the news of Fleance's escape. Macbeth's paranoia returns, 'Then comes my fit again', and he makes hasty arrangements to meet the murderers once more.

An unexpected appearance (lines 33–121)

Lady Macbeth gently reprimands her husband for neglecting their guests, 'You do not give the cheer.' He recovers sufficiently to hypocritically criticise Banquo's non-attendance at the banquet. In a dramatic turn of events, however, Macbeth suddenly has difficulty in finding a seat, 'the table's full'. His angry outburst, 'Which of you have done this?', heightens the dramatic tension.

The onlookers are understandably startled as Macbeth addresses what everyone else perceives as an empty chair, shouting 'Thou canst not say I did it.' The banquet hall is in disarray. Acting swiftly, Lady Macbeth comes to his rescue, calming the assembly, 'Sit, worthy friends', while offering a plausible-sounding excuse, 'The fit is momentary'. In an aside to her frantic husband, she appeals to his masculine strength ('Are you a man?') in an effort to coax Macbeth to control himself. When this fails, she then attacks his unstable personality ('these flaws and starts') and tries again to reason with him ('You look but on a stool').

Macbeth recovers temporarily, attributing his odd behaviour to a 'strange infirmity'. Within moments, however, his guilt-ridden imagination leads to the reappearance of the ghost. His erratic behaviour leaves Lady Macbeth with little alternative but to order all their guests to leave. Following the departure of the thanes, her agitated husband regains some of his former composure, but the banquet has been a disastrous failure – and a timely reminder of Macbeth's disorderly reign.

An unhappy couple (lines 122–45)

The bitter realisation dawns on Macbeth that 'blood will have blood'. In this murky, dehumanised world to which he and his wife have descended, nothing is as it seems – and they are even unsure about night and day, 'which is which'. Macbeth is preoccupied with Macduff's non-appearance at the banquet. It's clear that he will tolerate no one who questions his rule. Motivated by suspicion, he is desperate to hold on to power by eliminating all potential successors to the throne.

The terrible state of Scotland is evident when Macbeth admits to keeping a 'servant fee'd' in every thane's household. Having sacrificed everything for the kingship, all that he has left is a commitment to prolonging power through violence. He is now prepared to commit evil acts with or without his wife's support. This scene represents a significant turning point in the couple's relationship. As his confidence returns, Macbeth prepares to seek out the advice of the witches. There is no doubt that Lady Macbeth is losing her influence over him. In future, the self-absorbed Macbeth will act on impulse: 'We are yet but young in deed'.

Shakespeare's language

The playwright's staging of the play focuses the audience's attention on Macbeth's traumatic inner struggle. During the state banquet, Shakespeare places the protagonist's over-wrought imagination centre stage as he envisions the hideous apparition of Banquo, his former friend. Throughout the scene, **Macbeth's language changes in keeping with his divided self**. He begins by greeting the guests formally ('You know your own degrees'), but then echoes the murderers when discussing Banquo's death ('Thou art the best o' the cut-throats'). In his responses to the ghost, Macbeth's frenzied words reflect his fear-stricken mind: 'Avaunt, and quit my sight!' The contrasting language styles highlight the king's volatility and leave the audience in no doubt that Macbeth is rapidly losing control.

Blood imagery is prevalent throughout this intense scene, reinforcing the violent mood. The murderer who reports to Macbeth has blood on his face and Banquo shakes his 'gory locks'. Both the real and imagined blood symbolise guilt for the once-heroic Macbeth. He can no longer deny that 'blood will have blood'. His tragic stature is increased by making the audience concentrate on the fact that Macbeth is fully aware of the consequences of his actions. The graphic image of him wading through a sea of blood prepares the audience for the carnage to follow. Through this staging of Macbeth's thought processes, Shakespeare brings his audience with Macbeth on his descent into a hell of his own making and so enriches the dramatic experience.

Critical Analysis

1. 'Shakespeare's play *Macbeth* enables the audience to gain insights into Macbeth's complex character through a variety of dramatic techniques.' Discuss this statement, supporting your answer with reference to Act 3 Scene 4.

2. 'The relationship between Macbeth and Lady Macbeth changes significantly during the course of the play'. Discuss this view, with particular reference to Act 3 Scene 4.

Sample Paragraph 1 (Q1)

Macbeth to me is a very complex character and tragic hero of the play. One minute he is king and giving a welcome by going to sit in the middle of the invited people so as he might not be seen to be too proud, 'in their midst'. The next scene, he is shouting at an empty stool which he thinks in his imagination Banquo's ghost is sitting on. Macbeth isn't understood by the invited guests who are Scotland's thanes, so Lady Macbeth does her best to calm things down, telling everyone to keep 'seated'. He has many techniques to his complex character. First murdering the legal King Duncan and then paying the 'three cut throat' murderers to kill the innocent Banquo. But he is also afraid of his wife and the witches. He is both brave and evil. But he pays no intention as she used to be the strong partner of greatness. She has gave up and tells everyone to go. After seeing the ghost he snaps back to himself. He keeps discussing Macduff deciding not to attend the banquet after his coronation and how he is going to meet the three weird witches and do more evil things. He to me is a very complex tragic hero. *(210 words)*

Examiner's Comment

- This basic response relies mainly on summarising what happens during the banquet scene.
- The response lacks any focused engagement with the dramatic techniques that make Macbeth complex.
- Control of language is flawed and there are some grammatical errors.
- Much more engagement with the task, clear discussion points and the use of accurate quotations expected.

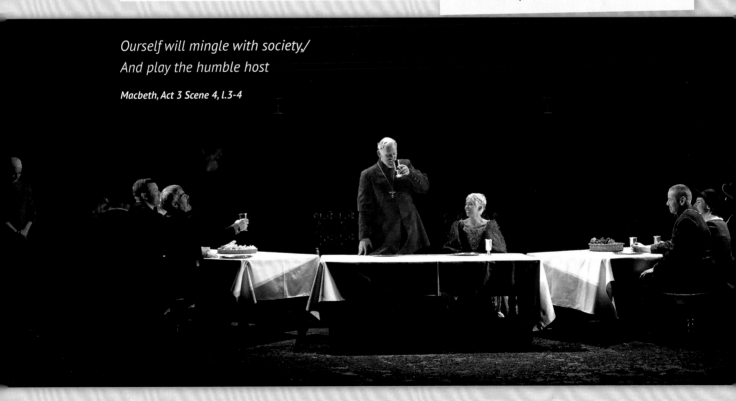

Ourself will mingle with society,/
And play the humble host

Macbeth, Act 3 Scene 4, l.3-4

Sample Paragraph 2 (Q1)

Shakespeare uses numerous techniques to show Macbeth. I thought you could really see into Macbeth's mind when you looked at the language he used at the banquet – including references to blood images. He talks about blood on the face of his paid murderers. Then he is filled with grief and sorrow, as he pictures himself wading in blood – the symbol of the river of blood. Macbeth also talks about graves sending their dead back – the image of disorder in his kingdom. He uses animals in his speech – the 'Hyrcan' tiger and a serpent. This shows how bad Macbeth has become in terms of morals. He has spies everywhere among the Scots noblemen. He wants to know everything about everyone and intends going to go to the wicked witches to find out more. Macbeth then decided he is not going to worry about his guilty conscience after this turning point scene. This has been a big problem for him, over-complicating everything and then not being able to act. So he decides he is just going to go ahead and act violently He sounds like the murderers too. You can see from his language used how mixed up he is. *(200 words)*

Examiner's Comment

- This mid-grade answer attempt to address the question through relevant points about imagery and language.
- However, the response is uneven, sometimes lacking clearly developed focus, e.g. when linking animal imagery to Macbeth's immorality.
- The absence of relevant quotes and awkward expression (e.g. the last sentence) also reduced the overall standard.

Sample Paragraph 3 (Q1)

Shakespeare's characterisation of Macbeth as a tortured man with various sides to his character shows the huge price he has paid psychologically for pursuing his ambition. The Banquet Scene illustrates his descent into his own private hell. Macbeth echoes the crude speech of his own hired assassins, 'Is he dispatched?' Shakespeare effectively demonstrates how Macbeth has sunk to the lowest human level, no longer the daring 'Bellona's bridegroom' of the opening scenes. Macbeth recognises his paranoia which flares at the news of Fleance's escape, 'I am cabined, cribbed, confined'. The technique of harsh alliterative phrasing show the effect of the tremendous pressure on Macbeth to secure his throne. But it is his realisation of how he has compromised himself, 'I am in blood / Stepped in so far', which best depicts this multi-faceted individual. A powerful image of a sea of blood shows his abysmal position. He has created this living nightmare himself and he knows that if he stopped now – 'Should I wade no more' – he can never return to be the respected military hero he once was. Shakespeare's portrayal of a man on the edge leaves the audience waiting for the next terrible deed that will be committed. *(200 words)*

Examiner's Comment

- Successful top-grade answer well organised around key points on characterisation, sound effects and imagery.
- Response focused firmly on both elements of the question (insights about Macbeth's character and dramatic techniques).
- Well-controlled, assured expression; impressive vocabulary ('flares', 'compromised', 'multi-faceted').
- Effective use of relevant, accurate quotations adds useful support to discussion points.

❝❞ Key Quotes

'Tis better thee without than he within./ Is he dispatched? *(Macbeth to First Murderer) l.14–15*	Macbeth's callous joke that Banquo's blood is better spattered on the murderer's face than keeping Banquo alive shows the extent of his moral decline. The euphemistic expression 'dispatched' indicates that he is at ease using the language of his hired assassins.
But now I am cabined, cribbed, confined *(Macbeth aside) l.24*	At the news of Fleance's escape, the new king's anxieties return. Macbeth feels the pressure of a paranoid fear that Banquo's descendants will succeed him to reign in Scotland. The hard alliterative 'c' stresses the force of these feelings.
Thou canst not say I did it. Never shake/ Thy gory locks at me *(Macbeth to Banquo's Ghost) l.50–1*	In a direct address to the ghost which only he can see, Macbeth tries to excuse himself from Banquo's silent accusation. Like the witches, he is equivocating and playing with words. Although Macbeth did not actually kill Banquo himself, he ordered the murder – which makes him culpable.
What, quite unmanned in folly? *(Lady Macbeth to Macbeth) l.73*	With a withering appeal to Macbeth's masculinity, Lady Macbeth tries once more to calm her disturbed husband by questioning his manliness. This tactic had been successful in encouraging Duncan's murder – but Macbeth was more easily influenced by his wife at that time.
I am in blood/ Stepped in so far that, should I wade no more,/ Returning were as tedious as go o'er *(Macbeth to Lady Macbeth) l.137–9*	Macbeth understands the evil of his actions, which is vividly conveyed through this terrifying image of a man making his way through a river of blood. He resigns himself to the fact that there is no going back.
We are yet but young in deed *(Macbeth to Lady Macbeth) l.145*	Macbeth's obsession with securing the safety of his powerful position as king makes him determined to do whatever it takes to succeed. He no longer needs his wife to strengthen his resolve. He has become brutalised, caring about nothing – and nobody – but himself.

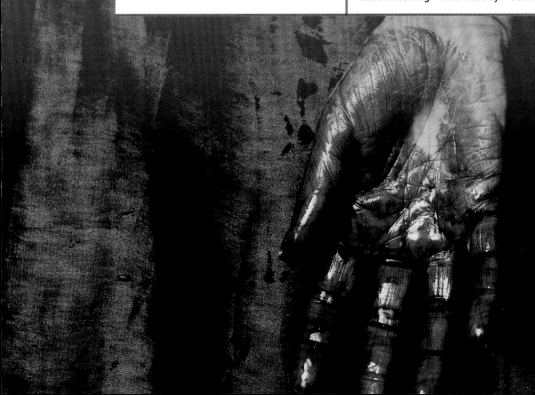

Act 3
Scene 5

OVERVIEW

Hecate, the goddess of witches, scolds the three weird sisters for not involving her in their dealings with Macbeth. She arranges a meeting with the witches for the next day. She then gives instructions that are designed to ensure Macbeth's downfall. Her plan is to deceive him with visions about his future. Hecate is called back to the underworld by another spirit and the witches hurry to carry out her orders and seal Macbeth's fate.

✳ Adds to supernatural theme of play

A heath

Thunder. Enter three Witches and Hecate

First Witch

Why, how now, Hecate, you look angerly.

Hecate

hags
Have I not reason, beldams as you are?

Saucy and overbold, how did you dare

To trade and traffic with Macbeth

5   In riddles and affairs of death;

And I, the mistress of your charms,   *— she never got to be apart of plan*

The close contriver of all harms,

Was never called to bear my part,

Or show the glory of our art?

10   And, which is worse, all you have done

Hath been but for a wayward son,

Spiteful and wrathful, who, as others do,

Loves for his own ends, not for you.

But make amends now: get you gone,

15   And at the pit of Acheron   *— hell*

Meet me in the morning. Thither he

Will come to know his destiny.   *Macbeth will come*

Your vessels and your spells provide,

Your charms and everything beside.

20   I am for the air; this night I'll spend

Unto a dismal and a fatal end.

Great business must be wrought ere noon.

Upon the corner of the moon

There hangs a vaporous drop profound;

25   I'll catch it ere it come to ground:

spell
And that, distilled by magic sleights

Shall raise such artificial sprites

As by the strength of their illusion

Shall draw him on to his confusion.   *— confuse Macbeth*

30   He shall spurn fate, scorn death, and bear   *} he thinks hes invicible*

His hopes above wisdom, grace and fear;

And you all know, security   *} too sure + cocky → things go wrong*

Is mortals' chiefest enemy.

Music and a song within: 'Come away, come away' etc.

Hark! I am called. My little spirit, see,

35   Sits in a foggy cloud, and stays for me.

Exit

First Witch

Come, let's make haste; she'll soon be back again.

Exeunt

---

1   angerly: *angry*

2   beldams: *malicious old women*

3   Saucy: *cheeky, presumptuous*

4   trade and traffic: *deal and negotiate with*

5   riddles: *mysteries*

7   close contriver: *secret plotter*

8   bear my part: *play my role*

11   wayward son: *the rebellious Macbeth*

12   Spiteful and wrathful: *vindictive and enraged*

14   make amends: *atone*

15   pit of Acheron: *a cave near the river Acheron in the Underworld in ancient Greek myth*

18–19   Your vessels ... beside: *bring your cauldrons, magic spells and whatever else you need*

21   fatal end: *dark and deadly result*

22   wrought: *done*

24   vaporous drop profound: *misty, heavy droplet*

26   sleights: *trickery*

27   artificial sprites: *false spirits*

28   illusion: *deception*

29   confusion: *turmoil, disorientation*

30   He ... fate: *Macbeth will scoff at destiny*

32   security: *over-confidence, desire for safety*

Study Notes

Supernatural manipulation (lines 1–36)

Some experts believe this scene was not in Shakespeare's original play. However, it does serve to increase suspense and establish a mood of evil and deception. As thunder sounds, Hecate appears and confronts the three weird sisters about their interference with Macbeth. She reasserts her superior position over them as 'mistress of your charms'. Without her, they are nothing. She criticises Macbeth's arrogant character and reminds the witches that he is self-obsessed, 'Loves for his own ends, not for you.' She believes that he is entirely to blame for his downfall.

Hecate then tells the witches that they can make amends by meeting her in hell, 'at the pit of Acheron'. Macbeth is about to discover his fate, so they should be prepared. Meanwhile, she is going to catch a 'vaporous drop profound'. The witches' malicious equivocation is apparent in this image of a misty, yet heavy, drop of water. Hecate intends to create illusions to deceive Macbeth and bring him to his doom, so that he will 'spurn fate, scorn death'.

A faint song is heard from Hecate's familiar spirit, suggesting that evil is always lurking nearby. While this scene is different in tone from the rest of the play, it adds to the suspense, foreshadowing the witches' involvement in the tragedy to come.

🙶 Key Quotes

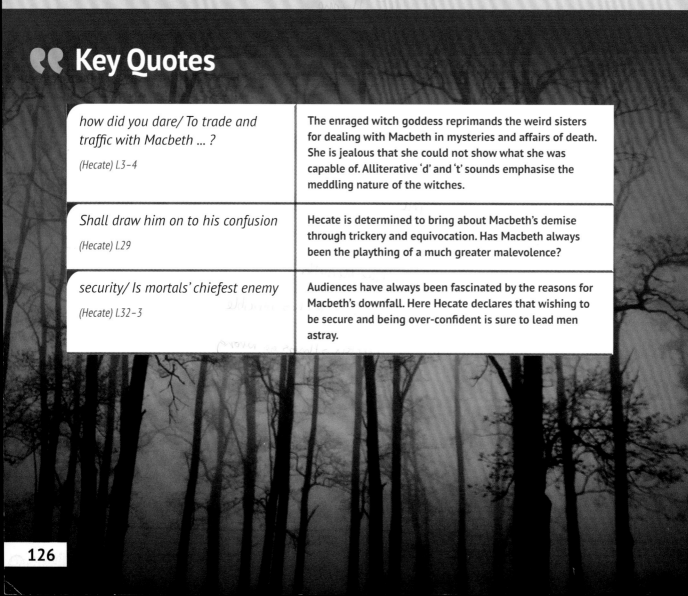

how did you dare/ To trade and traffic with Macbeth ... ? (Hecate) l.3–4	The enraged witch goddess reprimands the weird sisters for dealing with Macbeth in mysteries and affairs of death. She is jealous that she could not show what she was capable of. Alliterative 'd' and 't' sounds emphasise the meddling nature of the witches.
Shall draw him on to his confusion (Hecate) l.29	Hecate is determined to bring about Macbeth's demise through trickery and equivocation. Has Macbeth always been the plaything of a much greater malevolence?
security/ Is mortals' chiefest enemy (Hecate) l.32–3	Audiences have always been fascinated by the reasons for Macbeth's downfall. Here Hecate declares that wishing to be secure and being over-confident is sure to lead men astray.

OVERVIEW

Lennox and another Scottish lord discuss the rumours about Macbeth that are circulating throughout the country. Both men suspect the new king of being involved in the murders of Duncan and Banquo. Meanwhile, Macduff has gone to England to join Malcolm in pleading with England's King Edward for support. The forces of good are coming together.

The palace

Enter Lennox and another Lord

Lennox

My former speeches have but hit your thoughts,

Which can interpret farther: only, I say,

Things have been strangely borne. The gracious Duncan

Was pitied of Macbeth: marry, he was dead:

And the right-valiant Banquo walked too late;   5

Whom, you may say, if it please you, Fleance killed,

For Fleance fled: men must not walk too late.

Who cannot want the thought how monstrous

It was for Malcolm and for Donalbain

To kill their gracious father? Damnèd fact!   10

How it did grieve Macbeth! Did he not straight,

In pious rage, the two delinquents tear,

That were the slaves of drink and thralls of sleep?

Was not that nobly done? Ay, and wisely too;

For 'twould have angered any heart alive   15

To hear the men deny it. So that, I say,

He has borne all things well; and I do think

That had he Duncan's sons under his key –

As, an it please heaven, he shall not – they should find

What 'twere to kill a father; so should Fleance.   20

But, peace! For from broad words and 'cause he failed

His presence at the tyrant's feast, I hear

Macduff lives in disgrace. Sir, can you tell

Where he bestows himself?

Lord

　　　　　　　　　　　　The son of Duncan,

From whom this tyrant holds the due of birth,   25

Lives in the English court, and is received

Of the most pious Edward with such grace

That the malevolence of fortune nothing

Takes from his high respect. Thither Macduff

Is gone to pray the holy king, upon his aid   30

To wake Northumberland and warlike Siward:

That, by the help of these – with Him above

To ratify the work – we may again

Give to our tables meat, sleep to our nights,

Free from our feasts and banquets bloody knives,   35

Do faithful homage and receive free honours:

All which we pine for now. And this report
Hath so exasperate the king that he
Prepares for some attempt of war.

Lennox

40   Sent he to Macduff?

Lord

He did: and with an absolute 'Sir, not I!'
The cloudy messenger turns me his back,
And hums, as who should say 'You'll rue the time
That clogs me with this answer.'

Lennox

                     And that well might

45   Advise him to a caution, to hold what distance
His wisdom can provide. Some holy angel
Fly to the court of England and unfold
His message ere he come, that a swift blessing
May soon return to this our suffering country
Under a hand accursed!

Lord

50   I'll send my prayers with him.

Exeunt

37 pine for: *crave, miss*

42 cloudy: *bad-tempered*

43 rue: *regret*

47 unfold: *disclose*

50 Under a hand accursed: *ruled by terror*

how monstrous

Lennox, Act 3 Scene 6, l.8

Study Notes

Strange events (lines 1–50)

The exchange between Lennox and another noble Scotsman is circumspect because they know that Macbeth has many spies throughout the country. In a long list of ironic examples, Lennox warily comments that Macbeth was only sorry for 'the gracious Duncan' when the old king 'was dead'. He is equally sceptical of the rumours that Banquo was killed because he went walking 'too late' or that Fleance must have murdered his own father because he 'fled'. He also recalls how Macbeth killed Duncan's guards in a 'pious rage'. The sarcastic tone makes it clear that Lennox suspects Macbeth of being involved in the deaths of both Duncan and Banquo.

This summary of recent events reminds the audience of Macbeth's devious behaviour and inhumanity to date and shows how suspicious the people of Scotland are of their new king. But can anyone dare to challenge him? Shakespeare is building a solid case for a justifiable revolt against the king – something which in Elizabethan times would have been viewed as a shocking act.

This brief scene advances the political plot significantly. The audience learns that Malcolm has been well received in England. We also discover Macduff's whereabouts and his efforts to get help for his 'suffering country' from the 'most pious Edward'. England's king is presented as the complete opposite of the corrupt, autocratic Macbeth.

There is evidently a growing desire for peace in Scotland, to 'Give to our tables meat, sleep to our nights'. Macbeth is all too aware of the likely rebellion facing him and is preparing for war. Meanwhile, Lennox fears for Macduff's safety and expresses his hopes for a 'swift blessing' and the restoration of order in the country.

Shakespeare's language

The language in this short scene is in keeping with the widespread disorder of Macbeth's tyrannical reign. **Speech is fragmented**, interrupted by questions, pauses and disjointed thoughts: 'the right-valiant Banquo walked too late;/ Whom, you may say, if it please you, Fleance killed'. Lennox uses language guardedly because there is a pervading atmosphere of distrust. In the uncertain Scotland ruled over by Macbeth, it is dangerous to voice opinions openly.

The many **religious references** ('gone to pray', 'Some holy angel') underline the deeply held Elizabethan belief in the divine rule of kings, whose power was believed to come from God. Usurpers of the throne were seen as opposing God's will and creating chaos within the social order. Both Lennox and the unnamed Lord speak of Macbeth as a 'tyrant', indicating his increasing isolation. Three kings feature in this scene. The 'gracious Duncan' and the 'holy king' Edward are both lawfully appointed and provide a sharp contrast to the tyrannical despot, Macbeth, who seized the kingship improperly. The scene signals a growing opposition to Macbeth's 'accursed' regime. Can the forces of good eventually unite to challenge the unlawful ruler?

Key Quotes

The gracious Duncan/ Was pitied of Macbeth: marry, he was dead *(Lennox) l.3–4*	Lennox's ironic comment, that Macbeth only pitied Duncan after the respected former king was dead, is an example of his deep suspicions about Macbeth. With so many unanswered questions about Macbeth's sudden rise to power, it is not surprising that many of the thanes have doubts about him.
Give to our tables meat, sleep to our nights *(Unnamed Lord to Lennox) l.34*	Macbeth has not only created chaos within himself, he has also plunged Scotland into disarray – and all to satisfy his ambition for power. He is already widely regarded as a tyrant. It is ironic that ordinary people long to sleep just as he does – but there will be no peace for the country while this unlawful king occupies the throne.
Advise him to a caution, to hold what distance/ His wisdom can provide *(Lennox) l.45*	Macduff is seen as the avenger who could rescue Scotland and restore order. But knowing Macbeth's reputation for revenge, the thanes realise that Macduff's life is now in great danger.

Key Points | Act 3

- Act 3 marks a major turning point in the play, the murder of Banquo and attempted murder of Fleance. The shocking consequences of the Macbeths' evil actions are beginning to be felt. Nobody is safe in Scotland and there is growing estrangement between Macbeth and his wife.

- A series of tense scenes dramatise the protagonist's desperate struggle to regain control. Meanwhile, both the supernatural powers and the forces for good prepare to challenge the tyrannical king.

- Macbeth's coronation takes place offstage, highlighting its invalidity.

- Tortured soliloquies reveal the profound unhappiness of the newly crowned couple.

- Macbeth's association with hired assassins shows the moral depths to which this once-noble warrior has descended.

- Banquo's ghost terrifies Macbeth, exposing his weakness to the court, despite Lady Macbeth's repeated efforts to support her unpredictable husband.

- The state banquet, which should have been the new king's glittering triumph, ends in disarray.

- Macbeth's disappointment at Fleance's escape strengthens his determination to do whatever it takes to maintain power. He chooses to place his trust in supernatural forces.

- The relationship between Macbeth and his wife has changed. He is now in the ascendant, manipulative and secretive. This is the last time the Macbeths will appear together.

- The witches add an exciting, melodramatic quality to the play, foretelling Macbeth's tragic destiny.

- Act 3 highlights the protagonist's rapid moral descent. The balance of power is changing – not just within the Macbeths' relationship, but between the wider forces of good and evil.

Class/Homework Exercise

'Shakespeare uses vivid imagery (blood, horror, etc.) to create a disturbing atmosphere throughout Act 3 of *Macbeth*.'

Write a paragraph (150–200 words) discussing the impact of such imagery. Support your answer with reference to the play.

OVERVIEW

The witches complete their magic spell and summon up a series of apparitions. Macbeth arrives, anxious to know his destiny. Three apparitions appear – a helmeted head, a bloody child and a crowned child holding a branch from a tree. Macbeth is given some consolation; he will not be defeated by anyone born of woman or until Birnam Wood comes to Dunsinane hill. However, he is warned about Macduff and also shown that Banquo's descendants will be future kings. Lennox brings news that Macduff has fled to England. Macbeth reveals his determination to follow his instincts and kill every member of Macduff's family.

* A key scene requiring close, detailed study

A cave

Thunder. Enter three Witches

First Witch

Thrice the brinded cat hath mewed.

Second Witch

Thrice, and once the hedge-pig whined.

Third Witch

Spirit ande

Harpier cries; 'Tis time, 'tis time.

First Witch

Round about the cauldron go;

In the poisoned entrails throw.   5

Toad, that under cold stone

Days and nights has thirty-one

Sweltered venom sleeping got,

Boil thou first in the charmèd pot.

All

Double, double toil and trouble;   10

Fire burn, and cauldron bubble.

Second Witch

Fillet of a fenny snake,   nature, wild

In the cauldron boil and bake;

Eye of newt and toe of frog,

Wool of bat and tongue of dog,   15

Adder's fork and blind-worm's sting,

Lizard's leg and howlet's wing,

For a charm of powerful trouble,

Like a hell-broth boil and bubble.

All

Double, double toil and trouble;   20

Fire burn and cauldron bubble.

Third Witch

Scale of dragon, tooth of wolf,

Witches' mummy, maw and gulf

Of the ravined salt-sea shark,

poisonous

Root of hemlock digged i' th' dark,   *merchant of venice*   25

Liver of blaspheming Jew,   anti semetic → hatred of jew

Gall of goat, and slips of yew

Slivered in the moon's eclipse,

---

1 Thrice: *three times*

1 brinded: *tawny, striped*

2 hedge-pig: *hedgehog*

3 Harpier: *spirit, harpy (half bird, half woman)*

4 cauldron: *cooking pot*

5 entrails: *internal organs*

8 Sweltered venom: *sweated poison*

10 toil and trouble: *drudgery and pain*

12 Fillet: *slice*

14 newt: *small amphibian, like a lizard*

16 Adder's ... sting: *snake's poisonous tongue*

17 howlet: *young owl*

23 mummy: *embalmed flesh*

23 maw and gulf: *stomach and throat*

25 hemlock: *poisonous plant*

26 blaspheming: *profane, ungodly*

Turkey → muslim
↑   ↑
→ outsiders

Nose of Turk and Tartar's lips,

30 Finger of birth-strangled babe

Ditch-delivered by a drab,   *— baby ditched by prostitute*

Make the gruel thick and slab:

Add thereto a tiger's chaudron,

For the ingredients of our cauldron.

All

35 Double, double toil and trouble;

Fire burn and cauldron bubble.

Second Witch

Cool it with a baboon's blood,

Then the charm is firm and good.

Enter Hecate

Hecate

O! Well done! I commend your pains,

40 And every one shall share in the gains.

And now about the cauldron sing,

Live elves and fairies in a ring,

Enchanting all that you put in.

Music and a song: 'Black spirits' etc. Exit Hecate

Second Witch

By the pricking of my thumbs,

45 Something wicked this way comes. *→ Macbeth*

Open, locks, whoever knocks.

Enter Macbeth

Macbeth

How now, you secret, black, and midnight hags!

What is it you do?

All

A deed without a name. *→ spell*

Macbeth *→ wants to know future*

50 I conjure you, by that which you profess –

Howe'er you come to know it – answer me:

Though you untie the winds and let them fight

Against the churches; though the yesty waves

Confound and swallow navigation up;

55 Though bladed corn be lodged and trees blown down;

Though castles topple on their warders' heads;

Though palaces and pyramids do slope

29 Turk … Tartar: *races opposed to Christianity*

31 drab: *prostitute*

32 gruel: *thin porridge*

33 chaudron: *entrails*

Hecate: *goddess of witchcraft*

47 hags: *ugly old women*

50 conjure: *demand*

53 yesty: *frothy*

54 Confound: *destroy*

55 lodged: *flattened*

56 warders: *sentries, watchmen*

57 slope: *bend*

Their heads to their foundations; though the treasure

Of nature's germens tumble all together,

Even till destruction sicken; answer me   60

To what I ask you.

First Witch

Speak.

Second Witch

Demand.

Third Witch

We'll answer.

First Witch

Say, if thou'dst rather hear it from our mouths,   65

Or from our masters?

Macbeth

Call 'em; let me see 'em.

First Witch

Pour in sow's blood, that hath eaten

Her nine farrow; grease that's sweaten

From the murderer's gibbet throw   70

Into the flame.

All

Come, high or low; thyself and office deftly show.

Thunder. First Apparition: an armed Head

Macbeth

Tell me, thou unknown power –

First Witch

                                    He knows thy thought:

Hear his speech, but say thou nought.

First Apparition ➤ Demon

Macbeth! Macbeth! Macbeth! Beware Macduff;   75

Beware the Thane of Fife. Dismiss me. Enough.

Descends

Macbeth

Whate'er thou art, for thy good caution, thanks;

Thou hast harped my fear aright: but one word more –

66 masters: *powers who control us*

69 farrow: *young pigs*

70 gibbet: *scaffold*

72 thyself...deftly show: *reveal yourself and your work*
armed Head: *helmeted military figure*

78 harped: *predicted*

First Witch

He will not be commanded. Here's another,

80   More potent than the first.

Thunder. Second Apparition: A bloody Child

Second Apparition

Macbeth! Macbeth! Macbeth!

Macbeth

Had I three ears, I'd hear thee.

Second Apparition

Be bloody, bold, and resolute; laugh to scorn

The power of man, for none of woman born

85   Shall harm Macbeth.

Descends

Macbeth

Then live, Macduff: what need I fear of thee?

But yet I'll make assurance double sure,

And take a bond of fate: thou shalt not live;

That I may tell pale-hearted fear it lies,

And sleep in spite of thunder.

Thunder. Third Apparition: a Child crowned, with a tree in his hand

90   What is this

That rises like the issue of a king,

And wears upon his baby-brow the round

And top of sovereignty?

All

Listen, but speak not to it.

Third Apparition

95   Be lion-mettled, proud, and take no care

Who chafes, who frets, or where conspirers are:

Macbeth shall never vanquished be, until

Great Birnam wood to high Dunsinane hill

Shall come against him.

Descends

Macbeth

                          That will never be:

100 Who can impress the forest, bid the tree

Unfix his earth-bound root? Sweet bodements! Good!

Rebellion's head, rise never, till the wood

Handwritten margin notes:
- *continue bloody path*
- *no other human can harm you & invicible*
- *I'll make sure to kill Macduff to be sure.*
- *child king?*
- *until forest moves & improbable*
- *won't happen*

Glossary notes:
83 resolute: *determined*

87-8 But yet … bond of fate: *Macbeth wants a guarantee that Macduff will never harm him*

92-3 round … sovereignty: *highest symbol of royal power*

95 lion-mettled: *courageous*

96 chafes … frets: *provokes or worries*

97 vanquished: *defeated*

100 impress: *force into service*

101 bodements: *predictions*

103 rise: *out of the ground*

104 lease of nature: *full life*

104–5 pay ... custom: *die a natural death of old age*

Hautboys: *oboes, musical instruments*

Of Birnam rise, and our high-placed Macbeth

Shall live the lease of nature, pay his breath

To time and mortal custom. Yet my heart   105

Throbs to know one thing: tell me − if your art

Can tell so much − shall Banquo's issue ever

Reign in this kingdom?

All

Seek to know no more.

Macbeth

I will be satisfied. Deny me this,   110

And an eternal curse fall on you! Let me know.

Why sinks that cauldron?

Hautboys

        And what noise is this?

First Witch

Show!

Second Witch

Show!

Third Witch

Show!   115

All

Show his eyes, and grieve his heart;

Come like shadows, so depart.

A show of eight kings, the last with a glass in his hand, and the Ghost of Banquo following

Macbeth

[handwritten: 8 = symbol of infinity]

Thou art too like the spirit of Banquo: down!

Thy crown does sear mine eye-balls. And thy hair,

Thou other gold-bound brow, is like the first.   120

A third is like the former. Filthy hags! *[handwritten: → can see infinite Banquo children ruling forever.]*

Why do you show me this? A fourth? Start, eyes!

What, will the line stretch out to the crack of doom?

Another yet! A seventh? I'll see no more.

And yet the eighth appears, who bears a glass   125

Which shows me many more; and some I see *[handwritten: 3 kingdoms]*

That two-fold balls and treble sceptres carry.

Horrible sight! Now I see 'tis true;

For the blood-boltered Banquo smiles upon me,

And points at them for his.

119 sear: *blister, burn*

120 gold-bound brow: *crowned head*

122 Start: *recoil*

123 the line: *of Banquo's descendants, who will be kings*

127 two-fold ... sceptres: *King of Britain, France, Ireland*

129 blood-boltered: *Banquo with blood-covered hair*

The show vanishes

130   What! Is this so?

First Witch

Ay, sir, all this is so. But why

Stands Macbeth thus amazedly?

Come, sisters, cheer we up his sprites,

And show the best of our delights.

135   I'll charm the air to give a sound,

While you perform your antic round,

That this great king may kindly say,

Our duties did his welcome pay.

Music. Witches dance, and vanish

Macbeth

Where are they? Gone? Let this pernicious hour

140   Stand aye accursèd in the calendar!

Come in, without there!

Enter Lennox

Lennox

                        What's your grace's will?

Macbeth

Saw you the weird sisters?

Lennox

                    No, my lord.

Macbeth

Came they not by you?

Lennox

                    No, indeed, my lord.

Macbeth

Infected be the air whereon they ride;

145   And damned all those that trust them! – I did hear

The galloping of horse: who was it came by?

Lennox

'Tis two or three, my lord, that bring you word

Macduff is fled to England.

Macbeth

                    Fled to England?

Lennox

Ay, my good lord.

132 thus amazedly: *so astonished*

133 sprites: *spirits*

136 antic round: *bizarre dance*

139 pernicious: *malevolent, destructive*

140 aye: *for ever*

144 Infected: *diseased*

Macbeth

Aside

Time, thou anticipatest my dread exploits;   150

The flighty purpose never is overtook

Unless the deed go with it. From this moment

The very firstlings of my heart shall be

The firstlings of my hand. And even now,

To crown my thoughts with acts, be it thought and done: 155

The castle of Macduff I will surprise;

Seize upon Fife; give to the edge of the sword

His wife, his babes, and all unfortunate souls

That trace him in his line. No boasting like a fool:

This deed I'll do before this purpose cool.   160

But no more sights! – *[to Lennox]* Where are these gentlemen?

Come, bring me where they are.

Exeunt

151 flighty: *short-lived*

153 firstlings: *impulses*

156 surprise: *attack unexpectedly*

159 trace: *follow, stem from*

161 sights: *apparitions*
161 these gentlemen: *who brought news about Macduff's flight to England*

[handwritten note: ordered Macduff + entire family to be murdered –]

Study Notes

The spell (lines 1–46)

The three witches brew their grotesque spell using poisonous ingredients from the animal, natural and human world ('Adder's fork and blind-worm's sting'; 'Root of hemlock digged i' th' dark'; 'Finger of birth-strangled babe'). In their evil domain, nothing is as it seems. The 'harpier' is both animal and human, half-bird, half-woman. Even the 'newt' can live in two environments, land and water, just as the witches exist between reality and the supernatural. Their demonic incantation, 'Double, double toil and trouble', is the centrepiece of the dual meanings and contradictions that appear throughout the play. The 'weird sisters' seek to unleash 'powerful trouble' for Macbeth by subtly tempting him with assurances of security so that he descends into a state of half-man, half-monster.

Supernatural answers (lines 47–138)

A bold and reckless Macbeth arrives, determined to know his fate. He demands answers from the witches and is entirely focused on maintaining his hold on power, regardless of the consequences: 'Though palaces and pyramids do slope'. The witches present him with a sequence of apparitions. The first, 'an armed Head', is ambiguous. Does it represent Macduff's rebellion or Macbeth's eventual fate? In any case, the prediction confirms Macbeth's suspicions and he is satisfied that the spirit has 'harped my fear' about Macduff correctly.

The second apparition, 'a bloody Child', is also equivocal. What might be the connection with Macduff? As always, the witches delight in giving Macbeth apparent encouragement, urging him to be 'bloody, bold, and resolute' because 'none of woman born/ Shall harm Macbeth'. For a moment, these assurances of his security lead Macbeth to consider sparing

Macduff. But he quickly decides that his own safety is paramount, and bluntly declares, 'thou shalt not live'.

The third apparition ('a Child crowned, with a tree in his hand') seems to offer him further support: 'Macbeth shall never vanquished be, until/ Great Birnam wood to high Dunsinane hill/ Shall come against him'. His confidence grows, 'That will never be', so he is relieved to think that he can act without consequences. But Macbeth has one last concern: will Banquo's descendants take control of the Scottish throne? The vision of eight kings followed by Banquo has a horrifying impact on Macbeth, who is now appalled at the thought of failing to keep the crown within his own family. To his dismay, he is now more insecure than ever, 'Thy crown does sear mine eye-balls'.

Political reality (lines 139–62)

No sooner have the witches disappeared than Lennox arrives with news that Macduff has fled to England. Macbeth takes some encouragement from the witches' more favourable predictions and temporarily disregards his fears. He now resolves to act only on his evil impulses, 'The very firstlings of my heart shall be/ The firstlings of my hand'. His first horrendous decision is to take vengeance on the fugitive Macduff by slaughtering Macduff's wife and family. Ambition, paranoia and the witches' influence have combined to lure Macbeth into subhuman behaviour. The witches had earlier referred to him as 'Something wicked' – not a human being, but an object. The once-great warrior is now entirely corrupted and can be defined by his evil.

Shakespeare's language

This is an exhilarating scene of theatrical special effects which increases the sinister atmosphere of foreboding. The gruesome ingredients used for the spell, 'poisoned entrails', reveal the repulsive nature of malice and equivocation practised by the witches. The playwright employs spectacular **visual effects** to mesmerise the audience. The chanting creatures circling the bubbling cauldron and the three apparitions are unnerving. Shakespeare gives the eighth child in the line of kings a mirror to visually represent to Macbeth how Banquo's descendants will rule till the 'crack of doom'. This is a particularly cruel blow to the childless Macbeth, who has sacrificed everything for a 'fruitless crown'. The dramatic juxtaposition of a child, the symbol of innocence, with blood and warfare is terrifying.

Sound is also used effectively in this gripping scene, from the opening thunder signalling the moral chaos in Scotland caused by Macbeth's actions to the use of hypnotic, musical language. The witches speak in rhyming couplets (aabb), unlike the other characters, which highlights their weird presence. However, Macbeth also begins to echo them ('be'/'tree'; 'Good'/'word'). He has fallen for their 'Sweet bodements' and is increasingly at ease in their company. The hissing sibilance of 'Sweltered', 'slips' and 'Slivered' amplifies the malevolent atmosphere. Tension is increased through the repetition of the spell, 'Double, double toil and trouble'. Internal rhyme coupled with the alliteration of the explosive 'b' in 'burn' and 'bubble' musically evoke the bizarre scene.

The witches are symbols of spiritual treachery who ambiguously straddle the borders between reality and the supernatural, 'Where are they? Gone?' **Equivocation** permeates the entire scene. The weird sisters represent moral confusion – but do they control fate or are they the agents of fate? Blood is a symbol of sacrifice and guilt and the turbulent weather represents the disordered kingdom. Macbeth, desperate for security, accepts the prophecies at face value. Everyone on earth is born of woman; woods cannot walk. But what exactly did the apparitions really represent? Ironically, Macbeth foreshadows his own tragic fate, 'And damned all those that trust them!'

Critical Analysis

1. 'Shakespeare uses a range of dramatic techniques to convey a world of corruption in the play *Macbeth*.' Discuss this statement, with particular reference to Act 4 Scene 1.

2. The twin themes of deception and evil are central to the play *Macbeth*.' Discuss this view in relation to Act 4 Scene 1.

Sample Paragraph 1 (Q1)

I thought Shakespeare made a real world of evil in the play. The witch scene where they sing double, double was extremely evil. They throw real disgusting things into their 'gruel', snakes and toads and all sorts of awful things. The head witch comes to see if they did the spell right. Then when the spell is finished 'good and firm' they get ghosts up to tell Macbeth he is safe and not to worry. He believes the apparitions but just to make sure he decides to kill the whole lot of Macduff's family and wife and children because the witches warned him about Macduff saying 'Beware the Thane Macduff'. Macbeth couldn't get to Macduff because Macduff had fled away to England. I thought this was corrupt evil of the worst kind. *(130 words)*

Examiner's Comment

- Unfocused low-level response that fails to address dramatic techniques used to convey corruption in the scene.
- Relies mainly on rambling narrative.
- Inappropriate and inaccurate use of language, including incorrect quotations.
- Weak expression throughout.

Sample Paragraph 2 (Q1)

The world in the play is very corrupt. Macbeth is evil himself. He does not care what he does to get his own way, as it's all about him, 'answer me'. Everything in the scene is unnatural. Macbeth says 'Had I three ears'. The witches speak in riddles about a sow 'that had eaten her nine farrow'. The apparitions are 'an armed head' and 'a bloody child'. This is unnatural showing the corruption spreading in Macbeth's world since he murdered Duncan. The three apparitions are also corrupt because they say one thing but mean something else. This means they trick Macbeth by using this dramatic technique. The child says 'Macbeth shall never vanquished be' until the woods start moving. Macbeth is fooled by this. He believes this because he knows the trees are 'earth-bound'. But he can't see that the child is holding the tree, it is no longer 'earth-bound'. So he is tricked all the time by the corrupt witches and their deceiving evil spirits. This is how Shakespeare conveys a world of corruption. *(175 words)*

Examiner's Comment

- This mid-grade answer attempts to address the question, using references to corruption.
- Points are hit-and-miss, lacking development (e.g. about the scene being unnatural).
- Fails to show a convincing understanding of dramatic techniques.
- Expression lacks fluency and is repetitive throughout.

Sample Paragraph 3 (Q1)

From the ominous sound of thunder, through the visual spectacle of the 'weird sisters' chanting over the cauldron, to the equivocal, demonic apparitions, Shakespeare conjures up a fierce scene of evil deception in Act 4 Scene 1. The background storm signals Macbeth's fierce determination to turn the universe upside down to get his way, 'untie the winds and let them fight/ Against the churches'. His perverted nature is revealed by the witches, 'Something wicked this way comes.' The graphic description of the foul ingredients for the spell coupled with the repetitive chant ('Double, double toil and trouble') heighten the tense mood of pervasive malevolence. Equivocation dominates the entire scene. The witches take advantage of Macbeth's arrogance as

he boasts of being able to 'laugh to scorn/ The power of man'; they deceive him with favourable prophecies, 'none of woman born/ shall harm Macbeth'. The language of the scene is highly dramatic. Violent verbs echo this vindictive world, 'Sweltered', 'Slivered', 'birth-strangled', 'sear'. Yet, for me, it is not the corruption of the supernatural world that is most appalling. It is Macbeth's callous pledge to put Macduff's family to 'the edge of the sword', not for any obvious gain, but because he simply chooses to do so. Through the evil image of Macbeth, powerful language and sound and visual effects, Shakespeare creates a scene of terrible depravity. *(225 words)*

> **Examiner's Comment**
>
> - A successful top-grade standard based around clearly focused and well-illustrated points.
> - The impressive opening immediately engages with the key elements of the question.
> - Excellent discussion of effective techniques (characterisation, powerful language, etc.)
> - First-rate expression – fluent, varied and very well controlled (e.g. 'perverted nature is revealed', 'Equivocation dominates', 'Violent verbs echo this vindictive world').

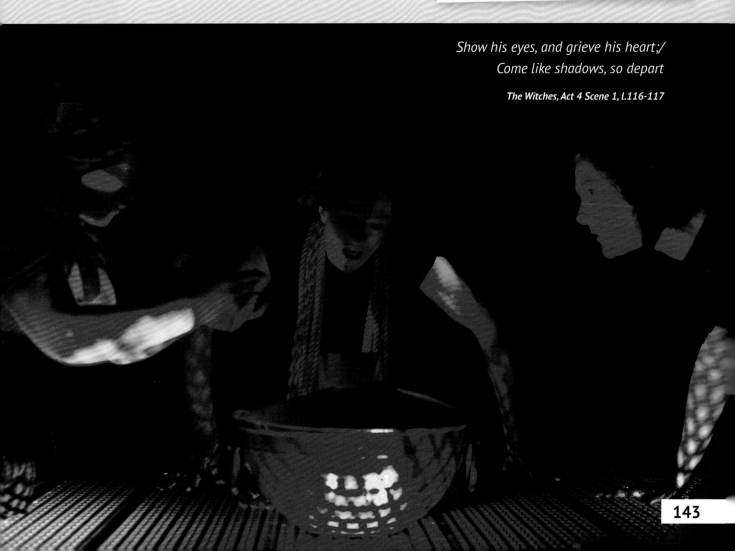

Show his eyes, and grieve his heart;/
Come like shadows, so depart

The Witches, Act 4 Scene 1, l.116-117

❝❝ Key Quotes

Double, double toil and trouble;/ Fire burn, and cauldron bubble (The witches) l.10–11	The weird sisters repeatedly chant this sinister refrain while they prepare their hideous spell. The heavy four beats of this magic verse, the alliterative 't' and 'b' sounds, internal rhyme and onomatopoeia effectively combine to produce a haunting chorus.
Beware Macduff;/ Beware the Thane of Fife (First Apparition to Macbeth) l.75–6	The 'armed head' makes the first prophecy, which corresponds closely with Macbeth's own deep-rooted fear of Macduff. However, the audience is left to consider exactly who or what the warrior head might symbolise.
laugh to scorn/ The power of man, for none of woman born/ Shall harm Macbeth (Second Apparition to Macbeth) l.83–5	A 'bloody child' seems to give an assurance that Macbeth can never be defeated because all human beings are born of woman. But is Macbeth forgetting that the witches always use language to deceive? Once again the prediction is ambiguous. What is the true significance of the 'bloody child'?
Macbeth shall never vanquished be, until/ Great Birnam wood to high Dunsinane hill/ Shall come against him (Third Apparition to Macbeth) l.97–9	A crowned child clutching a tree seems to reassure Macbeth. Trees cannot walk because they are rooted in the ground. But the child is holding a tree that has been uprooted. What does this mean? Who is this crowned child? Again, the audience is left to speculate.
Thy crown does sear mine eye-balls (Macbeth to the line of kings) l.119	Macbeth is obsessed with fears that Banquo's descendants will rule Scotland. He is shown a line of eight kings, all descended from Banquo, with the last child holding a mirror so that the line of succession stretches well into the future. Macbeth is immediately distraught at this vision. The violent onomatopoeic verb 'sear' vividly suggests the anguish felt by the childless Macbeth.
The castle of Macduff I will surprise;/ Seize upon Fife; give to the edge of the sword/ His wife, his babes (Macbeth soliloquy) l.156–8	This unjustified plan to massacre Macduff's household concludes a highly disturbing scene. Macbeth has now fallen to a subhuman level and expresses himself by carrying out evil acts for their own sake. As his steep moral decline continues, the audience begins to sense Macbeth's own imminent destruction.

OVERVIEW

Lady Macduff and her cousin, Ross, discuss her husband's sudden departure for England. She is bewildered and furious at his apparent desertion of her and her young family. Ross insists that Macduff has made a wise decision. An affectionate, though sharp, exchange between Lady Macduff and her son is suddenly interrupted by Macbeth's hired assassins. The child is killed and Lady Macduff tries to escape, but is pursued by the murderers.

Fife. Macduff's castle

Enter Lady Macduff, her Son and Ross

Lady Macduff

What had he done, to make him fly the land?

Ross

You must have patience, madam.

Lady Macduff

       He had none:
His flight was madness. When our actions do not,
Our fears do make us traitors.

Ross

      You know not
Whether it was his wisdom or his fear.   5

Lady Macduff

Wisdom! To leave his wife, to leave his babes,
His mansion and his titles, in a place
From whence himself does fly? He loves us not;
He wants the natural touch; for the poor wren,
The most diminutive of birds, will fight –   10
Her young ones in her nest – against the owl.
All is the fear and nothing is the love;
As little is the wisdom, where the flight
So runs against all reason.

Ross

      My dearest coz,
I pray you, school yourself. But, for your husband, 15
He is noble, wise, judicious, and best knows
The fits of the season. I dare not speak much further;
But cruel are the times, when we are traitors
And do not know ourselves; when we hold rumour
From what we fear, yet know not what we fear, 20
But float upon a wild and violent sea
Each way and move. I take my leave of you:
Shall not be long but I'll be here again.
Things at the worst will cease, or else climb upward
To what they were before. My pretty cousin,   25
Blessing upon you!

Lady Macduff

Fathered he is, and yet he's fatherless.

---

1 he: *Macduff*

4 make us traitors: *give the impression that we are cowardly*

7 titles: *property, possessions*

9 wants ... touch: *lacks normal feelings*

10 most diminutive: *smallest*

11 young ones: *chicks*

14 So ... reason: *his actions are irrational*

14 coz: *cousin*

15 school: *control*

17 fits of the season: *dangerous times we live in*

18 are traitors: *perceived as treacherous*

19 hold: *believe*

22 Each way and move: *in all directions*

24 climb upward: *get better*

25 cousin: *Lady Macduff's son*

Ross

I am so much a fool, should I stay longer,

It would be my disgrace and your discomfort:

I take my leave at once.

Exit

Lady Macduff

30   Sirrah, your father's dead;

And what will you do now? How will you live?

Son

As birds do, mother.

Lady Macduff

What, with worms and flies?

Son

With what I get, I mean; and so do they.

Lady Macduff

Poor bird! Thou'dst never fear the net nor lime,

35   The pitfall nor the gin.

Son

Why should I, mother? Poor birds they are not set for.

My father is not dead, for all your saying.

Lady Macduff

Yes, he is dead. How wilt thou do for a father?

Son

Nay, how will you do for a husband?

Lady Macduff

40   Why, I can buy me twenty at any market.

Son

Then you'll buy 'em to sell again.

Lady Macduff

Thou speak'st with all thy wit: and yet, i' faith,

With wit enough for thee.

Son

Was my father a traitor, mother?

Lady Macduff

45   Ay, that he was.

29 discomfort: *embarrassment*

30 Sirrah: *a term of affection*

34 net nor lime: *traps*

36 gin: *snare*

42 wit: *intelligence*

Son

What is a traitor?

Lady Macduff

Why, one that swears and lies.

Son

And be all traitors that do so?

Lady Macduff

Every one that does so is a traitor, and must be hanged.

Son

And must they all be hanged that swear and lie?   50

Lady Macduff

Every one.

Son

Who must hang them?

Lady Macduff

Why, the honest men.

Son

Then the liars and swearers are fools; for there are liars
and swearers enough to beat the honest men and hang   55
up them.

Lady Macduff

Now, God help thee, poor monkey! But how wilt thou do
for a father?

Son

If he were dead, you'd weep for him: if you would not, it
were a good sign that I should quickly have a new father.   60

Lady Macduff

Poor prattler, how thou talkest!

Enter a Messenger

Messenger

Bless you, fair dame. I am not to you known,
Though in your state of honour I am perfect.
I doubt some danger does approach you nearly.
If you will take a homely man's advice,   65
Be not found here; hence, with your little ones.
To fright you thus, methinks, I am too savage;
To do worse to you were fell cruelty,

47 swears: *makes a solemn oath*

57 poor monkey: *a term of affection*

61 prattler: *chatterer*

63 Though ... perfect: *I am aware of your
honourable situation*
64 doubt: *suspect*
65 homely: *plain, simple*
66 hence: *go away from here*

67 savage: *harsh*
68 fell: *dreadful*

Which is too nigh your person. Heaven preserve you!
I dare abide no longer.

Exit

Lady Macduff

70   Whither should I fly?
I have done no harm. But I remember now
I am in this earthly world, where to do harm
Is often laudable, to do good sometime
Accounted dangerous folly. Why then, alas,
75 Do I put up that womanly defence,
To say I have done no harm?

Enter Murderers

                    What are these faces?

First Murderer

Where is your husband?

Lady Macduff

I hope in no place so unsanctified
Where such as thou mayst find him.

First Murderer

                    He's a traitor.

Son

Thou liest, thou shag-haired villain!

First Murderer

80   What, you egg!

Stabbing him

Young fry of treachery!

Son

                He has killed me, mother:
Run away, I pray you!

Dies

Exeunt, with Lady Macduff crying 'Murder!'

---

69 nigh: *close to*

70 Whither: *to where*

73 laudable: *admirable, commendable*

74 folly: *foolishness*

75 womanly: *fearful*

76 faces: *people, strangers*

78 unsanctified: *dishonourable, unholy*

80 shag-haired: *long-haired*

80 egg: *youngster, brat*

81 fry of treachery: *child of a traitor*

Study Notes

Treacherous or wise? (lines 1–30)

Lady Macduff attempts to come to terms with her husband's flight to England, 'What had he done, to make him fly the land?' Ross urges 'patience'. Yet she feels abandoned, 'To leave his wife, to leave his babes,/ His mansion and his titles, in a place/ From whence himself does fly?' She accuses him of a lack of affection, referring to the 'poor wren', the smallest bird, which would fight the predatory owl to protect 'Her young ones in her nest'. Her paradoxical statement that her son is both 'Fathered' yet 'fatherless' troubles Ross so much that he takes his leave of his 'pretty cousin', promising to return soon.

Mother and son banter (lines 30–76)

A lively conversation follows between mother and son. Lady Macduff declares that her husband is 'dead' and that he was a traitor. From her point of view, Macduff has acted deceitfully, but her son comforts her with his response that the world is full of dishonest men. The treacherous atmosphere throughout Scotland has even found its way into the child's nursery, 'there are liars and swearers enough to beat the honest men and hang up them'. The arrival of a messenger advising Lady Macduff to flee increases the urgency of the scene.

A brutal murder (lines 76–82)

The murderers burst in. Lady Macduff courageously asserts herself, refusing to say where her husband is, 'in no place so unsanctified/ Where such as thou mayst find him'. Her son also challenges the murderer for calling his father a traitor. The boy's last words indicate his exceptional qualities – he thinks only of his mother when he cries 'Run away, I pray you!' She flees the horrendous scene pursued by the murderers, leaving the audience filled with horror.

Shakespeare's language

This short scene explores the nature of genuine courage, as opposed to the arrogant bravado of Macbeth. Questions have already been raised about the subject of manliness. Should a real man place his country above the safety of his family? Does Macduff lack 'the natural touch'? Through the use of the **emotive image** of the most 'diminutive of birds' which will always fight to defend her family, Shakespeare appeals to the audience's sympathies. **Verbal irony** ('Fathered he is, and yet he's fatherless') adds to the pathos. The natural warmth of the family atmosphere is juxtaposed against the corruption of Macbeth's world, underlining the key theme of good and evil.

This scene also functions as a **graphic depiction** of the depths to which the once-heroic and 'noble' Macbeth has fallen. Macduff has long suspected Macbeth, ever since the murder of Duncan's bodyguards. The appalling killing of Macduff's wife and son appears to be simply out of spite. Such sensational violence is common in Shakespeare's plays. There is a sharp **contrast** between the dishonourable act of a despotic king and the true bravery of a young mother and her child. As a result, the audience can relate to the victims' feelings of confusion and terror throughout this harrowing sequence.

❝❝ Key Quotes

His flight was madness (Lady Macduff to Ross) l.3	Lady Macduff fluctuates between anger and anguish. She feels that she has been deserted and regards her husband's flight to England as ill-judged. It gives the appearance of cowardice or guilt. Malcolm, Donalbain and Fleance have all been tainted with suspicion because they fled Scotland.
But, for your husband,/ He is noble, wise, judicious (Ross to Lady Macduff) l.15–16	Lady Macduff's cousin, Ross, knows the real reason why Macduff has gone to England, and he attempts to defend Macduff. Interestingly, he uses the same adjective, 'noble', that was used to describe Macbeth at the start of the play.
Whither should I fly?/ I have done no harm. (Lady Macduff) l.70–1	After being warned that she is in imminent danger and advised to flee, Lady Macduff is understandably confused – a reaction that elicits audience sympathy for this vulnerable woman and her young family. We are only too well aware that innocence is no protection in Macbeth's Scotland.
Young fry of treachery! (First Murderer to Macduff's son) l.81	In perhaps the most harrowing scene of the play, Macduff's young son is viciously murdered onstage. The contemptuous response of the murderer to this atrocity is reminiscent of the hired assassins who killed Banquo.

OVERVIEW

In England, Macduff meets Malcolm at the court of King Edward the Confessor. Duncan's son is suspicious of Macduff and tests his loyalty to Scotland by pretending to be an even less deserving leader than Macbeth. In response, Macduff is filled with despair and this convinces Malcolm that he is trustworthy. Ross then brings dreadful news that Macduff's family has been slaughtered. Malcolm urges Macduff to turn his grief to anger. The forces of good are moving closer to challenging the tyrant, Macbeth.

* A key scene requiring close, detailed study

England. Before the King's palace

Enter Malcolm and Macduff

Malcolm

Let us seek out some desolate shade, and there
Weep our sad bosoms empty.

Macduff

Let us rather
Hold fast the mortal sword, and like good men
Bestride our down-fall'n birthdom. Each new morn
5 New widows howl, new orphans cry, new sorrows
Strike heaven on the face, that it resounds
As if it felt with Scotland and yell'd out
Like syllable of dolour.

Malcolm

What I believe, I'll wail,
What know, believe; and what I can redress,
10 As I shall find the time to friend, I will.
What you have spoke, it may be so, perchance.
This tyrant, whose sole name blisters our tongues,
Was once thought honest. You have loved him well.
He hath not touched you yet. I am young; but something
15 You may deserve of him through me; and wisdom
To offer up a weak, poor, innocent lamb
To appease an angry god.

Macduff

I am not treacherous.

Malcolm

But Macbeth is.
A good and virtuous nature may recoil
20 In an imperial charge. But I shall crave your pardon.
That which you are my thoughts cannot transpose:
Angels are bright still, though the brightest fell;
Though all things foul would wear the brows of grace,
Yet grace must still look so.

Macduff

I have lost my hopes.

1 desolate: *bleak, empty*

3 mortal: *deadly*
4 birthdom: *native country*

8 dolour: *sorrow*

9 redress: *mend, put right*

11 perchance: *perhaps*
12 sole: *very*

16 innocent lamb: *Malcolm*
17 angry god: *Macbeth*

19 recoil: *change for the worse*
20 imperial charge: *royal command*

22 brightest fell: *Lucifer, the brightest angel, succumbed to evil*
23 brows: *facial expressions*

Malcolm

Perchance even there where I did find my doubts.   25
Why in that rawness left you wife and child,
Those precious motives, those strong knots of love,
Without leave-taking? I pray you,
Let not my jealousies be your dishonours,
But mine own safeties. You may be rightly just,   30
Whatever I shall think.

Macduff

                    Bleed, bleed, poor country!
Great tyranny, lay thou thy basis sure,
For goodness dare not check thee. Wear thou thy wrongs,
The title is affeered! Fare thee well, lord.
I would not be the villain that thou think'st   35
For the whole space that's in the tyrant's grasp,
And the rich east to boot.

Malcolm

                    Be not offended!
I speak not as in absolute fear of you.
I think our country sinks beneath the yoke;
It weeps, it bleeds; and each new day a gash   40
Is added to her wounds. I think withal
There would be hands uplifted in my right;
And here, from gracious England, have I offer
Of goodly thousands. But, for all this,
When I shall tread upon the tyrant's head,   45
Or wear it on my sword, yet my poor country
Shall have more vices than it had before,
More suffer, and more sundry ways than ever,
By him that shall succeed.

Macduff

                    What should he be?

Malcolm

It is myself I mean, in whom I know   50
All the particulars of vice so grafted
That, when they shall be opened, black Macbeth
Will seem as pure as snow, and the poor state
Esteem him as a lamb, being compared
With my confineless harms.

Macduff

55   Not in the legions
Of horrid hell can come a devil more damned
In evils to top Macbeth.

Malcolm

                                    I grant him bloody,
Luxurious, avaricious, false, deceitful,
Sudden, malicious, smacking of every sin

60   That has a name: but there's no bottom, none,
In my voluptuousness. Your wives, your daughters,
Your matrons and your maids, could not fill up
The cistern of my lust, and my desire
All continent impediments would o'erbear

65   That did oppose my will. Better Macbeth
Than such an one to reign.

Macduff

                                    Boundless intemperance
In nature is a tyranny; it hath been
The untimely emptying of the happy throne,
And fall of many kings. But fear not yet

70   To take upon you what is yours. You may
Convey your pleasures in a spacious plenty,
And yet seem cold; the time you may so hoodwink.
We have willing dames enough; there cannot be
That vulture in you to devour so many

75   As will to greatness dedicate themselves,
Finding it so inclined.

Malcolm

                                    With this there grows
In my most ill-composed affection such
A stanchless avarice that, were I king,
I should cut off the nobles for their lands,

80   Desire his jewels and this other's house:
And my more-having would be as a sauce
To make me hunger more, that I should forge
Quarrels unjust against the good and loyal,
Destroying them for wealth.

55 legions: *huge numbers*

58 smacking of: *practising*

61 voluptuousness: *lust*

63 cistern: *reservoir, container*
64 impediments: *obstructions*

71 Convey: *conduct*

73 dames: *women*

78 stanchless avarice: *unstoppable greed*

81 more-having: *getting more*

82 forge: *create, invent*

84–6 This avarice ... lust: *this greed is more deadly than a young man's desire*

88 foisons: *plenty*

89 portable: *endurable*

90 graces: *qualities*

92 verity ... stableness: *honesty, self-control, a steady nature*

93 Bounty: *generosity*

93 mercy, lowliness: *compassion, humility*

95 relish: *appreciation*

96 division: *variety*

98 concord: *harmony*

99 Uproar: *cause chaos to*

104 untitled: *one who has no right*

106 truest issue: *lawful heir*

107 interdiction: *words, accusation*

110 upon her knees: *at prayer*

113 breast: *heart*

Macduff

This avarice
Sticks deeper, grows with more pernicious root   85
Than summer-seeming lust; and it hath been
The sword of our slain kings. Yet do not fear;
Scotland hath foisons to fill up your will,
Of your mere own. All these are portable,
With other graces weighed.   90

Malcolm

But I have none. The king-becoming graces,
As justice, verity, temperance, stableness,
Bounty, perseverance, mercy, lowliness,
Devotion, patience, courage, fortitude,
I have no relish of them, but abound   95
In the division of each several crime,
Acting it many ways. Nay, had I power, I should
Pour the sweet milk of concord into hell,
Uproar the universal peace, confound
All unity on earth.

Macduff

O Scotland, Scotland!   100

Malcolm

If such a one be fit to govern, speak.
I am as I have spoken.

Macduff

Fit to govern!
No, not to live. O nation miserable,
With an untitled tyrant bloody-sceptered,
When shalt thou see thy wholesome days again,   105
Since that the truest issue of thy throne
By his own interdiction stands accused,
And does blaspheme his breed? Thy royal father
Was a most sainted king: the queen that bore thee,
Oftener upon her knees than on her feet,   110
Died every day she lived. Fare thee well!
These evils thou repeat'st upon thyself
Have banish'd me from Scotland. O my breast,
Thy hope ends here!

Malcolm

Macduff, this noble passion,

115 Child of integrity, hath from my soul

Wiped the black scruples, reconciled my thoughts

To thy good truth and honour. Devilish Macbeth

By many of these trains hath sought to win me

Into his power, and modest wisdom plucks me

120 From over-credulous haste; but God above

Deal between thee and me! For even now

I put myself to thy direction, and

Unspeak mine own detraction; here abjure

The taints and blames I laid upon myself

125 For strangers to my nature. I am yet

Unknown to woman, never was forsworn,

Scarcely have coveted what was mine own,

At no time broke my faith, would not betray

The devil to his fellow, and delight

130 No less in truth than life. My first false speaking

Was this upon myself. What I am truly

Is thine and my poor country's to command:

Whither indeed, before thy here-approach,

Old Siward, with ten thousand warlike men,

135 Already at a point, was setting forth.

Now we'll together; and the chance of goodness

Be like our warranted quarrel! Why are you silent?

Macduff

Such welcome and unwelcome things at once,

'Tis hard to reconcile.

Enter a Doctor

Malcolm

Well; more anon.

140 *[to Doctor]* Comes the king forth, I pray you?

Doctor

Ay, sir; there are a crew of wretched souls

That stay his cure. Their malady convinces

The great assay of art; but at his touch,

Such sanctity hath heaven given his hand,

They presently amend.

Malcolm

145 I thank you, doctor.

---

115 Child of integrity: *expression of goodness*
116 scruples: *suspicions*

123 detraction: *self-accusations*
123 abjure: *renounce*

126 forsworn: *perjured myself*
127 coveted: *desired*

133 here-approach: *recent request*

137 warranted quarrel: *justified struggle*

140 the king: *Edward the Confessor*

142 stay: *are awaiting*
142 malady: *sickness*
143 assay: *effort*

145 presently amend: *immediately recover*

146 the evil: *tuberculosis*

149 solicits heaven: *prays to God*
150 strangely visited people: *people with unusual diseases*

153 golden stamp: *holy icon*

156 benediction: *blessing*

158 sundry: *many*

160 My countryman: *Ross*

162 betimes: *quickly*

166 nothing: *no one*
167 once: *at any time*

Exit Doctor

Macduff

What's the disease he means?

Malcolm

      'Tis called the evil:

A most miraculous work in this good king;

Which often, since my here-remain in England,

I have seen him do. How he solicits heaven,

Himself best knows: but strangely visited people,   150

All swoln and ulcerous, pitiful to the eye,

The mere despair of surgery, he cures,

Hanging a golden stamp about their necks,

Put on with holy prayers: and 'tis spoken,

To the succeeding royalty he leaves   155

The healing benediction. With this strange virtue,

He hath a heavenly gift of prophecy,

And sundry blessings hang about his throne,

That speak him full of grace.

Enter Ross

Macduff

         See who comes here?

Malcolm

My countryman; but yet I know him not.   160

Macduff

My ever-gentle cousin, welcome hither.

Malcolm

I know him now. Good God, betimes remove

The means that makes us strangers!

Ross

          Sir, amen.

Macduff

Stands Scotland where it did?

Ross

         Alas, poor country!

Almost afraid to know itself! It cannot   165

Be called our mother, but our grave; where nothing,

But who knows nothing, is once seen to smile;

Where sighs and groans and shrieks that rend the air

Macduff

My children, too?

Ross

              Wife, children, servants, all

That could be found.

Macduff

                And I must be from thence!

My wife killed too?

Ross

              I have said.

Malcolm

                 Be comforted:

Let's make us medicines of our great revenge

215   To cure this deadly grief.

Macduff

He has no children. All my pretty ones?

Did you say all? – O hell-kite! – All?

What, all my pretty chickens and their dam

At one fell swoop?

Malcolm

             Dispute it like a man.

Macduff

220   I shall do so;

But I must also feel it as a man:

I cannot but remember such things were,

That were most precious to me. Did heaven look on,

And would not take their part? Sinful Macduff,

225   They were all struck for thee! Naught that I am;

Not for their own demerits, but for mine,

Fell slaughter on their souls. Heaven rest them now!

Malcolm

Be this the whetstone of your sword: let grief

Convert to anger; blunt not the heart, enrage it.

Macduff

230   O, I could play the woman with mine eyes

And braggart with my tongue. But, gentle heavens,

Cut short all intermission. Front to front

Bring thou this fiend of Scotland and myself;

214-15 Let's ... grief: *let us use revenge as a way of healing this terrible sorrow*

216 He: *could be either Malcolm or Macbeth*

217 hell-kite: *bird of prey: Macbeth*

218 dam: *mother*

219 Dispute: *fight*

224 take their part: *intervene on their behalf*

226-7 Not ... souls: *they were killed for my sins, not theirs*

228 whetstone: *sharpening stone*

229 blunt not: *don't soften*

231 braggart: *shout threats*

232 intermission: *pause, interruption*

235 tune: *attitude*

238 ripe for shaking: *ready to be cut down*

240 The night ... day: *bad times end eventually*

Within my sword's length set him; if he 'scape,

Heaven forgive him, too!

Malcolm

                        This tune goes manly.   235

Come, go we to the king; our power is ready;

Our lack is nothing but our leave. Macbeth

Is ripe for shaking, and the powers above

Put on their instruments. Receive what cheer you may:

The night is long that never finds the day.   240

Exeunt

Study Notes

Suspicious times (lines 1–159)

Malcolm has good reason to be cautious of those around him. Even within the safety of King Edward's palace, his initial instinct is to treat Macduff warily.

He fears that Macduff might be one of Macbeth's supporters. How else could Macduff's flight and abandonment of his family be explained? 'Why in that rawness left you wife and child ...?' Unlike the trusting Duncan, the more astute Malcolm has learnt not to trust appearances, 'all things foul would wear the brows of grace'. He challenges Macduff about his relationship with Macbeth, 'You have loved him well', but Macduff insists that he is 'not treacherous' and should therefore be trusted.

Despite this, Malcolm tests Macduff's loyalty. He pretends that he is even more corrupt than Macbeth and lists a series of character flaws – including uncontrolled lust – that would make him an unsuitable king. Initially, Macduff dismisses this as a young man's weakness and suggests that there are 'willing dames enough' to satisfy him. Malcolm goes on to say that his avarice is 'stanchless' and that he would pick quarrels with decent men simply to get his hands on their wealth. Again, Macduff refuses to condemn him, saying that Scotland has enough riches 'to fill up your will'.

It is only when Malcolm says that he has none of 'the king-becoming graces' and threatens that he would 'Pour the sweet milk of concord into hell' that Macduff reaches breaking point. In despair, he tells Malcolm that not only is he not 'Fit to govern', he is not fit to live. Malcolm is impressed by Macduff's integrity and recognises his true patriotism. He confesses that he has lied, 'My first false speaking/ Was this upon myself', leaving Macduff somewhat confused.

Contrasting news (lines 159–240)

A doctor arrives, speaking of the miraculous healing powers of the English king, which Malcolm describes as 'sundry blessings' that 'hang about his throne'. Ross enters, reminding the audience of the reality of Macbeth's tyranny, which has infected all of Scotland. He struggles to tell Macduff the terrible news: 'Your castle is surprised; your wife and babes/ Savagely slaughtered'.

Malcolm immediately urges Macduff to 'make us medicines of our great revenge'. However, the grief-stricken father poignantly points out, 'He has no children', and says that he must not only fight it like a man, but 'feel it as a man'. Macduff believes that he can blame himself alone for his family's deaths, but promises to avenge the massacre. 'Front to front/ Bring thou this fiend of Scotland and myself'.

Shakespeare's language

After the drama of the previous scenes, the pace of the play slows down, allowing the audience to consider the essential qualities of a rightful monarch. In a heavy-handed test of patriotism, Malcolm uses reverse psychology against Macduff. Contrasting images highlight the differences between a good king and a bad king. Edward the Confessor is portrayed as the epitome of grace and compassion, even promoting harmony ('the sweet milk of concord') beyond the boundaries of his own country. There is heart-breaking **dramatic irony** at work when Macduff repeatedly questions Ross about his family – as he is still unaware of their tragic fate.

Graphic descriptions of the terrible state of Scotland show the effects of Macbeth's 'untitled' and tyrannical rule. Violent verbs ('Strike', 'howl', 'sinks', 'bleeds', 'rend') vividly portray the country's turmoil and suffering. **Nature imagery** also reveals this chaos, 'good men's lives/ Expire before the flowers in their caps'. Macduff's agonising tragedy is conveyed through the innocent image of the slaughtered 'pretty chickens and their dam'. Macbeth is 'ripe for shaking'. He is likened to a predatory bird, 'hell-kite', and linked with satanic imagery, 'an angry god', 'black Macbeth', 'Devilish Macbeth', 'fiend of Scotland'. This provides a stark contrast to Edward, the 'gracious England' who constantly seeks heaven's help.

Critical Analysis

1. 'Shakespeare presents a compelling portrayal of both the use and abuse of power in the play *Macbeth*.' Discuss this statement, supporting your answer with reference to Act 4 Scene 3.

2. Disturbing imagery is used to powerful effect in Act 4 Scene 3. To what extent do you agree with this view? Support your answer with reference to the text.

Sample Paragraph 1 (Q1)

Macbeth really abused his power by killing Lady Macduff and her children, 'all my pretty ones'. Macduff is standing there, trying his best with Malcolm who says one thing one minute and something else the next and he is trying to figure this all out and then Ross tells Macduff 'the castle is surprised'. This is the worst abuse of power possible from Macbeth to kill innocent women and children. Malcolm just keeps saying get angry and kill Macbeth. At last Macduff pulls himself together and decides to oppose Macbeth. All of them have some power. But Macbeth abuses it. Malcolm also has some power and he is like Macbeth in this scene. We are left waiting to see who will win between them all. *(125 words)*

Examiner's Comment

- This basic response touches on aspects of power – its use and abuse.
- Confused comments about Malcolm contribute to the low grade.
- Note-like rambling narrative fails to address the task directly, however.
- Much of the language use is inappropriate and/or inaccurate.

Sample Paragraph 2 (Q1)

I thought the lists of faults which Malcolm said he had was good in making me think what a king should have. He said he was full of 'desire' and nothing could fill up the desire of his lust. He said he was greedy – 'avarice' – and wanted every nobleman's lands and wealth in Scotland. He said if he had 'power' he would create 'Uproar'. I thought then these are not the characteristics you would want in a king because this would lead to an abuse of power. Malcolm then listed the qualities he should have, 'temperance', 'mercy', 'patience', 'courage'. I thought these would be good in a proper king because then his country would be at peace and his people happy. The killing of Macduff's family also shows me how a tyrant has abused power. I thought this was an interesting way of looking at the abuse and use of power through lists. *(155 words)*

Examiner's Comment

- This mid-grade answer makes a reasonable attempt at examining how the use and abuse of power is treated in the scene.
- Some worthwhile illustration and use of reference showed engagement with the text.
- Uneven language control and over-use of 'I thought'.

Sample Paragraph 3 (Q1)

Through heart-rending descriptions of a country torn apart by an 'untitled' tyrant's rule, Shakespeare forces his audience to confront the shocking consequences of the abuse of power. Repetition emphasises the horror, 'each new morn/ New widows howl, new orphans cry, new sorrows/ Strike heaven'. Scotland, like an abused servant, 'sinks beneath the yoke'. 'Devilish Macbeth' rules for his own personal advancement, both in unlawfully grabbing power and seeking to retain it at any cost. The playwright then presents a stark contrast to this tyrannical rule in his portrait of 'gracious England'. King Edward cures rather than abuses his subjects, 'Such sanctity hath heaven given his hand'. When his people are 'All swoln and ulcerous', he 'solicits heaven', not the powers of darkness. Edward also spreads the 'sweet milk of concord' among his neighbours, lending 'Good Siward and ten thousand men' not to conquer, but to enable Malcolm to claim the throne as Duncan's rightful heir. Through this compelling juxtaposition of the 'good king' Edward with 'bloody-sceptred' Macbeth and the contrasting effects each has had on his own country, Shakespeare presents a powerful depiction of the use and abuse of power. *(190 words)*

Examiner's Comment

- This successful top-grade response addresses the question with great confidence.
- Informed discussion points contrast Edward with Macbeth.
- Accurate, detailed quotations support comments and show a close understanding of the play.
- Excellent expression – well-managed, varied vocabulary (e.g. 'confront the shocking consequences', 'compelling juxtaposition').

🙶 Key Quotes

Each new morn/ New widows howl, new orphans cry, new sorrows/ Strike heaven (Macduff to Malcolm) l.4–6	Macduff describes to Malcolm the horrendous state of Scotland to try to convince him to return and overthrow the tyrannical Macbeth. The repetition of the adjective 'new' underlines the routine atrocities that are occurring. Ironically, Macduff's family will be added to this terrible list.
I should cut off the nobles for their lands (Malcolm to Macduff) l.79	Malcolm is more astute than his father and is wary of trusting anyone. To test Macduff's patriotism, he declares that he has none of the 'king-becoming graces' and would confiscate the land and wealth of the Scottish thanes.
Fit to govern!/ No, not to live (Macduff to Malcolm) l.102–3	A disgusted Macduff shows his loyalty to his country by responding that Malcolm is unfit to be king. It has taken Macduff some time to express his principles, but now he is true to himself and shows his deep-rooted patriotism.
Your castle is surprised; your wife and babes/ Savagely slaughtered (Ross to Macduff) l.204–5	Ross has found it difficult to convey his devastating news to Macduff. The poignancy of the scene is almost unbearable. The tone is hesitant and hissing sibilant alliteration increases the tension.
Macbeth/ Is ripe for shaking, and the powers above/ Put on their instruments (Malcolm to Macduff and Ross) l.237–9	There is a renewed sense of urgency about the growing opposition to Macbeth. The strong rhythm and simple image from nature suggest that Macbeth can soon be toppled and order restored to Scotland. Even heaven is on the side of the forces for good. The scene ends on a purposeful note.

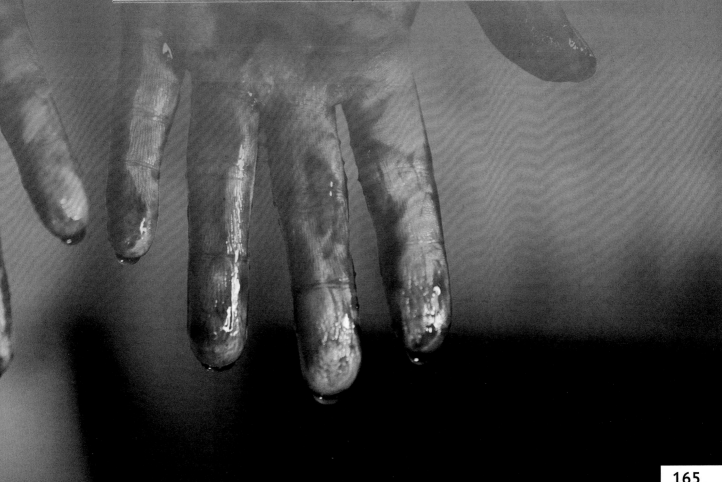

Key Points | Act 4

* Act 4 shows the depths of depravity to which Macbeth has sunk as well as the signs of an emerging challenge against him. His obsessive desire to secure his family's hold on the Scottish throne now leads him to rely on the reassurances of the witches, rather than his wife. A procession of equivocal apparitions serves both to embolden and enrage Macbeth.

* The opening scene of Act 4 is thrilling and spectacular. Macbeth is confronted by apparitions that appear to offer him security, yet tempt him to his downfall.

* Powerful visual effects and revolting details highlight the corruption of Macbeth's horrific world.

* Juxtaposed with this evil is a follow-up scene of human warmth and goodness.

* Such innocence is cruelly shattered by the hired assassins who slaughter Macduff's family. The playwright forces the audience to observe the reality of Macbeth's tyrannical reign, eroding any lingering sympathy for the former warrior.

* The genuine bravery of Macduff's wife and son is doomed to failure, leaving the audience in despair.

* Malcolm outlines the qualities required in a rightful king. The contrast between gracious and lawful kings (such as Duncan and Edward) and the malevolent Macbeth is stark.

* Act 4 once again highlights the protagonist's continuing moral descent. Corrupted by power, he is spiralling out of control. Yet the forces of good are determined to challenge this evil. Is there a possibility of hope?

Class/Homework Exercise

'Shakespeare makes effective use of dramatic contrasts between good and evil to reveal the character of Macbeth.'

In a short paragraph (150–200 words), discuss this statement, supporting your answer with reference to Act 4 of the play *Macbeth*.

OVERVIEW

An agitated Lady Macbeth is observed by a doctor and a lady-in-waiting. She sleepwalks and re-enacts fragmentary incidents from the murders of Duncan, Banquo and Lady Macduff, expressing guilt over her role in their deaths. She imagines blood on her hands and fears that nothing will ever wash it off. The doctor is shocked by her descent into madness and is concerned that she might harm herself.

Dunsinane. Macbeth's castle

Enter Doctor of Physic and Waiting-Gentlewoman

Doctor

I have two nights watched with you, but can perceive no truth in your report. When was it she last walked?

Gentlewoman

Since his majesty went into the field, I have seen her rise from her bed, throw her nightgown upon her, unlock her closet, take forth paper, fold it, write upon it, read it, afterwards seal it, and again return to bed; yet all this while in a most fast sleep. 5

Doctor

A great perturbation in nature, to receive at once the benefit of sleep and do the effects of watching. In this slumbery agitation, besides her walking and other actual performances, what, at any time, have you heard her say? 10

Gentlewoman

That, sir, which I will not report after her.

Doctor

You may to me, and 'tis most meet you should.

Gentlewoman

Neither to you nor any one, having no witness to confirm my speech. 15

Enter Lady Macbeth with a taper

Lo you, here she comes. This is her very guise; and, upon my life, fast asleep. Observe her. Stand close.

Doctor

How came she by that light?

Gentlewoman

Why, it stood by her: she has light by her continually, 'tis her command. → afraid of darkness 20

Doctor

You see, her eyes are open.

Gentlewoman

Ay, but their sense is shut.

Doctor

What is it she does now? Look how she rubs her hands.

Physic: *medicine*

1 perceive: *detect*

2 walked: *in her sleep*

3 field: *battlefield*

5 closet: *cabinet*

8 perturbation: *anxiety, disturbance*
9 effects of watching: *actions of being awake*

13 meet: *correct, suitable*

16 guise: *habit, conduct*

18 light: *candle*

22 their ... shut: *she can't actually see*

Gentlewoman

It is an accustomed action with her, to seem thus washing

25 her hands. I have known her continue in this a quarter of

an hour.

washing blood off her hands
→ guilt

Lady Macbeth

Yet here's a spot.

27 spot: *mark*

Doctor

Hark, she speaks! I will set down what comes from her, to

satisfy my remembrance the more strongly.

28 set down: *make a note*

29 satisfy: *assure*

Lady Macbeth

spot can remove from hands → her conscience.

30 Out, damned spot! Out, I say! One, two, why, then 'tis

time to do it. Hell is murky. Fie, my lord, fie! A soldier, and

afeard? What need we fear who knows it, when none can

nobody can go against

call our power to account? Yet who would have thought

the old man to have had so much blood in him?

31 murky: *dismal*

32 afeard: *afraid*

34 old man: *Duncan*

Doctor

35 Do you mark that?

Lady Macbeth

The Thane of Fife had a wife: where is she now? What, will

these hands ne'er be clean? No more o' that, my lord, no

more o' that: you mar all with this starting.

36 wife: *Lady Macduff*

38 mar all: *spoil everything*

Doctor

Go to, go to; you have known what you should not.

39 Go to: *come, come*

Gentlewoman

40 She has spoke what she should not, I am sure of that:

heaven knows what she has known.

Lady Macbeth

Here's the smell of the blood still: all the perfumes of

Arabia will not sweeten this little hand. Oh, oh, oh!

Doctor

What a sigh is there! The heart is sorely charged.

44 charged: *burdened*

Gentlewoman

45 I would not have such a heart in my bosom for the dignity

of the whole body.

45 dignity: *honour*

Doctor

Well, well, well.

Gentlewoman

Pray God it be, sir.

Doctor

not qualified in mental health.

This disease is beyond my practice. Yet I have known
those which have walked in their sleep who have died   50
holily in their beds.

Lady Macbeth

said to Macbeth when he killed Duncan

Wash your hands, put on your nightgown, look not so
pale. I tell you yet again, Banquo's buried; he cannot
come out on 's grave.

until this point → no confirmation of Banquo death

Doctor

Even so?   55

Lady Macbeth

To bed, to bed: there's knocking at the gate. Come, come,
come, come, give me your hand. What's done cannot be
undone. To bed, to bed, to bed.

Exit

Doctor

Will she go now to bed?

Gentlewoman

Directly.

Doctor

do something bad will be troubled by it

Foul whisperings are abroad. Unnatural deeds   60
Do breed unnatural troubles: infected minds
To their deaf pillows will discharge their secrets.
More needs she the divine than the physician.
God, God forgive us all! Look after her.   65
Remove from her the means of all annoyance,
And still keep eyes upon her. So, good night.
My mind she has mated, and amazed my sight.
I think, but dare not speak.

~ has figured it out but dare not speak as he will be killed

Gentlewoman

Good night, good doctor.   70

Exeunt

49   practice: *skill*

51   holily: *at peace*

52   Wash your hands: *advice given earlier to Macbeth*

61   Foul whisperings: *disgusting rumours*

63   discharge: *get rid of*

64   divine: *priest*

66   means of all annoyance: *instruments with which she might harm herself*

68   mated: *bewildered*

Study Notes

Unnatural deeds breed unnatural troubles (lines 1–70)

In this dramatic sleepwalking scene, Lady Macbeth has been reduced to a delirious state. Overwhelmed by the enormous guilt of the past, she is haunted by memories of her husband's murderous actions. The trauma of their shared complicity in killing the innocent king has finally unhinged her. She is obsessed with the imaginary spot of blood on her hands – an obvious metaphor for violence and shame.

The doctor describes her compulsive behaviour as a 'great perturbation in nature'. Her 'eyes are open' but 'their sense is shut'. She cannot bear the dark and keeps 'light by her continually'. Her obsessive nocturnal habits include fitful letter-writing – a reminder of the intimate correspondence between her husband and herself at the start of the play.

In contrast to her witchlike personality in earlier scenes, Lady Macbeth has emerged as a vulnerable character and this is particularly evident in her remorseful comment: 'The Thane of Fife had a wife: where is she now?' Her personal downfall anticipates the play's final tragic spectacle, evoking some degree of pity and fear in the audience.

Like so many others in Scotland, Lady Macbeth has been 'infected' by Macbeth's tyranny. The doctor admits that he cannot cure her, 'This disease is beyond my practice'. He advises the gentlewoman to 'Remove from her the means of all annoyance'. His concluding statement, 'I think but dare not speak', effectively sums up the dangerous state of the country.

Shakespeare's language

Shakespeare places his audience beside the doctor and gentlewoman as observers of one character's private hell. This allows us to truly experience the consequences of evil. The scene is written in **disjointed prose rather than verse**, in keeping with the disturbed, dreamlike atmosphere. As she sleepwalks, Lady Macbeth's language is fragmented and uneven. She speaks in short emphatic phrases, the staccato rhythm adding to the tension, 'Out, damned spot! Out, I say!'

Locked in her own damnation, Lady Macbeth's former role in life has been deleted. Now that she has been replaced by the witches, Macbeth no longer requires his wife's support. The running commentary of the doctor and gentlewoman compounds the **pathos and terror** of Lady Macbeth's disintegration, 'More needs she the divine than the physician'.

Echoing fragments of **irony** are found throughout this short scene. Lady Macbeth's incoherent recollections suggest that all the horrors the couple committed have become a great torrent of blood. The random, anguished references are out of sequence. In the aftermath of Duncan's murder, Lady Macbeth had presumed that 'a little water clears us of this deed'. Now she continually washes her hands. She had once relied on the evil powers of darkness, 'the dunnest smoke of hell', but this has all changed now and 'Hell is murky'. Poignantly, the final delusion for this broken woman is when she imagines that she is still alongside Macbeth, protecting and guiding him, 'come, give me your hand'. Shakespeare brings the audience into the abject terrors of spiritual darkness, the isolated soul's never-ending torment.

💬 Key Quotes

Here's the smell of the blood still; all the perfumes of Arabia will not sweeten this little hand (Lady Macbeth to herself) l.42–3	This harrowing statement emphasises how difficult it is to get rid of guilt. No matter what cosmetics are applied, the stench of evil seems to linger. The adjective 'little' adds a note of poignancy to Lady Macbeth's observation. Despite her earlier wishes, she has not been completely unsexed. Shakespeare's use of prose rather than the customary iambic pentameter heightens the effect of Lady Macbeth's mental disintegration.
Foul whisperings are abroad (Doctor to Gentlewoman) l.61	Under Macbeth's tyrannical regime, Scotland is rife with reports of heinous crimes. The onomatopoeic 'whisperings' effectively captures the spread of rumours in this dangerous environment where the king has paid spies watching everyone.
Unnatural deeds/ Do breed unnatural troubles (Doctor to Gentlewoman) l.61–2	Nature imagery is threaded through the play – often associated with the representatives of decency and goodness, such as Duncan. The Macbeths have performed unnatural deeds and so they are reaping the harvest of unnatural troubles, including the inability to sleep. Macbeth earlier declared that 'Glamis hath murdered sleep'. Ironically, his wife is now incapable of sleeping.

OVERVIEW

As more Scottish noblemen abandon Macbeth, the English army, led by Malcolm, Macduff and Siward, have assembled at Birnam Wood near Dunsinane Castle. Now that the forces of good are closing in on him, Macbeth is becoming increasingly isolated.

The countryside near Dunsinane

Enter with drums and colours, Menteith, Caithness, Angus, Lennox and Soldiers

Menteith

The English power is near, led on by Malcolm,

His uncle Siward, and the good Macduff.

Revenges burn in them; for their dear causes

Would to the bleeding and the grim alarm

Excite the mortified man. *— dead men would be seen so excited*

Angus

                    Near Birnam wood *→ prophecy → if woods moves Macbeth lose power.*

Shall we well meet them; that way are they coming.

Caithness

Who knows if Donalbain be with his brother?

Lennox

For certain, sir, he is not. I have a file

Of all the gentry: there is Siward's son,

And many unrough youths that even now   10

Protest their first of manhood.

Menteith

                    What does the tyrant? *→ Macbeth → on side of defeating him*

Caithness

Great Dunsinane he strongly fortifies. *→ preparing his castle.*

Some say he's mad; others that lesser hate him

Do call it valiant fury: but for certain

He cannot buckle his distempered cause   15

Within the belt of rule. *→ so corrupt, cant control own men.*

Angus

                    Now does he feel

His secret murders sticking on his hands; *→ blood drenched hands, ↳ Duncan Murder*

Now minutely revolts upbraid his faith-breach;

Those he commands move only in command, *→ dont love him just doing through fear.*

Nothing in love: now does he feel his title

Hang loose about him, like a giant's robe   20

Upon a dwarfish thief. *Noble Macbeth being described as dwarf thief.*

power greater, as a person less terrawy

Side glossary notes:

colours: *flags and banners*

1 power: *army*

3–5 for ... man: *their dedication would stir even the dead to battle*

8 file: *list*

10–11 unrough ... manhood: *many adolescents will show maturity*

11 the tyrant: *Macbeth*

14 valiant: *heroic*

16 buckle: *control*

17 sticking on: *clinging to*
18 minutely ... faith-breach: *small rebellions reveal his treachery*
19 in command: *when ordered*

20 title: *kingship*

Menteith

Who then shall blame

His pestered senses to recoil and start,

When all that is within him does condemn

Itself for being there?

Caithness

25   Well, march we on

To give obedience where 'tis truly owed:

Meet we the medicine of the sickly weal,

And with him pour we, in our country's purge,   *oath of alligiance*

Each drop of us.

Lennox

Or so much as it needs

30 To dew the sovereign flower and drown the weeds.

Make we our march towards Birnam.

Exeunt, marching

23 pestered: *traumatised*

27 medicine: *Malcolm's forces*
27 sickly weal: *diseased wound*
28 purge: *cleansing*

30 dew the sovereign flower: *encourage Malcolm*

Study Notes

An isolated king (lines 1–31)

This fast-moving scene depicts the mobilising of the armies opposed to Macbeth. As the preparations for battle gain momentum, four Scottish noblemen (Lennox, Menteith, Angus and Caithness) discuss the avenging 'English power' that is encamped nearby at Birnam Wood (mentioned earlier in the witches' prophecies). Most thanes have now abandoned Macbeth, who has lost control of the country. Meanwhile, mystery still surrounds the whereabouts of Donalbain, Malcolm's brother.

Conflicting opinions and rumours continue to circulate about Macbeth's volatile state of mind: 'Some say he's mad' while others call it 'valiant fury'. There is general agreement, however, that the 'tyrant' must be overthrown. Malcolm is now seen as Scotland's rightful king – the 'medicine' and 'sovereign flower' – who will ensure that the country recovers from its diseased state.

Shakespeare's language

The playwright makes striking use of **vivid clothing images** to highlight Macbeth's unsuitability for the position of king: 'now does he feel his title/ Hang loose about him, like a giant's robe/ Upon a dwarfish thief.' We are reminded of Macbeth's reaction when he first heard that he was to be Thane of Cawdor – and immediately compared it to being dressed in 'borrowed robes'. Now that the country is in chaos, Caithness sums up Macbeth's disastrous reign: 'He cannot buckle his distempered cause/ Within the belt of rule.'

Medical imagery describes how the gathering forces intend to make Scotland well again; Malcolm is the 'medicine of the sickly weal'. Using **images from nature**, Macbeth's enemies promise to shed blood, 'Each drop of us', to 'drown the weeds' and defeat the unlawful king. Their aim is to restore order in Scotland and establish the rightful king on the throne, 'dew the sovereign flower'. As the Scottish lords resolutely set out for Birnam Wood, the audience awaits the outcome of the final clash between the forces of good and evil.

🙶 Key Quotes

Near Birnam wood/ Shall we well meet them (Angus to Lords) l.5–6	In a shocking twist of fate, the forces of good are meeting close to Macbeth's castle. The witches had assured Macbeth that he was safe from defeat unless Birnam Wood 'shall come against him'. The audience must wait to see what will happen. Can a wood ever move? Macbeth did not believe it could.
Now does he feel/ His secret murders sticking on his hands (Angus to Lords) l.16–17	Macbeth's reign of terror is being revealed and the Scottish lords are determined to take their revenge. The onomatopoeic verb 'sticking' graphically describes how Macbeth (just like his wife) cannot escape guilt and responsibility.
like a giant's robe/ Upon a dwarfish thief (Angus to Lords) l.21–2	This vivid simile questions Macbeth's ability to be a fit monarch. His character does not have the 'king-becoming graces' to occupy the throne. He has never been the true heir to the Scottish crown.

OVERVIEW

Although Macbeth is under siege in Dunsinane Castle, he remains firmly convinced of his invincibility. Contemptuously, he dismisses a servant's news about thousands of enemy soldiers approaching and defiantly chooses to confront his opponents. The doctor informs him that Lady Macbeth is very ill, but says he is unable to treat her because her condition is purely mental, not physical.

1 fly all: *abandon me*

3 taint: *dishonour myself*
4-5 The spirits ... thus: *the apparitions who can see the future have assured me*

8 epicures: *pleasure-loving gluttons*

9 sway by: *am ruled by*

11 cream-faced loon: *white-faced fool*

12 goose: *foolish*

15 patch: *fearful fool*

16 linen: *pale*

17 whey-face: *pasty face*

20 push: *military advance*

21 disseat me: *lose me the throne*

23 fallen ... sere: *become withered*

Dunsinane. Macbeth's castle

Enter Macbeth, Doctor and Attendants

Macbeth

Bring me no more reports; let them fly all: *prophecies*

Till Birnam wood remove to Dunsinane

I cannot taint with fear. What's the boy Malcolm? — *prophacy*

Was he not born of woman? The spirits that know

All mortal consequences have pronounced me thus: *thinks he's* 5

'Fear not, Macbeth; no man that's born of woman *safe + invicible.*

Shall e'er have power upon thee.' Then fly, false thanes,

And mingle with the English epicures.

The mind I sway by and the heart I bear

Shall never sag with doubt nor shake with fear.   10

Enter a Servant

The devil damn thee black, thou cream-faced loon!

Where gott'st thou that goose look?

Servant

There is ten thousand −

Macbeth

                    Geese, villain?

Servant

                              Soldiers, sir.

Macbeth

Go prick thy face, and over-red thy fear,

Thou lily-livered boy. What soldiers, patch?   15

Death of thy soul, those linen cheeks of thine

Are counsellors to fear. What soldiers, whey-face? *Who are they.*

Servant

The English force, so please you.

Macbeth

Take thy face hence.

Exit Servant

                    Seyton! − I am sick at heart

When I behold − Seyton, I say! − This push   20

Will cheer me ever, or disseat me now.

I have lived long enough: my way of life

Is fallen into the sere, the yellow leaf;

[handwritten: fed up of this life]

And that which should accompany old age,
25 As honour, love, obedience, troops of friends,
I must not look to have; but, in their stead,
Curses, not loud but deep, mouth-honour, breath,
Which the poor heart would fain deny, and dare not.
Seyton!

Enter Seyton

Seyton

What's your gracious pleasure?

Macbeth

30   What news more? *[handwritten: asked for more news → worse]*

Seyton

All is confirmed, my lord, which was reported.

Macbeth

I'll fight till from my bones my flesh be hacked.
Give me my armour.

Seyton

                    'Tis not needed yet.

Macbeth

I'll put it on.
35 Send out more horses; skirr the country round;
[handwritten: tyrant] Hang those that talk of fear. Give me mine armour. – *[handwritten: Dying war]*
How does your patient, doctor? *[handwritten: Lady Macbeth]* *[handwritten: cares for his wife]*

Doctor

                    Not so sick, my lord,
As she is troubled with thick-coming fancies,
That keep her from her rest.

Macbeth

                    Cure her of that: *[handwritten: → can you not cure mental illness]*
40 Canst thou not minister to a mind diseased,
Pluck from the memory a rooted sorrow,
Raze out the written troubles of the brain,
And with some sweet oblivious antidote
Cleanse the stuffed bosom of that perilous stuff
Which weighs upon the heart?

Doctor

                              Therein the patient
45
Must minister to himself.

26 stead: *position*

28 fain deny: *prefer to reject*

32 hacked: *slashed*

35 skirr: *scour*

37 your patient: *Lady Macbeth*

38 thick-coming fancies: *numerous illusions*

40 minister to: *cure*

42 Raze ... brain: *erase her sad memories*

43 oblivious antidote: *drug to aid forgetfulness*

44-5 Cleanse ... heart: *cure her depression*

46 minister to himself: *self-help*

47 physic: *medicine*

50 dispatch: *hurry up*

52 pristine: *fresh*

55 senna: *medicinal plant*

58 it: *his armour*

59 bane: *murder*

62 Profit: *money*

Macbeth

Throw physic to the dogs; I'll none of it. –
Come, put mine armour on; give me my staff.
Seyton, send out. – Doctor, the thanes fly from me. –
Come, sir, dispatch. – If thou couldst, doctor, cast   50
The water of my land, find her disease,
And purge it to a sound and pristine health,
I would applaud thee to the very echo,
That should applaud again. – Pull't off, I say. –
What rhubarb, senna, or what purgative drug,   55
Would scour these English hence? Hear'st thou of them?

Doctor

Ay, my good lord; your royal preparation
Makes us hear something.

Macbeth

                          Bring it after me.
I will not be afraid of death and bane,
Till Birnam forest come to Dunsinane.   60

Exeunt all but Doctor

Doctor

Were I from Dunsinane away and clear,
Profit again should hardly draw me here.

Exit

As she is troubled with thick-coming
fancies,/ That keep her from her rest

Doctor, Act 5 Scene 3, l. 38-39

Study Notes

Contempt (lines 1–62)

This short, tense scene shows a defiant Macbeth repeating the 'assurances' of the witches to himself, 'Till Birnam wood remove to Dunsinane/ I cannot taint with fear.' He curtly dismisses the 'boy Malcolm' because he was 'born of woman'. His behaviour is highly erratic. A servant who brings news of the approaching army is treated with ridicule and scorn, 'lily-livered boy', 'whey-face'. Macbeth tells him to 'prick' his face and cover it with blood to hide his fear. Yet, ironically, there are signs of his own deep-seated anxiety in his repeated cries to Seyton.

As usual, Macbeth is fully aware of the truth of his desperate situation, 'this push/ Will cheer me ever, or disseat me now.' He is also conscious of how he has ruined his own life and paid such a terrible price for pursuing evil ambition. Macbeth has lost 'honour, love, obedience, troops of friends' in exchange for hatred ('Curses') and mere lip-service ('mouth-honour') from those who are afraid of him. He has become weary of his failed life, which has shrunk into the 'sere, the yellow leaf'. Nonetheless, a glimpse of the bold warrior of the early scenes emerges in his defiant declaration, 'I'll fight till from my bones my flesh be hacked.'

A doctor brings news of Lady Macbeth's growing insanity, 'thick-coming fancies'. Macbeth's reference to 'your patient' suggests that he himself is looking after his own patient, Scotland – and also thinking of how he might cure his country, 'cast/ The water of my land'. He longs for a 'purgative drug' to 'scour these English hence'. Having lost all faith in medicine, he repeats the witches' prophecies as he prepares for battle. The doctor, like the thanes, flees, vowing never to come to Dunsinane again, no matter what rewards are offered.

Shakespeare's language

Macbeth's lonely world is filled with tension as the avenging forces of good approach. His mood swings from bravado and brooding to disillusionment and determination. The unhappy king's ringing imperatives ('Bring me no more reports', 'fly, false thanes') are coupled with the abusive treatment of a hapless servant. The **ironic repetition** of the witches' prophecies increase the unsettling atmosphere. A poignant reflective note is introduced through the use of nature imagery, 'my way of life/ Is fallen into the sere, the yellow leaf'. The forlorn image of a leaf dropping from a tree in autumn is in keeping with the deeply despairing tone of Macbeth's short soliloquy.

Harsh-sounding **warlike verbs** heighten the violent mood, 'hacked', 'skirr', 'Raze'. Macbeth is not surrounded by loyalty or love but by 'Curses'. Shakespeare gives the audience a **visual representation** of Macbeth's inability to perform his role as king through his recurring agitation. Indecisive and fitful, he struggles to get into his body armour in an unconvincing attempt to lead his troops, 'put mine armour on', 'Pull't off, I say', 'Bring it after me'. In a state of near distraction, the former military hero – and the apprehensive audience – seems to understand that all is lost.

💬 Key Quotes

Bring me no more reports; let them fly all (Macbeth to attendants) l.1	Macbeth stubbornly refuses to hear any further updates about the approaching enemy army. Is his tone defiant or illogical? Or is he resigned to inevitable defeat? Might he even have a death wish? He also refuses to be daunted by the news that his thanes are deserting him.
I have lived long enough; my way of life/ Is fallen into the sere, the yellow leaf (Macbeth) l.22–3	One of Macbeth's better qualities is an ability to really see the truth of his situation – and to both acknowledge and articulate it. He knows that he has allowed ambition to destroy his life. Imagery from nature graphically depicts the wizened scraps of his life yellowed like an autumn leaf.
Pluck from the memory a rooted sorrow (Macbeth to Doctor) l.41	The deep breach in the relationship between Macbeth and his wife is evident in this scene. While he still cares for her, he no longer depends on her. Again using imagery from the world of nature, he urges the doctor to remove the hidden guilt that is driving Lady Macbeth insane.

Act 5
Scene 4

OVERVIEW

The joint English and Scottish armies meet at Birnam Wood. Malcolm orders them to cut down branches to camouflage their approach to Dunsinane.

Before Birnam Wood

Enter with drum and colours, Malcolm, Old Siward, Young Siward, Macduff, Menteith, Caithness, Angus, Lennox, Ross and Soldiers, marching

Malcolm

Cousins, I hope the days are near at hand

That chambers will be safe.

Menteith

We doubt it nothing.

Old Siward

What wood is this before us?

Menteith

The wood of Birnam.

Malcolm

Let every soldier hew him down a bough

And bear it before him. Thereby shall we shadow

The numbers of our host and make discovery

Err in report of us.

Soldiers

It shall be done.

Old Siward

We learn no other but the confident tyrant

Keeps still in Dunsinane, and will endure

Our setting down before it.

Malcolm

'Tis his main hope: 10

For where there is advantage to be given,

Both more and less have given him the revolt,

And none serve with him but constrainèd things

Whose hearts are absent too.

Macduff

Let our just censures

Attend the true event, and put we on   15

Industrious soldiership.

[margin notes]

2 chambers: *bedrooms*

2 We doubt it nothing: *we know it will happen*

4 hew: *cut*

5 shadow: *hide*

6 host: *army*

6–7 discovery ... us: *create a false report of our numbers*

10 setting down: *besieging*

12 have ... revolt: *have rebelled*

13 constrainèd things: *those forced to serve Macbeth*

14–15 Let our ... event: *let us judge later on*

[handwritten annotations]

→ soldier hold a branch of tree from woods to hide number of soldiers

ready for bloodshed / revenge

Old Siward

The time approaches

That will with due decision make us know

What we shall say we have, and what we owe.

Thoughts speculative their unsure hopes relate,

20 But certain issue strokes must arbitrate;

Towards which, advance the war.

Exeunt, marching

17 due decision: *result of the battle*

21 advance the war: *let us go and fight*

Study Notes

Trickery (lines 1–21)

This is the moment when the audience begins to understand that the witches' equivocal prophecies have all been malicious tricks. Malcolm's assured leadership contrasts sharply with Macbeth's disorganised behaviour in the previous scene. The woods of Birnam are coming to Dunsinane on Malcolm's orders, 'Let every soldier hew him down a bough/ And bear it before him'. His forces will create the illusion of a moving forest to confuse Macbeth about their numbers.

Yet again, Shakespeare emphasises Macbeth's isolation and the lack of loyalty among his troops, 'constrainèd things/ Whose hearts are absent'. The growing determination of his opponents – who 'put we on/ Industrious soldiership' – suggests that the end is near, raising the audience's hopes that perhaps, this time, the powers of good have a real chance of success.

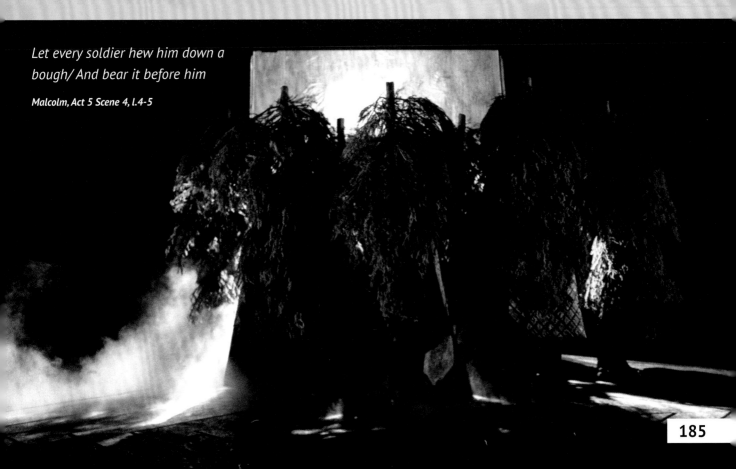

Let every soldier hew him down a bough/ And bear it before him

Malcolm, Act 5 Scene 4, l.4-5

❝❝ Key Quotes

Let every soldier hew him down a bough/ And bear it before him *(Malcolm to his army) l.4–5*	Malcolm shows himself to be a shrewd leader who knows that it is unwise to be completely open. It is good military strategy to have the element of surprise in battle. In an ironic twist of fate, he unknowingly proves the witches' promises to be untrue: 'Macbeth shall never vanquished be until/ Great Birnam wood to high Dunsinane hill/ Shall come against him.' Macbeth's reply was 'That will never be'.
And none serve with him but constrainèd things/ Whose hearts are absent too *(Malcolm) l.13–14*	The contrast between Malcolm and Macbeth is evident in their respective followers. Whereas Malcolm's supporters are fiercely loyal to Scotland's rightful heir, the tyrannical Macbeth has been deserted by all the thanes and now relies on mercenaries.

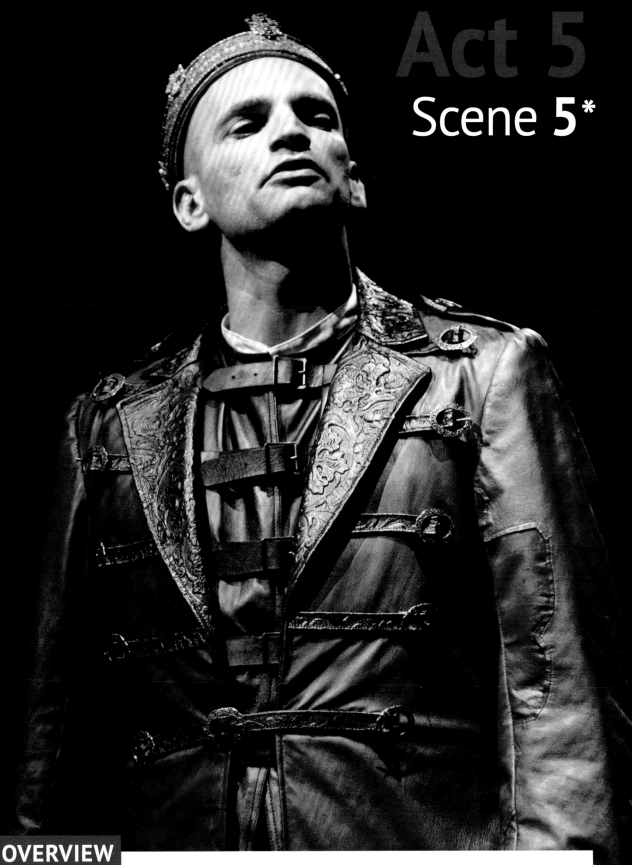

OVERVIEW

Fully armed and defiant, Macbeth prepares to fight to the death, still clinging to the witches' promises that his castle will withstand the enemy army. News is brought that Lady Macbeth has died, and he reflects on their unhappy lives. He also learns that Birnam Wood seems to be moving towards Dunsinane. Macbeth begins to wonder if the witches have tricked him, but remains determined to fight on.

* A key scene requiring close, detailed study

Dunsinane. Macbeth's castle

Enter, with drum and colours, Macbeth, Seyton and Soldiers

Macbeth

Hang out our banners on the outward walls.

The cry is still 'They come!' Our castle's strength

Will laugh a siege to scorn. Here let them lie

Till famine and the ague eat them up.

Were they not forced with those that should be ours,   5

We might have met them dareful, beard to beard,

And beat them backward home.

A cry of women within

What is that noise?

Seyton

It is the cry of women, my good lord.

Exit

Macbeth

I have almost forgot the taste of fears.

The time has been my senses would have cooled   10

To hear a night-shriek, and my fell of hair

Would at a dismal treatise rouse and stir

As life were in it. I have supped full with horrors;

Direness, familiar to my slaughterous thoughts

Cannot once start me.

Re-enter Seyton

Wherefore was that cry?   15

Seyton

The queen, my lord, is dead.

Macbeth

She should have died hereafter;

There would have been a time for such a word.

Tomorrow, and tomorrow, and tomorrow,

Creeps in this petty pace from day to day   20

To the last syllable of recorded time;

And all our yesterdays have lighted fools

The way to dusty death. Out, out, brief candle.

Life's but a walking shadow, a poor player

That struts and frets his hour upon the stage   25

---

2 cry: *battle cry*

3 scorn: *mockery*

4 ague: *sweating fever*

5 forced: *reinforced*

6 dareful: *defiantly*

10 my senses ... cooled: *I would have been afraid*

11 fell: *head*

12 treatise: *account, story*

13 horrors: *terrible deeds*

14 Direness: *appalling events*

15 start: *shock*

17 hereafter: *at a later time*

20 petty pace: *insignificant life*

21 syllable: *trace*

25 frets: *wastes*

And then is heard no more. It is a tale
Told by an idiot, full of sound and fury,
Signifying nothing.

Enter a Messenger

         Thou comest to use
Thy tongue: thy story quickly.

Messenger

          Gracious my lord,
30 I should report that which I say I saw,
But know not how to do it.

Macbeth

        Well, say, sir.

Messenger

As I did stand my watch upon the hill,
I looked toward Birnam, and anon, methought,
The wood began to move.

Macbeth

        Liar and slave!

Messenger

35 Let me endure your wrath if it be not so.
Within this three mile may you see it coming.
I say, a moving grove.

Macbeth

        If thou speak'st false,
Upon the next tree shalt thou hang alive,
Till famine cling thee. If thy speech be sooth,
40 I care not if thou dost for me as much. –
I pull in resolution, and begin
To doubt the equivocation of the fiend
That lies like truth: 'Fear not, till Birnam wood
Do come to Dunsinane'. And now a wood
45 Comes toward Dunsinane. – Arm, arm, and out! –
If this which he avouches does appear,
There is nor flying hence nor tarrying here.
I 'gin to be aweary of the sun,
And wish the estate of the world were now undone. –
50 Ring the alarum-bell! – Blow wind, come wrack,
At least we'll die with harness on our back.

Exeunt. Alarums

28 Signifying: *meaning*

30 should: *have to*

33 anon: *then*

37 grove: *copse, small wood*

39 sooth: *truth*

41 I pull in resolution: *I am less sure*
42 doubt ... fiend: *suspect the double-speak of evil spirits*

46 avouches: *asserts*

47 tarrying: *waiting*

48 'gin: *begin*

49 estate: *existence*

50 wrack: *destruction*

51 harness: *body armour*

Study Notes

Bold and poignant cries (lines 1–51)

Macbeth, still the resolute warrior at heart, prepares to defend his fortress, 'Our castle's strength/ Will laugh a siege to scorn'. An anguished cry rings out and Seyton announces, 'The queen, my lord, is dead'. In a distracted state, Macbeth reflects on the futility of life, but is interrupted by the news that Birnam Wood has begun to move. His anger turns to insecurity, 'I pull in resolution', and, for an instant, he wonders if the witches have lied to him, beginning 'To doubt the equivocation of the fiend'. However, he is soon moved to action, 'Arm, arm, and out!' Once again, the audience sees his physical bravery as he goes to confront his enemies on the battlefield – the only place where he is truly in his element, 'At least we'll die with harness on our back'.

Shakespeare's language

Macbeth's disdain for the approaching armies is expressed through **graphic personification**, 'Here let them lie/ Till famine and the ague eat them up'. The irony is that he himself is the one who has been devoured by his overwhelming appetite for power. Two compelling soliloquies remind us of former aspects of the heroic general. His earlier poetic imagination reasserts itself briefly at the news of his wife's death. Poignantly, he declares, 'She should have died hereafter'; at a later time, when he could have grieved for her properly, not now, when he is embattled by an approaching army.

The playwright uses effective **repetition**, **alliteration** and **onomatopoeia** to show how aware Macbeth is of his wasted life, 'Tomorrow, and tomorrow, and tomorrow,/ Creeps in this petty pace from day to day'. Vivid imagery captures the inevitable path to the end of life, 'all our yesterdays have lighted fools/ The way to dusty death'. The alliterative 'd' sound reminds the audience of the earth falling on the coffin and the inescapable finality of the grave.

A tragi-comic **metaphor** from the world of theatre illustrates how brief and inconsequential life actually is – of no more importance than an hour's performance on a stage where the 'poor player … struts and frets' and is heard of no more after the play ends. The audience is torn between disgust at Macbeth's destructive ambition and empathy for this tortured soul who realises that he has wasted such noble potential.

But his yearning for the end of life, 'I 'gin to be aweary of the sun', is still accompanied by an utter disregard for the destruction he has unleashed on his country through his unlawful accession, 'And wish the estate of the world were now undone'. The **jaded tone** conveys the utter disillusionment of a man who knows that he is doomed. With nothing left to lose, Macbeth makes his final choice to fight to the death.

Critical Analysis

1. 'Shakespeare presents a portrait of a powerful, multi-faceted leader in his dramatic tragedy *Macbeth*.' Discuss this view, supporting your answer with particular reference to the text of Act 5 Scene 5.

2. Throughout Act 5, Shakespeare uses a series of brief scenes that increase the tension of the imminent battle between the forces of good and evil. In your opinion, how successful are these short scenes in enhancing the audience's dramatic experience? Explain your response, supporting your answer with reference to the play.

Sample Paragraph 1 (Q1)

Macbeth is a strong leader. He is busy making his defences stronger in this scene, act five, scene 5 as he shows he doesn't care about anything, including Malcolm. He is also brave because even though his wife has just died hereafter he still goes out to battle Malcolm and Macduff's armies. He puts on his armour or 'harness'. He is very angry with the servants and lacking in basic discipline. A servant said he saw the army moving behind the trees that Malcolm had made them put in front of their faces so that it would keep Macbeth from knowing how many enemy soldiers there were. But Macbeth takes his anger out on the messenger in act 5, scene five, and says he will hang him on the 'next tree'. He now knows the witches were telling him lies but he still goes out to fight, 'Arm and arm'.
(150 words)

Examiner's Comment

- This basic response touches on some aspects of Macbeth's unstable character.
- Points lack clarity and cohesion, however, relying mainly on unfocused narrative.
- Answer is short of supportive references and quotation.
- Flawed language control – rambling sentences, note-like expression.

Sample Paragraph 2 (Q1)

This dramatic scene shows Macbeth's complex character. His domineering orders set the tone: 'Hang out our banners', 'Blow wind, come wrack'. Yet echoes of a more insecure man emerge in his confession, 'The time has been my senses would have cooled/ To hear a night shriek' and he admits: 'I have supped full with horrors'. But Shakespeare engages the audience's interest in this multi-layered character in his poetic outpouring after the news of his wife's death. He has always been unafraid to face reality, but now he brings the audience with him in confronting this uncomfortable truth – one day follows another, no matter what happens. Life means nothing to him. The onomatopoeic verb 'Creeps' evocatively expresses his weariness. His command, 'Out, out brief candle', shows his terrible apathy. However, a final glimpse of Macbeth's early bravery is contained in his statement, 'At least we'll die with harness on our back.' Shakespeare has presented us with a fascinating portrait of a strong leader, full of insecurity, possessing a poetic imagination, yet still capable of horrendous violence.
(175 words)

Examiner's Comment

- This successful paragraph shows close engagement with Macbeth's complex character.
- Clearly focused discussion on several characteristics – including his poetic imagination.
- Effective use of supportive references and apt quotations.
- Very good use of language and impressive vocabulary ('echoes of a more insecure man emerge', 'confronting this uncomfortable truth').
- Excellent concluding sentence rounds off this top-grade response.

🙶 Key Quotes

Our castle's strength/ Will laugh a siege to scorn (Macbeth) l.2–3	Personification is used to describe the defiant attitude of Macbeth to the approaching armies. The hissing sibilance adds to the menacing mood.
I have supped full with horrors (Macbeth) l.13	Macbeth has had his fill of horrendous acts. The audience is reminded of the litany of horrific murders in which he has been involved. But nothing can startle him anymore; he has become desensitised to evil.
Tomorrow, and tomorrow, and tomorrow,/ Creeps in this petty pace from day to day/ To the last syllable of recorded time (Macbeth) l.19–21	This poetic declaration of Macbeth's weariness with life is vividly caught in the personification of time loitering aimlessly from day to day. The alliterative phrase 'petty pace' adds to the sluggish rhythm of the line, emphasising the slow movement of time.
I pull in resolution, and begin/ To doubt the equivocation of the fiend/ That lies like truth (Macbeth) l.41–3	Macbeth doubts the witches' prophecies, giving hope to the audience that good might overcome evil. We are reminded of Banquo's warning that sometimes the powers of evil tempt us with truths 'And oftentimes, to win us to our harm'. Is it possible that Macbeth has been aware of his self-delusion all along?
Blow wind, come wrack,/ At least we'll die with harness on our back (Macbeth) l.50–1	Shakespeare concludes the scene on a defiant note. Macbeth is determined to fight, no matter what the outcome. This marks the re-emergence of the old Macbeth who excelled on the battlefield. But despite this final act of courage, is it likely that the audience will have any sympathy for him?

OVERVIEW

Outside Dunsinane Castle, Malcolm orders his troops to lay down the branches they had cut from Birnam Wood and reveal their true numbers to Macbeth. Siward and his son will lead the first charge; Malcolm and Macduff will follow.

Dunsinane. Before Macbeth's castle

Enter, with drum and colours, Malcolm, Old Siward,
Macduff and their army, with boughs

Malcolm

Now, near enough: your leafy screens throw down,
And show like those you are. – You, worthy uncle,
Shall, with my cousin, your right noble son,
Lead our first battle. Worthy Macduff and we
Shall take upon us what else remains to do,   5
According to our order.

Old Siward

                Fare you well.
Do we but find the tyrant's power tonight,
Let us be beaten, if we cannot fight.

Macduff

Make all our trumpets speak; give them all breath,
Those clamorous harbingers of blood and death.   10

Exeunt. Alarums

1 leafy screens: *cut branches*
2 show ... are: *disclose the scale of our numbers*
3 cousin: *young Siward*
4 first battle: *opening onslaught*

6 According to our order: *as we have planned*

7 tyrant's power: *Macbeth's forces*
8 Let ... fight: *we deserve to lose if we can't beat such an army*

10 clamorous harbingers: *deafening messengers*

Now, near enough: your leafy screens throw down,/ And show like those you are.

Malcolm, Act 5 Scene 6, l.1-2

Study Notes

A prophecy fulfilled (lines 1–10)

This brief scene shows Malcolm's competence as a military leader. When his soldiers approach Macbeth's castle, he orders them to discard their camouflage and reveal their true numbers, so as to unnerve Macbeth's army. Malcolm addresses Old Siward respectfully as his 'worthy uncle' and invites him to lead the first attack, while Macduff and he follow, 'According to our order.' Such reverence for Old Siward's seniority reflects the propriety shown in Malcolm's army, in contrast to the disorder within Macbeth's depleted forces.

Malcolm also unknowingly fulfils one of the witches' prophecies – 'Macbeth shall never vanquished be, until/ Great Birnam wood to high Dunsinane hill/ Shall come against him.' Macbeth took the witches' words at face value, believing that a tree cannot 'Unfix his earth-bound root'. In his haste to retain power, he did not take sufficient notice of the bearer of the message, 'a child crowned, with a tree in his hand'. The apprehensive audience now waits to see the outcome of the battle.

❝❝ Key Quotes

your leafy screens throw down,/ And show like those you are (Malcolm to soldiers) l.1–2	Malcolm shows himself to be a much more effective leader than his father. Unlike Duncan, he accompanies his army into battle and astutely uses the element of surprise against his enemy, Macbeth. His stratagem of camouflage also fulfils one of the witches' equivocal prophecies.

Act 5
Scene 7

The great battle between the forces of good and evil is under way. Macbeth is challenged by the courageous son of Siward while Macduff eagerly searches for the man who was responsible for the murder of his family. Although Macbeth is still reliant on the witches' predictions, his soldiers are soon forced to surrender.

Another part of the field

Alarums. Enter Macbeth

Macbeth

They have tied me to a stake; I cannot fly,
But, bear-like, I must fight the course. What's he
That was not born of woman? Such a one
Am I to fear, or none.

Enter Young Siward

Young Siward

What is thy name?

Macbeth

5   Thou'lt be afraid to hear it.

Young Siward

No; though thou callest thyself a hotter name
Than any is in hell.

Macbeth

                My name's Macbeth.

Young Siward

The devil himself could not pronounce a title
More hateful to mine ear.

Macbeth

                        No, nor more fearful.

Young Siward

10   Thou liest, abhorred tyrant; with my sword
I'll prove the lie thou speakest.

They fight; Young Siward is slain

Macbeth

                            Thou wast born of woman.
But swords I smile at, weapons laugh to scorn,
Brandished by man that's of a woman born.

Exit

Alarums. Enter Macduff

Macduff

That way the noise is. Tyrant, show thy face!
15   If thou be'st slain and with no stroke of mine,
My wife and children's ghosts will haunt me still.

2 course: *duration, an attack in bear-baiting*

6 hotter: *worse*

9 fearful: *alarming*

10 abhorred: *detested*

16 still: *always*

197

17 kerns: *mercenaries, hired soldiers*

18 staves: *spears*

20 undeeded: *unused*

21 clatter: *noise*

22 bruited: *reported*

24 gently rendered: *easily forced to surrender*

27 professes: *announces*

29 beside us: *on our side*

I cannot strike at wretched kerns, whose arms
Are hired to bear their staves: either thou, Macbeth,
Or else my sword with an unbattered edge
I sheathe again undeeded.

Alarums

                    There thou shouldst be;   20
By this great clatter, one of greatest note
Seems bruited. Let me find him, Fortune,
And more I beg not.

Exit. Alarums

Enter Malcolm and Old Siward

Old Siward

This way, my lord; the castle's gently rendered:
The tyrant's people on both sides do fight;   25
The noble thanes do bravely in the war;
The day almost itself professes yours,
And little is to do.

Malcolm

                We have met with foes
That strike beside us.

Old Siward

                Enter, sir, the castle.

Exeunt. Alarums

Study Notes

Foreshadowing doom (lines 1–29)

Macbeth realises that he is in jeopardy and has no choice but to face his enemies. He uses the vivid image of bear-baiting, comparing himself to a captured wild animal, frantic yet unable to move: 'They have tied me to a stake; I cannot fly.' All that he can do is await his fate. Shakespeare stirs the audience's emotions through Macbeth's repetition of one of the witches' prophecies, 'What's he/ That was not born of woman?' Young Siward challenges Macbeth, but is easily slain. This increases Macbeth's feelings of superiority that he cannot be hurt by weapons 'Brandished by man that's of a woman born'.

Ironically, the imposing figure of Macduff appears. Revenge must be his and his alone if he is to escape his deep feelings of guilt at having abandoned his family. Old Siward announces that Macbeth's castle has been 'gently rendered'. Even some of Macbeth's own soldiers are now fighting on Malcolm's side. The scene is set for the final confrontation between Macduff and Macbeth.

❝❝ Key Quotes

bear-like, I must fight the course (Macbeth) l.2	In this comment by Macbeth, an image of the brave warrior reasserts itself. Now that he is fully aware of the grave danger facing him, Macbeth refuses to surrender. He compares himself to a trapped bear at the mercy of wild dogs – and is more determined than ever to fight to the end.
Thou wast born of woman (Macbeth) l.11	To reassure himself, Macbeth clings desperately to reassurances given to him by the weird sisters. He has just killed Young Siward and feels buoyed up because he believes this vindicates the truth of the witches' prophecies.
Let me find him, Fortune,/ And more I beg not (Macduff) l.22–3	Macduff eagerly searches for Macbeth and prays that fate will let him find the tyrant so that he can avenge his family's slaughter. The tension increases as Shakespeare prepares the audience for the final confrontation between these two great enemies.

OVERVIEW

Macbeth and Macduff finally come face to face. At first, Macbeth is reluctant to engage in combat, but at Macduff's challenge, he boasts about how he can never be defeated. Macduff proves that the witches' prophecy is yet another trick when he reveals the details of his birth. Although greatly shaken, Macbeth vows to fight to the end.

Another part of the field

Enter Macbeth

Macbeth

suicide

Why should I play the Roman fool, and die

On mine own sword? Whiles I see lives, the gashes

Do better upon them.

Enter Macduff

Macduff

        Turn, hell-hound, turn!

Macbeth

Of all men else I have avoided thee:

5   But get thee back; my soul is too much charged

With blood of thine already.

Macduff

        I have no words:

My voice is in my sword, thou bloodier villain

Than terms can give thee out.

They fight

Macbeth

        Thou losest labour:

As easy mayst thou the intrenchant air

10   With thy keen sword impress as make me bleed.

Let fall thy blade on vulnerable crests;

I bear a charmèd life, which must not yield

To one of woman born. — *prophecy*

Macduff

        Despair thy charm;

And let the angel whom thou still hast served

15   Tell thee Macduff was from his mother's womb

Untimely ripped. — *aka caesarian → c-section*

Macbeth

Accursed be that tongue that tells me so,

For it hath cowed my better part of man.

And be these juggling fiends no more believed,

20   That palter with us in a double sense,

That keep the word of promise to our ear

And break it to our hope. I'll not fight with thee. — *old personality coming through*

1 play ... fool: *commit suicide*

2 lives: *living enemies*

4 men else: *other men*

5 charged: *guilt-ridden*

8 losest labour: *waste your efforts*

9 intrenchant: *immovable*

10 impress: *mark*

11 crests: *helmets*

12 charmèd: *enchanted*

13 Despair thy charm: *lose faith in your magic*

14 angel: *Satan*

16 Untimely ripped: *born by Caesarean section*

19 juggling fiends: *deceiving witches*

20 palter: *deal crookedly*

23 yield: *surrender*

24 gaze: *laughing stock*

26 Painted: *depicted*

29 baited … curse: *ridiculed by the common people*

31 opposed: *opposite me*

33 Lay on: *draw your sword and fight*

Macduff

Then yield thee, coward,

And live to be the show and gaze of the time:

We'll have thee, as our rarer monsters are,   25

Painted upon a pole, and underwrit,

'Here may you see the tyrant.'

Macbeth

                                   I will not yield   *[refuses to accept Malcolm as king]*

To kiss the ground before young Malcolm's feet,

And to be baited with the rabble's curse.

Though Birnam wood be come to Dunsinane,   30

And thou opposed, being of no woman born,

Yet I will try the last. Before my body   *[puts down shield, says kill me.]*

I throw my warlike shield. Lay on, Macduff,

And damned be him that first cries, 'Hold, enough!'

Exeunt, fighting. Alarums. Re-enter, fighting. Macbeth is slain. Exit Macduff

Study Notes

False promises exposed (lines 1–34)

Macbeth refuses to consider suicide to avoid being taken prisoner, asking, 'Why should I play the Roman fool'? He envisages no circumstances that involve recognising Malcolm as Scotland's king. When confronted by Macduff, he is initially reluctant to fight, confessing, 'my soul is too much charged/ With blood of thine already.' But the wronged husband and father, Macduff, can only focus on revenge, 'My voice is in my sword'.

Macbeth tells him that it is useless to engage in combat because 'I bear a charmèd life, which must not yield/ To one of woman born.' However, Macduff shatters Macbeth's self-delusion by informing him that he was born by Caesarean section ('from his mother's womb/ Untimely ripped'). On hearing the words, 'Despair thy charm', Macbeth realises that nothing can save him now.

Acknowledging that he has been duped by the witches ('these juggling fiends') shakes Macbeth's confidence. Yet he is still unwilling to face Macduff, 'I'll not fight with thee'. It is now Macduff's turn to mock his adversary: 'Then yield thee, coward'. He also threatens to have Macbeth publicly humiliated – 'baited with the rabble's curse'. His warning has the desired effect and Macbeth finally rises to the challenge, 'I will not yield/ To kiss the ground before young Malcolm's feet'.

Macbeth would prefer to die than lose his tyrannical hold on power. His final speech is resolute and defiant, echoing his earlier heroism on the battlefield. Even though he knows that all the witches' prophecies have been proven false, he raises his 'warlike shield', shouting 'damned be him that first cries, "Hold, enough!"' This inevitable contest between Macduff and Macbeth clearly symbolises the struggle between good and evil that has been central to the entire play. It will end with Macbeth's death and Macduff's triumph. The audience is likely to experience conflicting emotions – relief that good has triumphed mixed with sadness and regret at the wasted potential of 'Bellona's bridegroom'.

❝❝ Key Quotes

But get thee back; my soul is too much charged/ With blood of thine already (Macbeth to Macduff) l.5–6	Macbeth is carrying a heavy burden of guilt since ordering the slaughter of Macduff's family. He does not want Macduff's blood on his soul as well. Ironically, he still believes the witches' prophecy that he can defeat any man born of woman.
Macduff was from his mother's womb/ Untimely ripped (Macduff to Macbeth) l.15–16	Macbeth's faith in the witches is dealt a fatal blow when Macduff tells him that he was not born naturally, but by Caesarean section. This is yet another example of the double-speak of the equivocating witches, who have deceived him with false assurances.
be these juggling fiends no more believed (Macbeth) l.19	Ruefully, Macbeth now understands Banquo's former warning, that the witches use double-speak to destroy people. The adjective 'juggling' vividly conveys their malevolent trickery.
I will not yield/ To kiss the ground before young Malcolm's feet,/ And to be baited with the rabble's curse (Macbeth to Macduff) l.27–9	In his defiant final speech, Macbeth refuses to surrender his royal status – and particularly not to an inexperienced youth. He will never swear allegiance to the true heir, Malcolm, nor allow himself to become an object of ridicule by the common people.
Yet I will try the last (Macbeth to Macduff) l.32	Although all seems lost, Macbeth retains some of the pride that made him a hero on the battlefield. He will resist once more – even if it is for the last time. He intends to die as a soldier, leaving the audience admiring, at least, his physical bravery.

Act 5
Scene 9

OVERVIEW

Shakespeare's great tragedy reaches its natural conclusion. Malcolm and
Old Siward take stock of their victorious troops. Macduff displays Macbeth's
severed head and proclaims Malcolm as Scotland's rightful king. Malcolm
promises to reward all his noble supporters for their services and invites those
who have fought with him to attend his coronation at Scone. Order and justice
will be restored.

Inside Macbeth's castle

Retreat and flourish. Enter, with drum and colours, Malcolm, Old Siward, Ross, Thanes and Soldiers

Malcolm

I would the friends we miss were safe arrived.

Old Siward

Some must go off; and yet, by these I see,

So great a day as this is cheaply bought.

Malcolm

Macduff is missing, and your noble son.

Ross

5 Your son, my lord, has paid a soldier's debt.

He only lived but till he was a man, — barely an adult.

The which no sooner had his prowess confirmed

In the unshrinking station where he fought,

But like a man he died.

Old Siward

Then he is dead?

Ross

10 Ay, and brought off the field. Your cause of sorrow

Must not be measured by his worth, for then

It hath no end.

Old Siward

Had he his hurts before? — did he die like a man, fighting not running away

Ross

Ay, on the front.

Old Siward

Why then, God's soldier be he.

Had I as many sons as I have hairs,

15 I would not wish them to a fairer death;

And so, his knell is knolled.

Malcolm

He's worth more sorrow,

And that I'll spend for him.

Old Siward

He's worth no more;

1 we miss: *who are absent*

2 go off: *die*
2 these: *survivors*
3 cheaply bought: *won with few casualties*

5 soldier's debt: *death in battle*

7 prowess: *bravery*
8 unshrinking station: *unyielding manner*

12 Had ... before?: *Were his wounds on the front of his body?*

16 knell is knolled: *funeral bell is rung*

18 score: *debt*

20-21 where ... head: *where Macbeth's head is placed*
22 compassed ... pearl: *surrounded by noblemen*
23 salutation: *greeting*

27 reckon with: *reward*

30 more: *yet*

34 forth: *to face justice*
34 ministers: *supporters*

36 self: *herself*

38 grace of Grace: *God's blessing*
39 measure: *the proper*

They say he parted well, and paid his score,

And so God be with him. Here comes newer comfort.

Enter Macduff with Macbeth's head

Macduff

Hail, king, for so thou art. Behold, where stands   20

The usurper's cursèd head. The time is free.

I see thee compassed with thy kingdom's pearl,

That speak my salutation in their minds;

Whose voices I desire aloud with mine:

Hail, King of Scotland!

All

                    Hail, King of Scotland!   25

Flourish

Malcolm

We shall not spend a large expense of time   *reward*

Before we reckon with your several loves,

And make us even with you. My thanes and kinsmen,

Henceforth be earls, the first that ever Scotland

In such an honour named. What's more to do,   30

Which would be planted newly with the time,

As calling home our exiled friends abroad

That fled the snares of watchful tyranny;

Producing forth the cruel ministers

Of this dead butcher and his fiend-like queen,   *referring to Macbeth's*   35

– Who, as 'tis thought, by self and violent hands   *suicide.*

Took off her life – this, and what needful else

That calls upon us, by the grace of Grace,   *rhyming lines*

We will perform in measure, time and place.

So, thanks to all at once, and to each one,   40

Whom we invite to see us crowned at Scone.

Flourish. Exeunt

Study Notes

A gracious finale (lines 1–41)

This victorious scene is tinged with poignancy. Malcolm acknowledges the terrible reality of the struggle to overthrow evil, 'I would the friends we miss were safe arrived.' The seasoned warrior Old Siward regards this great day as 'cheaply bought', unaware that his son has paid the ultimate price. Young Siward's sacrifice is made even more tragic due to his age, 'He only lived but till he was a man'. However, his grieving father accepts that his son is 'God's soldier' now. The personal sacrifice of this heroic youth is sharply contrasted with the self-serving Macbeths.

Macduff appears, carrying Macbeth's decapitated head impaled on a staff. He is the first to greet Malcolm with his new title, 'King of Scotland'. In his acceptance speech, Malcolm echoes his chivalrous father, promising that those who fought bravely will be well rewarded. His thanes will be proclaimed, 'earls, the first that ever Scotland/ In such an honour named.' He also wishes to call home those who have fled the country in fear of Macbeth, reminding us particularly of his own brother, Donalbain.

The play ends with the promise of a new start for Scotland as Malcolm invites his supporters to come to Scone to see him crowned. The country's rightful king is now in place and the natural order has been restored. Despite the apparent peace, however, the audience might well wonder if Malcolm's power is truly secure. Is it possible that the cycle of blood-letting might begin again?

Shakespeare's language

Shakespeare fills the final act with several significant **contrasts**. The plain speech and lack of triumphalism in this concluding scene stand out against the poetic heights of previous occasions when the drama was much more intense. In the exhausted aftermath of battle, its calm atmosphere differs from the turmoil and tension of earlier scenes. The news that Young Siward has been killed in action characterises the subdued mood. Once again, true courage is distinguished from selfish ambition.

The killing of Macbeth takes place offstage, like so many other pivotal events in the play. This allows Shakespeare to explore the consequences of this crucial development. We have been left to imagine the ignominious deaths of the 'dead butcher and his fiend-like queen'. **Malcolm's timely epitaph** reminds us of Macbeth's bloody actions and Lady Macbeth's links to the spirits of darkness.

In his accession speech, Malcolm adopts the royal plural ('we'), establishing his status as Scotland's rightful king. His speech is gracious and humble, reminding the audience of his father. Is there already a sense that the old cycle of power and rebellion is starting again? Malcolm's 'What's more to do,/ Which would be planted newly with the time' echoes his father's metaphor when first addressing Macbeth. Such **nature imagery** has been associated with the forces of good throughout the play. For the moment, Macbeth's oppressive rule is over, 'the snare of watchful tyranny' has finished and 'The time is free'. Order is finally being established after the chaos which Macbeth and Lady Macbeth unleashed on 'bleeding' Scotland.

The final near-**rhyming couplets** ('Grace'/'place', 'one'/'Scone') mirror the serenity and calm which is now descending on the ruined land. For the moment, we are left reassured and satisfied that good has overcome evil. Yet this has been achieved at a great personal cost, particularly to Macduff and Old Siward. The tragic drama has reached its resolution.

Critical Analysis

1. 'Shakespeare's play *Macbeth* leaves audiences in no doubt that good overcomes evil.' Discuss this statement, supporting your answer with particular reference to Act 5 Scene 9.

2. 'Malcolm's closing speech in Act 5 Scene 9 is a model of astute political judgement after all the turmoil of Macbeth's reign.' Discuss this view, using suitable reference to the play.

Sample Paragraph 1 (Q1)

I really liked that Macbeth and his evil queen were defeated. I was sad that young Siward died. Old Siward could have been a lot more sorry for him. He was only concerned if his son had wounds on his front so that he didn't die running away. I thought he should of showed much more sympathy. Also, many other good characters have been killed in the war. So good isn't always the only winner. Malcolm is friendly and is a good king who is not another Macbeth. Which is a good thing for the Scotland population. He has overcome evil but there was a long time good while by which Macbeth ruled but he is now dead by beheading. Also, they say Malcolm is the good king now. Then they were all going to Scone to see him king. I think this is the right end to the play, with evil overcome by good. *(155 words)*

Examiner's Comment

- This very basic response takes a hit-and-miss approach to the question and only touches on the central issue.
- Random unfocused narrative fails to produce any coherent discussion.
- Lack of relevant reference or apt quotation.
- Language flaws throughout (e.g. 'should of showed', 'the Scotland population').

Sample Paragraph 2 (Q1)

The ending of the play, 'Macbeth', was very satisfactory. The 'dead butcher and his fiendish queen' were properly punished. Justice has been done. Macbeth was killed by Macduff, whose wife and children had been slaughtered by the 'tyrant'. Lady Macbeth committed suicide and was driven insane by guilt. Malcolm had been named by Duncan as his lawful successor and was deprived by the evil tyrant Macbeth of his rightful place. King of Scotland. The audience is left in no doubt. It was only right that the thanes of Scotland proclaimed him king at the end of the play. There has been a conflict and contrast over the whole play – good versus evil. The witches represent evil. Malcolm and Macduff represent good. The fight at the climax of the play is a symbol of which is the greater power. Good or evil. Macbeth 'the turncoat hellhound' is defeated, so bleeding Scotland is healed, so to speak. The proper king gains power. Good wins. End of story. *(165 words)*

Examiner's Comment

- This mid-grade answer makes a reasonable attempt at addressing the question.
- Includes several good basic points about the restoration of justice and a rightful king.
- Useful reference, overall, despite some misquotes ('fiendish queen', 'the turncoat hellhound').
- Some repetition and note-like expression.

Sample Paragraph 3 (Q1)

After all the chaos and destruction, good finally overcomes evil in the play's final scene and order is restored, 'The time is free'. But is it as simple as that? Where is Donalbain, the brother of Malcolm? Will there be another challenge to the new king? I felt a sense of anti-climax at the end. The vigour and strength of the 'dead butcher and his fiend-like queen' have disappeared – but their replacement seems lacklustre. Malcolm intends to proceed 'in measure, time and place'. Yet, for me, although he is gracious, like his father, he seems uninspiring. If good has truly overcome evil, then it has been at a terrible cost – in terms of innocent lives and political upheaval. Scotland has suffered from various conflicts right throughout the story. Macbeth was certainly an appalling tyrant, but it could be argued that Duncan was also a political failure who failed to unite Scotland and maintain order. I believe that Malcolm is likely to be challenged as well – if not by his brother, then by some other ambitious thane. This is why I felt a slight apprehension at the end – and unconvinced that the victory of good over evil will last long. *(200 words)*

Examiner's Comment

* Lively and thought-provoking discursive response that challenges the question effectively.

* Close engagement with the play; discussion aptly supported by reference to events.

* Central point about the continuing power struggle was well developed.

* Clear confident expression (e.g. 'I felt a sense of anti-climax', 'replacement seems lacklustre'). Top-grade standard.

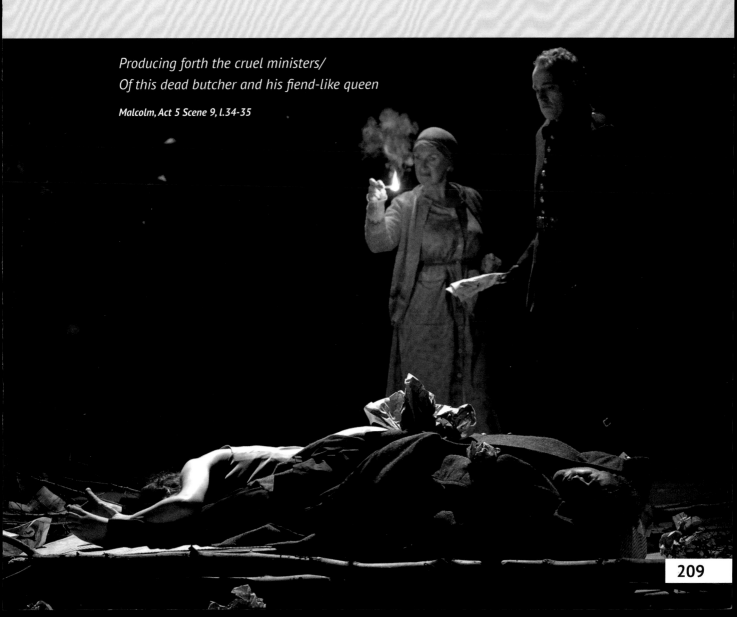

Producing forth the cruel ministers/
Of this dead butcher and his fiend-like queen

Malcolm, Act 5 Scene 9, l.34-35

Key Quotes

So great a day as this is cheaply bought *(Old Siward to Malcolm) l.3*	Old Siward's ironic comment that the battle has been won with few casualties becomes much more poignant when he learns of his young son's heroic death on the battlefield. It is a traumatic reminder that any conflict between good and evil is achieved through personal sacrifice and individual sorrow.
The time is free *(Macduff) l.21*	Macduff has good reason to acknowledge that Scotland is well rid of Macbeth. On a personal level, he has avenged his slaughtered family and also ended the tyrant's rule. People will no longer be oppressed now that order has been restored.
this dead butcher and his fiend-like queen *(Malcolm) l.35*	This reference highlights Macbeth's horrendous reign of terror and bloodshed (the murders of Duncan, the bodyguards, Banquo, Macduff's entire household). The adjective 'fiend-like' recalls Lady Macbeth's chilling speech when she invited the spirits of darkness to fill her from 'the crown to the toe top-full/ Of direst cruelty'.
So, thanks ... to each one,/ Whom we invite to see us crowned at Scone *(Malcolm) l.40–1*	Malcolm's gracious, inclusive tone reflects his efforts to restore harmony to his troubled country. This is what Malcolm hopes will be the hallmark of his reign. Is the audience equally hopeful? Or will it just be a matter of time before there is another power struggle to seize the Scottish throne?

Key Points | Act 5

- In Act 5, we are presented with the resolution of the drama. Through a fast-moving sequence of nine brief scenes, the monumental clash between the forces of good and evil moves towards its inevitable conclusion. The rightful heir, Malcolm, is reinstated and order is restored once more to the kingdom of Scotland.

- 'Bloody instructions' have returned to 'plague the inventor'. Lady Macbeth's once invincible façade crumbles beneath the weight of accumulated guilt and her estrangement from her husband.

- Macbeth's realisation of what he has lost and his weary view of life as 'a tale told by an idiot' highlights his utter despair. The tragic hero learns that actions do have consequences. Once unified in their shared 'vaulting ambition', Macbeth and his wife are now isolated in their own private hells.

- In contrast to Macbeth's nihilism, the forces of good have a more positive view of life and a Christian vision of redemption. They see themselves as instruments of a benevolent force.

- Macbeth's death takes place offstage, like so many of the significant events of the play. This increases the tension, allowing the audience to consider the consequences of the killing rather than the event itself.

- Health and disease are powerful symbols of good and evil throughout Act 5.

- Malcolm's description of Macbeth as a 'butcher' is understandable, but dismisses the protagonist's tragic heroism.

- Violated nature repairs itself through the visual spectacle of Birnam Wood coming to Dunsinane. The balance of power in the state and in nature is finally restored.

Class/Homework Exercise

'Shakespeare makes effective use of striking imagery (light and darkness, medicine and disease, natural and unnatural events) to highlight the restoration of order at the end of the play.'

In a short paragraph (150–200 words), discuss this statement, supporting your answer with reference to Act 5 of the play *Macbeth*.

Characterisation

Macbeth

First Impressions

courageous   manly heroic   patriotic   ambitious sensitive   imaginative

'Yet do I fear thy nature' (Act 1 Scene 5, l.15)

- Macbeth is mentioned at the start of the play when the witches speak about their plans to meet with him. We know at once that **something suspicious or evil will happen** involving Macbeth. Their hypnotic chant, 'Fair is foul, and foul is fair', suggests a central theme for the drama: good and evil may not be what they seem. The witches clearly represent the forces of evil, however, and their association with Macbeth raises a crucial question: will he become a victim of their destructive supernatural power? From the outset, Shakespeare presents the play's protagonist in a manner that makes him ambiguous.

- Our initial impressions of Macbeth are also based on the Captain's report of his extraordinary courage in battle. He is filled with admiration for 'brave Macbeth – well he deserves that name'. In his description of Macbeth's heroic actions, the Captain highlights images of bloodshed that suggest **a sadistic side** to Macbeth's behaviour. Is he a soldier who actually takes pleasure in killing his enemies? We learn that when he confronted the rebellious Macdonwald, 'he unseamed him from the nave to th' chops'. Was such a gruesome slaughter necessary – even in the heat of battle?

> *'Macbeth is somebody who is very fractured from the beginning.'*
> ***Michael Fassbender***

- The gory murders that will soon fill the play are foreshadowed by the bloody victory of the Scottish forces over their opponents. For the moment, however, Macbeth has led his army in defeating the king's foes. **Duncan is grateful for such loyalty** and salutes him as a 'valiant cousin, worthy gentlemen' – an acknowledgement that is in stark contrast to the previous scene's association of Macbeth with the witches. The Thane of Ross brings further news of Macbeth's heroism on the battlefield in the victory over the Norwegian invaders. His **lavish praise** of 'Bellona's bridegroom' prompts the king to reward Macbeth with the newly vacant position of Thane of Cawdor.

- When Macbeth first appears on stage, **his opening words ironically echo the witches**: 'So foul and fair a day I have not seen'. The weird sisters inform him that he will become the new Thane of Cawdor and also the next king of Scotland. Unlike Banquo (who is told that his descendants will be future kings), Macbeth reacts to the witches' words with surprise, followed by spellbound silence.

- Lady Macbeth provides interesting insights into her husband's character. She acknowledges that he is highly ambitious, but she fears the way in which, whatever Macbeth desires, he wants to have it 'holily'. In her pragmatic view, he is 'too full o' the milk of human kindness'. Lady Macbeth is well aware of her husband's weaknesses, and taunts him with accusations of cowardice, irresolution and lack of manliness. Her influence at this crucial stage reveals that Macbeth can be **easily manipulated**.

- Although the audience might see him as a victim of his witch-like wife, there can be little or no sympathy for Macbeth's moral weakness.

'I dare do all that may become a man'

'I dare do all that may become a man'

His confused mental state is evident in the early soliloquies, when he repeatedly considers the implications of killing the king, Caught between evil ambition and a deep-rooted sense of honour, Macbeth reluctantly acts. Despite his better judgement, he **chooses to do something that he knows is wrong**.

- His guilty conscience emerges in the immediate aftermath of the horrific murder. Macbeth is tormented by shame and terrified by his **deep sense of depravity**. He knows that he will always have to live with the moral choice he made to kill the old king. Even though he had little enthusiasm for the assassination, there is no denying the truth. Duncan was not murdered by either Lady Macbeth or the witches. Filled with remorse, Macbeth imagines that he will never rest peacefully again: 'Methought I heard a voice cry "Sleep no more!"'. His guilt can never be erased: 'Will all great Neptune's ocean wash this blood/ Clean from my hand?'

Character Development

volatile	fearful	delusional
complex	indecisive	weak

'Something wicked this way comes' (Act 4 Scene 1, l.45)

- Having chosen to rule the country by violence and intimidation, Macbeth's actions become increasingly callous. Anguished and paranoid, he admits that his mind is 'full of scorpions'. He even envies Duncan, who now sleeps peacefully in his grave. **Macbeth's degeneration is also seen in the collapse of his marital relationship**. Following the banquet scene in Act 3, it is clear that he is becoming estranged from his wife, speaking only of what must be done for 'mine own good'. The marriage is all but over and we never see the couple together again. Instead, Macbeth relies more and more on the witches.

- Throughout his time as king, Macbeth resorts to the routine abuse of power. He has spies everywhere. **No longer troubled by his conscience**, he pays hired assassins to murder Banquo and his son, Fleance, in a failed attempt to prevent Banquo's heirs becoming kings. Taking heed of the witches' advice to 'be bloody, bold and resolute', he is responsible for the greatest atrocity in the play. Unable to find

Macduff, he orders that everyone in his enemy's household is to be massacred – a vengeful bloodbath that appals audiences. All of Scotland now suffers under Macbeth's tyranny.

- With his corrupt kingship immersed in deceit and unspeakable evil, the unhappy king is becoming increasingly isolated. At this stage, there is a clear sense that **Macbeth knows he is doomed** – and the audience might possibly have some sympathy for him. He has exchanged his former popularity and self-respect for a powerful royal position – but it has brought him no peace of mind. Haunted by insecurity, he seeks out the witches in the hope of discovering what the future holds for him. Through apparitions and ambiguous promises, they assure him that he will never be defeated.

Final View

evil	tyrannical	
philosophical	poetic	isolated
tragic	defiant	

'a charmed life' (Act 5 Scene 8, l.12)

- As his **moral decline** continues, Macbeth is irritated by news that Malcolm's avenging forces have come to Dunsinane, but he still chooses to believe the witches' assurances and refuses to be afraid.

- Macbeth has become a victim of the disordered world he himself created and from which he cannot escape: 'Methought I heard a voice cry, "Sleep no more!"' He is worn out with bloodshed and dismay: 'I have supped full with horrors'. For him, **terror has slowly degenerated into tedium** – and all that remains is death.

- Intensely aware that he has forfeited his nobility and will never even have the respect that normally accompanies old age, Macbeth is no longer capable of caring. His wife's suicide makes little impact on him. Lady Macbeth's death does not strike him so much with grief but rather unleashes his **disenchantment**. He bitterly reflects that life is 'a tale/ Told by an idiot, full of sound and fury,/ Signifying nothing'. Considering the Christian world of the play, this is a shocking expression of his despair and atheism.

- In their final confrontation, Macbeth initially refuses to fight Macduff because he is already too guilt-stricken about the deaths of his innocent family. The moment offers a brief glimpse of Macbeth's former moral consciousness. It also marks the end of his self-delusion (his so-called 'charmed life') when Macduff reveals the truth about his Caesarean birth. The disintegration of Macbeth's world is now complete. Only when Macduff threatens to tie him to a pole and make a public spectacle of him does Macbeth engage in combat. His **final words are characteristically defiant**: 'I will not yield/ To kiss the ground before young Malcolm's feet'.

- In the end, Macbeth suffers the consequences of his horrendous treachery, but he still dies like a brave soldier. Moral weakness has always been at the core of his **tragic downfall**. As a soldier, his courage has never really been in doubt. Away from the battlefield, however, he has few redeeming features and is flawed by an inability to reject evil. Macbeth is one of Shakespeare's most intense and multi-faceted characters. Whether or not he is a true tragic hero remains open to question.

> 'When you think of violent murders, brutal crimes, nightmarish horrors, you might think of a big city, or if you're like me, you might think of a 400-year-old play named Macbeth.'
>
> *Ethan Hawke*

Macbeth's Dramatic Role

- Shakespeare presents Macbeth's **changing character** primarily through powerful soliloquies. For the audience, of course, Macbeth is always the tragic focus of attention. He speaks almost one-third of the lines of the play. Originally a faithful and respected man, his descent into betrayal is the tale of how warped ambition can tarnish any individual. Driven by loyalty to Duncan, his own 'Vaulting ambition'

leads to him killing the ageing king to secure his own destiny. The 'dead butcher' at the end of the play is barely recognisable as the noble Macbeth we hear about at the beginning.

- Macbeth is a tragic figure because of the combination of good and evil in his character. He does some appalling things, yet his conscience and imagination trouble and punish him. His guilt is revealed through subconscious imaginings and visions. Macbeth's **vivid imagination** is obvious from his first encounter with the witches when he visualises murdering Duncan. Later, he imagines the creatures of evil, 'night's black agents', gathering in the darkness as Banquo's murder is imminent.

- Much of the drama takes place within the protagonist's haunted mind. Before the first murder, he struggles with good and evil, sometimes thinking that his fate is decided by sinister forces beyond his control. In the final scenes, Macbeth is alone and almost deranged, clinging to the security of the witches' twisted promises. His wife is driven mad with guilt, but he is so detached from her that he feels nothing. While audiences can sympathise with a man who is tempted by his own natural weakness, they might also see Macbeth as **reaping what he has sown**.

- However, there is a moment when Shakespeare's words remind us of Macbeth's awareness of how futile his life has been. Just after his wife's tragic death, he realises that he has been tricked by the witches when he sees the trees of Birnam Wood appear to move, and for a moment it is possible to feel sorry for a man who is so completely unhappy and whose 'way of life/ Is fallen into the sere, the yellow leaf'. For the audience, Macbeth's **moral decay** and ruinous journey into evil is at an end – and it has been both horrifying and engrossing.

❝❝ Macbeth – Key Quotes

I have no spur/ To prick the sides of my intent, but only/ Vaulting ambition, which o'erleaps itself/ And falls on the other (Macbeth) Act 1 Scene 7, l.25–8	**Macbeth is a reluctant murderer. From a logical perspective, he can find no good reason to justify the horrendous murder of Scotland's rightful king. At this early stage, he has been tempted by power, but has not yet given in to his black and deep desires.**

Will all great Neptune's ocean wash this blood/ Clean from my hand? (Macbeth after the murder of Duncan) Act 2 Scene 2, l.58–9	The exaggerated language demonstrates the heightened extent of Macbeth's guilt. Ironically, as his moral decline takes hold, he will soon feel no remorse for the murders of Banquo and Macduff's family.
Thou hast it now: king, Cawdor, Glamis, all/ As the weird women promised; and I fear/ Thou played'st most foully for it (Banquo on Macbeth) Act 3 Scene 1, l.1–3	Banquo and Macbeth were both tempted by the witches – but their contrasting responses reflect their distinctive moral characters. The comment traces Macbeth's downfall resulting from his evil ambition to gain his ill-gotten power.
This tyrant, whose sole name blisters our tongues (Malcolm) Act 4 Scene 3, l.12	Scotland has suffered a dire fate under Macbeth's evil reign. His kingship is now widely associated with tyranny, violence and corruption. Macbeth is universally seen as a terrible disease that is destroying the entire country.
Out, out, brief candle./ Life's but a walking shadow (Macbeth) Act 5 Scene 5, l.23	Macbeth's utter despair is summed up in this nihilistic view of his wasted life. His personal tragedy is the horrifying awareness that he has made a catastrophic moral choice, destroying the better part of himself. His poignant words are bitter and disappointed.

Macbeth: the Tragic Hero

In ancient Greek drama, a **tragic hero** was someone of noble birth who made a serious error of judgement or had a personality flaw that brought about great suffering and his eventual downfall.

In Shakespeare's plays, tragic heroes are powerful and admired figures, occupying positions of importance in society. Their **character weaknesses** (frequently combining excessive pride, moral blindness and self-deception) lead to obsessive behaviour.

The hero himself is responsible for initiating a course of action that unleashes forces beyond his control. As a result, his emotional distress affects the welfare of the entire nation. Everyone is drawn into the turmoil as **order descends into chaos**.

Through the process of suffering, the tragic hero usually learns to recognise his faults and to take responsibility for his actions. Unfortunately, this **self-knowledge** comes too late to save him.

Tragedy should arouse strong emotions of pity and fear, but leave the audience with a **sense of release** at the end. In *Macbeth*, however, the play's final scenes are so distressing that there is little sense of catharsis or relief.

Nevertheless, *Macbeth* is one of Shakespeare's most powerful dramas. The central tragedy lies in the demise of a man **capable of great heroism** and nobility, but whose self-destructive personality is deeply flawed.

Class/Homework Exercise

At the end of the play, Malcolm describes Macbeth as 'this dead butcher'. To what extent do you agree with this assessment of Macbeth's character? Write a paragraph (150–200 words), supporting your answer with suitable reference to the play.

Prompt!
- Does Shakespeare present Macbeth as a villain without any good qualities?
- Is Macbeth a killing machine or is he a much more complex character?
- Is Macbeth the plaything of a much greater supernatural evil?
- Does his poetic language suggest that he is a tragic figure?
- Is Macbeth physically brave but morally weak?

Lady Macbeth

First Impressions

strong   ambitious   ruthless
false   unnatural
manipulative   focused

'direst cruelty' (Act 1 Scene 5, l.42)

- Lady Macbeth is one of Shakespeare's most powerful female characters. At the start of the play, she is much more **ambitious and determined** than her husband. Unlike Macbeth, she needs no supernatural temptations to urge her on. Her first appearance alone on stage means that we are given direct access to her innermost thoughts. While reading her husband's letter about encountering the witches, she immediately decides on the course of action that they will pursue, never doubting that Macbeth 'shalt be/ What thou art promised'. Her words are filled with the imagery of darkness and death, creating a strong verbal association between herself and her husband.

- All through the play's early stages, Lady Macbeth is the dominant partner in the marriage. She is fully aware of the influence she has on her weak-willed 'partner in greatness' and she is supremely confident of overcoming every obstacle 'that impedes [him] from the golden round'. **Unscrupulous and single-minded**, she greets Macbeth fervently, showing that her plans for him had already been formed: 'Great Glamis! Worthy Cawdor!/ Greater than both, by the all-hail hereafter.'

- Obsessed by the thought of becoming the next queen of Scotland, she does not reflect on conscience. Royal status offers her everything she wishes for: greatness and glory, 'sovereign sway and masterdom'. Lady Macbeth chooses evil without equivocation, viewing her husband's 'human kindness' as a shameful failing. Whereas Macbeth did not seek out the witches directly, his wife urges evil spirits to 'unsex' her. Eager to remove any trace of feeling that might weaken her resolve, she is **fully prepared to sacrifice her natural femininity** to pursue her passion for power and social position.

- Macbeth is completely overwhelmed by her manipulative character. Knowing his weaknesses better than anyone, she flatters her husband at first and then taunts him about his masculinity, accusing him of cowardice. Lady Macbeth even goes as far as to question his love for her. Because their relationship is so intense, this personal insult affects Macbeth deeply. She **arouses horror** and revulsion when she cold-bloodedly states that she would kill her own child rather than break a promise.

> *'She had no illusions about the evil she was embracing, but the thrill of it drew her back.'*
>
> **Judi Dench**

- When she tells her husband to 'Leave all the rest to me', Lady Macbeth is convinced that by deceit and cunning, she herself could organise and carry out Duncan's murder, so that no suspicion would rest upon either Macbeth or herself. When she welcomes the unsuspecting king to their castle – offering him 'All our service' – her conduct shows that she is a natural liar and hypocrite. In the aftermath of the killing, Lady Macbeth's self-control is unwavering.

- She remains **calm and focused** despite her husband's panic. Macbeth is terror-stricken when he returns from the crime scene, but she does everything possible to ease his fears. On discovering that he has forgotten to smear the grooms with blood, and that he has brought the daggers from Duncan's chamber, she urges him to go back and carry out the unfinished details of the plot. His refusal leads to a heated exchange and she accuses him of being cowardly, 'Infirm of purpose!'

- Her sharp insults no longer have the desired effect, however, and she is forced to carry out the fearful task herself. On her return, she again exhibits **remarkable self-possession**. While the knocking is going on at the castle gate, she persuades Macbeth to retire to his chamber. In a rare moment of humanity, she claims that she herself would have been prepared to kill the old man – 'had he not resembled [her] father as he slept'. Her fainting spell during the confusion following the discovery of Duncan's body is unexpected. Whether it is genuine or not, it succeeds in distracting attention from Macbeth.

Character Development

loyal	unscrupulous	worldly
composed	pragmatic	isolated

'Nought's had, all's spent' (Act 3 Scene 2, l.6)

- It could be argued that what really destroys Lady Macbeth is her sense of increasing **estrangement within her marriage**. By Act 3, it is evident that she is losing influence over her volatile husband: 'How now, my lord! Why do you keep alone …?' Finding no satisfaction or peace of mind in her new role as queen, she is distressed by the way Macbeth's personality has been transformed. He has become secretive and paranoid, no longer confiding in her – in particular about his plans to have Banquo and Fleance murdered. As he grows more and more independent, he no longer relies on her support. Indeed, the couple's roles have become reversed and Lady Macbeth is increasingly marginalised, reduced to asking her husband, 'What's to be done?'

- During the banquet scene, she is helplessly unaware of what is happening, but remains **completely loyal** to her distraught husband. It soon becomes clear that neither her desperate appeals to Macbeth's remaining sense of reason nor scathing insults about his masculinity are having any effect. As the couple struggle to communicate, all she can suggest is that Macbeth should rest: 'You lack the season of all natures, sleep'. These are the last words she ever speaks to him.

Final View

delusional	remorseful	pitiful
traumatised	tragic	vulnerable

'fiend-like queen' (Act 5 Scene 9, l.35)

- By Act 5, Lady Macbeth has been reduced to a **pitiful figure** who is terrified of the dark. She sleepwalks, continuously tries to wash away imaginary blood from her hands, and talks in her sleep of murder. Consumed by the repressed guilt of her evil past, she withdraws into herself, re-enacts the earlier murders and eventually loses her mind. The doctor caring for her can do nothing for her 'disease'.

- Her incoherent words (''tis time to do it. Hell is murky') reflect a combination of desperate remorse with an awareness that she is hopelessly **tormented**. The relationship between Lady Macbeth and her husband has been mutually destructive, ending in her tragic death.

> 'She finally loses herself, and once she's lost him, I feel as though she can't live anymore.'
> **Samantha Spiro**

- Significantly, Lady Macbeth's earlier threats of violence, for all their force and brutality, have always been empty fantasies. It is Macbeth who converts them into hard reality. Is she to be pitied or is she entirely lacking in saving graces? Audiences may well form a more complex interpretation of her striking character. It is understandable that Malcolm describes her as a 'fiend-like queen'. His comment emphasises her evil nature and is a reminder of the link between her and the witches. Ultimately, Lady Macbeth fails the test of her own hardened ruthlessness and is a **victim of evil ambition**.

Lady Macbeth's Dramatic Role

- Lady Macbeth has a significant dramatic function in the tragedy and her influence on Macbeth plays a crucial part in developing the action of the plot. She adopts various roles at different stages, symbolising the danger of

'*Look like the innocent flower*'

uncontrolled ambition and the nature of evil. Shakespeare presents the heroine as a stronger character than her husband for much of the play, a **reversal of the typical gender roles** of Elizabethan times. By the end, however, it is unlikely that Lady Macbeth will be judged as a tragic heroine.

♦ Not only is she inherently amoral, but she also brings out the worst in her husband. Her lust for power and domination incites him to make active choices to fulfil his secret longings. She is also a **mirror image of Macbeth**, who is impressionable and nervous early on, but becomes much stronger and less human as the play unfolds. Lady Macbeth develops in exactly the opposite way. By the time of the sleepwalking scene she has become as vulnerable and distressed as her husband was immediately following Duncan's murder. Guilty, troubled and sleepless, she is tormented by similar remorse and struggles with the burden of conscience.

♦ The report of his wife's death prompts Macbeth to consider for one last time the cycle of life and its absurdity. For both of them, everything became ultimately meaningless. Some critics argue that Lady Macbeth's late transformation from a powerful and unnaturally masculine figure into a sensitive woman **re-establishes a sense of natural order**. Despite her obvious immorality and rapid decline, Lady Macbeth remains a powerful presence. In the end, she dies offstage, an event that seems to emphasise how peripheral she has become in her husband's life.

❝❞ Lady Macbeth – Key Quotes

Glamis thou art, and Cawdor, and shalt be/ What thou art promised. Yet do I fear thy nature (Lady Macbeth) Act 1 Scene 5, l.14–15	After reading the letter from her husband (which recounts the witches' prophecy), Lady Macbeth's ambitious and evil thoughts immediately turn to killing the king. She knows Macbeth very well and is sure that he lacks the nerve to murder Duncan.
look like the innocent flower,/ But be the serpent under it (Lady Macbeth's advice to Macbeth) Act 1 Scene 5, l.64–5	Deception comes naturally to Lady Macbeth, who dominates her morally weak husband and persuades him to act falsely. Her determined tone reflects her fierce desire to become Queen of Scotland no matter what treachery is necessary.
Be innocent of the knowledge, dearest chuck,/ Till thou applaud the deed (Macbeth to Lady Macbeth) Act 3 Scene 2, l.47–8	Lady Macbeth's relationship with her husband changes significantly over the course of the play. Her influence is reduced as he becomes more independent and tyrannical. By the time he decides to have Banquo killed, he no longer seeks his wife's approval.
Yet who would have thought the old man to have had so much blood in him? (Lady Macbeth) Act 5 Scene 1, l.33–4	It is one of the play's many great ironies that a guilt-ridden Lady Macbeth is eventually driven insane by the memory of what has happened to Duncan. In the aftermath of the murder, she was confident that 'A little water clears us of this deed'. Her conscience now haunts her and she has become a pathetic victim of her earlier wrong-doing.
She should have died hereafter (Macbeth's reaction to his wife's death) Act 5 Scene 5, l.17	Macbeth is strangely unmoved by his wife's death. Ever since the banquet scene, Lady Macbeth has had no influence over him – and this estrangement has destroyed her. Like her unfeeling husband, however, Lady Macbeth's life has been one of tragic failure.

Class/Homework Exercise

In your opinion, is it possible to ever feel any lasting sympathy for Lady Macbeth? Write a paragraph (150–200 words), supporting your answer with suitable reference to the play.

Prompt!

- Lady Macbeth is a loyal, loving and supportive wife.
- Her memory of her father would suggest that she once had human feelings.
- Lady Macbeth struggles to keep Macbeth under control.
- She is devastated when he distances himself from her.
- Lady Macbeth is a monstrous character without any redeeming features.
- Her sleep-walking and guilt-ridden madness make her a pathetic figure.
- Ultimately, Lady Macbeth is so distraught that she cannot bear to live with herself.

Duncan

'The Lord's anointed temple'

First Impressions

gracious	trusting	gullible
noble	fair-minded	decisive
just	generous	

'So clear in his great office' (Act 1 Scene 7, l.18)

- We first meet King Duncan on the edge of the battlefield, where he rejoices in the news of

his army's triumph over the rebel Scottish forces. He is full of praise for all who have fought, but particularly for Macbeth, whom he acknowledges as a 'valiant cousin, worthy gentleman'. Duncan is an elderly man, no longer a warrior king. However, his **innate kindness** is seen when he sends for a surgeon to help the wounded army captain. His language is characteristically formal, in keeping with the royal position he holds.

- Duncan shows himself as **firm and decisive** when he orders the execution of the traitorous Thane of Cawdor, and then rewards Macbeth with the title. Yet his **gullibility** is also evident when he admits his earlier failure in recognising Cawdor's treachery: 'There's no art/ To find the mind's construction in the face.' The comment is highly ironic, of course. Duncan fails to practise what he preaches and will soon repeat his error of judgement by placing all his trust in Macbeth. This deadly flaw of naivety will have tragic consequences both for himself and for Scotland.

- Duncan's kingdom has already been engulfed in rebellion precisely because he is such a **poor judge of character**. The audience is only too aware of Macbeth's 'Vaulting ambition' and watches aghast as Duncan greets Macbeth, 'O worthiest cousin!' Similarly, when the ageing monarch innocently remarks, 'This castle hath a pleasant seat', we have only just heard Lady Macbeth ominously declare, 'The raven himself is hoarse/ That croaks the fatal entrance of Duncan/ Under my battlements.' The king completely fails to recognise that he is surrounded by duplicitous evil.

- Nonetheless, Duncan is clearly a **sensitive and generous man** who is generally well respected by his Scottish subjects. Victories against rebellious thanes and the Norwegians have made him a popular and honoured figure. There is little doubt that he places the needs of his country above his own interests and he tries to provide unity and stable governance within the kingdom. Despite his best intentions, though, his **decision to transfer power to his son** Malcolm hastens his own untimely death.

- Yet even the devious Macbeth acknowledges the old king's **saintly qualities** and expresses his doubts about proceeding with the murder: 'this Duncan/ Hath borne his faculties so meek, hath been/ So clear in his great office, that his virtues/ Will plead like angels, trumpet-tongued against/ The deep damnation of his taking-off.' The king's essential decency is apparent in everything he does. Duncan is so incapable of suspicion that he is truly perplexed by the deception around him.

- During his short exchange with Lady Macbeth, he uses the word 'love' four times. The **unconscious irony** is obvious when he courteously greets the woman who is actively plotting against him, providing the audience with further evidence of the underlying atmosphere of betrayal that exists throughout the play.

Final View

tragic	compassionate	respected
honourable	idealistic	shallow
	weak humane	

'a most sainted king' (Act 4 Scene 3, l.109)

- Shakespeare presents Duncan as the **representative of God** on earth, ruling by divine right. This feature of kingship was widely believed during the playwright's lifetime. The act of regicide establishes one of the play's central themes: the disturbance of the natural order. Duncan's 'divinity' is emphasised when Macbeth hypocritically speaks of the dead king's 'silver skin laced with his golden blood'. Macduff is more genuinely horrified at the killing of 'The Lord's anointed temple'.

- Despite Duncan's many attributes, **questions remain about the quality of his leadership as king**. Even though his officers and army are prepared to fight for him, there are rebellions against him elsewhere – from both within and outside Scotland. Do these uprisings suggest that he is seen as a weak ruler?

- Duncan's natural **tendency to see only the good in others might well be his great tragic flaw**. However, he is everything that Macbeth is not. As Scotland's lawful ruler, he is a symbol of order. Although he is only seen for a brief time at the start of the play, his virtuous nature contrasts strikingly with the evil around him.

- Duncan's fatherly affection for Macbeth makes his brutal murder all the more appalling. Throughout the play, he embodies important values that are to be initially defeated and eventually restored – particularly Scotland's political and social order. Duncan might be a good man, but he **is not a very effective king**.

Duncan's Dramatic Role

- Shakespeare wrote *Macbeth* in 1606, less than a year after the Gunpowder Plot to blow up the Houses of Parliament in London. King James I was on the throne and was fascinated by what made a good king. This theme is central to the play, which presents the audience with four kings: Duncan; Macbeth; Edward of England; and, finally, Malcolm. Duncan, Scotland's lawful king, **symbolises honour** and common decency.

- **Dialogue** is cleverly used by the playwright to examine the emotional relationships between characters. Duncan speaks formally when addressing Lady Macbeth: 'The love that follows us sometime is our trouble, / Which still we thank as love.' Her response is equally reserved: 'All our service/ In every point twice done, and then done double,/ Were poor and single business'. This contrasts sharply with the simplicity and warmth of the king's exchange with Banquo: 'let me enfold thee/ And hold thee to my heart', and in Banquo's direct reply, 'There if I grow,/ The harvest is your own.'

- Duncan **delivers no soliloquies**, emphasising the fact that he has nothing to hide; there is no need to see inside his mind to discover his intentions, hopes and fears. The playwright presents Duncan in sharp contrast to Macbeth, who frequently agonises over murdering the king. In one early soliloquy, Macbeth lists the reasons against regicide. He is Duncan's 'kinsman and his subject'. He also acknowledges that Duncan has been a merciful and honest ruler who 'Hath borne his faculties so meek, hath been/ So clear in his great office'.

- The moral order which Duncan represented as Scotland's rightful king is destroyed by Macbeth and will only be restored when the lawful heir, Malcolm, succeeds his father. While Duncan has many of the necessary 'king-becoming graces', his weak political judgement makes him an **ineffective ruler**, leaves him open to betrayal and ultimately contributes to the tragedy of Macbeth's tyrannical reign.

🎜 Duncan – Key Quotes

O valiant cousin, worthy gentleman! (Duncan praises Macbeth) Act 1 Scene 2, l.24	Duncan is presented as a dignified character. His formal speech and manners reflect his nobility and graciousness.
He was a gentleman on whom I built/ An absolute trust (Duncan speaking about the rebellious Cawdor) Act 1 Scene 4, l.14	It is highly ironic that Duncan is so out of touch with reality that he cannot imagine threats to his leadership. The king's lack of judgement is his greatest character flaw and raises questions about the nature of kingship.
this Duncan/ Hath borne his faculties so meek, hath been/ So clear in his great office (Macbeth describes Duncan) Act 1 Scene 7, l.16–18	For a brief moment, Macbeth's sense of right and wrong troubles him. He is also burdened by secrecy and shame. In terms of natural justice, he can find no reason for killing a man who possesses the qualities of an ideal king.
Had he not resembled/ My father as he slept, I had done't (Lady Macbeth to Macbeth) Act 2 Scene 2, l.12–13	Even Lady Macbeth recognises the humanity in Duncan and shows him the dutiful respect that she once had for her own father.
Thy royal father/ Was a most sainted king (Macduff to Malcolm) Act 4 Scene 3, l.108	Macduff's heartfelt assessment is a reminder of Duncan's fundamental goodness. His murder is a crime against God and the laws of the natural world.

Class/Homework Exercise

In your opinion, to what extent is Duncan responsible for his own downfall? Write a short paragraph (150–200 words), supporting your answer with suitable reference to the play.

Prompt!

- Does Shakespeare present Duncan as the ideal king?
- Why is there so much resistance to Duncan's rule?
- Does Duncan ever learn from experience?
- Are those who take advantage of Duncan's decency the real villains?
- Is he a foolish old man who is out of touch with reality?
- Does he depend too much on the support of his thanes?
- Is he simply not shrewd enough to be an effective king?
- In the end, is Duncan partly to blame for the tragic events that take place?

Banquo

First Impressions

brave	noble	trusting
ambitious	loyal	honest

'Noble Banquo,/ That hast no less deserved'
(Act 1 Scene 4, l.29–30)

- Banquo is first presented as the equal to Macbeth. Fiercely loyal to Scotland, he has **fought heroically** against Duncan's enemies on the battlefield. The king acknowledges these qualities and is keen to praise his courageous general, comparing him favourably with Macbeth: 'Noble Banquo,/ That hast no less deserved'.

- Macbeth and Banquo **react differently** to the witches' prophecies. Banquo immediately senses that they are evil and is genuinely suspicious of their powers. The questions he asks come from natural curiosity; unlike Macbeth, he has no hidden ambition to be king. However, Banquo is subject to human desires and is just as keen to hear what the three weird sisters have in store for him: 'Speak then to me, who neither beg nor fear/ Your favours nor your hate.'

- While both men are clearly shocked and intrigued by what has been promised,

'the right-valiant Banquo'

224

Banquo is more sceptical. He even **warns Macbeth** to be careful of the witches: 'oftentimes, to win us to our harm,/ The instruments of darkness tell us truths'. Yet there is no doubt about his growing fascination at the prospect of his descendants becoming kings of Scotland at some time in the future.

- At the start of Act 2, we learn that Banquo has been **troubled** by 'cursèd thoughts' that have kept him from sleeping. However, he makes no secret of this: 'I dreamt last night of the three weird sisters.' In contrast to Macbeth, who is becoming obsessed with what he has been promised, Banquo remains fearful of the witches and prays that some 'Merciful powers' will protect him from them.

Character Development

	cautious	sly
resentful	sceptical	self-serving

'Our fears in Banquo/ Stick deep' (Act 3 Scene 1, l.48)

- In his revealing soliloquy at the start of Act 3, Banquo expresses **deep distrust** of Macbeth: 'Thou hast it now: king, Cawdor, Glamis, all,/ As the weird women promised; and I fear/ Thou played'st most foully for it.' There is more than a hint of resentment – and even the same secret ambition that first led Macbeth astray. Banquo has no conclusive proof that Macbeth committed regicide to gain the throne, and he publicly approves Macbeth's election as king, presumably choosing to put aside his misgivings in pursuit of his own interests.

- Caught between his fundamental decency and his longing to be the 'root and father/ Of many kings', Banquo reveals his **crucial moral weakness**. In deciding to do nothing about Macbeth's evil ascent to power, Banquo not only contributes to the tyranny and chaos that will overwhelm Scotland, he also hastens his own untimely death. There is no sign that he ever imagines that his own life – and Fleance's – will be in grave danger when Macbeth becomes king.

- Meanwhile, Macbeth continues to see Banquo as a **serious threat**: 'Our fears in Banquo/ Stick deep'.

To begin with, he knows too much about their fateful meeting with the witches. The new king is also jealous of Banquo's many qualities (particularly his 'royalty of nature') and convinced that he is an ambitious rival. Macbeth admires his former friend's courage, but is increasingly worried about his shrewdness, the 'wisdom that doth guide his valour'. He is also dismayed that he has sacrificed his soul to benefit Banquo's descendants.

- Interestingly, this resentment of Banquo's natural superiority motivates Macbeth to immerse himself in even greater evil. From the paranoid king's point of view, Banquo is **perceptive** enough to work out the truth about all that has happened. After all, immediately following Duncan's murder, it was Banquo who advised the helpless thanes to 'meet,/ And question this most bloody piece of work'.

Final View

	cowardly	truthful
patriotic	tragic	unfortunate

'the right-valiant Banquo walked too late' (Act 3 Scene 6, l.5)

- Throughout the play, Banquo's primary dramatic function is to provide an **effective contrast** to the evil Macbeth. His horrific murder exemplifies Macbeth's tyrannous reign in Scotland. It also leads noblemen, such as Lennox, to come to their own conclusions about everything that occurred on the night of King Duncan's death. Lennox's sarcastic comment that 'the right-valiant Banquo walked too late' expresses the anger felt by Macbeth's Scottish lords, who are now all too aware of his terrifying abuse of power.

- After being killed by Macbeth's assassins, Banquo's blood-spattered ghost makes several brief appearances at a ceremonial banquet. By this stage, Macbeth is almost completely guilt-ridden and frequently hallucinating. He is forced to put his faith in the weird sisters once more and seems incapable of escaping Banquo's presence. Even when the witches show the deranged Macbeth their three apparitions, the **final vision is of Banquo and his line of kings**.

* Despite his character flaws, Banquo is a **sympathetic figure** for several reasons. First, he is ignorant of what the audience knows concerning the murder of the king and of his own impending downfall. He is also an affectionate father. To some extent, he equivocates – and keeps equivocating until his dreadful death. The fact that he chooses good over evil reminds us that Macbeth also acts

from free will. In the end, however, Banquo is a victim of malevolence and his own ambivalent morality.

Key Character Traits

* A loyal Scottish thane
* Courageous in battle
* A shrewd judge of character
* Essentially honourable
* Morally weak at times

Banquo – Key Quotes

And oftentimes, to win us to our harm,/ The instruments of darkness tell us truths,/ Win us with honest trifles, to betray us/ In deepest consequence. *(Banquo warns Macbeth)* Act 1 Scene 3, l.124–7	A central theme in the play is that appearances can be deceptive. Banquo warns Macbeth that half-truths can be used to trick people and lead them astray. Banquo's view of the witches as truly evil is evidence of his essentially moral character.
Speak then to me, who neither beg nor fear/ Your favours nor your hate *(Banquo to the witches)* Act 1 Scene 3, l.61–2	After seeing the witches promise so much to Macbeth, Banquo is naturally interested in finding out what the future might hold for him. At no stage during the encounter, however, does he become as 'rapt' and spellbound by their prophecies.
I dreamt last night of the three weird sisters *(Banquo confides in Macbeth)* Act 2 Scene 1, l.20	Over time, Banquo has considered the witches' prophecies and is keen to discuss them. His open nature contrasts with the secretive Macbeth, who pretends to have no interest in what was promised.
Thou hast it now: king, Cawdor, Glamis, all,/ As the weird women promised; and I fear/ Thou played'st most foully for it *(Banquo considers Macbeth's sudden rise to power)* Act 3 Scene 1, l.1–3	Audiences eventually get a glimpse of Banquo's moral decline. He may not be as honourable as he once appeared. Although he suspects Macbeth of foul play, he is not prepared to confront the new king or share his concerns with other thanes. He pays dearly for his lack of moral courage.

Class/Homework Exercise

'In Shakespeare's play *Macbeth*, the audience is presented with an ambiguous portrait of Banquo.'

To what extent do you agree with this view? Write a short paragraph (150–200 words), supporting your answer with suitable reference to the play.

Prompt!

- Banquo is initially praised for his courage and loyalty.
- He is more astute in suspecting the witches.
- Banquo is unimaginative and a poor judge of Macbeth's character.
- His naivety endangers his son's life.
- He hides his suspicions about Macbeth out of self-interest.
- Banquo must share the responsibility for the play's tragic events.

Macduff

First Impressions

brave	loyal	perceptive
noble	moral	

'I am not treacherous' (Act 4 Scene 3, l.18)

- Macduff, the Thane of Fife, is a **respected Scottish nobleman**. Although there is little development in his character during the course of the play, his patriotism is beyond question and he is motivated to kill Macbeth because he is duty-bound to rid Scotland of a tyrannical king.

- Macduff travels to Macbeth's castle, arriving the morning after Duncan has been murdered. He is genuinely **shocked and appalled** to discover the king's body. He is almost speechless at such 'horror' and describes the dead monarch as the 'Lord's anointed temple', indicating his firmly held belief that kings receive their power directly from God.

- When Macbeth announces that he has killed Duncan's bodyguards, Macduff is the only one to demand an explanation: 'Wherefore did you so?' Clearly **unhappy with Macbeth's fine words**, he refuses to attend his coronation and banquet – something for which he will pay dearly.

- Like Banquo, he is suspicious of Macbeth, but he chooses to act rather than play the part of the deferential courtier. He tells Ross that Duncan's

'I have lost my hopes'

bodyguards were 'suborned' and that they may have been bribed by Malcolm and Donalbain, so 'Suspicion of the deed' is now directed against the king's sons. It is likely, however, that Macduff **remains sceptical** about Duncan's demise and is keeping an open mind about the murder.

- From his first appearance, Macduff distinguishes himself as an independent and honourable character. Over the course of the play, he becomes the **epitome of the avenging hero**, not simply out for revenge but with a much greater moral intent. His loyalty to Scotland is never in doubt. However, his impulsive decision to flee to England and offer his support to Malcolm leaves his family unprotected, suggesting that he has underestimated Macbeth's barbaric nature.

Final View

vengeful	emotional	patriotic
dignified	tragic	heroic

'I have no words' (Act 5 Scene 8, l.7)

- Audiences can see further evidence of Macduff's **patriotism** when Malcolm tests his loyalty by pretending that he would be an even worse king than Macbeth. Macduff is dismayed by what he hears and finally breaks down, crying 'O Scotland, Scotland'. In typically candid fashion, he tells Malcolm that he is not 'Fit to govern!/ No, not to live.'

- When he learns the shocking news of his own family's slaughter, Macduff immediately blames himself, acknowledging that he has been 'Sinful' – his abandoned wife and children were slain because of his opposition to Macbeth. Urged by Malcolm to 'Dispute it like a man', Macduff agrees on the need for vengeance, but tells the prince, 'I shall do so;/ But I must also feel it as a man'. Macduff is **worthy of sympathy** throughout the story – not least at this poignant moment when he grapples with overwhelming grief as a loving husband and father.

- In the final confrontation with Macbeth's depleted forces, Macduff's entire focus is on seeking out the tyrant who is responsible for the deaths of his family: 'Let me find him, Fortune,/ And more I beg not'. His most dramatic scene is when he **reveals the witches' half-truths**, highlighting the fact that Macbeth's sense of power was largely based on illusion.

- When Macduff emerges victorious and holds up Macbeth's severed head, the theatrical image is one of **good finally triumphing** over evil. We are reminded that justice cannot be done without the vigilance and actions of virtuous individuals who loyally devote their efforts to upholding what is right.

- As a symbol of honour and goodness, Macduff serves as a constant contrast to Macbeth. His integrity and decency highlight Macbeth's moral perversion. Although Macduff's character does not change very much during the story, he is never corrupt or unheroic. In the end, he can be seen as an important character, the **play's functional hero**, who kills Macbeth and restores Scotland's leadership to Malcolm's family.

Key Character Traits

- Straightforward, honest and well-intentioned
- A man of principle who follows his conscience
- Always places his country before self-interest
- A caring father and a courageous soldier
- Restores Malcolm as the rightful Scottish king

❞❞ Macduff – Key Quotes

Confusion now hath made his masterpiece!/ Most sacrilegious murder hath broke ope/ The Lord's anointed temple *(Macduff's response to Duncan's murder)* *Act 2 Scene 3, l.61–3*	Macduff's personal integrity is obvious in his horrified reaction to finding Duncan's body. He believes in the divine right of kings and views this murder as an act of blasphemy. Shakespeare describes the killing in forceful religious terms to highlight the enormity of such an evil deed.
Bleed, bleed, poor country! *(Macduff to Malcolm)* *Act 4 Scene 3, l.31*	Blood imagery will define Macbeth's tyrannical reign. In complete contrast, Macduff's unconditional patriotism is never in doubt.
He has no children. All my pretty ones?/ Did you say all? *(Macduff reacts to the dreadful news about his family)* *Act 4 Scene 3, l.216–17*	In this heartbreaking scene, Macduff shows his innate humanity as he struggles to come to terms with the murder of his entire family. The comment is usually taken to refer to either Macbeth or Malcolm. From Macduff's viewpoint, neither man can understand what he is feeling.
I have no words:/ My voice is in my sword *(Macduff finally confronts Macbeth)* *Act 5 Scene 8, l.6–7*	For Macduff, all-out revenge is imperative. His moral choice to kill the tyrannical Macbeth is beyond discussion. He has always been a man of few words – unlike Macbeth, who has been bewitched by the witches' promises and his wife's arguments.

Class/Homework Exercise

'Macduff is the real hero of Shakespeare's play *Macbeth*.'

To what extent do you agree with this view? Write a short paragraph (150–200 words), supporting your answer with suitable reference to the text.

Prompt!

* Macduff's bravery and loyalty are evident throughout.
* He is the first to challenge Macbeth's account of Duncan's death.
* Unlike Banquo, he does not support the new king's coronation.
* His hunger for revenge and his naivety endanger his family's lives.
* He is slow to oppose Malcolm during the loyalty test.
* Macduff is a man of feeling as well as courage.
* In the end, he re-establishes order and justice in Scotland.

Malcolm

First Impressions

> royal   wary
> unemotional   dutiful

'Let's not consort with them'
(Act 2 Scene 3, l.130)

- Malcolm is King Duncan's eldest son, nominated by his father as the Prince of Cumberland, heir to the Scottish throne. While Duncan has no doubts about Malcolm's potential as his **successor**, there is little evidence of his son's qualities during the play's early scenes.

- While Malcolm seems to have inherited his father's sense of honour, he displays much **greater judgement**. Following Duncan's violent death, he fears – quite rightly – for his own life and flees to England, saying: 'This murderous shaft that's shot/ Hath not yet lighted, and our safest way/ Is to avoid the aim.'

- Malcolm is wise enough to understand that **nobody around him can be trusted**: 'Let's not consort with them'. Of course, while his sudden disappearance ensures his immediate safety, it also allows Macbeth to blame him for Duncan's murder.

- During his exile, Malcolm **matures significantly** and he assumes responsibility for avenging his father's untimely death. Displaying a strong sense of purpose, he asks for military assistance from Siward and King Edward. His own patriotism is never in question as he becomes increasingly concerned with Macbeth's abuse of power: 'I think our country sinks beneath the yoke'.

- There is no doubting Malcolm's resolution to assemble an army that will allow him to **challenge Macbeth** and regain the Scottish throne. He also gains importance when Macduff visits him in England. As a result, he becomes well established at the English court.

- Before fully trusting Macduff, Malcolm **tests his loyalty**. He displays his shrewd nature when he pretends to be even more corrupt than Macbeth and unworthy of ever being Scotland's king. The

'by the grace of Grace'

test provides further evidence of both men's patriotic characters. Malcolm is also acutely aware of the duties of kingship, listing the ideal 'virtues' required in a sovereign ruler: 'justice, verity, temperance, stableness,/ Bounty, perseverance, mercy, lowliness,/ Devotion, patience, courage, fortitude'.

- Later, he attempts to comfort Macduff after the horrendous massacre of his family at their castle in Fife, encouraging him to 'Dispute it like a man'. Although he is trying to be supportive, he does, however, appear somewhat **insensitive** to the enormity of Macduff's loss. Instead, his complete focus is on asserting good over evil by ending the tyranny of Macbeth – who is 'ripe for shaking'.

Final View

capable	intuitive	honourable
astute	virtuous	patriotic
far-sighted		generous

'At no time broke my faith'
(Act 4 Scene 3, l.128)

- Malcolm's **leadership qualities** are clearly seen on the battlefield. While he values the military experience of those around him, he shows himself to be a courageous and competent general, organising his armed forces with great assurance. He also comes up with the innovative idea of using branches from Birnam Wood as camouflage for his soldiers.

- Shakespeare highlights Malcolm's most impressive attributes at the end of the play. As Duncan's rightful heir, it is appropriate that the new king is the last to speak. His vision for Scotland's future is all that his father would have wished. In a carefully measured speech, he **looks ahead to a new order**, setting out his plans to re-establish justice and civilised rule.

- Malcolm acknowledges the loyal support of his thanes, calls back the exiles who have fled the country in fear, and pledges to reunite the kingdom once more. His assured tone leaves the audience with a clear sense of his innate virtue and royal nature. Malcolm is ready to take over as king and **restore stability** to Scotland. He will rule 'by the grace of Grace'.

Key Character Traits

- A dutiful son and astute judge of character
- An effective leader on the battlefield
- Proves himself fit to be king
- Willing to learn from the past
- Restores order and harmony to Scotland

❝❞ Malcolm – Key Quotes

Nothing in his life/ Became him like the leaving it (Malcolm speaking of Cawdor's execution) Act 1 Scene 4, l.7–8	Malcolm's dignified style of speaking reflects his father's moral attitude. The rebel Thane of Cawdor faced death with dignity. Malcolm clearly believes in the importance of virtue and honour – even if it comes late in life.
O! By whom? (Malcolm to Macduff) Act 2 Scene 3, l.95	The response Malcolm makes to the news of Duncan's murder indicates his immediate shock. He is lost for words and overwhelmed by the occasion. Is his reaction a natural one or a sign of weakness?
Be comforted:/ Let's make us medicines of our great revenge (Malcolm to Macduff) Act 4 Scene 3, l.212–14	In trying to console Macduff after the slaughter of his family, Malcolm's main concern is overthrowing Macbeth. He seems insensitive to Macduff's remorse. Is there a suggestion that he is self-interested and cold-hearted?
We shall not spend a large expense of time/ Before we reckon with your several loves (Malcolm to his army) Act 5 Scene 9, l.26	In the aftermath of Macbeth's death, Malcolm promises to act quickly by rewarding all those who have been loyal to him and to Scotland. He knows how important it is to unite the kingdom and he is more realistic than his father. The signs are that he will be a deserving and successful king.

The Witches

First Impressions

mysterious	theatrical	gifted
insightful	fascinating	

'Fair is foul, and foul is fair' (Act 1 Scene 1, l.12)

- The witches are not really characters in the conventional sense – individuals who develop during the course of the play. They are usually seen as symbols or **agents of evil** who are closely associated with Macbeth from the start. They deliver the infamous lines that set the sinister tone for the drama: 'Fair is foul, and foul is fair'. In this play, nothing is certain. The witches are present in just three main scenes: Act 1 Scene 1; Act 1 Scene 3; and Act 4 Scene 1. (Act 3 Scene 5, in which they appear with Hecate, is thought to have been added to the play at a later date.) Nevertheless, these three scenes are critical to Macbeth's fate.

- We first see the three witches in the foulest of weather – thunder, lightning, 'fog and filthy air'. This establishes the play's dark, supernatural setting and also introduces the central **theme of disorder**. The weird sisters often speak in verse, uttering equivocal incantations that are intended to confuse. Although they communicate in riddles and half-truths, Macbeth chooses to interpret these to suit his own interests. The witches also maintain the play's tense, supernatural atmosphere. Their hypnotic rhyming couplets and chanting of grotesque magic spells vibrate with fearful, unspoken malice.

- Interestingly, when Macbeth first speaks, he echoes their ominous words: 'So foul and fair a day I have not seen'. He is immediately susceptible to the witches' influence and takes their prophecies very seriously. He becomes 'rapt' in wonder (unlike the more sceptical Banquo), perhaps indicating that the weird sisters are simply articulating his own evil ambitions. It's clear that they **understand Macbeth's weak moral nature** and they take the utmost delight in exploiting it.

- As the story develops, Macbeth becomes increasingly isolated from his wife and relies more and more on the witches. In their second encounter, the witches conjure up compelling visions of his future, **reassuring him** that no man born of woman will ever kill him and that he will not be defeated until a forest advances upon him. In his unstable state, the apparitions confirm Macbeth's false sense of invincibility – something that will inevitably lead to his violent death.

Final View

sinister	callous	repulsive
equivocal	devilish	malicious

'these juggling fiends' (Act 5 Scene 8, l.19)

- Throughout the play, the three sisters are repeatedly referred to as 'weird' (originating from the old English word 'wyrd', meaning 'fate'). Some critics believe that Shakespeare is suggesting that Macbeth doesn't have control over his own actions, and that his **tragic downfall** is predestined.

- Only at the end of the play does Macbeth face the truth about the witches and their double-dealing. On learning of Macduff's birth, he is forced to accept that he has been tricked by the **false promises** of 'these juggling fiends'.

- The witches are seen for the last time in Act 4 Scene 1, just as the apparitions vanish. Their final words are **typically devious**. Having filled Macbeth with false hope, their 'antic' dancing is accompanied by a bizarre promise: 'cheer we up his sprites'. For audiences observing the deluded king go to his doom, the dramatic irony of this scene could hardly be more devastating.

- The three weird sisters are an important dramatic device and have a **profound influence** on events in the story; their prophecies drive Macbeth's thirst for power and enable Lady Macbeth to pursue her own dark ambitions. Overall, their deceptive prophecies, malevolent presence and outlandish – and sometimes comic – rituals heighten the impact of this tragic drama.

'What are these ...'

◆ While the witches do not specifically tell Macbeth to kill Duncan, they use a subtle form of temptation in prophesying that he is destined to be king. By placing this thought in his mind, they effectively aid his own destruction. Right to the end, however, Shakespeare keeps us guessing about the relationship between the witches and Macbeth, so that the extent of their control over him remains debatable. Ultimately, the weird sisters are not presented as human, but rather as **manifestations of the forces of evil**. However, they have such a powerful effect on the plot of the play that their influence is certainly not insignificant.

Key Character Traits

- ◆ The witches are instruments of absolute evil
- ◆ They introduce the dark supernatural atmosphere
- ◆ They expose Macbeth's hidden ambition
- ◆ They are striking voices of a chaotic world
- ◆ They represent motiveless malignancy
- ◆ They hasten Macbeth's moral decline

❝❝ The Witches – Key Quotes

What are these,/ So withered, and so wild in their attire,/ That look not like the inhabitants o'th'earth ...? (Banquo questions the nature of the witches) Act 1 Scene 3, l.39–40	The witches establish the supernatural context of Macbeth's downfall. In Shakespeare's time, people were much more superstitious than we are today. They would have accepted the existence of occult forces and the power of evil spirits.
What, can the devil speak true? (Banquo considers their motives) Act 1 Scene 3, l.108	Banquo's response to the witches reflects the widespread belief that absolute evil was a powerful force in the world. As agents of the devil, their purpose is to deceive their victims and create disorder in the world.
Glamis thou art, and Cawdor; and shalt be/ What thou art promised (Lady Macbeth reacts to the witches' promises) Act 1 Scene 5, l.14–15	With the witches, nothing is ever quite what it appears. What exactly are they promising? Glory? Misery? While the weird sisters tempt Macbeth by encouraging his secret desires, Lady Macbeth goes a stage further and directs him more forcibly to murder Duncan.
He shall spurn fate, scorn death, and bear/ His hopes above wisdom, grace and fear (Hecate describes Macbeth) Act 3 Scene 5, l.30–1	Hecate identifies Macbeth's great flaw; he is so self-obsessed and over-confident that he has convinced himself that he can cheat death. Her comment suggests that he has little or no control over his destiny.

(For sample Leaving Cert examination questions on the play's central characters, see page 267.)

Themes in *Macbeth*

Introduction

A theme is an idea or a common thread that goes through a story. In any interpretation of dramatic themes, there is bound to be some **overlap**: power and kingship are obvious examples in *Macbeth*. Another prominent theme is the conflict between good and evil, which embraces various sub-themes, such as honour and the supernatural. Shakespeare's themes are also closely associated with the main characters and are reflected in the play's language and imagery.

Leaving Certificate questions usually include **several elements**. It is unlikely that candidates will be asked to write about a single theme. Rather, questions tend to focus on comparing themes or linking themes to characters and what they represent, for example:

> 'Shakespeare offers significant insights into aspects of appearances and reality in the play *Macbeth*.' To what extent do you agree with this view? Support your answer with reference to the text.

Another typical question might be linked to aspects of language:

> 'In the play *Macbeth*, Shakespeare makes effective use of a variety of dramatic devices to explore issues of trust and betrayal'. Discuss this statement, supporting your answer with reference to the play.

In the examination, it is essential to study the wording of questions closely and identify the key elements that are to be addressed. When planning and writing the 60-minute essay, follow the Exam Technique guidelines on page 250. Use your **critical thinking skills** to organise relevant discussion points based on a clear understanding of the play.

Appearance and Reality

In *Macbeth*, Shakespeare creates a world where not only the characters but also the audience are often unsure of the distinction between what appears to be real and what actually is real. The playwright uses the theme of appearance and reality for two purposes: to show **how easily a person can deceive and be deceived**; and to set out the **disastrous consequences for a society** in which 'nothing is/ But what is not'. The world of this great tragedy is filled with rumours, fears, uncertainty and half-truths. Shakespeare makes full use of equivocation (language that can be understood in more than one way) to reveal truth.

The story is filled with equivocation, concealment and deception

The witches ... 'imperfect speakers'

The gulf between 'seeing' and 'being' is established from the outset of the play. Three witches on a windy heath talk about a mysterious battle that is 'lost and won'. These weird sisters – who seem to 'Hover through the fog and filthy air' – **set the menacing atmosphere of confusion and illusion**. Their physical appearance is disturbing. They 'should be women', yet their beards suggest otherwise. They 'seemed corporal' but 'melted as breath into the wind'. The witches target Macbeth, nurturing in him the seed of his evil ambition to be king. They prompt him to allow his festering 'black and deep desires' to overwhelm his better nature.

Lady Macbeth … 'sleek o'er your rugged looks'

Lady Macbeth's outward appearance is a **masquerade** of the perfect hostess. Inwardly, she seethes with a lust for power and cannot wait for the unsuspecting Duncan to come through the 'fatal entrance' of her castle. No 'compunctious visitings of nature' will shake her 'fell purpose'. She repeatedly counsels her husband in deceit, declaring that his face 'is as a book, where men/ May read strange matters'. Aligning herself with the temptress Eve in the Garden of Eden, she advises him to 'Look like the innocent flower,/ But be the serpent under it'.

Deception comes easily to Lady Macbeth and she practises what she preaches by taking control. She returns to the scene of the crime to 'gild the faces of the grooms', crudely implicating them in the murder, 'For it must seem their guilt'. Later, she pretends to faint when Macbeth is coming under suspicion for the assassination. During the chaotic banquet, when Macbeth loses self-control she attempts to restore order by coolly dismissing his erratic behaviour: 'My lord is often thus … The fit is momentary'. However, in the sleepwalking scene, the once-dominant Lady Macbeth, overwhelmed by the burden of remorse, has become a shadow of her former self.

Shakespeare graphically depicts the consequences of deceit. Wandering aimlessly in her isolated 'murky' hell, Macbeth's distracted wife is now completely unaware of the difference between reality and illusion. Continuously washing her hands to rid herself of guilt, she presents a pathetic and chilling spectacle: 'all the perfumes of Arabia' cannot wash away the smell of blood. Audiences are left in no doubt that 'Unnatural deeds/ Do breed unnatural troubles' for even the most powerful personality.

Duncan and Malcolm … 'Angels are bright still, though the brightest fell'

Throughout the play, Shakespeare uses the theme of appearance and deception to show that it is **not enough simply to be honourable and trusting**.

Duncan is not only duped by the rebel Thane of Cawdor, 'a gentleman on whom I built/ An absolute trust', but also by his 'peerless kinsman' Macbeth. Learning little from experience, he ruefully concludes, 'There's no art/ To find the mind's construction in the face'. His son and heir, Malcolm, is much more astute. During his uneasy encounter with Macduff in the English court, he makes it clear that successful political leaders need to be wary of everyone around them. Malcolm's elaborate test of Macduff's loyalty is based on bitter experience. Because of his father's death, he trusts no one – 'all things foul would wear the brows of grace'.

Malcolm eventually breaks Macduff by declaring that he would 'Pour the sweet milk of concord into hell' if he had power. He has learned the foolishness of 'over-credulous haste'. Duncan's faith in Macbeth showed that naivety leads to ruin – and Malcolm will not make the same mistake. By ordering his **soldiers to camouflage themselves with branches**, he tricks Macbeth about the size of his army: so deception is sometimes necessary for the forces of good to overcome evil. The audience can be confident that when Malcolm eventually restores order to Scotland, his power is likely to last.

Macbeth … 'A dagger of the mind'

Macbeth's tragic fate is his ability to face reality – but only when he chooses. He has no difficulty in listing the reasons not to kill the king; he is Duncan's host, kinsman and subject. But 'Vaulting ambition' overrides all these considerations, and he deliberately chooses to let the 'eye wink at the hand'. Macbeth is fully aware that there will be **consequences** for his decision to commit regicide. He appreciates that kingship is a 'poisoned chalice' – only achievable by evil means that will surely come back to haunt him. Yet he cannot restrain himself and chooses to join forces with his duplicitous wife, echoing her unnerving words, 'False face must hide what the false heart doth know'.

Like his wife, Macbeth suffers hallucinations – a bloodstained dagger and Banquo's ghost – because he decided to bend every 'corporeal agent' to the act of murder. He knows that he is acting against his own nature ('I dare do all that may become a man'), but he pours 'rancours in the vessel' of his peace to gain the throne. This **clarity of vision** engages the audience's interest in his personality.

Macbeth puts his complete **trust in the witches' equivocal prophecies**, only listening to the literal meaning of their words. As a result, he is betrayed 'In deepest consequence' as Banquo had advised on their first encounter with the 'midnight hags'. Nor does Macbeth fully 'see' the apparitions (the helmeted head, the bloody child, the child crowned with a tree), instead deluding himself with the false promises that 'none of woman born/ Shall harm Macbeth' and that his safety is guaranteed until 'great Birnam wood' comes to high Dunsinane.

All through the play, Shakespeare illustrates how there is none so blind as those who will not see. Only when every prophecy has been disproved does Macbeth finally realise that he has been cheated by the 'juggling fiends'. Finally, all his illusions have been stripped away and truth restored. By the end of *Macbeth*, it is all too evident that **a world built on dishonesty is doomed to fail**. Is Shakespeare suggesting that the tragedy of life is not death, but what we allow to die inside us while we live?

Isolation

Macbeth's disastrous kingship leads to abandonment and alienation

Initially portrayed as courageous and daring, Macbeth is described by one of Duncan's sergeants as 'Valour's minion', fiercely attacking enemy soldiers with his smoking sword. Always at the centre of the fighting, he is a popular figure who earns widespread respect, particularly from the grateful king: 'he is full so valiant'. On his first appearance, this great military leader is surrounded by supporters and his comrades Banquo, Ross and Angus. What fascinates audiences is the character flaw that makes Macbeth jeopardise all the 'Golden opinions ... Which would be worn now in their newest gloss'. These are cast aside to satisfy his intense ambition to be king, an ambition that will lead to a **terrifying journey into total isolation** for him and his wife. Sooner than he imagines – immediately after the murder of Duncan, when 'renown and grace is dead' – he will experience the desolation of losing his potential for true greatness.

Macbeth becomes increasingly **isolated in his thoughts**, 'Look, how our partner's rapt', and starts to live more intensely in his own mind. His 'black and deep desires' take centre stage in his soliloquies. In their planning and execution of the regicide, the Macbeths break the bonds of nature and orderly society and become divorced from mainstream Scotland. The first crucial step into the world of darkness is expressed in disturbing invocations. Lady Macbeth calls on the 'spirits/ That tend on mortal thoughts', while Macbeth implores the earth, 'Thou sure and firm-set earth,/ Hear not my steps'. The couple retreat more and more from reality and normal behaviour, choosing to hide beneath the cover of darkness, 'Come, thick night'. In breaking the divine right of lawful accession, Macbeth and his wife are clearly prepared to completely isolate themselves – regardless of the outcome.

The murder of a friend ... 'A deed of dreadful note'

The murder of Duncan marks the crucial turning point in Macbeth's development. He quickly grows obsessed with the future and securing power. In particular, he fears Banquo, 'under him,/ My genius is rebuked'. However, he hesitates about telling his wife his plan to have his friend killed, 'Be innocent of the knowledge'. **Self-absorbed and paranoid**, Macbeth's behaviour becomes much more extreme as he terrorises Scotland, keeping 'a servant fee'd' in every house. Following the news of Fleance's escape, he feels 'cabined, cribbed, confined'. Hopelessly engulfed, his moral downfall continues at a relentless pace.

The slaughter of a family ... 'Strange things I have in head'

When Macduff 'denies his person' at Macbeth's banquet, the new king decides to have his entire family slaughtered. Macduff's young son is butchered before our eyes in an attack on nature and the vulnerable that seems even worse than killing Duncan. Macbeth is now prepared to destroy all for 'sovereign sway'. His king, friend and now an innocent child are all sacrificed for his selfish agenda. He soon becomes the subject of adverse gossip throughout Scotland, 'Now does he feel/ His secret murders sticking on his hands'. Macbeth's journey towards **utter depravity and isolation** is rapidly reaching its end.

Lady Macbeth ... 'dearest partner of greatness'

Ironically, the relationship between Macbeth and his wife is shattered by their relentless pursuit of power. Her ambition has always been primarily for him. She is determined that he 'shalt be/ What thou art promised'. Tragically, each partner destroys the other – he by initially considering killing the king, she by her relentless insistence that he commit the murder against his better judgement. Their **estrangement** becomes apparent when Lady Macbeth is reduced to asking him, 'Why do you keep alone,/ Of sorriest fancies your companions making ...?'

Macbeth has now retreated from society and from his wife. In turn, Lady Macbeth has isolated herself from her feminine nature in order to support her husband, 'unsex me here, / And fill me from the crown to the toe top-full/ Of direst cruelty'. But her greatest tragedy is that she is unable to follow her husband in his great outbursts of imaginative eloquence. When he is transported beyond her comprehension – ' I am in blood/ Stepped in so far that, should I wade no more,/ Returning were as tedious as go o'er' – she listlessly replies, 'You lack the season of all natures, sleep'. Almost inevitably, **the couple are finally isolated from each other** in their depths of despair.

Life's tragic tale ... 'full of sound and fury, Signifying nothing'

The resolution of the play shows a clear-sighted Macbeth fully aware of what he has forsaken in pursuit of the crown: 'honour, love, obedience, troops of friends'. He has lost his army, 'We have met with foes/ That strike beside us'. **Lady**

Macbeth is also imprisoned in her own friendless 'murky' hell, reliving dreadful moments from the couple's shared past: 'who would have thought the old man to have had so much blood in him?' Pathetically, she discharges her secrets to 'deaf pillows'. She is beyond help and eventually takes her own life, the ultimate act of loneliness.

Macbeth's life is also forsaken, and filled with self-interrogation and confession. The relationships he forms are as fragile as the values by which he lives in a world that he can never fully understand. Like his distraught wife, he is trapped – but much more defiant – in the end. An image from bear-baiting illustrates his **alienation**: 'They have tied me to a stake; I cannot fly,/ But, bear-like, I must fight the course'. Bitterly disappointed, he has been driven almost mad by his own actions and is paying an enormous price, 'To know my deed, 'twere best not know myself'.

The Macbeths never express contrition for their actions, but remain focused on their unhappiness. For most audiences, this isolation is likely to induce a sense of pity for the protagonists, and an empathy for their suffering – even though it was brought on by their own evil choices. It also evokes fear in the audience; we know that there are **chilling consequences** of allowing our evil desires to conquer our better natures.

Power and Tyranny

The use and abuse of power is a central theme throughout the play. Power suggests authority, privilege, control, dominance and oppression. In *Macbeth*, Shakespeare presents the audience with the uncomfortable truth that **the desire to overthrow authority leads to personal and societal destruction**. The story (of ambition, betrayal, revenge and eventual justice) traces the downfall of a potentially honourable man who trades everything to satisfy his lust for power and then loses all humanity. Macbeth 'filed' his mind and 'Put rancours in the vessel' of his peace, plunging his country into chaos.

Both kings and tyrants require power, but it is **how they use power** that distinguishes a rightful king from a tyrant. An oppressive monarch acts irresponsibly and rules unjustly; a true king is conscious of his duty and leads his people fairly. Tyrants subjugate; lawful kings provide security. As Macbeth demonstrates, a despot will do anything to seize power. Ambition can be a force for good, driving a character to accomplish great things in life; but evil ambition is a different matter. At the start of the story, Macbeth heroically drives the rebels from Scotland, but within a remarkably short time, he has discarded all honour and loyalty. Shakespeare's play demonstrates that **uncontrolled avarice for power corrodes the individual and leads to his destruction**.

Acquiring power ... 'black and deep desires'

Macbeth has an irrepressible lust for power. He is delighted by the witches' 'truths' and sees them 'As happy prologues to the swelling act/ Of the imperial theme', when he will become Scotland's new king. Nevertheless, he is not naturally inclined to commit evil deeds. At first, he seems content to wait: 'If chance will have me king, why, chance may crown me,/ Without my stir'. But when Duncan publicly names Malcolm as his heir, everything changes. For Macbeth, that development is 'a step/ On which I must fall down, or else o'erleap'. He is fully aware that the only 'spur' he has to murder Duncan is his 'Vaulting ambition'. With his image of an uncontrolled horse that 'o'erleaps itself/ And falls', Macbeth leaves us in no doubt that **uninhibited hunger for power is extremely dangerous**.

Lady Macbeth sums up her husband's character; 'not without ambition, but without/The illness should attend it'. Macbeth himself is acutely conscious of Duncan's legitimate claim to the Scottish throne. In an early soliloquy, he emphasises his obligations to the king: as Duncan's 'kinsman and his subject' and his host, Macbeth should do everything he can to protect him. But Macbeth's yearning for royal status overwhelms all other considerations. He has to 'bend up/ Each corporal agent to this terrible feat'. Shakespeare is highlighting the **sheer force of unrestrained desire for power**. Macbeth is willing to break all laws – natural, societal, moral and divine – to secure the throne. Through regicide, he becomes an 'untitled tyrant bloody-sceptred'.

Securing power ... 'but to be safely thus'

Once the decision is made to use violence to satisfy his quest for power, Macbeth finds it impossible to stop. Ironically, his **fear of losing power**, 'To be thus is nothing', drives him to commit more and more despicable crimes. Macbeth murders his friend Banquo, because his fears about him 'Stick deep' and he is wary of Banquo's 'royalty

Power struggles of various kinds are central to the play

of nature'. Desperate to guarantee his family's position into the future, Macbeth is furious that he has a 'barren sceptre' and will have 'No son of mine succeeding'. Bitterly, he realises that power without long-term security is not worth having.

This leads to paranoia. Because Macbeth feels 'cabined, cribbed, confined', he decides that 'For mine own good/ All causes shall give way'. Instigating a tyrannical reign of intimidation, he keeps a 'servant fee'd' in every house, murdering innocent women and children at will. His power is now maintained entirely through sheer tyranny: 'Each new morn/ New widows howl, new orphans cry, new sorrows/ Strike heaven on the face'. Through the course of this violent story, Shakespeare illustrates how **acquiring power illegally leads to the use of terror to retain it**.

Of course, **power is not evil in itself and does not always corrupt**. Malcolm, the legal heir to the throne, is the 'medicine of the sickly weal' of Scotland. In his shrewd testing of Macduff's

Malcom

patriotism, we see a leader, who, unlike Macbeth, chooses intellect and honour over intemperate emotion. Yet he is also capable of showing his feelings after Macduff shows him that it is insufficient to merely 'Dispute' sorrow 'like a man', he 'must also 'feel it as a man'. Later on, Malcolm puts this advice into practice in expressing grief for young Siward. At the play's conclusion, Shakespeare presents the audience with a selfless leader in stark contrast to Macbeth.

Malcolm is a measured and controlled ruler, who carefully balances punishments with rewards to his loyal supporters. He is not self-seeking, but inclusive ('thanks to all at once') and invites all Scotland's noblemen to see him crowned at Scone. Malcolm has clearly learned valuable lessons from his father's naivety, and he seems destined to rule fairly. Shakespeare has shown his audience that while **tyranny causes lawlessness, suffering and insecurity, true kingship brings order, justice and security.**

Men and Women

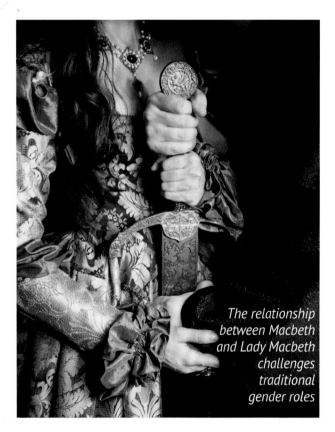

The relationship between Macbeth and Lady Macbeth challenges traditional gender roles

In Elizabethan times, social expectations and personal status differed greatly between the sexes. Men were regarded as natural leaders, while women were expected to support men, rather than having a distinct role in their own right. **Shakespeare challenges this stereotype** with the creation of strong women characters in his

plays. Lady Macbeth is a powerful, dominant woman, with some typically 'male' characteristics, and the playwright also dares to give feminine traits to his male protagonist. Macbeth is 'too full o' the milk of human kindness/ To catch the nearest way'; he has to be manipulated by the 'valour' of his wife's influential personality. Lady Macbeth is quick to abandon her feminine qualities, 'unsex me here', 'take my milk for gall'. Her admiring husband describes her as possessing 'undaunted mettle'.

Macbeth is emotional, full of doubts, haunted by the enormity of the deed, 'If we should fail?' In contrast, Lady Macbeth is forceful and determined, 'screw your courage to the sticking-place'. She assumes the leading role in the couple's marriage, commanding her impressionable husband to 'put/ This night's great business into my despatch'. **Lady Macbeth manipulates her husband** by attacking his masculinity, 'Art thou afeard … ?' and asking if he is prepared to 'live a coward in thine own esteem'. Both before and after the murder of Duncan, her loyalty to Macbeth is never in doubt, as she encourages, supports and protects him.

Yet there is a cost to denying one's nature. In the sleepwalking scene, Lady Macbeth's **femininity reasserts itself.** Broken by guilt, she poignantly cries, 'all the perfumes of Arabia will not sweeten this little hand'. The dominant mistress of the castle who announced Duncan's 'fatal entrance' now cannot bear the dark, but must have light by her constantly. Alone and forlorn, she has also lost her husband through their terrible lust for power.

The witches are another support for Macbeth. From the outset, the weird sisters **manipulate Macbeth**, seemingly offering him encouragement, 'Be bloody, bold, and resolute, laugh to scorn/ The power of man'. But, of course, they are 'juggling fiends' who confuse and conceal, either by omission or ambiguity, 'for none of woman born/ Shall harm Macbeth'. Interestingly, while Lady Macbeth uses her influence to empower Macbeth, the witches use power to destroy him.

All through the play, Shakespeare has brought his audience on a terrifying journey exploring the allure and danger of power. The destruction that happens when evil ambition goes unchecked by moral constraints is clearly evident in the two protagonists. The playwright's conclusion is that – for both men and women – **power must be acquired legally,** used wisely and exercised for the greater good, 'by the grace of Grace'.

Dramatic Techniques

Imagery

Imagery involves using emotionally charged words and phrases to **create vivid pictures** in the minds of the audience. The main function of imagery and symbolism in *Macbeth* is to aid characterisation and reinforce themes in the play. Patterns of imagery also help to create specific atmospheres and heighten evocative moods in the drama.

We come to know Macbeth's developing character through a series of images and symbols, often associated with clothing, nature and blood. Other recurring images **sharpen our appreciation** of important aspects of the play, including key relationships, deception and the supernatural.

Macbeth contains some of the most powerful language in all of Shakespeare's work. In addition to imagery relating to light and darkness and animals, the play uses images of children, masculinity, fate, sleep and the theatre. The play's rich images give us a **deeper understanding** of the main characters and their situations, describe emotions, foreshadow key events and create atmosphere, thus heightening the audience's appreciation of Shakespeare's great tragedy.

Light and Darkness

Contrasts are central to *Macbeth* and the story includes recurring references to the tension between good and evil. Macbeth's tyranny is closely connected with dark forces. Darkness is linked to corruption, cruelty and guilt; light to grace, truth and honour. The two opposing sets of images **emphasise the moral force** of this tragic drama.

As Scotland's divinely appointed king, Duncan would have been associated with light and sunshine. In the play's melodramatic opening scene (amid thunder and lightning), the equivocating witches introduce a **mood of moral**

Light and darkness are used as recurring metaphors for good and evil

confusion and foreshadow the king's death by promising to meet again 'ere the set of sun'. References to darkness reinforce the recurring theme of immorality. Macbeth demonstrates his inclination towards malevolence when he asks the stars to 'hide your fires!/ Let not light see my black and deep desires'.

Of course, the witches' presence intensifies the **ominous atmosphere** that pervades the drama. Banquo rightly considers them 'instruments of darkness', and their relentless malice and deception reflect the Macbeths' moral decay. In the hours before Duncan's killing, Lady Macbeth expresses her longing to be hidden from daylight, urging the foulest spirits to surround her with 'thick night' and a 'blanket of the dark'.

Immediately following Macbeth's accession as king, there is a remarkable change in the atmosphere throughout Scotland. Ross comments on the strange turn of events: 'by the clock 'tis day,/ And yet dark night strangles the travelling lamp'. His observation emphasises just how unnatural Duncan's murder was; the assassination of the lawful king has **unsettled the natural world**. It seems that night has overpowered day, just as evil has conquered good.

Most of the abnormal and corrupt events in the drama occur in darkness; the murders of Duncan and Banquo, the sleepwalking scene, the appearance of the witches all take place at night. Lady Macbeth once craved the darkness, but now needs a candle to dispel it, symbolising her deep-rooted insecurity and guilt. Shakespeare shows how the horror of her deeds has possessed her, and does so by dramatising the most elemental and childlike of fears: **terror of darkness**.

Through much of the play, night serves as an effective **metaphor** for Macbeth's oppressive reign. Order is not restored until Macduff takes his revenge and Scotland is finally purged of corruption and depravity. It is only then that the audience can fully appreciate Malcolm's earlier remark: 'The night is long that never finds the day.'

Throughout *Macbeth*, the struggle between good and evil is repeatedly reinforced by **compelling images** of light and darkness, all of which contribute to the play's pervasive sense of evil.

Blood

Blood symbolises murder and guilt throughout the tragedy

Macbeth is one of Shakespeare's **most violent plays**. Even when blood is not being shed onstage, characters frequently refer to it. Our first impressions of Scotland are of a country at war. 'What bloody man is that?' The play's second scene begins with a wounded soldier bringing news from the battlefield that Macbeth's sword 'smoked with bloody execution'. Does the description suggest heroism or sadism?

During times of war, such accounts of bloody encounters were proof of courage and loyalty. Macbeth and Banquo are highly regarded for their ferocious fighting skills. When Macbeth begins to focus on killing Duncan, he is tortured by the vision of a dagger ('And on thy blade and dudgeon gouts of blood'), in a revealing glimpse of his **powerful imagination** – a character trait that will continue to torment him.

Blood is everywhere in this play. Lady Macbeth 'smears' the grooms with it, so that they will seem 'steep'd' in the colours of their trade. Images of blood both reflect the murderous thoughts and actions of Macbeth and his wife and signify the sheer force of their **heartlessness**.

Nor does the blood wash away. Many of the references to blood are closely associated with

guilt and remorse. 'This is a sorry sight,' Macbeth says as he stares at his hands after returning from Duncan's room. Lady Macbeth advises her agitated husband to wash away the 'filthy witness', but Macbeth knows that even an entire ocean will not cleanse him. The murderer who reports Banquo's death has blood on his face. Shortly afterwards, Banquo's 'blood-boltered' ghost appears at the banquet and shakes his 'gory locks' at the terrified king. By this stage, Macbeth is all too conscious of his own moral descent and expresses his **savage nature** graphically: 'I am in blood/ Stepped in so far that, should I wade no more,/ Returning were as tedious as go o'er.' His desolate words reveal the increasing sense of **despair** that signals his imminent downfall. In Act 4, the horrific effects of Macbeth's violent reign are highlighted when Macduff cries, 'Bleed, bleed, poor country!'

While blood has always been a common symbol of brutality and suffering, Shakespeare makes effective use of blood symbolism to characterise the Macbeths. References to blood are a constant reminder of the wrongful acts they have committed and their hideous **descent into inhumanity**. As they lose all sense of reality, both Macbeth and his wife are haunted by imagined blood.

When Macbeth is finally confronted by Macduff, their terse exchange is dominated by talk of blood-letting. The two men are **inextricably linked by blood**. For a moment, the tyrant king acknowledges the appalling deeds for which he was responsible, saying: 'my soul is too much charged/ With blood of thine already'. But Macduff has long gone beyond words, and tells his great enemy: 'My voice is in my sword, thou bloodier villain'.

The drama begins and ends with bloody battles, and blood images carry huge **emotional force** throughout the tragedy. As one of the play's central images, the symbolic meaning of blood changes over the course of the story. Initially, it represents honour and courage in battle. As Macbeth's ambition grows, however, blood is directly linked to treachery and murder. In the end, it is a powerful reminder of the central characters' shameful lives.

> *The most frequently occurring words in the play are 'blood' and 'night' – each of which appears in various forms more than* **40 times**.

Clothing

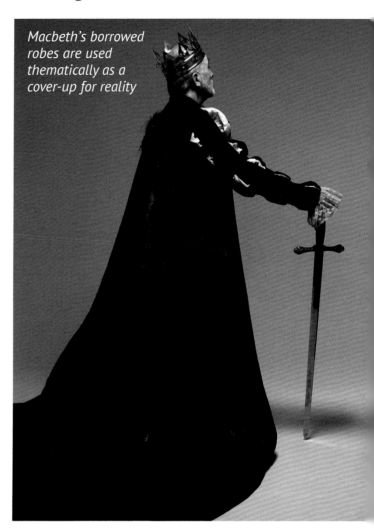

Macbeth's borrowed robes are used thematically as a cover-up for reality

Shakespeare uses clothes as a metaphor throughout *Macbeth*. In Act 1 Scene 3, Macbeth questions his new title: 'The Thane of Cawdor lives; why do you dress me/ In borrowed robes?'' He can hardly believe his luck that the witches' prophecy has come true. Right from the start, there are already **foreboding signs** that the change of clothing is also changing Macbeth's character for the worse.

Although his thoughts become increasingly treacherous, Macbeth is still **reluctant to claim the throne**. There are good reasons to remain loyal to Duncan, who has publicly acknowledged his heroism. Macbeth is a proud man with a reputation to protect. He also relishes the glory of 'golden opinions' and honours: 'Which would be worn now in their newest gloss,/ Not cast aside so soon.' The clothing comparison reveals another layer of Macbeth's personality, suggesting that he **likes to play the role** of the heroic military leader. But Lady Macbeth demands that he shows a different kind of strength – the courage to kill

Duncan. She quickly turns the clothing reference against her husband by taunting his apparent cowardice: 'Was the hope drunk/ Wherein you dressed yourself?'

From the moment he becomes king, there is no doubt that the royal garments Macbeth wears are stolen. He himself is always conscious that they do not belong to him, and he is deeply uncomfortable at **concealing his true nature** under a disguise. Before the final battle that will overthrow him, Macbeth is widely regarded as a tyrant who was never fit to rule Scotland. Caithness's comment is appropriate: 'He cannot buckle his distempered cause/ Within the belt of rule'. Angus agrees, commenting that Macbeth's title hangs 'loose about him, like a giant's robe/ Upon a dwarfish thief'.

The use of clothing imagery in *Macbeth* symbolises the **dramatic changes** that happen in the story. Most of the images refer to one of the play's central themes – the protagonist's failure to fit into his role as king – and illustrate the tragic development of a highly complex character.

Disease and Disorder

Macbeth is typical of Shakespeare's tragedies in that the natural world of the play reflects key aspects of the plot. In particular, the imagery of disease acts as a **metaphor for evil**. From the play's opening anarchic scene, the witches, immersed in 'fog and filthy air', are associated with disorder ('hurlyburly') as they make plans to meet again 'In thunder, lightning, or in rain'. There are also early signs that Macbeth already has some links with the supernatural.

The 'withered and wild' **witches represent chaos**. There are numerous references to their malicious spells, the disgusting poisons they throw into their cauldron and the 'infected' air that is their natural element. Disorder is evident in their delight in wickedness, reflected in their paradoxical language. Macbeth is soon drawn into their grotesque world, transformed from an honourable general defending order to a double-dealing assassin intent on causing havoc in Scotland.

As the power-hungry and ambitious Macbeth kills the country's rightful king and everyone else he distrusts, the **natural world begins to unravel**. The weather becomes unruly, darkness replaces daylight and submissive animals become predators. Shakespeare's figurative language suggests deception, corruption and unnaturalness. For the audience, this raises a crucial question about Macbeth. Is he a victim of fate or an agent of free will?

Metaphors of disorder and decay reinforce key themes of evil and corruption

In the hours before the assassination of the king, Macbeth complains of suffering from a 'heat-oppressèd brain' and his wife describes him as 'sickly'. **Sickness and disease spread**, affecting all of Scotland ('the sickly weal') as well as the play's central characters. After Duncan is slain, Lennox describes the earth as 'feverous'. Even the landscape reflects the moral order.

Inevitably, the country's social order slides into disarray. During the state banquet – an occasion that should showcase royalty at its best – Macbeth is clearly out of control, haunted by guilty visions of Banquo's ghost. One of the hired assassins says that Banquo's body lies in a ditch with 'twenty trenchèd gashes on his head'. Such **graphic descriptions** reflect the new king's vicious reign. As the banquet descends into uproar, Lady Macbeth struggles to restrain her husband and is forced to frantically dismiss all the guests. Having **disrupted the divine order** of lawful royal rule, Macbeth has now destroyed his relationship with his wife and left the suspicious Scottish lords longing for peace and normality.

Towards the end of the play, Macduff views Macbeth as Scotland's disease, directly responsible for violating society ('Bleed, bleed poor country'). Lady Macbeth's mind is also 'diseased', tormented by recreating Duncan's murder, even in her dreams. Her madness, of course, is yet another symbolic form of disorder. Ironically, Macbeth asks her physician to cure his wife, still unaware that their **evil is the root cause of all their suffering**.

For most of the play, images of chaos and sickness highlight Macbeth's **disastrous kingship**. Shakespeare keeps reminding the audience that political stability is the natural reflection of a good ruler. But Macbeth has never shown any interest in serving the ordinary people of Scotland. It is only after his death and the return of Malcolm, King Duncan's lawful heir, that order can be restored.

Animals

Animal imagery is used extensively in *Macbeth*. Duncan's murder is **foreshadowed** in Lady Macbeth's words: 'The raven himself is hoarse/ That croaks the fatal entrance of Duncan/ Under my battlements.' This stark image of the raven, a long-established symbol of death, suggests the savagery of what will soon occur in Macbeth's castle.

References to animals are closely associated with the prevailing inhumanity in the drama

The whole earth seems to rebel against the noble king's death. Birds scream, crickets cry, horses break out of their stalls and eat one another. In the hierarchy of the animal kingdom, every creature has its place, but following Duncan's murder, 'A falcon, towering in her pride of place,/ Was by a mousing owl hawked at and killed.' Shakespeare's incisive image shows the chaotic state Scotland has entered.

Macbeth himself admits that his mind is 'full of scorpions', a vivid symbol of his disturbed mental condition. The language he uses to describe his growing fears of Banquo and Fleance further reflects his **loss of humanity**: 'We have scorched the snake, not killed it'.

As Macbeth falls into irreversible decline, he uses more **threatening** animal imagery. By the end of Act 5, isolated, besieged and finally facing death, he describes himself as 'bear-like'. In the play's closing scene, Macduff addresses him simply as a 'hellhound'. Despite everything, Macbeth is determined to fight to the finish. For the audience, it is a timely reminder that Macbeth's only claim to heroism was his fearlessness in battle.

Soliloquies

The **soliloquy**, a speech delivered by a single character on stage, originated in Greek tragedy. The term comes from two Latin words, *solo* ('to oneself') and *loquor* ('I talk'). The character who is alone on stage will appear to be thinking aloud. Shakespeare's soliloquies are modern in that they break through what is often referred to as the 'fourth wall' that separates the audience from the stage.

An **aside** is a similar dramatic device, except that the character is not alone. When a character makes an aside, while the audience can hear every word, other characters on stage are completely oblivious of what is being said.

Some of the play's most powerful language is found in Macbeth's speeches. Soliloquies contribute greatly to his characterisation as a tragic hero. Because we know the true state of Macbeth's mind, we understand his dilemma as he contemplates the murder of Duncan. He is acutely aware that this course of action is wrong, but the temptation to be king is so strong that it eventually overrides all his concerns. In *Macbeth*, the protagonist himself has the greatest number of soliloquies. This **adds to our experience of the drama** as we share in his fears and anxieties.

> *Macbeth speaks more than*
> **30 per cent** *of the lines in the play – a dominance unmatched by any of the other tragic heroes in Shakespearean dramas. Lady Macbeth speaks* **11 per cent**.

Macbeth's key soliloquies are:

- Act 1 Scene 3: 'Two truths are told/ As happy prologues to the swelling act ...'
- Act 1 Scene 7: 'If it were done, when 'tis done ...'
- Act 2 Scene 1: 'Is this a dagger which I see before me ...?'
- Act 3 Scene 1: 'To be thus is nothing/ But to be safely thus ...'
- Act 5 Scene 3: 'I have lived long enough ...'
- Act 5 Scene 5: 'Tomorrow, and tomorrow, and tomorrow ...'

In Macbeth's **first soliloquy** (Act 1 Scene 3), he is considering what the witches have promised him. Their prophecies have already made a deep impact and his desire for power is starting to take hold. He ignores Banquo's warning and focuses instead on the possibility of becoming Scotland's next king.

Soliloquies contribute greatly to Macbeth's characterisation as a tragic hero

The witches have been proved right on two counts: they recognised that Macbeth was Thane of Glamis; and now he has been rewarded with the new title of Thane of Cawdor. Yet he wonders if their 'soliciting' is to be fully trusted. What disturbs him most is **his own evil ambition** (the 'suggestion'). His heart beats faster and his hair stands on end at the 'horrid image' of things to come. How can the prospect of becoming king be good if it creates such 'horrible imaginings'?

It's clear to the audience that the unnerving idea of killing Duncan is now firmly lodged in his mind. Macbeth's nervous tone reflects his inner conflict and the sibilant effect of 'Shakes so my single state of man' has a sinister quality that foreshadows his future actions. With so many lingering doubts, Macbeth decides not to take action until he is certain. In the interim, **he will let destiny take its course**: 'chance may crown me'. While he is impatient with his own indecisiveness, he resigns himself to wait: 'Come what come may'.

Macbeth's first soliloquy not only engages the audience, it also **heightens the dramatic tension**, develops the plot and **reveals Macbeth's complex nature**. The audience has already seen two sides to his character: he was first associated with the witches, but he is also a loyal and courageous soldier. This soliloquy lays bare his thoughts, confirming that he is a highly ambitious man who is motivated to kill Duncan. But Macbeth has been confused by the witches' prophecies and is reluctant to make a firm decision.

The critical soliloquy in **Act 3** ('To be thus is nothing') highlights Macbeth's growing obsession with securing his family's control of the Scottish throne. If the witches' promises come true, he will have murdered Duncan to benefit Banquo's heirs. Macbeth feels threatened because he considers himself inferior to Banquo in courage and nobility. The deliberate rhythm and violent language reflect his murderous thoughts, 'Our fears in Banquo stick deep'.

Macbeth is acutely aware that he has no legitimate right to be king. Duncan had already named Malcolm as his lawful successor. Shakespeare's audience would have believed in the divine right of kings. So Macbeth was not entitled to the kingship on either count. Yet his **arrogant ambition** is greater than ever now that he fears his 'genius is rebuked'. He refers to another great power struggle between the Roman

generals Mark Antony and Octavian (later Caesar Augustus).

The **repetitive structure** of Macbeth's speech also shows his deep-rooted uncertainty. He repeatedly returns to his anxieties about Banquo and the unresolved subject of safeguarding his kingship. Again, this illustrates his anxiety and unsettled state of mind. He is now determined to eliminate any threats – real or imagined – that could undermine his long-term control of the Scottish throne.

Dismissive references to the 'fruitless crown' and 'barren sceptre' emphasise Macbeth's dissatisfaction and sense of self-pity. He is also conscious of the irony of sacrificing his immortal soul ('mine eternal jewel') – and all to advance the political interests of 'the seeds of Banquo'. In contrast to earlier soliloquies, in which he reflected on the morality of his plans, **Macbeth shows no humanity**. The enormity of committing murder no longer affects him; now it is merely a means to an end.

Some of the play's most compelling language is found in the soliloquies

This crucial soliloquy **marks the point at which Macbeth's complete moral downfall begins**. No longer satisfied with power for himself, his discontent grows to ferocious antagonism as he vows to challenge what the weird sisters have foretold. His tone varies from despair and insecurity to resentment and defiance, but he is always conscious of his own evil choices. This is what saves him from becoming a one-dimensional monster and makes him a truly tragic character.

Macbeth's second soliloquy in Act 5 ('Tomorrow, and tomorrow, and tomorrow ...') addresses the subject of time, which has become an intolerable burden for him. His response to the news of Lady Macbeth's death is not altogether surprising. Beyond all feeling, he can only say, 'She should have died hereafter'. For him, time itself no longer makes sense and the 'hereafter' does not exist. The word he focuses on is 'tomorrow'. A rhythmic, childlike pace suggests the relentless passage of time, and the compulsive repetition reflects Macbeth's growing madness.

In soliloquies lies truth

Macbeth considers that our short lives 'have lighted fools/ The way to dusty death': people are excited by the prospect of success and happiness when their desires are fulfilled, only to be disappointed in the end. The alliteration of the consonant sound in 'dusty death' creates a starkly negative tone, contributing to a **sense of nihilism**. The plodding rhythm becomes harsh and the tone more indignant when he introduces a powerful image signifying life's transience and vulnerability: 'Out, out, brief candle'.

He personifies life as 'a walking shadow', similar to a talentless actor ('a poor player') who exaggerates his performance on stage and then leaves, never to be heard of again. Shakespeare develops the metaphor, comparing human existence to the play itself. Not only are the actors ridiculous in themselves, they are taking part in an **absurd drama** written by an idiot and filled with pointless 'sound and fury'. Now that Macbeth has ceased to care about anything, the phrase encapsulates the empty mockery that his kingship has become.

In this final soliloquy, we see the play's ultimate tragedy as Shakespeare invites us to identify with the central character. Macbeth is **poignantly aware of the rapid deterioration of his humanity** and concludes that existence is entirely meaningless. The short concluding phrase ('Signifying nothing') fades away, leaving only silence. Macbeth's pathos makes a devastating impact and his sickness of heart is likely to awaken some sympathy in the audience.

> *Macbeth is probably the most performed play ever written. It is claimed that a performance is staged somewhere in the world* **every four hours**.

Dramatic Irony

Dramatic irony means that **the audience knows something the characters do not**. Because of this awareness, the characters' words take on a different meaning, often giving rise to increased suspense or – on some occasions – humour. Shakespeare shows that people can be blind to the truth of a situation by enabling his audience to see things as they really are.

Throughout *Macbeth*, various forms of dramatic irony are used to create **tension** and involve the audience. An early example occurs in Act 1 Scene 3 when the witches greet Macbeth as 'Thane of Cawdor'. He is bemused, saying, 'The Thane of Cawdor lives'. However, we have already seen Duncan condemn the traitor to death and grant the title to Macbeth. Later, when Ross arrives to announce this news, Macbeth's reaction is one of shock.

There is more dramatic irony when Duncan arrives at Macbeth's castle at Inverness and is struck by the peaceful atmosphere of the place: 'This castle hath a pleasant seat.' His words follow the dramatic exchange in which Macbeth and his wife begin plotting the king's murder. Lady Macbeth's behaviour is also ironic in this same scene, particularly in the refined and formal language with which she welcomes the unsuspecting king. Duncan's complete unawareness of the danger he is in **engages the audience and builds suspense**.

Perhaps the most powerful example of dramatic irony is Macbeth's reliance on the witches' apparitions. He is desperate to believe their assurance that no man 'of woman born shall harm Macbeth' and that he will remain protected until the trees in Birnam Wood begin to move. The audience **recognises the equivocations** of the witches long before Macbeth does.

A more subtle form of irony is when a character's words only become significant later in the story. For example, during the murder scene, Lady Macbeth confidently says, 'A little water clears us of the deed'. By the end of the play – when she has become weak and deranged – she will be haunted by the smell of the blood and obsessively trying to wash her hands. Before her powers began to slip, Lady Macbeth supported her guilt-ridden husband, dismissing his talk of hearing voices: 'So, it will make us mad'. **This is an ironic foreshadowing of her sleep-walking scene**, when she is finally overwhelmed by conscience and descends into insanity.

Shakespeare's use of dramatic irony places his characters' weaknesses into sharp relief. Their errors of judgement stand out all the more when the audience is aware of their impending doom. The fact that we know what lies ahead when some of the characters do not **enhances the emotional experience of the play**, creating feelings of suspense, sympathy, fear, disbelief and even anger in the audience.

(For sample Leaving Cert examination questions on Shakespeare's use of dramatic techniques, see page 267.)

When the audience knows more than the characters, dramatic tension results from such irony

Exam Technique

Purposeful Use of Key Scenes

Successful *Macbeth* Leaving Cert answers will be assessed on four basic criteria:

* knowledge and understanding of the play
* answering the question relevantly
* use of suitable reference and quotation
* quality of the written expression.

'Reading' Questions

Question wording should be scrutinised to identify the various key aspects that you are being asked to discuss. The three key elements (underlined) of the following question all need to be addressed:

> Q. 'In the play *Macbeth*, Shakespeare presents a <u>powerful vision</u> of <u>human triumph</u> in a <u>world of equivocation and evil</u>.'
>
> Discuss this view, supporting your answer with reference to the play.

Planning Answers

* Take time (at least five minutes) to plan, so that you construct a **succinct, cogent response** based on the evidence of the text. Your essay should have a clear sense of purpose, starting with a simple, coherent viewpoint rather than an imprecise, rambling approach. Every paragraph should be a step in a developing argument. Effective critical literacy skills and incisive analysis will be well rewarded.
* **Avoid unfocused narrative** or general summary. You will need to be selective and refer to specific moments from the play that are appropriate to the question.
* The examination questions are framed to invite candidates to engage with them but not necessarily to agree completely with the premise put forward in the question. Always **be prepared to challenge** the key terms of a question, perhaps disagreeing with some part/s or the entire premise outlined.

Paragraphing Guide

* A paragraph is a unit of writing that usually focuses on **one main idea**. This central idea (or point) is simply what the paragraph is about. It may be stated in a topic sentence (often early in the paragraph), or it may be so obvious that it is implied. An effective paragraph develops the main idea with enough relevant detail to hold the examiner's attention while clearly conveying your views. A paragraph is much more than a collection of connected sentences. It is a building block of essay development.

* Most paragraphs consist of at least six or seven sentences; therefore, several supporting details (illustrated by suitable reference or quotation) are needed to build on the topic sentence. Each new sentence in the paragraph should relate to the overall topic so as to **develop the analysis**.

* The examiner has to understand your train of thought, so what you write should always be clear and **coherent** and form a unified passage.

- Since most Single Text Leaving Cert examination essays are at least 800 words in length, it makes sense to plan five or six key points as the basis of your response. Main paragraphs would likely be about 150 words on average. Of course, **a paragraph can be any length**, depending on its purpose.

- Your own language skills are crucial to success. Aim for **controlled expression** that is fresh, varied and assured. A common flaw is repetition of key words or phrases from the question in an attempt to maintain a relevant approach. Look for alternatives to invigorate your discussion, e.g. a character's 'admirable qualities' can also be described as 'personal attributes', 'attractive features', 'appealing traits', etc.

- You usually start **a new paragraph**:
  - after ending your introduction
  - to begin a new discussion point
  - when contrasting ideas
  - when starting your conclusion.

- Aim to **structure** your paragraphs in the same way as a full essay, with an introduction, main body and conclusion.
  - Introduce the paragraph's main point.
  - Develop and support the point.
  - Show the significance of the point you are making.

The pursuit of power

Quoting Effectively

As a general guide, quotations should be **accurate, brief and relevant**. Quotes should always support the point you are making. Words taken directly from the play should be placed within quotation marks, e.g. 'Fair is foul, and foul is fair.'

A well-chosen quotation **enables you to comment effectively** on theme, character/s and style. Apt quotes, derived from a thorough knowledge of the text, will help to develop your analysis.

Try to **integrate quotations** seamlessly into your own sentences, e.g. *Macbeth's sword is said to have 'smoked with bloody execution'.*

You will be penalised for mechanical errors, so **take great care** with spelling, grammar and punctuation. Remember – examiners award marks for 'quality of language'.

How the Single Text Shakespeare Question is Marked

The Single Text English (Higher Level) question is allocated 60 minutes in the exam and is worth 60 marks in total. These are awarded by reference to the **PCLM** criteria for assessment (i.e. 3 x 18 marks for each of P, C and L plus 6 marks for M):

> P = Clarity of **Purpose**: 18 marks (30%)
>
> C = **Coherence** of Delivery: 18 marks (30%)
>
> L = Efficiency of **Language** Use: 18 marks (30%)
>
> M = Accuracy of **Mechanics**: 6 marks (10%)

Clarity of Purpose

In assessing Clarity of Purpose, examiners will judge how successfully the candidate has addressed the question and engaged with the set task. This refers to the quality of engagement, relevance, focus, originality, and understanding of the appropriate genre.

The marks awarded for Coherence of Delivery and Efficiency of Language Use will not normally be higher than those awarded for Clarity of Purpose.

Coherence of Delivery

In awarding the marks for Coherence of Delivery, examiners will assess how well the candidate has sustained the response and developed the entire answer. This refers to the quality and management of ideas, supporting points, sequencing, and engagement with texts, appropriate to the task.

Efficiency of Language Use

Marks for Efficiency of Language Use are awarded for the management and control of language. This refers to the quality of language used to achieve clear communication in terms of vocabulary, paragraph structure, syntax, punctuation, fluency, style and expression, appropriate to the task.

Accuracy of Mechanics

Marks awarded for Accuracy of Mechanics refer to spelling and grammar, appropriate to the register. Marks for M are essentially independent of P, C and L marks.

Chief Examiner's Report Observations

- It is the question set which must be answered.
- Students should be assisted to develop the skills needed to shape, manipulate and adapt their knowledge to produce measured, informed and reflective responses.
- Some examiners identified candidates who were able to demonstrate knowledge of a text ... but were less able to deliver this knowledge in a lucid and coherent fashion.
- It is essential that candidates fully engage with the terms of any question attempted, challenging the terms of the question, perhaps disagreeing with some part or the entire premise outlined.
- Examiners were impressed when candidates presented lucid responses to questions based on their knowledge and understanding of the texts, augmented by a well-reasoned argument, point of view or opinion.
- Examiners were pleased when they saw candidates trust in their own personal response and demonstrate a willingness to challenge the 'fixed meaning' of texts.
- Careless use of quotation served to undermine answers.

www.examinations.ie

Evil ambition leads only to isolation and tragedy

Writing Top-Grade Essays

Responding to the Task (Clarity of Purpose)

Clarity of Purpose (P) refers to **identifying the task clearly and addressing the question**.

It is crucial when developing a response to the exam question to identify all the key elements and to decide whether you agree and/or disagree with the given statement.

> **Remember!**
> *The marking scheme awards 18/60 marks for this skill.*

Sample Leaving Cert Question

Q. 'Macbeth and Lady Macbeth share a variety of character traits that contribute to the tragic aspects of the drama.' Discuss this statement, supporting your answer with reference to the play *Macbeth*.

How do I Approach the Question?

Identify the task by checking all the key terms:

'Macbeth <u>and</u> Lady Macbeth <u>share</u> a variety of <u>character traits</u> that <u>contribute</u> to the <u>tragic aspects</u> of the drama.'

+ Both characters should be discussed (although not necessarily equally).

+ Adopt a viewpoint or stance: agree/disagree wholly or in part.

+ Identify both the shared personality traits and individual characteristics.

+ Discuss what these character traits contribute to the tragic aspects of the play.

Possible Viewpoints

Both characters share common character traits, such as ambition, courage and ruthlessness. This leads the couple to perform deeds that have tragic consequences (murder, intimidation, disorder, suicide, etc.). At different stages, both suffer from guilt, which contributes to their personal tragedy.

(The candidate is in full agreement with the given statement.)

OR

While they share some characteristics initially (such as ambition and courage), Macbeth is weak and his wife's influence is largely responsible for Duncan's murder. This results in tension between them and Macbeth becomes increasingly dominant and tyrannical. Because of his moral decline, Scotland suffers, Lady Macbeth cannot live with her guilt and the disillusioned Macbeth is eventually killed.

(The candidate is in partial agreement with the given statement.)

Sourcing Evidence from Act 1 to back Discussion Points

Prompt!

+ Macbeth and Lady Macbeth are highly ambitious individuals. She is cold-blooded while he is easily tempted and conflicted morally – and this will result in violence, suffering and loss.

+ At the outset, Macbeth is weak-willed and manipulated by the amoral Lady Macbeth who persuades him to kill Duncan. He grapples with his conscience, intensifying the tragedy.

+ Lady Macbeth is more practical than her husband and she plans the king's murder. Macbeth could be viewed as a victim of the greater evil around him.

Class/Homework Exercise

Based on your study of **Act 1**, write down three short bullet points (supported by suitable quotation) that could be used in a response to the following statement:

'Shakespeare's effective use of a variety of contrasts creates a darkly intriguing world in the play *Macbeth*.'

Prompt!

- Identify all aspects of the task by studying all the key terms.
- Adopt a clear viewpoint (agree/disagree wholly or in part).
- Witches introduce a sinister atmosphere of mischief and deception.
- Battlefield scene presents Macbeth as both courageous and bloodthirsty.
- Duncan is respected but also susceptible to treachery.
- The ambitious Lady Macbeth is an evil influence on her morally weak husband.

Planning Your Essay (Coherence of Delivery)

Having clearly identified the task in the Leaving Cert *Macbeth* question, it is important to develop the ability to sustain a coherent response over the entire answer. This requires careful planning. The response demands clear management of ideas, the choice of suitable references and close engagement with the text of the play.

suitable reference and/or quotation, and engaging with the text of the play.

> **Remember!**
> *The marking scheme awards 18/60 marks for this skill.*

A Sustained Response

Coherence of Delivery (C) refers to **sustaining an effective response over the entire answer**. This involves managing relevant ideas and discussion points, sustaining continuity of argument, using

Note! Unfocused narrative is a recurring flaw that will be penalised by examiners. Always avoid re-telling the story of the play or merely summarising key scenes without any analysis or comment.

Is Macbeth the victim of a greater malevolence?

Sample Leaving Cert Question

Q. 'The changing relationship between Macbeth and Lady Macbeth engages audiences and adds poignancy to the play *Macbeth*.' Discuss this view, supporting your answer with reference to the text.

How do I Approach the Question?

Identify the task by checking the key terms ('changing relationship', 'engages audiences', 'adds poignancy').

Sample Essay Plan

Sample viewpoint or stance: Agree.

Intro: Ambitious couple bound by the strength of their love and shared ambition. Their contrasting moral characters engages interest from the start and leads to tragic consequences for both of them.

Point 1: Initial loving relationship may not be what it seems. Lady Macbeth's knowledge of her husband's nature, 'too full o' the milk of human kindness'. Questions arise about the balance of power within the Macbeths' marriage.

Point 2: Dominance of Lady Macbeth over her indecisive husband, 'Look like the innocent flower'. Yet he admires his wife's ruthless desire, 'bring forth men-children only'. Dramatic impact of

tension between the different views about killing Duncan enriches the theatrical experience.

Point 3: Practical Lady Macbeth plans the murder, 'Leave all the rest to me'. Macbeth hesitates, deciding, 'We will proceed no further in this business'. Lady Macbeth bitterly criticises him. The growing tension between the couple adds depth to the drama.

Point 4: The killing of Duncan marks a dramatic turning point in the couple's relationship. Lady Macbeth is delighted, 'My husband!' Macbeth is disgusted with himself. 'Wake Duncan with thy knocking! I would thou couldst!' Macbeth's action has not only killed Duncan, but poignantly has put a deadly rift in the couple's close relationship.

Point 5: Following the climactic banquet scene, the couple become estranged. Guilt drives Lady Macbeth to take her own life and her tyrannical husband loses all humanity, 'She should have died hereafter'. Audiences left with mixed feelings.

Develop one of the above points into a paragraph.

Point 2: Sample Paragraph

Shakespeare unnerves the audience with the spectacle of Lady Macbeth calling on evil spirits to help her achieve the couple's plans to become Scotland's next king and queen. Her powerful language reflects her demonic character. She wishes to 'pour' her 'spirits' in Macbeth's ear, to 'chastise' him 'with the valour of' her tongue. When her husband arrives, she assumes control, 'you shall put/ This night's great business into my dispatch'. She commands, 'Leave all the rest to me.' When Macbeth displays his indecision, 'We will proceed no further in this business', she reverts to disdainful sarcasm to make him act, 'From this time/ Such I account thy love.' In a horrifying speech she declares that she would have 'dashed the brains' of her child onto the ground if she had 'so sworn' as Macbeth had done to murder Duncan. Before this terrifying attack, Macbeth gives way, 'If we should fail?' But the practical Lady Macbeth devises the plan and leaves an admiring Macbeth to declare, 'Bring forth men-children only'. With the tension mounting, we are appalled by the couple's cruel plans, as they get ready to 'mock the time with fairest show'. *(190 words)*

Examiner's Comment

- Well-informed response that tackles the question of the couple's intense relationship.
- Sustained focus on the impact of their interaction on the audience ('unnerves', 'horrifying speech', 'we are appalled').
- Apt and accurate quotations used effectively.
- Excellent expression throughout enhances the top-grade standard.

Class/Homework Exercises

1. Choose another one of the points from the sample plan and write your own developed paragraph (150–200 words).

2. Using the sample plan above as a guide, write your own essay plan for an answer to the following question:

   'Lady Macbeth is portrayed as more ruthless and amoral than her husband, and this results in her suffering less than Macbeth.' Discuss this statement, supporting your answer with close reference to the play.

Prompt!
- Identify all the key aspects in the question.
- Decide on a clear viewpoint or approach.
- Audience has some initial regard for the conflicted Macbeth.
- Lady Macbeth is strong and evil from the start – and less sympathetic.
- Soliloquies show Macbeth's vulnerability and pain.
- Both characters suffer equally – but at different times.

Macbeth and his wife – a complex, changing relationship

Sample Essays

Sample Essay 1

Q. 'In the play *Macbeth*, audiences are presented with a horrifying vision of an evil world dominated by the use and abuse of power.'

Discuss this view, supporting your answer with reference to the text.

Marking Scheme Guidelines

Candidates are free to agree and/or disagree with the view expressed in the question, but must focus on the 'horrifying vision of an evil world dominated by the use and/or abuse of power'.

Allow for a broad interpretation of 'power' including political, physical, emotional, moral, divine, etc.

MICHAEL FASSBENDER MARION COTILLARD

MACBETH

UN FILM DE **JUSTIN KURZEL**

'The sovereignty will fall upon Macbeth'

Indicative Material

- Witches' supernatural power creates evil/gothic atmosphere.
- Impact of Macbeth's powerful military presence on the battlefield.
- Influence of Lady Macbeth's destructive ambition/emotional blackmail.
- Duncan's use of political power is idealised/ineffectual.
- Banquo and Macduff make positive moral choices and are/are not forces for good.
- Malcolm represents the ideal of moral/divine power.
- Shocking violence/tyranny/despair pervades the play. Etc.

1 The Elizabethans believed that kings were appointed by God and had a divine right to maintain order in the natural world. In 'Macbeth', the central character, through a great flaw in his personality, 'vaulting ambition', breaks this order by killing the rightful King Duncan and seizing power in Scotland. His tyrannous rule creates chaos and invites the audience into a nightmarish world of violence, gloom and hopelessness. Over the course of the play, Shakespeare uses four portraits of very different kings (Duncan, Macbeth, Edward the Confessor and Malcolm) to examine the use and abuse of power.

2 Duncan is introduced as a weak ageing king trying to rule over a rebellious country. He does not directly lead his soldiers, but depends on Macbeth, 'Bellona's bridegroom', for victory. With remarkably poor timing, Duncan then names his eldest son Malcolm as his heir, thus removing any possibility of Macbeth being crowned king by chance. In failing to use his power wisely, he gives Macbeth a motive for acting against him. Duncan also trusts too easily, remarking, 'There's no art to find the mind's construction in the face'. He had misplaced his trust in Cawdor, 'a man on whom I built an absolute trust'. Yet he proceeds to act in exactly the same way with Macbeth. His gentleness is even praised by Macbeth, 'Hath borne his faculties so meek'. But this mildness is seen as weakness and from an early stage, we are involved in Macbeth's tense agony as we wonder whether or not he will choose to kill rightful king.

3 His 'rapt' fascination with the witches associates him with falseness and corruption – and he struggles with 'horrible imaginings'. Through a series of anguished soliloquies, we recognise his overwhelming moral dilemma and get a glimpse of his disturbed mind when he imagines a bloodstained dagger leading him to Duncan's chamber. His language is sinister, filled with references to 'gouts of blood' and 'dark and deep desires'. As he wrestles with his conscience, his amoral wife exerts her influence, demanding that he prove himself to her by killing the king and fulfilling her dreams. By the end of Act 1, we see two monstrous figures who have given in to a warped lust for power. Lady Macbeth's speeches are particularly shocking. Mocking the brooding Macbeth, she demonstrates her heartlessness by claiming that she would kill her own nursing child ('dashed the brains out') rather than break her promise.

4 The playwright uses setting very effectively to illustrate the enormous evil surrounding Macbeth's rise to power. On the night of the actual murder, there are storms, 'the night has been unruly', 'Our chimneys were blown down', and there were 'strange screams of death'. Shakespeare's audience would instinctively have recognised the consequences of Macbeth's misuse of power. Unnatural acts are reported, a falcon was killed by an owl, Duncan's horses were said to have eaten each other.

5 Macbeth's rule as king could hardly be more horrifying. He unleashes a reign of terror to try to secure his illegal royal position, 'There's not a one of them but in his house I keep a servant fee'd'. Exploitation and oppression are the hallmarks of his sovereignty. The 'suffering country' is 'Under a hand accursed'. Macbeth then descends into 'murky' hell when he decides to attack his enemy, Macduff, by killing his family, 'Seize upon Fife; give to the edge of the sword/ His wife, his babes and all unfortunate souls/ That trace him to his line'. In such distressing scenes that shock audiences, everyone suffers under the oppression of the tyrant.

6 However, Macbeth's evil time in power eventually ends. Malcolm, like the English King Edward, is shown as the antithesis to a despot. He is the epitome of the proper use of power, but is sceptical when Macduff approaches him to come to Scotland's aid. More astute in exercising power than his naive father, Malcolm will bring a new order to the poor bleeding homeland when he takes over. After the horrendous suffering, the nightmare will soon be over.

7 Not only is Malcolm the rightful heir but he shows the necessary 'king-becoming graces' – 'courage', 'bounty', 'justice', 'perseverance', 'lowliness'. He is brave in battle, unlike Duncan, who did not lead, but let others fight on his behalf. Malcolm also engenders loyalty, again unlike his father, 'We have met with foes that strike beside us'. He is careful in his use of power, repaying all his chief supporters by making the thanes earls and stating that 'what needful else ... We will perform in measure, time and place'. He invites all to Scone to see him rightfully crowned because unlike Macbeth he is there 'by the Grace of God'. The divine line of kingship has finally been re-established.

8 After witnessing the horrific spectacle of evil witchcraft and gratuitous violence, the audience is left to speculate on the potential of Malcolm to restore the natural order. Through the proper application of power, unlike his predecessors – ineffectual Duncan and unlawful Macbeth – it seems likely that harmony will reign once more in Scotland. 'The night is long that never finds the day.'

(c. 850 words)

Marking Scheme		
P	18	18
C	18	18
L	18	18
M	6	6
	60	60

GRADE: H1

Examiner's Comment

- ◆ A very well-informed and sustained top-grade essay that addresses all aspects of the question.
- ◆ The discussion is well structured; points are clearly developed and supported with suitable reference and accurate quotation.
- ◆ Interesting exploration of the contrasting attitudes to power of Duncan, Macbeth and Malcolm.
- ◆ Range of perceptive points including the way language and setting amplify the world of evil.
- ◆ Controlled expression and syntax. Vocabulary is impressive (e.g. 'overwhelming moral dilemma', 'Exploitation and oppression are the hallmarks of his sovereignty').

Sample Essay 2

Q. 'Shakespeare's portrayal of Macbeth and Lady Macbeth's relationship is both fascinating and repellent.'

Discuss this view, supporting your answer with reference to the play *Macbeth*.

Marking Scheme Guidelines

Candidates are free to agree and/or disagree with the view expressed in the question, but should focus on the playwright's 'portrayal of Macbeth and Lady Macbeth' and how their relationship is 'both fascinating and repellent' (although not necessarily equally).

Allow for a broad interpretation of 'fascinating and repellent'.

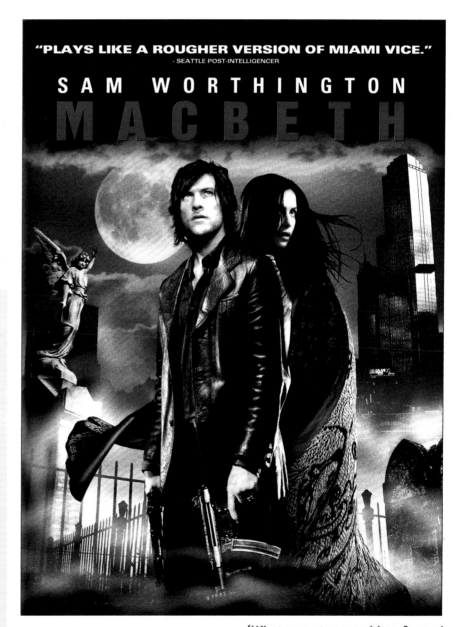

'What cannot you and I perform...'

Indicative Material

- Riveting opening portrayal of a close couple's joint ambition.
- Impressive/off-putting dominance of Lady Macbeth in the lead-up to Duncan's murder.
- Couple's battle of wills engages audience, creating sympathy/antipathy.
- Clever/despicable behaviour immediately after the king's death.
- Distressing/unsurprising estrangement of couple following the banquet scene.
- Reversal of roles fascinates/repels.
- Impact of self-destructive development and downfall of both characters.
- Poignancy/poetic justice of final scenes. Etc.

1 In the tragedy 'Macbeth', Shakespeare explores the changing dynamic in the relationship of a modern-style marriage between equals. This provides a dramatic experience which is riveting and compelling, but is certainly not fascinating in the sense of delightful or enchanting. For the most part, the audience is moved to revulsion and disgust at the Macbeths' obsessive lust for power. From the rushed opening letter to his 'dearest partner in greatness' to the forlorn statement, 'She should have died hereafter', we are engrossed as each of these compelling central characters hastens towards 'dusty death'.

2 After hearing the witches' prophecies, Macbeth wrote a hurried letter to his wife to tell her of 'what greatness is promised thee'. This is a husband who needs to impress. In a powerful soliloquy, Lady Macbeth criticises his 'human kindness', clearly showing that she has the dominant role in their relationship. She will 'chastise with the valour of my tongue/ all that impedes thee from the golden round'. She desires what her husband wants and will do all in her power to encourage him to proceed. But the audience then becomes sickened when she calls on the powers of darkness to 'unsex me here'. Lady Macbeth wishes to deny her feminine nature, suggesting that power matters more to her than respect for Macbeth.

3 When he attempts to follow his conscience and proceed no futher in the 'business' of murder, Lady Macbeth begins to 'chastise' her weak-willed husband. She starts by comparing him to the 'poor cat in the adage', afraid to get its feet wet while desiring to catch the fish. Then in a most repugnant image. she describes how she would kill her own child if she had sworn 'as you/ Have done to this'. Yet surprisingly, Macbeth, instead of being horrified, as is the audience, bends to her strong will, 'If we should fail?' Now Lady Macbeth reaches the height of her monstrous powers, dismissing her husband's fears, 'screw your courage to the sticking place/ And we'll not fail'. She then sets out the plan for Duncan's murder to an admiring Macbeth, 'Bring forth men-children only'. To our disgust, he surrenders full stop to his powerful wife, echoing her hypocritical words, 'false face must hide what the false heart doth know'.

4 The reaction to this couple is now one of revulsion at their evil ambition. But Shakespeare now shows another side to this intriguing marriage. The focus is now placed on the effect of the murder on the couple. A nervous Lady Macbeth is seen pacing anxiously, awaiting the return of her husband from the crime scene, 'The attempt and not the deed/ Confounds us'. An uneasy exchange between the couple vividly conveys the enormous pressure on them both in the undertaking of this horrific enterprise, 'Did you not speak?'/ 'When'/ 'Now?'. Lady Macbeth is the more practical of the two and just as she assumed control in the planning of the murder, she now takes care of the situation. Macbeth has returned with the daggers which should have remained in Duncan's room so as to incriminate the bodyguards. She returns them and scolds him, almost like a naughty child, for his regret at his bloody hands, 'I shame/ To wear a heart so white'.

5 Interestingly, the murder transforms their relationship. Lady Macbeth can no longer communicate so easily with her guilt-stricken

husband whose imagination makes him distracted. However, his hard-headed wife regains some control again when the knocking at the gate requires her to act in a rational way. She barks out instructions, 'Retire we to our chamber', 'Get on your nightgown'. Ironically she believes deep consideration of their deed 'will make us mad'. She even convinces herself that 'A little water clears us of this deed'. We know that this pragmatic woman is only fooling herself. She is unaware that not only have the couple destroyed Duncan, but also their own peace of mind, their relationship and the well-being of the country. A tense audience waits to see developments disgusted, yet intrigued.

6 The Banquet Scene marks the end of their original close relationship. Abandoned by Macbeth, who has now put all his hope in witchcraft, Lady Macbeth is a pathetic, broken woman. When we next see her, she is acting almost as if deranged and even obsessively washing blood off her imaginary blood-stained hands, 'Out damn spot'. By making us watch the meltdown, both physically, emotionally and mentally of this once all-powerful woman, Shakespeare looks for sympathy for her. Her lonely cry of 'all the perfumes of Arabia will sweeten this little hand' is pathetic.

7 Of course, Macbeth is otherwise preoccupied, trying to resist the threat of his opponents' armies. When he is informed of his wife's tragic death, his reply shocks us, 'She should have died hereafter'. The audience is left to wondering whether this man who has just experienced his 'dearest partner in greatness' end her life is beyond all feeling. The relationship has already been dead for a long time. Like Lady Macbeth, he is only aware of the futility of their evil choices. The once glittering couple have gone to their 'dusty death' alone, leaving us both gripped and horrified by the Macbeths' evolving relationship.

(c. 860 words)

Marking Scheme		
P	18	18
C	17	18
L	16	18
M	6	6
	57	60

GRADE: H1

Examiner's Comment

- Clear, concise introduction that engages directly with the full question.
- Effectively traces the development of the central relationship.
- Very well illustrated references to the changing roles of both characters.
- First-rate use of suitable supportive quotes integrated into discussion points.
- Generally well controlled expression, apart from the odd problem with repetition (e.g. par 4)
- Paragraph 6 is the least successful and the undeveloped point here is awkwardly phrased.
- Informed and insightful response showing very good understanding of the play.

Power corrupts

Sample Essay 3

Q. 'The dramatic portrayal of Macbeth makes him the play's dominant character from start to finish.'

Discuss this view, supporting your answer with reference to the play *Macbeth*.

Marking Scheme Guidelines

Candidates are free to agree and/or disagree with the view expressed in the question, but must focus on the 'dramatic portrayal of Macbeth' and 'dominant character from start to finish'.

Allow for a broad interpretation of 'dramatic portrayal' – including plot, structure, staging, references, soliloquies, imagery, dialogue, audience reaction, etc.

'I cannot taint with fear'

Indicative Material

- Shakespeare's structuring of the play places Macbeth centre stage.
- Anticipatory beginning and compelling ending serve to strengthen Macbeth's dominance.
- Soliloquies provide engrossing insights into Macbeth's conflicted interior life.
- Poetic power of the language elicits audience sympathy.
- Dramatic impact of other characters is focused on Macbeth.
- Single plot intensifies audience's experience of the tragic hero.
- Consequences of Macbeth's actions totally disrupt the world of the play. Etc.

1 In the play 'Macbeth', Shakespeare creates a character of high status, who is fallible, and with whom the audience can sympathise. Macbeth brings about his own downfall through human frailty (a lust for power) and suffers the consequences of his actions. The spotlight, throughout the play, remains firmly focused on the protagonist while the playwright explores his moral degeneration.

This central character's story demonstrates the dangers of blind ambition for an audience whose response alternates between pity to terror and back again.

2 Shakespeare chooses to delay Macbeth's entrance. This creates a state of fevered anticipation while we await his appearance in Scene 3. Other characters have already been speaking about him. The witches will go

to the heath 'to meet with Macbeth'. The army captain speaks in glowing terms of 'brave Macbeth' who fearlessly strode into battle with 'his brandished steel, /Which smoked with bloody execution'. Ross regards him as 'Bellona's bridegroom', while Duncan calls him 'noble Macbeth'. Then the playwright chooses to have Macbeth's first words, 'So foul and fair a day I have not seen', echo the witches' 'Fair is foul, and foul is fair'. Dialogue is used to associate Macbeth with the 'instruments of evil', adding to the sense of ambiguity. This man, 'Valour's minion', full of the 'milk of human kindness' dominates the opening of the play.

3 But it is Macbeth's fascinating soliloquies that illuminate the agony of this flawed hero. His initial loyalty can be seen in the list of reasons he gives not to kill the king, 'I am his kinsman and his subject', 'his host', he recognises that Duncan has been a 'meek' king. He is propelled by such a lust for power that when he hears Duncan name his son Malcolm as his heir, he decides to act to further his ambition. Appropriately for a man of action, Macbeth uses an image from hunting, adding to his tragic dilemma, 'I have no spur/ To prick the side of my intent, but only/ Vaulting ambition'. Not only does he recognise his weakness, but he understands the consequences which will follow if he allows it sway, it then 'o'er leaps itself/ And falls on the other'.

4 Only the audience is aware of the agony within Macbeth's 'heat oppressed brain'. The playwright brings audience and tragic hero into a world which is both an imaginary 'false creation' and at the same time an inner reality. The 'bloody business' of Duncan's murder creates a hellish experience conveyed through the vivid personification of 'withered Murder' stalking the land. The imagery of light and darkness is used by Macbeth to conjure up this nightmare vision into which he and the audience will descend, 'Stars hide your fires!/ Let not light see my dark and deep desires'. The effective alliterative phrase beats out the strength of Macbeth's evil ambition.

5 The choice made by Shakespeare not to present the murder of Duncan onstage focuses the audience's attention solely on the consequences of the killing on Macbeth himself to generate empathy. Macbeth gazes at his bloody hands, 'This is a sorry sight'. The hushed sibilance underlines his vulnerability. He admits he is 'afraid to think what I have done'. Again, his self-knowledge is shocking. He knows he has destroyed his own peace of mind for ever, 'Macbeth does murder sleep'. Despite the fact that Macbeth has committed regicide, the audience is being invited to feel sympathy with the murderer, not the victim. Macbeth's horror at the effects of his action are poetically phrased in the vivid image, 'the multitudinous seas incarnadine'. Such poetic language will further engage the audience as it suggests the tragic hero's horrifying sense of his own terrible fate as well as Duncan's.

6 Everything that happens in the play is centred on Macbeth. The witches plot to bring about his downfall, 'draw him on to confusion'. Banquo is used as a foil to Macbeth, resisting the witches' temptation. Minor characters discuss the horrors Macbeth has brought on the land, which are mirrored in nature's disorder, 'dark night strangles the travelling lamp'. Duncan's horses 'ate each other'. Lady Macbeth devotes herself to making him king and then fades into the background when he excludes her from his plans, 'be innocent of the knowledge, dearest chuck'. Malcolm and Macduff dedicate themselves to bringing about his downfall. In every scene in the drama, all the characters spiral around the central dominant figure.

7 But it is Macbeth's eloquent soliloquy after Lady Macbeth's suicide which lingers in the mind. We witness the catastrophic results of his misjudged ambition. He has nothing left but endless days, 'Tomorrow, and tomorrow, and tomorrow, / Creeps in this petty pace from day to day/ To the last syllable of recorded time'. The repetition and laboured rhythm mimic the slow movement of the passing days. Slender-vowelled onomatopoeia ('Creeps') and the alliterative phrase 'petty pace' highlight the dreariness of life. Shakespeare has succeeded in his attempt to gain some sympathy for a tyrannical murderer.

8 Macbeth, however, who has shown no remorse nor attempted to reform himself, is given a dignified exit. Throwing on his 'warlike shield', he goes to inhabit the only place where he has been truly great, the battlefield. Throughout the play, his desires, thoughts and actions have propelled the plot. The presence of Macbeth pervades the play from start to finish. Even at the end, we do not see him being killed, but we can imagine that he died courageously.

(c. 900 words)

Marking Scheme		
P	18	18
C	18	18
L	18	18
M	6	6
	60	60

GRADE: H1

Examiner's Comment

◆ An excellent response that tackles both elements of the question with confidence.

◆ Insightful discussion points on structure, imagery, soliloquies and poetic language.

◆ Strong emphasis on the audience's involvement with Macbeth.

◆ Good use of suitable quotations and informative references.

◆ Quotes effectively integrated into critical commentary.

◆ Well-organised paragraphs and assured language use.

◆ Expression is clear, varied and incisive throughout.

Sample Essay 4

Q. 'Throughout the play *Macbeth*, Shakespeare makes effective use of a variety of dramatic devices to explore what makes a successful king.'

Discuss this statement, with reference to at least two dramatic devices used by the playwright. Support your answer with reference to the text.

Marking Scheme Guidelines

Candidates are free to agree and/or disagree with the view expressed in the question, but must focus on 'effective use of a variety of dramatic devices' and 'what makes a successful king'.

Allow for a broad interpretation of 'dramatic devices' to include characterisation, contrast, setting, dialogue, imagery, soliloquy, irony, etc.

'If such a one be fit to govern'

Indicative Material

- Characterisation of four kings reveals qualities required for successful leadership.
- Contrast between unlawful accession to the throne and the lawful, divine right of kings.
- Vivid imagery dramatically highlights the consequences of effective/ineffective rule.
- Soliloquies offer significant insights into attitudes to kingship.
- Exchanges of dialogue investigate the necessary requirements for a successful monarch.
- Plot of the play focuses on key aspects of the 'king-becoming graces'. Etc.

1 Shakespeare presents contrasting portraits of four different kings in 'Macbeth' – 'Gracious' Duncan, the 'holy king' Edward the Confessor, the 'tyrant' Macbeth and the rightful heir, Malcolm. An examination of their qualities and flaws is undertaken by the playwright to find what is important in a good king. What are the essential good qualities which he must possess? This play was written in 1606 and reflects the belief that kings were appointed by God. So the context of the divine right of kings and legal accession is explored. Through soliloquies, Shakespeare allows us into the mind of the central character who is obsessed by kingship. The use and abuse of royal power is also dramatised through dialogue and imagery.

2 Shakespeare emphasises the rightful position of Duncan as king, 'The Lord's anointed temple'. Through the use of imagery, the playwright highlights this aspect of Duncan's kingship, 'His silver skin laced with his golden blood'. Macbeth associates him with heaven, 'his virtues will plead like angels trumpet-tongued'. When this order is destroyed by his murder, all is plunged into chaos, 'our country sinks beneath the yoke;/ It weeps, it bleeds'. Yet to a modern audience Duncan can seem incompetent and easily deceived. He was betrayed by the Thane of Cawdor, 'a gentleman on whom I built an absolute trust'. Duncan is unaware of the danger around him, 'This castle hath a pleasant seat'. It is his flaw of naivety which prevents him from being an effective king.

3 Macbeth allows 'Vaulting ambition' to take precedence over lawful accession to the throne. He has many noble characteristics. He is brave, 'Bellona's bridegroom', a fine military leader who defeats the country's rebels. But he refuses to wait until he can be rightfully crowned king. Aided by his wife, the ruthless pair set out on a bloody journey to seize the throne. Shakespeare fills the play with blood imagery. Macbeth's regicide pollutes the natural world, 'Will all great Neptune's ocean wash this blood/ Clean from my hand?' Yet a defiant Macbeth loses all humanity, 'I am in blood stepped in so far that should I wade no more/ Returning were as tedious as go o'er'. Under his tyrannical rule, Scotland sinks 'bleeding'. Macbeth's violent reign is a disaster because he is an evil king.

4 His oppressive and unjust behaviour shows how unfit he is for office, 'There's not a one of them, but in his house/ I keep a servant fee'd'. This 'hellhound' hires assassins to murder Banquo and his son, he has Lady Macduff, her children and household put to the sword. He demands absolute obedience, but those he commands 'move only in command, nothing in love'. Vivid clothing imagery is used to highlight his unfitness for office, he 'cannot buckle', the country 'within the belt of rule'. He is portrayed as ridiculous, 'his title' hangs loose 'about him like a giant's robe upon a dwarfish thief'. Effective use of imagery and vivid language define Macbeth.

5 In contrast, Shakespeare presents a positive image of Edward the Confessor. Unlike the self-obsessed 'Devilish Macbeth', Edward's concern is for justice and peace. We are given an idealised portrait of a saintly king conveyed through the use of religious imagery. He, like Duncan, is associated with heaven. Edward promises to help Malcolm restore order back in Scotland. Care for one's people is an obvious quality Edward possesses – something that never entered Macbeth's head.

6 Malcolm is the rightful heir to the throne. He is realistic and acts on his insight, unlike his father, that men are not as they appear. He

lists the 'king becoming graces' that a good king requires and is clearly prepared to take his royal responsibilities seriously. Malcolm even suspects Macduff when he appears in the English court, fearing that Macduff could betray him as 'a sacrifice' to Macbeth. In a tense exchange, he tests Macduff's loyalty by pretending that he is too corrupt to ever become king. The plan works and Malcolm learns that Macduff is noble and can be trusted. The discussion between the two men shows how a good king needs to be astute.

7 In contrast to his father, Malcolm chooses to lead his army into battle. He shows himself a shrewd and capable leader, ordering the soldiers to 'hew him down a bough' to 'shadow/ The numbers of our host'. Another attribute of a good king is to lead. Yet, like Duncan, he is associated with natural imagery through the verb 'plant'. Malcolm will wait to

'be planted with time' whereas Macbeth is associated with a 'fruitless crown' and 'barren sceptre'. Under Macbeth's reign, there is chaos. The natural order is destroyed. (Duncan's horses are rumoured to have turned 'wild' and 'ate each other'.) Pathetic fallacy, bizarre events in the weather, 'dark night strangles the travelling lamp', adds to the general confusion under Macbeth's evil reign.

8 In the end, order is restored. Malcolm promises to undertake his duties in 'measure, time and place'. Lawful accession is restored. Throughout the drama, Shakespeare has explored many aspects of what makes an effective monarch. Malcolm is the rightful ruler combining all of the main 'graces' – not only is he virtuous and responsible, he is also shrewd enough to learn from experience – a fitting person to be king.

(c. 875 words)

Marking Scheme		
P	18	18
C	16	18
L	16	18
M	6	6
	56	60

GRADE: H1

Examiner's Comment

- Opening addresses question of kingship and introduces key discussion points.
- Follow-up paragraphs focus on characterisation, contrast and imagery.
- Clear analysis and insightful critical discussion.
- Well-developed study of Macbeth's actions explore the failure of his reign.
- Excellent support based on apt references and accurate quotations.
- Paragraph 5 points would benefit from more thorough development.
- Good controlled expression and varied vocabulary (e.g. 'regicide pollutes the natural world', 'Lawful accession is restored').

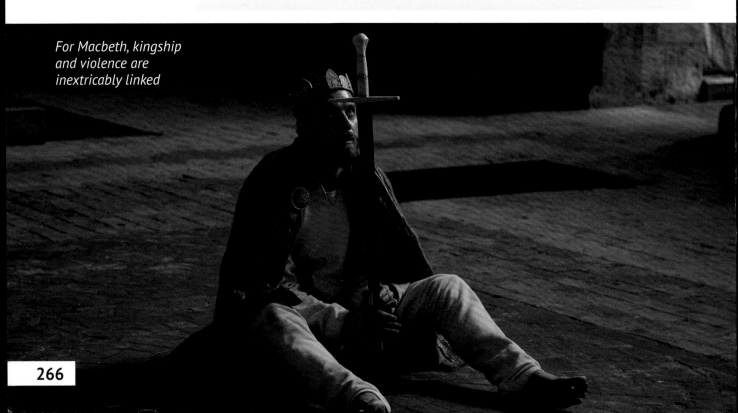

For Macbeth, kingship and violence are inextricably linked

Essay Questions on *Macbeth*

Note: 60 marks/60 minutes. Aim for at least 800 words.

1. 'Over the course of the play *Macbeth*, Shakespeare powerfully portrays a world dominated by equivocation and deception.'

   To what extent do you agree with this view? Support your answer with suitable reference to the text.

2. 'In the play *Macbeth*, Shakespeare makes effective use of a variety of dramatic devices to explore issues of tragic heroism.'

   Discuss this view, with reference to at least two dramatic devices used by the playwright. Support your answer with reference to the text.

3. 'Throughout the play *Macbeth*, Shakespeare addresses the compelling theme of progressive isolation where the central character is faced with confronting his tragic destiny.'

   Discuss this statement, supporting your answer with reference to the play.

4. 'Lady Macbeth is a complex villain who ultimately fails to bear the torments of her guilt.'

   Discuss this view, supporting your answer with suitable reference to Shakespeare's play *Macbeth*.

5. 'Shakespeare's play *Macbeth* presents audiences with many dramatic moments of despair contrasted with some rare glimpses of hope.'

   Discuss this statement, supporting your answer with suitable reference to the text.

6. 'Macbeth and Lady Macbeth share a variety of character traits from which they learn bitter lessons.'

   To what extent do you agree with this statement? Support your answer with suitable reference to the play *Macbeth*.

7. 'Shakespeare raises important questions about moral responsibility and free will in the play *Macbeth*.'

   Discuss this view, supporting your answer with reference to the text.

8. 'The supernatural events that occur throughout the play create moments of dramatic tension and maintain suspense.'

   To what extent do you agree with this view? Support your answer with reference to the play *Macbeth*.

9. 'Macbeth is both a ruthless villain capable of appalling cruelty and also a troubled hero who compels our sympathy.'

   To what extent do you agree with this view? Support your answer with suitable reference to the play *Macbeth*.

10. 'In the play *Macbeth*, Shakespeare uses a range of dramatic techniques to heighten our experience of evil and disorder.'

    Discuss this statement, supporting your answer with reference to at least two dramatic techniques used by the playwright.

Is Macbeth's heroism confined to the battlefield?

Using *Macbeth* as a Comparative Text

Introduction

The Leaving Cert Comparative Study section is worth **70 marks** – the second most important question on the exam paper.

In the comparative section, novels, plays and films are all referred to as **texts**.

A **mode** of comparison is simply a framework in which to explore a text.

There are four prescribed Higher Level modes:

1   The Cultural Context
2   Theme or Issue
3   Literary Genre
4   The General Vision and Viewpoint

You are required to study **at least two** of the three prescribed modes. Only **two** of the three prescribed modes will appear on the exam paper. Students can check the details with their teachers or by accessing www.education.ie for circulars regarding prescribed material.

Each mode on the paper will offer a **choice of two questions**:

* *either* a single essay question comparing three prescribed texts (70 marks)
* *or* a **two-part** question:
  – part (a) requires discussion of **one prescribed text** (30 marks)
  – part (b) requires comparison of **two other prescribed texts** (40 marks)

You are allocated **70 minutes** for the Comparative section. Aim to write at least 1,000 words in the single 70-mark answer.

For the two-part question, aim to write at least 400 words for Part (a) and at least 600 words for Part (b).

When answering Comparative questions, candidates may compare and/or contrast, i.e. address similarities and/or differences in both the subject matter and style of their chosen texts.

Note: At **Higher Level,** a play by Shakespeare **must be one of the texts chosen**. This can be studied on its own (for the Single Text section) or as an element in the Comparative Study section.

The fatal entrance to Macbeth's castle, Dunsinane

The Cultural Context

The cultural context is often described as the **society or 'world' of the text**. It refers to the social setting, values, attitudes and practices. Our understanding of a text is enriched by knowing about the culture in which the story is set. Revealing features of a society include:

- power
- morality/values
- violence
- patriarchy

- freedom
- family
- social class
- superstition

> ### Remember!
> *Various aspects of cultural context will overlap at times. For example, order and anarchy are closely interlinked with society's ideas of masculinity and femininity in the play* Macbeth.

The Cultural Context in *Macbeth*

Shakespeare's *Macbeth* is set in eleventh-century Scotland during a turbulent time in the country's history. **Political power struggles** and murders often resulted from bitter rivalries between important families and clans over the ownership of land or trade. The play touches on enduring social issues such as relationships, ambition and political control. Shakespeare invites us into an intense drama where we see the corrupting nature of power.

Banquo's response to the witches ('What, can the devil speak true?') suggests that the world of *Macbeth* is a **Christian** one. There is an underlying moral sense throughout the story and Macbeth himself struggles initially with wrongdoing.

The playwright has also created a disturbing social setting, filled with rumour and mystery. The first characters to appear on stage are the witches. Are they natural or unnatural? They establish the play's **atmosphere of evil and superstition**.

Scottish society is patriarchal (male-dominated), with men and women expected to maintain their traditional roles.

- Will Macbeth and Lady Macbeth conform to society's expectations?

- Or will they rebel against the confines of their world?
- What will be the consequences of their actions?

Power

As in modern times, when there is a change of government, it is important to follow the correct procedures for the transfer of power. Shakespeare believed that **citizens' happiness depends on those in power**. In *Macbeth*, power struggles affect all the central characters.

- **Honour and loyalty are important values** in the play. When the natural order is disrupted, the world is thrown into chaos, and this disruption is reflected in nature through storms, disease and abnormal events.

- Macbeth, once a loyal army general, gives in to 'Vaulting ambition' and kills Duncan, his lawful king. The Elizabethans believed that the monarch's power came from God, so this rebellion against God is seen as a **perversion of the natural order**.

- **Duncan's Scotland is far from peaceful**. The play opens with a rebellion by Macdonwald, aided by 'Norweyan' invaders. It is defeated by loyal soldiers under the leadership of Macbeth and Banquo. Order is restored and the grateful king rewards his trusted supporters.

- **The witches oppose order.** The atmosphere of the opening scenes is continual unrest: 'Fair is foul, and foul is fair'.

- In **uncertain and dangerous times**, there are many unanswered questions about the succession to the Scottish throne. Duncan nominates his son Malcolm as heir – and his decision is accepted.

- It is only later, when Macbeth's tyranny becomes apparent, that there is growing awareness that the **natural order has been destroyed**. The natural world is plunged into revolt on the night of Duncan's murder, 'the earth/ Was feverous and did shake'.

- For most of Macbeth's reign, **Scotland is in chaos**. By contrast, there is order and harmony at the English court of Edward the Confessor, who reigns with the approval of God, not the spirits of darkness.

Class/Homework Exercise (Comparing the Cultural Context in Texts)

Copy the following table about power in your comparative texts, adding your own responses with reference to the texts that you are studying.

	First Text (*Macbeth*)	Second Text	Third Text
Who has **power** or influence?			
Is **power used responsibly** or abused?			
Briefly describe a scene which illustrates how power is used.			
Outline what happens as a result.			
Name one **image** the author used to indicate power.			

Power in Macbeth

Ambition for power

Temptation of the witches

Use/abuse of power

Masculinity/ femininity

Christianity/evil

Class/Homework Exercise (Comparing the Cultural Context in Texts)

'Understanding where power lies can offer the reader valuable insights into the cultural context of texts.' With reference to **three** of the texts on your comparative course, write two paragraphs in response to this question. (Aim for at least 200 words.)

Masculinity and Femininity

• In the violent, unstable world of *Macbeth*, notions of manhood are repeatedly challenged. **Courage in battle is greatly admired** – physical strength, soldierly skill, masculine honour. 'Brave Macbeth' defeats the rebels 'with his brandished steel,/ Which smoked with bloody execution'. In such a world, men express themselves through violence.

• But **Lady Macbeth presents a challenge to this masculine world**. She sees herself as the source of power that will transform Macbeth into the epitome of the heroic male ideal. She interprets her husband's essential sense of honour as a sign of weakness ('too full o' the milk of human kindness').

• **Lady Macbeth does not adopt the traditional woman's role** – a moral compass leading men from evil ways. Instead, she assumes the role of Eve, the instrument of corruption, 'Look like the innocent flower,/ But be the serpent under it'.

She also seeks to discard her own femininity, pleading with the powers of darkness to 'unsex' her. She taunts Macbeth about his masculinity.

• Lady Macbeth is an unlikely character in this male-dominated world. She is **a woman before her time**. Until the banquet scene, she is vicious, ambitious, without conscience and willing to do whatever it takes to become queen. As Macbeth becomes more independent, the couple become estranged.

• In the end, the play traces the terrible consequences of her unnatural behaviour. Lady Macbeth reverts to her traditional female role. She is broken by guilt and despair: 'all the perfumes of Arabia will not sweeten this little hand'. Unable to endure the breakdown of trust in her marriage, she is left stranded in a 'murky' hell of remorse, finally taking her own life. She has paid an enormous price for **daring to break society's expectations** of masculinity and femininity.

Useful Quotes Cultural Context

Ross *Bellona's bridegroom* *(Act 1 Scene 2, l.54)*	Courage and skill on the battlefield are qualities that are greatly admired in the **patriarchal world** of the play. Ross tells Duncan that Macbeth was so brave that he deserved to be respected as though he were the husband of the Roman goddess of war.
Macbeth *This supernatural soliciting* *Cannot be ill, cannot be good* *(Act 1 Scene 3, l.132–3)*	Macbeth is confused about the witches' forecast that he will be king. Should he wait for fate to take its course or actively pursue the kingship? The witches' equivocal language lures Macbeth to **break the social order** – which will unleash destruction for him and for Scotland.
Lady Macbeth *Come to my woman's breasts,* *And take my milk for gall* *(Act 1 Scene 5, l.46–7)*	Lady Macbeth is willing to deny her innate womanly nature to advance her own and her husband's political ambitions. As a central female character, she **defies the traditional image of the nurturing maternal figure**. This subversion of the natural order will have tragic consequences for her.
Lady Macbeth *My hands are of your colour;* * but I shame* *To wear a heart so white* *(Act 2 Scene 2, l.62–3)*	Not for the first time, Lady Macbeth takes charge, mocking her husband's cowardice. Once again, she **challenges conventional gender roles**. While Macbeth is relegated to anxiety and dependence, his wife's behaviour becomes more decisive, proactive, masculine.
Malcolm *… by the grace of Grace,* *We will perform in measure, time* * and place* *(Act 5 Scene 9, l.38–9)*	The idea of the **divine right of kings** was widely accepted in Scotland in the 11th century. At the end of the play, Malcolm becomes the new king. He believes that order has been restored and that he is the rightful heir to the throne. Malcolm sees himself as God's appointed ruler, unlike Macbeth, whose tyrannous reign was aided by the supernatural powers of evil.

Using *Macbeth* in Comparative Questions

> **Remember!**
>
> *Discussion points in the 30-mark Part (a) sample answer can also provide the basis for developed comparisons in the 40-mark Part (b) and 70-mark single questions.*

Sample Part (a) Question

Q. 'The opening scene (or scenes) of a text can reveal valuable insights into the impact the cultural context of a narrative is likely to have on the outcome of the story.'

Discuss this view in relation to your study of one text on your comparative course. (30 marks)

Indicative Material

- Initial impact of setting/atmosphere on characters and events.
- Dramatic/narrative features and language/imagery illustrate social norms and affect plot.
- Society's expectations can influence the narrative outcome.
- Cultural aspects of opening scene/s often foreshadow tragic developments.
- Effect of attitudes to power, ambition and morality reveal cultural values/traditions, etc.

The tempting of Macbeth

Sample Answer

Shakespeare opens his play, *Macbeth*, while **turmoil rages**. A battle is 'being lost and won'. Three witches meet on an 'open place' in a storm, 'withered and wild'. They are there to 'meet with Macbeth', clearly signalling to the audience that they intend to target him as a likely victim of their malice.

These **'instruments of darkness' tempt** an overly-ambitious Macbeth with 'honest trifles' to commit regicide. These women are not of the natural order, they 'look not like the inhabitants of the earth/ And yet are on it'. They upturn the natural order, 'fair is foul, and foul is fair'. Their equivocation sets the tone for the morally ambivalent Macbeths who intend to 'look like the innocent flower,/ But be the serpent under it'. Macbeth himself reminds us of their devious words, 'So foul and fair a day I have not seen'.

The **Macbeths willingly embrace this 'murky' world**. They become associated with darkness and the supernatural. Macbeth commands, 'Stars hide your fires!/ Let not light see my black and deep desires'. Lady Macbeth echoes his command, 'Come thick night and pall thee in the dunnest smoke of hell,/ That my keen knife see not the wound it makes'. These opening scenes set the mood for the breakdown of order instigated by the power-hungry couple.

Macbeth is less determined than his ruthless wife. He lists the reasons why he should not kill Duncan. This man is his noble relation and his king, 'I am his kinsman and his subject'. Macbeth is Duncan's 'host' who should protect his guest, not 'bear the knife myself'. He is aware to 'do more' brings him from being human to the level of a beast. But his wife's savage criticism of his manhood changes him. Her persuasive arguments soon control him, 'What beast was it, then,/ That made you break this enterprise to me?' His weak response ('If we should fail?') shows that the balance of power has moved in this couple's relationship. The murder will take place and Scotland will be plunged into chaos to satisfy a couple's ambition.

The mayhem of the opening scenes involving the witches and the brutality of battle only worsens as the play reaches its **tragic conclusion**. Scotland endures appalling suffering over the course of this story. The play's opening scenes provide a powerful insight into an unstable and disturbing world that only ends with the death of Macbeth. *(400 words)*

Examiner's Comment

- Very well-focused answer that addresses the question in an informed way.
- Excellent use of close reference and quotations to support key points
- Well-developed central points about the reversal of moral codes and the natural order.
- Very impressive use of language and controlled expression throughout this top-grade response.

Class/Homework Exercise

Using some of the points from the indicative material above, write your own response to the Part (a) question. (Aim for about 400 words.)

Exam Advice

To help you structure your comparative essay answer on the Cultural Context, a useful exercise is to practise making an outline of the key points you want to include. The draft plan below uses *Macbeth* as one of the three comparative texts.

Foul and fair witches

Sample 70-mark Question

Q. 'The way in which social forces affect the freedom of central characters can broaden our understanding of the cultural context of a text.'

Compare the way in which the effect of social forces on the freedom of central characters broadened your understanding of the cultural context when studying **three texts** on your comparative course.

Indicative Material

- Individuals can be liberated/restricted by power, class, race, money, religion.
- Impact of social expectations, relationships, marriage and traditional gender roles.
- Reader's understanding of culture often informed by characters and/or key events.
- Effect of law, violence, and tensions between power and freedom.
- Freedom expressed through setting, narrative voice, language, symbolism, music, etc.

Conforming to societal expectations

Sample Draft Plan

INTRODUCTION

Opening of *Macbeth* focuses on the army general Macbeth, who is subject to societal expectations of bravery, loyalty, honour and masculinity. Banquo, another heroic soldier, is also subject to these expectations. Both are tempted by the lure of evil to break these norms. One resists, the other gives in. One conforms to society's rules, the other rebels. **Choosing freedom from society's expectations results in paying a heavy price.** *In my other two texts, the two central characters also have to choose between freedom and conforming to society's expected standards – each with different results ...*

POINT 1 Conforming to society's norms

Duncan appoints Malcolm as his successor, going against the conventions of Scotland – where the king was chosen by the vote of the thanes. This leads to Duncan's murder by Macbeth – 'That is a step/ On which I must fall down, or else o'erleap'. Play's conclusion: Macduff restores order by killing the tyrant, but also reinstates Scotland's rules of choosing the king by the thanes – 'Whose voices I desire aloud with mine'. *In contrast/similarly, my second text also explores the tension between freedom and conformity ...*

POINT 2 Gender roles

Reversal of traditional gender roles results in horrifying consequences. Lady Macbeth assumes masculine role of action – 'you shall put/ This night's great business into my dispatch'. She is an instigator of evil, not the traditionally female force for good. She manipulates Macbeth, who is overwhelmed by her powerful personality and agrees to follow her advice –'I am settled'. This freedom of action on her part results in the eventual downfall of Scotland as well as the breakdown of the Macbeths' relationship. *Gender constrictions play a similar/different role in my third text ...*

POINT 3 Loss of freedom leads to new insight

As the play develops, central characters find wisdom/truth despite/because of their loss of freedom. Society places enormous demands on its political leaders. Macbeth begins to realise, too late, what is important: peace of mind ('Macbeth shall sleep no more'); 'honour, love, obedience, troops of friends', which he will never have because he broke the customs of his country when seizing the crown. *There are some equally interesting and revealing similarities/contrasts in my other texts …*

POINT 4 Terrifying conclusion

There are instructive insights into social traits in Act 5 of the play when Macbeth and Lady Macbeth are isolated – 'What's done cannot be undone'. She is broken by guilt and cannot endure her own terrible alienation. He has been crushed by failure to secure his power as king and feels that he has 'lived long enough'. His life has become a 'walking shadow'. The couple broke all the constrictions of society, reaping a whirlwind of destruction. *This is very like/unlike the ending of my second text …*

CONCLUDING PARAGRAPH

All three texts reveal much about the range and influence of cultural influences. In particular, Shakespeare's play explores a rigid, brutal world where personal freedom is always threatened. *My knowledge of how society affects individuals was also broadened by my other two texts …*

Remember!

Examiners will expect you to take a comparative approach. However, it can sometimes be difficult to compare three texts in a single paragraph. Effective paragraph responses often focus on a key moment/ reference from one text, usually making a comparison at the start or end of the paragraph. This can lead to useful discussion of the second and/or third text in follow-up paragraphs.

Sample Paragraph: POINT 1 Conforming to society's norms

The plot of *Macbeth* emphasises a social order that oppresses the freedom to deviate from the accepted rules of society. The opening scenes include a captain's report of the fierce battle being waged against the rebel 'merciless Macdonwald'. Banquo and Macbeth's prowess on the battlefield is recounted in glowing terms, 'They doubly redoubled strokes upon the foe'. They are clearly conforming to society's expectations of masculinity and honour in this heroic effort to restore order to Scotland. The witches tempt both men. Macbeth is lured by the promise that he 'shalt be king hereafter'. Banquo is promised that he 'shalt get kings'. However, the two men respond differently. Banquo regards the weird sisters as the 'devil', while Macbeth is fascinated by the thoughts of fulfilling personal ambition – and is 'rapt' by what they promise. Banquo advises his companion that evil seeks to 'win us to our harm' through 'honest trifles'. But Macbeth, unlike Banquo, has no desire to keep his 'bosom franchised and allegiance clear'. He decides to exercise his freedom of choice and break the great social taboo of regicide in order to seize the throne. In choosing this option, he unleashes society's 'Bloody instructions, which, being taught, return/To plague the inventor. *(200 words)*

In the novel that I have studied, the central character also has the freedom to choose between accepting the confines of the society in which they live or rebelling against its constrictions …

Examiner's Comment

- Successful top-grade answer tackles question confidently.
- Focused discussion points, supported effectively by apt reference and quotations.
- Well-developed central point re Macbeth's response to pressure of political ambition.
- Impressive expression (e.g. 'break the great social taboo of regicide'). Good use of comparative language towards end of paragraph.

Class/Homework Exercises

1. Choose **one** of the other points in the sample draft plan and write a paragraph of your own in response to the question above. (Aim for at least 150 words.)

2. 'An awareness of who is powerful and who is powerless often helps to reveal the cultural context in texts.'

   Compare how the distribution of power within each of **three** texts on your comparative course helps to reveal the cultural contexts in these texts. Support your answer with reference to your chosen texts. (70 marks)

> **Remember!**
> *The world of a text is often shown through the experience of a central character who is trying to overcome obstacles in his/ her life.*

Breaking the social taboo of regicide

Theme or Issue

A theme or issue in a text is a **central idea or subject of interest** in the story. The universal themes in *Macbeth* include:

- ambition
- power
- relationships
- conflict
- morality
- appearance and reality
- isolation

The **presentation of a theme or issue often challenges the reader** to think about human nature and to distinguish between right and wrong. Comparing different treatments of themes can broaden our understanding of life, allowing us to experience at one remove the struggles characters go through as they respond to challenges.

We all **need to know ourselves**, to distinguish between appearance and reality, come to terms with growing up, face the finality of death, understand the destructive consequences of hatred and violence – and the redeeming power of love. Great writers help us to do this.

The **impact of a key scene** or turning point in a text will influence our understanding of a particular theme or issue. What questions are raised about the topic? Is the treatment comic or tragic? What techniques does the playwright use? What do we learn about the theme?

> **Remember!**
> *Do not confuse **theme** (the message of the text) with **plot** (the storyline).*

Exploring the Theme of Relationships

Relationships can be **functional** (successful and good for the individuals involved) or **dysfunctional** (unsuccessful). Functional relationships guide characters to do good, to improve themselves and to enhance society. Dysfunctional relationships steer characters towards evil, which can harm themselves as well as society. Over the course of the play, Macbeth's different relationships with various people all contribute to the tragic storyline.

> **Remember!**
> *In* Macbeth, *Shakespeare explores the theme of relationships through the interaction of characters.*

The gracious hostess greets her king

Class/Homework Exercise (Comparing the Theme or Issue)

Copy the following table about relationships in your comparative texts, adding your own responses with reference to the texts that you are studying.

	First Text (*Macbeth*)	Second Text	Third Text
Central character's relationship with self: Functional/dysfunctional? Has self-knowledge? Protects own integrity? Gains insight?			
Central character's relationship with society: Rebels against authority? Conforms to society? Consequences?			
Central character's relationship with others: Supportive or hostile relationships? Dependent on or independent of others? Gains maturity through relationships with others?			
Conclusion: Isolated or surrounded by friends? Approved or disapproved of by society? Treatment of theme of relationships tragic or positive?			

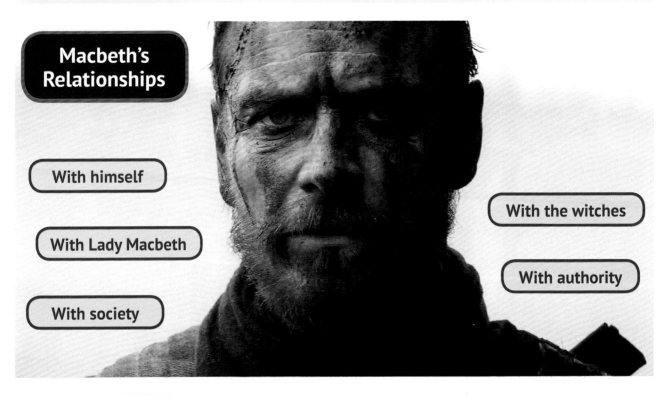

Macbeth's Relationships

- With himself
- With Lady Macbeth
- With society
- With the witches
- With authority

Macbeth and his King

- Duncan and Macbeth are **closely related** – they refer to each other as 'cousin' and 'kinsman'. Macbeth is at first a loyal subject who courageously leads the king's troops to defeat the rebel Thane of Cawdor. The grateful monarch rewards Macbeth with Cawdor's former title.

- However, when the witches predict that Macbeth 'shalt be king hereafter', the Macbeth–Duncan **relationship changes drastically**. From his first soliloquy, we learn that Macbeth has given serious thought to seizing the throne, 'why do I yield to that suggestion/ Whose horrid image doth unfix my hair ...?' Not long afterwards, when Duncan announces that his son, Malcolm, is to be his heir, Macbeth decides to pursue his own desires through evil means. Aided by his ruthless wife, he allows 'Vaulting ambition' to overcome his initial hesitancy.

- Duncan is everything Macbeth is not. He was deceived by Macdonwald and will also be betrayed by the devious Macbeth, whom he regards as a 'peerless kinsman'. The unreliable **relationship between Duncan and Macbeth** highlights the underlying **conflict between good and evil** that is always present in the drama. The rightful king was 'meek' and 'clear', with a mind incapable of suspicion. Yet Macbeth's distorted ambition makes him break all the ties of loyalty, service, duty and morality by committing regicide.

- The play charts the significant **changes in the relationship** between two contrasting characters, which is central to the tragedy. Macbeth immediately regrets his murderous deed, but he must live with the terrible truth that he has destroyed the sacred link between subject and ruler, 'renown and grace is dead'.

Macbeth and his Friend

- Banquo and Macbeth were comrades-in-arms on the battlefield. As a true friend, Banquo offers Macbeth some astute advice after they meet the witches: 'oftentimes, to win us to our harm,/ The instruments of darkness tell us truths'. At first, Macbeth wants to confide in Banquo, 'let us speak/ Our free hearts each to other', but Banquo lays down a strict condition;

to 'keep/ My bosom franchised and my allegiance clear'. With these words, **Banquo sets limits on his loyalty to Macbeth**.

- **Macbeth's desire for power is greater than any relationship** and he has no hesitation in sacrificing his friendship with Banquo. He is also suspicious of Banquo, who has become just another obstacle to be overcome, 'To be thus is nothing,/ But to be safely thus'. Fearing his former friend's 'royalty of nature', he hires assassins to murder Banquo and his son.

- The **relationship between Macbeth and Banquo shows how power can corrupt.** It also reveals their true characters. Both men are tempted, but while Macbeth surrenders to his evil instincts, Banquo waits and watches.

Macbeth and his Wife

- Macbeth and Lady Macbeth appear to have a **close and rather modern relationship.** At the start of the play, she is his 'dearest partner in greatness' and shares in his plans for the future. This formidable lady is utterly committed to her husband's advancement. When she reads his letter about the witches' prophecies, she quickly decides that he 'shalt be/ What thou art promised'.

- **Lady Macbeth knows his personality well** and fears that he is 'too full o' the milk of human kindness/ To catch the nearest way'. Throughout the first half of the play, Lady Macbeth dominates their relationship by assuming control, 'Leave all the rest to me'.

- **Provoking Macbeth**, she declares that she would have 'dashed the brains out' of her child rather than go back on her word as he is doing. Awestricken at her verbal onslaught, **Macbeth gives in to her advice**, promising to 'mock the time with fairest show'.

- In the immediate aftermath of Duncan's murder, **Lady Macbeth adopts another role** – the pragmatist. As Macbeth ruefully regards his bloodstained hands, she notices that he has brought the incriminating evidence of the grooms' daggers from the king's bedchamber. When he refuses to return the knives, she scolds him, 'infirm of purpose'.

- She repeatedly comes to his rescue when he loses his composure in public at his vision of

Banquo's ghost. Always quick-thinking, she advises their guests to 'Sit, worthy friends.' But this crucial scene marks a **critical turning point in the couple's relationship**. Further communication between them has become impossible.

- Having characterised their relationship as equal, **Shakespeare now breaks down the equality**: Macbeth, once crowned, rises in power as his wife descends in importance. He abandons his 'great love' and removes from her the only purpose in her life – himself. She is unable to cope with their estrangement. Instead, she sleepwalks, reliving their shared crimes.

- The closeness between husband and wife now lies shattered by their common pursuit of power ('Nought's had, all's spent'). In the end, their **relationship cannot endure the breakdown of trust and intimacy** that they had taken for granted.

Macbeth and Himself

- Macbeth's **powerful soliloquies** ensure that the audience never fully disengages from the play's central character. We know that Macbeth desires the throne, but 'holily', hoping that 'chance may crown me,/ Without my stir'. It is when presented with the obstacle of the heir, Malcolm, that he resolves to act, 'for in my way

it lies'. The impact of the witches' temptation on Macbeth exposes his **deeply divided self**.

- From the moment he murders Duncan, Macbeth is aware that he will never be able to rid himself of guilt. He is truly appalled by himself, 'To know my deed, 'twere best not know myself'. Despite his **self-delusion**, he can never fully escape the truth. He is so anxious to secure his family's power on the throne that he takes the witches' prophecies at face value.

- From Act 3 onwards, it is clear that Macbeth is unable to live with himself. Shakespeare holds our interest in this complex character by showing us that he **understands exactly what he has sacrificed**. Any potential for nobility or heroism has been squandered in exchange for tyranny and despair. Having lost all humanity, Macbeth is left viewing existence as wearisome, no more than 'a poor player/ That struts and frets his hour upon the stage'.

- The **overall treatment of the theme of relationships is tragic**. Throughout the drama, Macbeth's relationships veer from the positive belief that he has 'bought/ Golden opinions from all sorts of people' to the heart-rending insight that he has, by his own choice, missed out on 'that which should accompany old age,/ As honour, love obedience, troops of friends'.

The deeply divided tragic hero

Useful Quotes Theme or Issue

Lady Macbeth *wouldst not play false,* *And yet wouldst wrongly win* *(Act 1 Scene 5, l.20–1)*	**Lady Macbeth sums up her husband's character** succinctly. He desperately wants to be king, but lacks the ruthlessness to achieve his ambition by criminal means. As the dominant marriage partner, this astute and determined woman will put pressure on her husband to commit the heinous crime of regicide by challenging what he holds most dear, his masculinity.
Macbeth *He's here in double trust:* *First, as I am his kinsman and his subject –* *Strong both against the deed; then, as his host,* *Who should against his murderer shut the door,* *Not bear the knife myself* *(Act 1 Scene 7, l.12–15)*	**Macbeth considers his special relationship with Duncan** and lists the reasons why he should not commit the murder. However, this is the rational side of Macbeth's divided character. He is also a moral coward who will soon discard all these reasons to satisfy his headlong desire for the throne. Duncan is an obstacle to his callous ambition.
Macbeth *There is none but he* *Whose being I do fear; and under him* *My genius is rebuked* *(Act 3 Scene 1, l.53–5)*	Although Macbeth has secured the Scottish throne, **he feels threatened by Banquo** (who is already becoming suspicious). Neither friendship nor decency matter any longer to the increasingly paranoid Macbeth. Although Banquo was also tempted, he has refused to compromise his loyalty to Duncan. As a result, he is another obstruction to Macbeth's evil plans – and must therefore be removed.
Macbeth *I bear a charmèd life, which must not yield* *To one of woman born* *(Act 5 Scene 8, l.12–13)*	**Macbeth has chosen to rely entirely on the witches' ambivalent promises.** In this final confrontation between good and evil, Macduff aims to avenge his family. He proves how misleading the witches' words were when he tells Macbeth that he was 'Untimely ripped' from his mother's womb. Only now does Macbeth realise that he has been duped by the 'juggling fiends'.

Remember!

Discussion points in the 30-mark Part (a) sample answer can also provide the basis for developed comparisons in the 40-mark Part (b) and 70-mark single questions. To write successful examination answers, it is essential to study the wording of questions closely. Marks can easily be lost if attention is not paid to each element of the question.

Sample Part (a) Question

Q. 'In many texts, a theme or issue may not be resolved to the complete satisfaction of the reader.'

Discuss the extent to which a theme or issue is resolved to your satisfaction in **one** text on your comparative course. Support your answer by reference to the text. (30 marks)

Indicative Material

- Establishment/development of theme leads to a convincing/unconvincing conclusion.
- Plot and memorable events may/may not be credible or realistic.
- Other key moments highlight expectations of satisfactory/unsatisfactory conclusions.
- Characterisation, language, symbols, theatrical effects can be fulfilling/unfulfilling.
- Impact of author's approach to the story's denouement, etc..

Sample Answer

Shakespeare's play 'Macbeth' extensively **explores the central theme of relationships** with great success. He presented the predicament of a main character with a flaw of over-reaching ambition, who, as a result of not controlling that defect, destroyed all of his key relationships. Macbeth smashed all his ties with his lawful king, his country, his own wife, his fellow thanes and even himself. Ambition drove Macbeth to destroy the bond which unites subject and king, comrades-in-arms, husband and wife and even his own personal integrity. The act of regicide unleashed a terrifying sequence of events engulfing individuals and country.

Macbeth has a **tense relationship with Duncan**. He serves him well as 'Bellona's bridegroom' on the battlefield. But the announcement of Malcolm becoming heir to Duncan catapults him into action. This obstruction transforms the relationship. Although Duncan has 'honoured' Macbeth recently with the title Thane of Cawdor, Macbeth now sees the king as an object rather than a person. He casts aside all the reasons why he should not kill Duncan – he is his 'kinsman', his king, he is Duncan's 'host',

Duncan has been a good king. His lust for power, 'vaulting ambition' is too great to resist, so his relationship with the king becomes another casualty.

Scotland as a country to be cared for is not on Macbeth's list of priorities, since he is only concerned with his security on the throne – and therefore **betrays and kills his friend Banquo** to attain that, 'There is none but he /Whose being I do fear'. Macbeth's reign is one of secrecy ('There's not a one of them, but in his house/ I keep a servant fee'd') and terror, ('each new morn/ New widows howl'). He never shows remorse for the state in which he has left his country. Macbeth wants power for power's sake, rather than use it for good. Even at the conclusion of the play, he is happy that 'the estate of the world were now undone'. His **relationship with Scotland suffers** underneath his uncontrollable desire for complete control.

Shakespeare explores the theme of relationships in his play, 'Macbeth', through the central character's dysfunctional relationships with king, country and friend. The **audience has had the theme resolved satisfactorily** because the playwright has traced the catastrophic effects on all the key relationships when a character allows evil ambition to obliterate his natural humanity. The result is chaos where the 'sweet milk of concord' has been transformed into 'hell'. *(410 words)*

Examiner's Comment

- Focused answer addresses question in informed way.
- Effective use of close reference and quotations support discussion.
- Well-developed points about the disintegration of relationships.
- Good language use, overall, but some sentences over-long (paras 1 and 3)
- Impressive vocabulary ('personal integrity', 'dysfunctional relationships') throughout this solid high-grade response.

Class/Homework Exercise

Using some of the points from the indicative material above, write your own response to the Part (a) question.

Exam Advice

To help you structure your comparative essay answer on Theme or Issue, a useful exercise is to practise making an outline of the key points you want to include. The following draft plan uses *Macbeth* as one of the comparative texts.

Partners in greatness

Sample 70-mark Question

Q. 'Studying a particular theme or issue in a text enables a reader to form a range of insightful reflections on that theme or issue.'

Compare the various reflections that you formed on a common theme or issue in the **three texts** that you studied for your comparative course.

Indicative Material

◆ Plot, narrative voice, characters' behaviour provide thought-provoking insights.

◆ Key moments/scenes offer revealing considerations and perspectives.

◆ Impact of language (imagery, symbolism, visual and aural effects) shapes perceptions.

◆ Resolution of a theme enables a reader to draw personal/broader conclusions, etc.

Sample Draft Plan

INTRODUCTION

The three texts I studied allowed me to focus on the **theme of relationships and how these ties helped or hindered the character on his journey to personal growth**. In *Macbeth*, key moments involving Lady Macbeth, Malcolm, Macduff and Macbeth's soliloquies exposed useful perspectives on this central theme. *My **other two texts** presented similar/ contrasting views …*

POINT 1 Lady Macbeth's dominance in relationship

Key moments: reading Macbeth's letter; goading him to commit murder; banquet scene. Her initial supportive role, to ensure her husband gets what 'thou art promised', changes to terrifying dominance when she ridicules and scolds her husband to force him to commit the crime, 'When you durst do it, then you were a man'. **She forces him to act against his better nature.** Shakespeare presents a useful perspective on a relationship consumed by a couple's lust for power. *Key moments in my second text were similar/different …*

POINT 2 Mistrust in a relationship

The uneasy relationship between Macduff and Malcolm is shown in Malcolm's lack of trust in Macduff, 'He hath not touched you yet'. This key scene in Act 4 shows that Malcolm learns from others. He knows from his father's experience not to trust too readily, and he **learns compassion** from Macduff. The playwright shows how relationships can enhance an individual and lead to personal growth. *Such personal growth is/is not seen in the relationships in my second text …*

POINT 3 Betrayal of oneself

In Macbeth's soliloquies, Shakespeare reveals how the protagonist has betrayed his own integrity in pursuit of power. This chills the audience while teaching a valuable lesson about being true to your essential nature. Recognising Macbeth's flaw of warped ambition, Shakespeare's language provides a revealing depiction of this process of unstoppable consequences. Macbeth does achieve an awareness of his failed life, so **his honour is salvaged to a degree** at the play's conclusion. *In my third text, the central character does/does not reach this state of self-awareness …*

CONCLUDING PARAGRAPH

The **playwright resolves his tragic theme of dysfunctional relationships** by detailing the trail of destruction that an individual can create by breaking bonds for the sake of one desire – political power and royal status. Despite all the obstacles, the character will achieve personal growth through suffering when he recognises his flaws. However, Shakespeare does not spare the audience in this horrific exploration of the theme of relationships and self-growth. *My other two texts also gave me a range of interesting insights …*

Sample Paragraph: **POINT 2 Mistrust in a relationship**

By contrast, all the characters in *Macbeth* are **forced to learn the hard way**. Through the bitter experience of his murdered father, Malcolm has learned not to trust others without good reason. He has the 'wisdom' to see that Macduff could possibly be a spy from Macbeth to trap a 'weak, poor innocent lamb'. Therefore he challenges Macduff's loyalty to Scotland by pretending he has numerous vices, including lust and avarice. Macduff cannot bear the thought of yet another corrupt king replacing Macbeth, so when Malcolm threatens to 'Uproar the universal peace', Macduff shows his 'noble passion', proving his noble character. This test of patriotism shows the harsh life lesson Malcolm has had to learn from his relationships with others. Shortly afterwards, Macduff is told his wife and children have been savagely

slaughtered. Malcolm encourages Macduff to turn his grief to anger, but Macduff teaches him he has to 'also feel it as a man'. Malcolm puts this lesson to good use when Old Siward accepts his son's death as a brave soldier. Malcolm comments: 'He's worth more sorrow,/ And that I'll spend for him'. Although this is a lengthy scene, it demonstrated the way relationships can teach valuable life lessons and enhance a character's progress to self-growth. *(210 words)*

In my third text, the central character does/does not attain this state of self-growth ...

Examiner's Comment

- Solid high-grade standard that focuses directly on the question.
- Clear discussion, supported effectively by apt reference to a key scene.
- Some good turns of phrase (e.g. 'forced to learn the hard way', 'enhance a character's progress to self-growth').
- Uses comparative language effectively at the beginning and end of the paragraph.

Class/Homework Exercises

1. Choose **one** of the other points in the sample draft plan and write a paragraph of your own in response to the question above. (Aim for about 200 words.)

2. 'Some texts offer a largely unrealistic presentation of a theme or issue, while others leave readers with a more convincing and accurate impression of the same theme or issue.'

   With reference to the above statement, compare the impression of the same theme or issue when studying **three texts** on your comparative course. Support your answer with reference to your chosen texts. (Aim for at least 1,000 words.) (70 marks)

Remember!
Drama usually conveys its message through:

- *character*
- *plot*
- *atmosphere*
- *sound*
- *setting*
- *dialogue*
- *movement*
- *imagery/symbolism*

The new king and queen extend their hospitality

Literary Genre

Literary genre refers to **the craft of story-telling**.

> ### Remember!
> *Common **narrative techniques** in novels, plays and films include:*
>
> - *plot or storyline*
> - *characterisation*
> - *setting*
> - *dialogue*
> - *conflict and tension*
> - *resolution*

Macbeth: Literary Genre

Macbeth is a Shakespearean **tragedy** in five acts. A **tragic hero has the potential for greatness** but has a **fatal character fault** (*hamartia*) that leads to his **downfall**, with disastrous consequences for himself and others. Macbeth's flaw is his all-consuming ambition. At the beginning of the play, encouraged by the witches and Lady Macbeth, he makes the decision to kill Duncan and seize the crown. Macbeth's betrayal of his own nature leads to his demise and to chaos in Scotland. *Macbeth* can also be seen as a **moral tale** – crime does not pay. It is a political story about the use and abuse of power.

Key Aspects of Literary Genre in *Macbeth*

- The early part of the play is full of mystery and a sequence of intriguing questions. This keeps the audience enthralled.
- This fast-paced structure intensifies the audience's participation in Shakespeare's exploration of the key themes of evil ambition and power.

Structure

The genre of tragedy is rooted in ancient Greek drama. Shakespeare's famous tragedies have a five-act structure, which corresponds to sections of the story. Analysing the **plot structure** can help us see the play's action as purposeful and unified. In *Macbeth*, the tight **one-strand plot and chronological timeline** (events are revealed in the order in which they happen) focuses the audience's attention throughout the drama.

Shakespeare structures *Macbeth* to proceed at a **fast pace**:

- He sets up a series of **conflicts** to be resolved.
- The early part of the play is filled with **mystery and a sequence of questions**, keeping the audience enthralled.

This **intensifies the audience's participation** in Shakespeare's exploration of the key themes of evil ambition and power.

Macbeth desires to know the worst

Macbeth: Structure

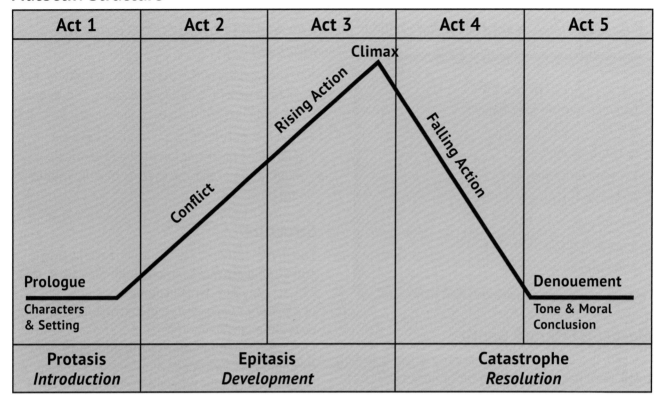

Act 1

Exposition:

- Time and place (setting)
- Main characters introduced
- Source/s of conflict established

Eleventh-century Scotland; a time of rebellion. The characters of Macbeth and Banquo are contrasted; the witches' prophecy about accession to the throne sets in motion the source of conflict.

Act 2

Rising Action:

- Complications arise to thwart the protagonist's desires
- Build-up of tension
- Characters respond to the opening conflict

Macbeth and Lady Macbeth plot and carry out the murder of Duncan. Macbeth is conflicted by the enormity of what he has done. Lady Macbeth takes control. Suspicions grow about the horrendous crime and the security of Macbeth's powerful position is in doubt.

Act 3

The Climax:

- Turning point of the play – the tension is at its height
- Protagonist successful in achieving his aim
- Faces increasing pressures and struggles to cope

Macbeth is king, but becomes obsessed with maintaining power. In an attempt to secure his royal position, he orders the killing of Banquo and his son (who escapes). As he becomes more and more guilt-ridden, Macbeth imagines seeing Banquo's ghost at the state banquet, which ends in total confusion. Meanwhile, the forces opposed to his tyranny (led by Macduff and Malcolm) assemble in England.

Act 4

Falling Action:

- Consequences of action taken by protagonist begin to arise
- Antagonists gather to challenge the main character
- Protagonist is becoming anxious

As he distances himself from reality, Macbeth returns to the witches, seeking assurances. Lady Macduff and her family are slaughtered. There are signs that Macbeth's evil reign is nearing its end. The rebellion against him is being organised by Malcolm, aided by Macduff and forces from England.

Act 5
Resolution:

- Main conflict between the protagonist and antagonists takes place
- Protagonist dies, having achieved a profound insight into life
- Political and moral order is restored at great cost
- Tragedy evokes pity and fear, resulting in catharsis for the audience

Lady Macbeth dies. Macbeth realises that he has been tricked by the witches and that his own evil choices have ruined his life. He and his wife have risked all and achieved nothing of worth. He is killed by Macduff and the forces of good take control. The rightful heir, Malcolm, becomes king and harmony returns to Scotland. The audience has also learned two valuable lessons: power seized unlawfully brings social chaos; and uncontrolled ambition leads to personal misery.

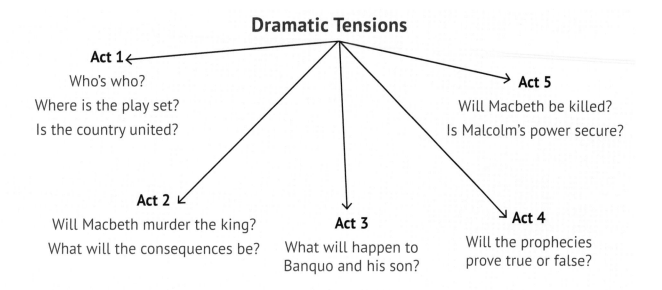

Dramatic Tensions

Act 1
Who's who?
Where is the play set?
Is the country united?

Act 5
Will Macbeth be killed?
Is Malcolm's power secure?

Act 2
Will Macbeth murder the king?
What will the consequences be?

Act 3
What will happen to Banquo and his son?

Act 4
Will the prophecies prove true or false?

Characterisation

The development of the central characters is a key narrative element in drama. *Macbeth* is a story of a moral hero of potential greatness, but with a fatal flaw that has disastrous consequences for him and others. Although he is initially courageous and noble, Macbeth is morally weak. Inspired by his evil ambition, he murders the king and breaks the divinely appointed order, thus unleashing devastation on his country. Macbeth's **soliloquies reveal his inner torment** before and after the murders, so that the audience is always aware of his suffering.

The playwright also uses **asides** – when a character 'thinks aloud' and is not heard by others on stage – which allows the audience to learn details that other characters do not know. For example, during the banquet, the guests are unaware of the turmoil between Macbeth and his wife – something that makes this tense scene all the more absorbing for the audience.

Macbeth's **intense inner conflict** reflects his deeply divided self. In surrendering to warped ambition, he discards his innate sense of morality.

Shakespeare's characterisation highlights the utter failure of Macbeth's life and his horror at what he has forfeited. Ironically, his ability to endure extreme suffering and his acquisition of **moral insight** sends a positive message to the audience about the strength of the human spirit.

Symbols and Imagery Patterns

Key words and phrases are threaded through the play, adding to the dramatic atmosphere and intensifying the themes. Two of the most important are **blood** and **night**.

Blood

- Shakespeare wants the audience to understand the magnitude of Macbeth's crime in assassinating Scotland's lawful king. The recurring references to blood highlight the fact that **regicide is not only a crime, but a mortal sin.** The entire play, like the country, seems to be drowning in blood.

- A **bloodstained captain** reports on the battle to Duncan with bloody descriptions of Macbeth's exploits. Later on, when he considers the witches' promises, Macbeth hallucinates, thinking that he sees a dagger with 'gouts of blood' and that he will 'incarnadine' all the seas of the world because of his action.

- The **protagonist** is doomed to wade through a sea of blood. It is spilt in the murders of Duncan, Banquo, Lady Macduff and young Siward. Lady

Macbeth, in vain, attempts to wash the illusory bloodstains from her hand.

- The **witches** use animal blood in their charms; a bloody child appears as one of their apparitions; Macbeth's severed head is held aloft by Macduff. The continual references to blood unnerve the audience and are a constant reminder of the horrific consequences of Macbeth's violent actions.

Useful Quotes Images of Blood

Lady Macbeth *Make thick my blood* *(Act 1 Scene 5, l.43)*	**Lady Macbeth's inhumanity** is evident when she calls on the evil spirits of darkness to take from her any feelings of pity. Her urgent tone reflects her overwhelming ambition and her determination to support her husband in their horrendous crime.
Macbeth *Will all great Neptune's ocean wash* *this blood* *Clean from my hand?* *(Act 2 Scene 2, l.58–9)*	**Macbeth realises the devastating consequences** of his murder of Duncan. The desolate tone of his rhetorical question suggests that he understands the awful truth – nothing can assuage his guilt. He will have to live with what he has done for ever.
Macbeth *It will have blood; they say, blood will* *have blood* *(Act 3 Scene 4, l.122)*	Macbeth remembers the saying that when blood is shed through violence, it creates a **cycle of violence**; more blood will be spilt in revenge. Macbeth feels trapped by the inevitability of future violence. The repetition of 'blood' reflects his obsession with the reality of his tyrannous reign.
Macbeth *I am in blood* *Stepped in so far that, should I wade no more,* *Returning were as tedious as go o'er* *(Act 3 Scene 4, l.137–9)*	The metaphor of being trapped in a river of blood is entirely appropriate. Macbeth understands that he has been responsible for so many murders that it is not possible to undo them. There is **no turning back on his evil journey**; he will have to go on killing to maintain any kind of power.
Lady Macbeth *Here's the smell of the blood still* *(Act 5 Scene 1, l.42)*	The once-strong queen has become a **pitiable figure**. Lady Macbeth has lost control of her mind and is hallucinating under the strain of guilt and isolation. Ironically, she can find no escape from the incriminating evidence of her crimes.

The realisation that blood will have blood

Night

- Shakespeare had to convey the time of day in his characters' dialogue because the plays were usually performed out of doors and during daylight.

- He uses night as a device to show how evil deeds are linked with darkness.

- Many of the most **horrifying scenes take place at night** under cover of darkness, such as the murders of Duncan and Banquo.

- Even when it is daylight, many of the characters remark that it **feels more like night** because of the unnatural state of the country.

- Night is also used repeatedly to **show the evil wishes and feelings** of the characters.

Lady Macbeth craves light in her murky world

Useful Quotes Images of Night

Lady Macbeth *Come, thick night,* *And pall thee in the dunnest smoke of hell* *(Act 1 Scene 5, l.49–50)*	Macbeth's wife calls on the spirits of darkness to bring on the dark of night quickly to conceal the murder she is planning. She echoes her husband's wish, 'Stars, hide your fires!' The startling imagery reflects her **ruthless, immoral nature**.
Ross *By the clock 'tis day* *And yet dark night strangles the travelling lamp* *(Act 2 Scene 4, l.6–7)*	Shakespeare creates a **surreal mood** in the aftermath of Duncan's untimely death. All of Scotland seems sunk in an unnatural gloominess, even though it is daytime. The graphic verb 'strangles' adds to the tense atmosphere.
Macbeth *Come, seeling night,* *Scarf up the tender eye of pitiful day* *(Act 3 Scene 2, l.48–9)*	Macbeth reminds us of his wife's earlier prayer to the forces of darkness. He hopes that the night will hide the vicious killing of Banquo. His language shows how **deeply immersed in evil** he has become. Daylight would expose his murderous acts.

Poetic Structure

Macbeth is written in poetry and prose.

- Shakespeare uses **iambic pentameter** (five beats, each consisting of an unstressed syllable followed by a stressed syllable):

    So fair and foul a day I have not seen.

    The use of poetic language is a signal to the audience that these are noble characters occupying a high position in Scottish society. Poetry is powerful. The use of rhythm focuses the audience on the **heightened emotions** involved, similar to the language of musicals or opera, when 'ordinary speech' is insufficient to express strong feelings. The use of this metre sounds natural, yet lends itself to dramatic delivery.

- Sometimes **a half-line** is used to quicken the pace, often denoting anxiety. The exchange between Macbeth and Lady Macbeth on his return from the murder of Duncan is an example. The rapid interchange of half-lines shows the couple's extreme nervousness:

    Did not you speak?

    When?

    Now.

    As I descended?

- The supernatural characters are given a different rhythm, a **four-beat line** (a stressed syllable followed by an unstressed syllable). The unnatural rhythm lends a sinister air to their speech.

    Fair is foul, and foul is fair.

- **Prose** is used for the more **common characters**, such as the Porter, or to show an **extreme emotional state**. When Lady Macbeth sleepwalks, Shakespeare has her speak in prose to show her intense personal turmoil.

Sample Part (a) Question

Q. 'Different techniques may be used to heighten the impact of moments of crisis in texts.'

Discuss the techniques used to heighten the impact of at least one moment of crisis in **one** of the texts you have studied for your comparative course. Support your answer with reference to the text. (30 marks)

Indicative Material

- Characterisation, key events, dialogue and setting are vital elements in creating crises.
- Imagery, symbolism and motifs used to increase dramatic and emotional intensity.
- Dialogue, soliloquy, language, dramatic irony, etc. employed to heighten tension, conflict/crises.
- Intense moments created through stage directions, costumes, props, music, special effects, lighting, camera shots, etc.
- Flashbacks, foreshadowing, interior monologues and contrasts can intensify mood/atmosphere.

Sample Answer

Shakespeare uses **motifs like blood and night** to increase dramatic and emotional intensity at key moments in *Macbeth*. In this rapid moving play, the playwright not only uses a **single storyline** and the **chronological sequencing** of events to keep the action flowing. He also uses many references to time. The action increases towards the play's climax and resolution, particularly in the brief scenes in Act 5. Events become more intense and the consequences have much more significance.

Looking into the future is important to Macbeth, to ensure his peace of mind. It gives him a sense, as it turns out, of misplaced power. Then Lady Macbeth counsels her husband how to deceive the naive Duncan, saying 'To beguile the time, look like the time'. At the news of his wife's death, a rueful Macbeth muses, 'there would have been a time for such a word'. Bitterly, he comes to the realisation that he has destroyed his life through his own evil actions and is now left to time which 'Creeps in this petty pace from day to day/ To the last syllable of recorded time'. The constant beat of the **motif of time** adds not only **dramatic tension**, but highlights **how different characters perceive time through their own experiences**.

The **use of the short half-lines** in the sharp exchanges between the murderous couple in the immediate aftermath of Duncan's murder also **heightens the audience's experience of dramatic impact**. The couple seem to step on top of each other in their extreme anxiety, ('Did you not speak?/ When?/ Now./ As I descended? Ay'). This is a graphic illustration of how Macbeth has actually murdered sleep for his household. Their peace has been forever shattered by the despicable deeds they have done.

Dramatic irony is used to great effect **to intensify the play's claustrophobic mood**. There is no escape from evil consequences. Lady Macbeth has laughed at her husband's anxiety and guilt with the offhand, ironic comment, 'A little water clears us of this deed'. Then, in the sleepwalking scene the audience watches her trying to wash her own hands, crying, 'Out damned spot'. Her previous comment echoes strongly. Shakespeare is reminding us that evil cannot be denied. Lady Macbeth has to come to the tragic truth that not all the perfumes of Arabia 'will sweeten this little hand'.

Shakespeare's effective use of the dramatic techniques of the drama including such as time as a motif, half-lines and dramatic irony are all very successful in adding to the audience's dramatic experience of this tragedy of the 'dead butcher and his fiend-like queen'. *(430 words)*

Tyrannical rule cannot unite a country

Sample 70-mark Question

Q. 'An engaging aspect of texts is that authors rarely tell their stories in exactly the same way.'
Compare the extent to which this statement applies to each of the **three texts** that you have studied on your comparative course.

Class/Homework Exercise

Using some of the other points from the indicative material above, write your own response to the Part (a) question.

Exam Advice

To help you structure your comparative essay answer on Literary Genre, a useful exercise is to practise making an outline of the key points you want to include. The following draft plan uses *Macbeth* as one of the comparative texts.

Indicative Material

- Contrasting introductions and settings invite readers to enter the unique world of the text.
- Varying presentation of individual characters adds to our enjoyment/interest.
- Range of narrative perspectives and structures affects the reader's engagement.
- Distinctive plots and dialogue create degrees of emotional intensity.
- Specific imagery, symbolism, descriptive detail intensify/reduce appreciation.
- Music, camerawork, special effects all heighten/lessen the drama/tension, etc.

Sample Draft Plan

INTRODUCTION

The three texts on my comparative course have very different literary genres, but share some common aspects. *Macbeth* – a play in five acts – follows a conventional structure for Shakespearean tragedy. *This is very different from the organisation of events in my other two texts …*

POINT 1 Contrasting settings invite audience into story

Setting moves between the wild heath, violent battlefield, 'fatal' Dunsinane, innocent Macduff's castle, English court of Edward the Confessor. Establishes a contrast between family love and civilised Christian values of caring and self-sacrifice, and selfish ambition, duplicity, violence and chaos. *However, in my second text the setting is …*

POINT 2 Powerful imagery intensifies dramatic experience

The play is rich in revealing imagery. Repeated references to 'sleep' and 'nature' create a sense of loss and suffering. Macbeth is haunted by the consequences of what he has done, but is determined to sleep without fear. *In contrast, the author of my third text relies on dialogue to reveal character …*

POINT 3 Intense soliloquies engage audience interest in character

Shakespeare uses dramatic soliloquies and monologues to reveal the truth about characters and to engage the audience's interest – particularly Macbeth. *A similar effect is achieved through the use of flashback to reveal the truth about characters in both my other texts …*

POINT 4 Dramatic irony discloses chilling truth

Significance of irony in the story – brings insights and understanding. *The best example of irony in my second text is …*

CONCLUDING PARAGRAPH

Dual ending of *Macbeth* – dominated by death and the restoration of order. Evil has been defeated, but at an enormous cost. *While the conclusions are realistic in my other two texts, they are not nearly as bleak …*

Sample Paragraph: **POINT 3 Intense soliloquies engage audience interest in character**

A prominent feature of 'Macbeth' is Shakespeare's **use of soliloquies**. These monologues not only inform the audience about plot and character, they **involve us in the story**. The playwright brings the audience directly into the mind of Macbeth, full as it is of 'scorpions' in his anguished soliloquy, 'Is this a dagger which I see before me?' He is not without 'ambition, but without/ The illness should attend it'. So, lured by the witches and taunted by his cunning wife, he gives in to his great character flaw, moral weakness. In his highly emotional state, the blood-stained weapon seems to him 'palpable'. Macbeth's poetic imagination creates the dagger after the murder with horrifying 'dudgeon gouts of blood' on the blade. The soliloquy ends with the simple line, 'I go and it is done'. Denying his better nature which would have liked to have worn the 'Golden opinions' he had won so nobly in battle, he now descends into a hell of his own making. The bell he hears is not only a death knell for Duncan, but for Macbeth, once 'Bellona's bridegroom'. *(180 words)*

A similar effect in advancing the plot is achieved through the use of flashbacks in both of my other texts…

Examiner's Comment

- High-grade standard, based on solid discussion of use of soliloquy in play.
- Points clearly stated, supported with suitable reference and well-integrated quotation.
- Developed discussion on effectiveness of dagger image in revealing Macbeth's character.
- Language coherent and controlled; a comparative approach taken throughout.

Class/Homework Exercises

1. Choose one of the other points in the sample draft plan and write a paragraph of your own in response to the question above. (Aim for at least 150 words.)

2. 'Authors can use a range of narrative techniques to make settings authentic and engaging.'

   Compare how the authors of **three** of the texts on your comparative course make the settings in these texts authentic and engaging. (Aim for at least 1,000 words) (70 marks)

Macbeth's volatile emotional state is revealed in his soliloquies

Exploring Comparisons under Literary Genre

1. How is the Story Told?

Macbeth: Conflict	Other texts: Conflict
Individual vs Other (Macbeth vs Macduff)	Individual vs Other
Individual vs Society (Regicide)	Individual vs Society
Internal conflict (Soliloquies)	Internal conflict
State conflict (Good vs evil, order vs chaos)	State conflict?
Macbeth: Conclusion	**Other texts: Conclusion**
Conflict resolved	Conflict resolved/unresolved?
Insight gained	Redemption/bleak outlook?
Protagonist dies	Happy/sad?
Order restored	
Cathartic experience for audience	

Expectations are raised by genre

- A fairy story demands that the wicked are punished and the good are rewarded.
- Shakespearean tragedy is resolved by the restoration of order and the central character's acquisition of spiritual insight.

2. Who Tells the Story?

Elizabethan Stagecraft

- In Shakespeare's plays, there is minimal use of scenery and props.
- Setting and mood are established through play's dialogue.
- Minimal stage directions.
- Form, structure and language are used to create tension and drama.

A powerful wife convinces her hesitant husband

3. How is the Protagonist Portrayed?

Macbeth	Other texts
• The audience sees and hears what is said and done onstage. The character's actions, tone of voice, facial expression, etc. give us clues about him. • Soliloquies show the inner emotions and thoughts of the character. • The attitudes of other characters also inform us about the protagonist. • Further insights are conveyed through imagery, humour, dramatic irony, foreshadowing, music, costume, special effects, etc.	**Novel** We get to know central characters through reading about what is said and done. The plot and narrative voice also reveal the protagonist. Stream of consciousness shows inner emotions and thoughts. Additional insights are conveyed through imagery, symbols, humour, dramatic irony, foreshadowing, etc. **Film** Viewers learn about onscreen characters through action, tone of voice, facial expression, etc. Plot and the attitudes of other characters can frequently be revealing. Voice-overs, camera angles and lighting show the inner emotions and thoughts of the protagonist. Characteristics are often evident in key images, symbols, humour, colour, music, sound effects, etc. **Second Play** We see and hear the dialogue and action. Detailed stage directions give costumes and character mannerisms, etc. Lighting, colour, sound effects, music, costume and imagery, etc. can also be informative.

Humour in a text

Humour can be gentle, satirical, mocking or slapstick. It allows the author to comment on the story/character.

> **Remember!**
> *Modes overlap. For example, the general vision and viewpoint is often influenced by both the cultural context and aspects of literary genre of a text.*

Macbeth is entranced by the duplicitous witches

The General Vision and Viewpoint

Authors **challenge us** to look afresh at our assumptions, beliefs and prejudices, while entertaining us with the craft of story-telling. Stories can show us different ways of looking at people and the world.

The General Vision and Viewpoint mode refers to the broad outlook of a particular text. For example, if a writer is critical of a society, events or central characters, the vision of the text is likely to be dark and **negative**. If the outlook in the text is **positive** and life-affirming, the author might well be praising the courage and resilience of characters as they overcome or come to terms with their problems and circumstances.

Texts can usually be described as pessimistic, optimistic or realistic, or any combination of these. The **reader/audience will have their own views** of the outlook of the text.

The **ending** of a story is very important in determining the viewpoint. Whether happy or sad (or both), the ending must be credible within the context or 'world' of the story.

Students will be expected to compare **the broad outlooks on life** presented in texts.

- Is Macbeth's story told sympathetically, compassionately or cynically?
- Is the play generally optimistic or pessimistic? Is it realistic?
- Does the story reflect the era in which it is set?
- Is the social setting secular or religious?
- Is the storyline moral or political?
- What aspects of life does the text concentrate on?
- How effectively is the viewpoint expressed?
- Are the characters happy, free and fulfilled or unhappy, constrained and unfulfilled?
- Is the ending resolved, unresolved or contradictory?

We can identify the general viewpoint as something that is expressed through the narrative voice (Shakespeare's own view), a central character or a group of characters, e.g. Macbeth, Lady Macbeth and the witches all epitomise evil and disorder.

In studying the General Vision and Viewpoint of *Macbeth*, it is important to focus on the **overall impact the drama makes on the audience** – and on how this is communicated.

Dramatic features, including key moments, dialogue, soliloquies, setting, poetic language, etc., convey the atmosphere of the text.

- **Imagery and language** can also affect the atmosphere.
- **Visual and aural effects** (lighting, sound, music and costume) can show a world of beauty or terror, and influence the audience's perception of the play's vision as optimistic or pessimistic.
- The impact of a crucial scene or **turning point** in the play will usually shape our viewpoint.
- In particular, the **concluding scenes** usually have a huge effect.
  - Are issues raised by the story resolved happily or unhappily?
  - Or do they remain unresolved?

> ### Remember!
> *The vision of a text is usually set by the author's use of character, plot, language and narrative voice.*

The Tragic Vision in *Macbeth*

Plays 'hold, as it were, the mirror up to nature' (*Hamlet*). A mirror does more than reflect reality; it **shows reality from a different perspective**. In *Macbeth*, Shakespeare gives us a dual vision – hopeful and despairing – while exploring the depths of depravity to which humans will descend to satisfy their needs.

The playwright shows how anarchy and destruction occur when order is broken by uncontrolled desire. Lady Macbeth sums up the intense unhappiness she and her husband experience following the murder of Duncan: 'Nought's had, all's spent/ Where our desire is got without content.'

Order is restored – for the moment

Class/Homework Exercise (Comparing the Vision and Viewpoint)

Copy the following table about the general vision and viewpoint in your comparative texts, adding your own responses with reference to the texts you are studying.

	First Text (*Macbeth*)	Second Text	Third Text
What **mood** is established by the **setting** of the text?			
What is the character's **aim/wish**?			
What are the **obstacles** preventing this aim?			
Has the main character **supporters or enemies** to help or obstruct?			
What is the **critical decision** made by the main character? Is the aim achieved? Is the conclusion happy/sad?			

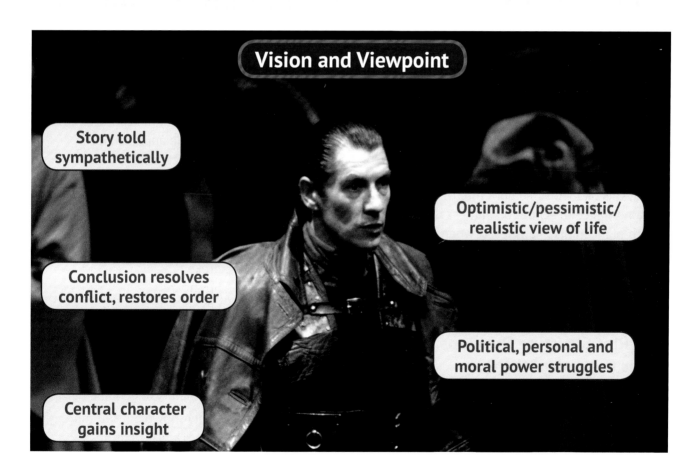

Vision and Viewpoint

Story told sympathetically

Optimistic/pessimistic/realistic view of life

Conclusion resolves conflict, restores order

Political, personal and moral power struggles

Central character gains insight

How Language and Imagery Establish the Outlook of the Play

- The ringing, equivocal chanting of the witches, 'Fair is foul, and foul is fair', sets the **unsettling tone** of *Macbeth*. The play opens dramatically, with thunder and lightning, inviting the audience into a world of moral uncertainty. Even the outcome of the battle between the rebels and Duncan's forces is 'Doubtful' at first.

- The first four scenes begin with questions – all of which help establish the edgy atmosphere and the play's disturbingly **dark outlook**. Lady Macbeth advises her husband to 'Look like the innocent flower,/ But be the serpent under it'. The audience is enveloped in a **shadowy world of duplicity** that foreshadows the violence ahead.

- Shakespeare also uses powerful imagery to convey a sense of evil. Macbeth's crime of regicide brings about his horrendous descent that is reflected in striking references, such as the hallucinatory dagger with its 'gouts of blood'. This is a **horrifying vision**, a swirling tide of blood through which Macbeth wades.

- Audiences can hardly fail to view Macbeth's fall from grace as both **tragic and depressing**. The play's protagonist makes a **crucial decision** to act against nature's defined order. Macbeth's heart knocks at his ribs 'against the use of nature' before he commits the murder.

- All through the play, the forces of good are associated with nature imagery. Shakespeare uses this to shed some light into this dark drama. Malcolm echoes his father's use of the verb 'plant' in his final speech, when he restores political order. After all the violence and chaos, **the play ends on a cautiously hopeful note**. While evil has pervaded *Macbeth,* it is only temporary. Ultimately, order is restored.

How Plot Structure Develops the Tragic Outlook of the Play

- Shakespeare carefully arranges the plot of *Macbeth* so that many of the **pivotal events** – the murder of Duncan and his guards, the slaughter of Lady Macduff and her household, Lady Macbeth's suicide and the killing of Macbeth himself – all **take place offstage**. This leaves the focus of the play on the psychological torment of Macbeth and Lady Macbeth.

- To a significant extent, the **story is told sympathetically**. The dominant outlook is truly tragic. Shakespeare exposes the tortured soul of Macbeth, who sees with piercing clarity that he is paying the most terrible price for his heinous crimes.

- Macbeth has a nihilistic view of life, 'Tomorrow, and tomorrow, and tomorrow,/ Creeps in this petty pace from day to day'. The playwright brings the audience on this harrowing journey of **bitter insight**.

- The play's **conclusion is neither totally optimistic nor totally pessimistic.** While Macbeth gains some self-awareness, it is all too late – both for his unfortunate victims and himself. His own moral weakness enticed him to seek power for the sake of glory, not to enable him to do good for his country. As he faces death, he resorts to unleashing destruction again ('I ... wish the estate of the world were now undone').

How Plot Structure Establishes the Play's Positive Conclusion

- Shakespeare's great tragedy is crafted to show how – despite the strength of evil – **good triumphs in the end**. Acts of **self-sacrifice counterbalance the play's negative view** of life. A messenger, at great peril to himself, attempts to warn Lady Macduff of the approaching murderers. Her son bravely defends his father's honour. His courage is mirrored by young Siward, who dies battling the 'abhorrent villain' Macbeth.

- As Macbeth's tyranny draws to its inevitable end, the play's **viewpoint becomes more positive**. Although he has paid a terrible price, Macduff emerges as the real hero. In avenging the murder of his wife and children, he initiates the restoration of order in Scotland. Macduff has also clarified the question of what it is to be 'manly'. His response to the heart-breaking news of his family's slaughter ('I must also feel it as a man') reflects the humanity of genuine heroism.

- Malcolm has certainly shown himself more astute than his father, Duncan, but he is inexperienced. Yet he leads his troops with 'industrious soldiership' into the battlefield, unlike his father, who relied on Macbeth and Banquo. He also shows a military tactician's skill when he orders his soldiers to 'hew him down a bough/ And bear it before him' to 'shadow/ The numbers of our host'. The **outlook for Scotland during Malcolm's reign is hopeful**.

♦ Malcolm embodies his father's 'virtues' of humility and generosity. His final speech is carefully measured to unite the country and avoid disorder. It seems that he will rule, unlike Macbeth, with 'the grace of Grace' and the unanimous support of the thanes. Shakespeare has brought the audience through the dark and pessimistic world of wrongdoing and malevolence to the **brighter, optimistic vision** of order and civilisation.

Royal power will lead to suffering and chaos

Useful **Quotes** The General Vision and Viewpoint

The witches *Fair is foul, and foul is fair* *(Act 1 Scene 1, l.12)*	The **tone of moral ambiguity** is struck at the very beginning of the play. Are the witches real or imaginary? They introduce us to a disturbing world of malice and confusion. Nothing is ever quite as it seems in this drama, where appearance and reality are so closely associated.
Lady Macbeth *Come, thick night,* *And pall thee in the dunnest smoke of hell,* *That my keen knife see not the wound it makes* *(Act 1 Scene 5, l.49–51)*	A terrifying vision of evil incarnate is conjured by this **soliloquy by Macbeth's resolute wife**. She is determined that her husband shall have the crown he has been promised, no matter what evil acts must to be done to achieve it. Lady Macbeth's ruthlessness foreshadows the violence ahead.
Lennox *Some say, the earth* *Was feverous and did shake* *(Act 2 Scene 3, l.55–6)*	Events in the play become darker and more disturbing. On the night of Duncan's murder, Scotland is wracked by mighty storms. **Nature reflects the turmoil** unleashed on the country by Macbeth's act. The natural order has been overthrown by the Macbeths' all-consuming desire for the throne.
Malcolm *by the grace of Grace,* *We will perform in measure, time and place* *(Act 5 Scene 9, l.38–9)*	After the turmoil of the Macbeths' unlawful reign, **order has been restored** – but at a terrible cost. The lawful king is on the Scottish throne again, with his divine right to rule. Will there be permanent peace? Or will the cycle of blood-letting begin again? The even pace and rhyming couplet highlights the harmony that reigns for the present.

Remember!

Discussion points in the 30-mark Part (a) sample answer can also provide the basis for developed comparisons in the 40-mark Part (b) and 70-mark single questions. To write successful examination answers, it is essential to study the wording of questions closely. Marks can easily be lost if attention is not paid to each element of the questions.

Sample Part (a) Question

Q. 'Authors make effective use of a range of techniques to dramatically heighten the impact of the general vision and viewpoint in texts.'

Discuss the technique(s) used to dramatically heighten the impact of the general vision and viewpoint in **one** of the texts you have studied for your comparative course. (30 marks)

A tragic heroine?

Indicative Material

- Plot and/or the experiences of central characters often shape the general vision and viewpoint.
- Setting, narrative voice, contrasts, etc. can intensify mood/ atmosphere in establishing vision.
- Imagery, symbolism and motifs can be used to increase awareness of vision and viewpoint.
- Dialogue, soliloquy, irony, etc. heighten tension/conflict in exploring dark/bright outlook.
- Intense moments created through stage directions, costumes, props, music, special effects, lighting, camera shots, etc. add to the pessimistic/optimistic/realistic vision, etc.

Sample Answer

In the play 'Macbeth', Shakespeare repeatedly uses the **imagery of clothing** to illustrate the tragic vision of the play. From the start, we see that kingship is not Macbeth's proper role. When informed by Ross that Duncan has promoted him to Thane of Cawdor, he replies, 'The Thane of Cawdor lives; why do you dress me in borrowed robes?' When he is reluctant to kill Duncan, he uses a clothing image to express how he wishes to wear the 'golden opinions' he has earned 'in their newest gloss/ Not cast aside so soon'. Later in the play, as the forces of good are gathering against Macbeth, one of the thanes, Angus, remarks: 'now does he feel his title /Hang loose about him, like a giant's robe/ Upon a dwarfish thief'. The image is a reminder of Macbeth's vicious tranny and reflects the tragic outlook of the story.

Macbeth's selfish rule has caused chaos, 'He cannot buckle his distempered cause/ Within the belt of rule.' At the end of the play, when he realises he has been fooled by the witches, he calls for his armour and – once again dressed in military uniform – fights to the end, 'Before my body/ I throw my warlike shield'. This final clothing imagery adds to the dark vision of the play and emphasises the violent disorder of Macbeth's dismal reign.

In contrast, imagery from the world of medicine brings an optimistic element to the story. The English king, 'pious Edward', is portrayed as the epitome of a successful monarch. His 'touch' cures 'wretched souls' in his kingdom. He is using his power to do good, to care for his people with 'healing benediction', unlike Macbeth, who is only interested in self-advancement. The thanes regard Malcolm as the 'medicine of the sickly weal' in Scotland, who, with their help, will 'purge' the 'suffering country' of Macbeth's tyranny. In a play where there is so much cruelty and corruption, such positive imagery makes all the greater impact on the audience's mood.

The playwright has used the dramatic impact of **clothing imagery** to show his **pessimistic view that the illegal seizing of power** does not suit the thief. Macbeth is not a great enough man to fill the position of king, even though he once excelled on the battlefield. The imagery of medicine is used to show how although evil cannot be cured, goodness can eventually triumph over evil. This dual optimistic/pessimistic viewpoint adds greatly to the audience's appreciation of the dramatic story of Macbeth. *(415 words)*

Examiner's Comment

- Solid high-grade standard, focusing well on imagery as a key technique that shapes play's vision.
- Displays a close knowledge – clear understanding – of both text and mode.
- Some developed discussion, well supported by apt reference and accurate quotes.
- Good control of language, overall (e.g. 'violent disorder of Macbeth's dismal reign', 'epitome of a successful monarch').

Class/Homework Exercise

Using some of the points from the indicative material above, write your own response to the Part (a) question.

Exam Advice

To structure your comparative essay answer on the General Vision and Viewpoint, a useful exercise is to practise making an outline of the key points you wish to include. The following draft plan uses *Macbeth* as one of the three comparative texts.

Sample 70-mark Question

Q. 'Significant events in texts and the impact they have on readers often help to clarify the general vision and viewpoint of those texts.'

With reference to **three texts** on your comparative course, compare the ways in which at least one significant event in each text, and its impact on you, helped to clarify the general vision and viewpoint of these texts.

Indicative Material

- Impact of the opening/ending of a text influences understanding of outlook.
- Sense of optimism, pessimism, shock, joy, etc. experienced in response to key events.
- Characters' experiences affect readers' perspective on the vision/viewpoint of texts.
- Language/imagery, music, special effects can all shape vision.
- Effect of historical, cultural, political, social events clarifies the general outlook, etc.

Sample Draft Plan

INTRODUCTION

The three texts in my comparative course offer **a diverse selection of viewpoints with varying degrees of optimism and pessimism**. I have learnt from my comparative study that the vision and viewpoint is the general outlook on life presented by the playwright in the text. In particular, Shakespeare's 'Macbeth' presented a bleak, negative view of the world, but ended on a more hopeful note. *My other two texts presented similar/contrasting views ...*

POINT 1 Characters' outlooks impact on audience's emotions

Optimistic/pessimistic outlooks shown by characters make an impact on the audience/reader. The kings Duncan, Edward, the heir Malcolm and the thane Macduff all show how love for country is necessary for the well-being of society. This affects our view of the viewpoint in the play. Evil is shown through the self-serving couple, Macbeth and Lady Macbeth, who destroy Scotland for their selfish ambition. Various violent scenes are truly shocking. These affect the reader in a negative fashion. *In contrast/similarly, my second text ...*

POINT 2 Dialogue conveys vision of text

Dramatic dialogue used to convey the central tragic vision. Shakespeare's powerful language conveys Macbeth's psychological turmoil before he commits the crime of regicide Act 2 Scene 1 (the dagger scene). We are aghast at his torment and dreadful determination. He is fully aware of the terrible deed he is about to do, yet goes ahead – the audience is caught between awe at such clarity of insight and revulsion at such an evil deed. *An equally revealing scene in my third text shares/does not share ...*

POINT 3 Key point illuminates viewpoint of texts

The private exchange between Macbeth and Lady Macbeth, prior to Banquo's killing, discloses the 'doubtful joy' the couple now live in. It is evident that neither character has achieved contentment, even though they have gained power and royal status. The banquet scene is particularly bleak, foreshadowing isolation and despair for Macbeth and his wife. *This dramatic scene is mirrored in my other texts ...*

POINT 4 Conclusions of texts illustrate vision

Endings contribute to the viewpoint in a text and leave the reader with lasting impression of the text's vision. Macbeth and Lady Macbeth have learnt through suffering that getting a desire 'without content' is useless. Shakespeare's dual vision is both optimistic and pessimistic. *The ending of my second text is like/unlike ...*

CONCLUDING PARAGRAPH

A play that has been dominated by pessimism, violence and corruption ends with healing, insight and hope. A new rule of law is established under Malcolm with the aid of Macduff and the English forces, so the ending is redemptive. Good triumphs but at a terrible cost to both innocent and guilty. Overall, I found this life-affirming. *Similarly, the conclusions of my other two texts ...*

The ghost of Banquo appears to Macbeth alone

Sample Paragraph: **POINT 3 Key point illuminates viewpoint of texts**

In the **crucial exchanges** between Macbeth and his wife surrounding Duncan's death, the language used **influences the readers' understanding of the bleak view on life** that is present throughout the tragedy. Macbeth is full of 'sorriest fancies'. His torment is expressed using animal imagery, 'O full of scorpions is my mind'. He feels insecure on the throne. He believes 'we have scorched the snake, not killed it'. In his determination to be safe and get royal family power for his descendants, he creates a hellish scene of terror, referring to 'night's black agents' on their hunt for 'prey'. Other menacing sounds of night-time are used, the 'cloistered flight' of the bat, the 'drowsy hum' of the 'shard-borne beetle'. He associates himself with this nightmare scene, 'Come seeling night,/ Scarf up the tender eye of pitiful day' in which he means Banquo's murder. The audience is left disturbed by the intensity of Macbeth's determination to secure power in Scotland, no matter what the cost, 'let the frame of things disjoint, both the worlds suffer,/ Ere we will eat our meal in fear'. This important exchange between the Macbeths uses language which really clarifies the dark outlook in the play. *(200 words)*

There is an equally revealing scene in my second text ...

> **Examiner's Comment**
>
> - Uneven response.
> - Includes some impressive points on how imagery shapes the play's disturbingly bleak vision.
> - Very effective use of apt reference and accurate quotation.
> - Some awkward expression (e.g. 'and get royal family power', 'in which he means').
> - Uses comparative language effectively towards the end of the paragraph.
> - Solid mid-grade standard, overall.

Class/Homework Exercises

1. Choose **one** of the other points in the sample draft plan and write a paragraph of your own in response to the question above. (Aim for at least 150 words)

2. Compare the key moments (or series of moments) that you feel were most representative of the general vision and viewpoint of each of three texts on your comparative course. (Aim for at least 1,000 words.) (70 marks)

Useful Comparative Links

Successful comparative answers include clear links between texts.

The following phrases might be useful in pointing out similarities and differences between texts.

Similarities	Differences
• Both authors take a similar approach	• These two texts could not be more different
• The two stories have much in common	• These two key moments illustrate contrasting aspects of ...
• This is also evident in the film's most disturbing scene	• In an entirely different way ...
• Common to all three narratives is ...	• In contrast, the opening scene in the novel ...
• In an almost identical way ...	• The complete opposite is seen in ...
• This is mirrored in way the heroine of the story acts when ...	• On the other hand ...
• The same effect occurs later in the text	• This is certainly not the case in the film, where ...
• Likewise, in my other texts ...	• All three endings are completely different
• This viewpoint is echoed at the end of my second text ...	• The novel takes a much more unexpected approach
	• This aspect is contrasted in my second/ third text, when ...

Leaving Certificate Comparative Study Practice Questions

Theme or Issue

1. 'Exploring a significant theme or issue in different texts can often challenge or change the preconceived ideas of a reader.'

   With reference to **three texts** on your comparative course, compare the extent to which your study of a significant theme or issue challenged or changed some of your preconceived ideas. (70 marks)

OR

2. 'The experience of the central character can highlight the complexity of a theme or issue for a reader.'

   (a) Discuss the extent to which the experience of the central character highlighted the complexity of a theme or issue in **one** of the texts you have studied on your comparative course. (30 marks)

   (b) Compare the extent to which the experience of the central character highlighted the complexity of the same theme or issue in each of **two other** comparative texts you have studied. (40 marks)

Literary Genre

1. 'A variety of techniques can be used in a text to shape a compelling storyline.'

   Identify and compare the techniques used to shape compelling storylines in **three texts** you have studied on your comparative course. (70 marks)

OR

2. 'The author's use of imagery and symbolism can help to create the mood in a text.'

   (a) Discuss how the author's use of imagery and symbolism helped to create the mood in **one** of the texts on your comparative course. (30 marks)

   (b) With reference to **two other** comparative texts, compare how the author's use of imagery and symbolism helped to create the mood in these texts. (40 marks)

The Cultural Context

1. 'The way in which family or social expectations liberate or restrict central characters can broaden our understanding of the cultural context of a text.'

   Compare the way in which central characters were liberated or restricted by family or social expectations helped to broaden your understanding of the cultural context in **three texts** on your comparative course. (70 marks)

OR

2. 'Understanding attitudes to gender roles can offer the reader a valuable insight into the cultural context of the text.'

   (a) Discuss how understanding attitudes to gender roles offered you a valuable insight into the cultural context of **one text** that you have studied on your comparative course. (30 marks)

   (b) Compare the way in which attitudes to gender roles offered you a valuable insight into **two other** comparative texts that you have studied. (40 marks)

The General Vision and Viewpoint

1. 'Relationships between central characters which prove valuable or damaging often shape a reader's understanding of the general vision and viewpoint of a text.'

   In the light of this statement, compare the extent to which the relationships in **three texts** you have studied on your comparative course helped to shape your understanding of the general vision and viewpoint. (70 marks)

OR

2. 'The general vision and viewpoint of a text can be interpreted by a reader's response to key scenes or significant moments in that text.'

   (a) With reference to **one text** on your comparative course, discuss how key scenes or significant moments shaped your personal response and helped you to interpret the general vision and viewpoint. (30 marks)

   (b) With reference to **two other** comparative texts, compare how key scenes or significant moments shaped your personal response and helped you to interpret the general vision and viewpoint in these texts. (30 marks)

The new king and queen trade everything for power

Comparative Study Guidelines

(SEC Leaving Cert English Marking Scheme)

In all answers to questions in this section, candidates may compare **and/or** contrast, i.e. address similarities **and/or** differences in both the content and style of their chosen texts

In shaping their responses to the questions set on the Comparative Study, it is expected that candidates will be involved in some/all of the following kinds of activities:

- Description/analysis of the text/s in the light of the modes for comparison
- Making general observations about texts in relation to each other
- Making connections between similar aspects of texts
- Recognising differences between texts
- Showing that similarities/differences need to be qualified
- Demonstrating awareness of themselves as readers, their reactions/responses/involvement.

Expect a wide variety of approaches both in the patterns of discussion and the manner of illustration.

> **Remember!**
>
> *In your introductory paragraph, it's important to name the text/s, author/s and mode that you have chosen.*

FAQs

Q. How many comparisons are expected?

A. There is no set number. Some candidates will focus in depth on a few key comparisons; others will range widely over texts, finding numerous similarities and/or differences.

Q. Do examiners expect a detailed summary of the plot of each text?

A. Writing detailed summaries is generally wasteful and time-consuming. In most cases, a brief outline will be sufficient. For example, 'Shakespeare's tragic play *Macbeth* traces the rise and fall of an ambitious Scottish nobleman.'

Q. What exactly is a 'key moment'?

A. This term usually refers to a revealing moment or scene, sometimes indicating a turning point in the story. It can be a brief exchange between characters, a soliloquy, an ironic remark, a violent incident, a grand occasion or even a seemingly unimportant event.

Q. How many key moments are expected?

A. Again, there is no set number. While some developed discussions include a range of references to revealing moments, others select a few and explore these in greater depth.

Q. Is it necessary to compare all three texts in every paragraph?

A. A paragraph will frequently refer to a key moment/scene from one text. A valid comparison with a second and/or third might be made – often at the start or end of the paragraph. Occasionally, there could be reference to all three texts.

Q. Should comparative texts be given equal attention in answers?

A. Although examiners are unlikely to have strict expectations, merely nominal or token discussion of any text will be penalised.

> **Remember!**
>
> *The **main aim is to take a comparative approach** and engage with the terms of the question. Examiners will reward relevant, well-written answers that demonstrate a good understanding of the chosen mode and the three texts.*

Chief Examiner's Report

Many examiners reported genuine engagement with the terms of the questions, combined with a fluid comparative approach. As in previous years, examiners also noted that a significant minority of candidates were hampered by a rigid and formulaic approach. In recent years there have been few instances of the use of invalid texts in answer to the questions on Comparative Studies. Nevertheless, it is worth noting that the use of some texts is not permitted in the Comparative Studies Section. Texts that are not valid are:

- a text already answered on as a Single Text
- a text not on the prescribed list for the current year
- the use of two films.

The Comparative Study is one of the areas where candidates have an opportunity to demonstrate skills in critical literacy. It is possible for candidates to challenge, wholly or in part, not only the premise put forward in questions but also the views and opinions they encountered in the course of studying texts. Many candidates showed **evidence of critical engagement** with the texts they had studied and a mature critical literacy was seen in the work of some candidates. Examiners were pleased when they saw candidates trust in their own personal response and demonstrate a willingness to challenge the 'fixed meaning' of texts. The best answers managed to remain grounded, both in the question asked and in the text.

www.examinations.ie

*A despondent Macbeth counts
the cost of his ambition*

Glossary of Dramatic Terms

Aside: when a character says something that is only heard by the audience.

Blank verse: unrhymed verse in iambic pentameter, relatively close to spoken English.

Catharsis: the purging of emotion (usually pity and fear) that the audience experiences at the end of a tragedy.

Characterisation: the way a playwright creates characters so as to attract or repel the audience.

Conflict: there is no drama without conflict or tension. The conflict between opposing forces can be external (between characters) or internal (within a character) and is usually resolved by the end of the story.

Denouement: resolution or unfolding of a plot when the expectations of the audience are satisfied or denied.

Dramatic irony: the audience is aware of some impending catastrophe or important fact of which some characters are either totally ignorant or not fully aware. For example, we know about Macbeth's murderous plans while Duncan still trusts him.

Exeunt: Latin for 'they leave'. Plural of 'exit'.

Foreshadowing: hints of what is to happen later in the story.

Genre: type or classification of literature, e.g. drama, tragedy, etc.

Iambic pentameter: ten-syllable lines in which unstressed syllables alternate with stressed syllables.

Imagery: figurative or literary language (including symbols, metaphors and similes) that creates pictures in the mind.

Metaphor: a figure of speech that makes an implicit comparison between two things, e.g. 'There's daggers in men's smiles.'

Pathos: a quality of a text that arouses feelings of pity or deep sorrow.

Patriarchy: a society where men hold most of the power and where women have none.

Personification: a type of metaphor in which an object is described as if it were alive, e.g. 'Blood will have blood.'

Plot: the storyline or sequence of events making up a narrative.

Poetic justice: the idea that characters should get what they deserve, based on their behaviour.

Protagonist: the central or main character in a story.

Rhetoric: the use of language techniques to make speech or writing more powerful and persuasive.

Rhythm: a pattern of sounds created by the arrangement of stressed and unstressed syllables.

Soliloquy: a speech in which a character reveals his or her thoughts and feelings exclusively to the audience.

Symbol: usually an object that represents an idea, e.g. the blood on Macbeth's hands is a symbol of the guilt he feels for his crimes.

Theme: a central idea or issue explored in the play, e.g. power in *Macbeth*.

Tone: dominant mood or feeling suggested by the playwright.

Tragedy: genre of drama in which characters experience a reversal of fortune, usually for the worse. The downfall of a potentially heroic individual usually results from a serious character weakness.

Tragic flaw: the main fault or character weakness that leads to the tragic hero's downfall, e.g. Macbeth's evil ambition.